KU-576-375

Multiplicity of Nationalism in Contemporary Europe

Multiplicity of Nationalism in Contemporary Europe

Edited by
Ireneusz Paweł Karolewski
and Andrzej Marcin Suszycki

LEXINGTON BOOKS
A division of
ROWMAN & LITTLEFIELD PUBLISHERS, INC.
Lanham • Boulder • New York • Toronto • Plymouth, UK

Published by Lexington Books
A division of Rowman & Littlefield Publishers, Inc.
A wholly owned subsidiary of The Rowman & Littlefield Publishing Group, Inc.
4501 Forbes Boulevard, Suite 200, Lanham, Maryland 20706
http://www.lexingtonbooks.com

Estover Road, Plymouth PL6 7PY, United Kingdom

British Library Cataloguing in Publication Information Available

Library of Congress Cataloging-in-Publication Data

Multiplicity of nationalism in contemporary Europe / edited by Ireneusz Pawel Karolewski and Andrzej Marcin Suszycki.
p. cm.
Includes bibliographical references and index.
ISBN 978-0-7391-2307-2 (cloth : alk. paper) — ISBN 978-0-7391-3956-1 (electronic)
1. Europe—Politics and government—1989– 2. Europe—Ethnic relations. 3. Nationalism—Europe. 4. Nationalism—Europe—Case studies. 5. National characteristics, European. 6. Boundaries—Political aspects—Europe. 7. Supranationalism—Europe. 8. Regionalism—Europe. I. Karolewski, Ireneusz Pawel. II. Suszycki, Andrzej Marcin.
D2009.M85 2010
320.54094—dc22 2009030615

™ The paper used in this publication meets the minimum requirements of American National Standard for Information Sciences—Permanence of Paper for Printed Library Materials, ANSI/NISO Z39.48-1992.

Printed in the United States of America

Contents

Chapter 1
Nationalism in Contemporary Europe: Is There Still Anything to Explore?

Andrzej Marcin Suszycki
and Ireneusz Paweł Karolewski

Nationalism remains one of the key political, societal, and sociopsychological phenomena in contemporary Europe. Its significance for the justification of state policies and the stability of political systems, particularly in the context of advanced democracies, and—more generally—its significance for people's basic needs for a political and cultural identity and a sense of national pride continue to challenge scholars.

A great number of approaches and theories have been developed with regard to the nature and forms of nationalism. However, the various debates have brought about rather more conceptual, theoretical, and methodological controversies and unresolved questions than clarified questions and well-defined terms, making nationalism one of the most controversial subjects in the field of political science, sociology, and anthropology. Paradoxically, the more nationalism has been studied, the greater the need for new theoretical and empirical insights seems to be.

Nationalism is not limited to Europe, but Europe is the only part of the world where the complex political, social, and economic reality resulting from European integration, the ongoing processes of nation-building, and regionalism allows for the viewing of nationalism simultaneously and concurrently in several dimensions. In this volume, we examine three perspectives of nationalism.

Firstly, we focus on the term "European nationalism." By this, we mean attempts by the institutions of the European Union to form a collective "European" identity. In this regard, our research question is the extent to which the European Union can indeed weaken national identities of the member states and produce a new form of nationalism going beyond the nationalism of the European nation-states. We apply the term supranationalism to this phenomenon. This term has at least two major aspects. On the one hand, supranationalism should strengthen unity, solidarity and parity between the member states and their citizens; hence it is believed to have "good" or calming effects on the European politics. On the other hand, however, it might have excluding and discriminating effects with regard to non-members, even if the strategies of exclusion and discrimination occur in a subtle way. This aspect is by far the less perceptible one. The positive integrative force of Euronationalism and the negative discriminating one show its ambivalent character.

Secondly, we focus on the traditional nationalism of European nations. This type of nationalism is predominantly linked to boundary-making and discrimination of non-members. It emphasizes differences and its integrative elements are clearly limited to the members of the nation. Since it often generates negative feelings toward others, exclusion, chauvinism, and even violence and ethnic cleansing are associated with this form of nationalism.

Thirdly, we speak of regional nationalism. Here, we concentrate on recent regional political developments in the EU member states. We can observe that the regional nationalism is in direct interaction with the European nationalism of the EU and the traditional nation-state nationalism. On the one hand, it might be seen as a reaction to the centralist nation-state nationalism; on the other hand, it might also be generated by the process of European integration, in particular as an instrument used by the EU to weaken nationalism of the member-states. Hence, regional nationalism can have both a modern character, in the sense of state and nation-building processes with their fragmenting tendencies, and a post-modern character in the sense of a reference to a significant number of political identities and authorities.

The Aims and the Structure of the Volume

Using these three meanings of nationalism in contemporary Europe, this volume has three aims.

First, in part I we intend to question the conceptual grounds of the contemporary discourse on nationalism. We will focus on two influential schools of thought pervasive in scholarly debates on nationalism. On the one hand, this section takes up the traditional dichotomy of civic and ethnic nationalism. Many scholars still confirm the old division of nationalism into the enlightened Western type, i.e., supportive of democracy and liberalism, and the backward Eastern type, which is seen as a major problem for democratic and liberal developments. Against the background of newer developments in Western and Eastern Europe, we pose the question if we can really speak of differences between "Western" and "Eastern" nationalism. In particular, we ask if the transformations that the East (Central and Eastern Europe and the three Baltic states) has undergone in recent decades and its ability to fulfill the criteria for membership of the EU and NATO are evidence of a tendency toward the convergence of Western and Eastern nationalism. We also ask if nationalism in the East was *ever* different to the Western form of nationalism. On the other hand, Section A deals with the recently popular concept of liberal nationalism. With this regard, we will empirically evaluate the theoretical claim that "liberal" nationalism has a "friendly" core element. We ask if there is empirical evidence supporting the argument that nationalism helps regain citizens' solidarity and support for the welfare state as well as citizens' confidence in their political system.

Second, in part II, we attempt to shift our examination from the civic-ethnic dichotomy of nationalism and the liberal nationalist approach toward three perspectives on nationalism in Europe: Regional nationalism, supranational nationalism, and boundary-making nationalism. These new perspectives correspond to our three meanings of nationalism mentioned above. They are not conceptualized as fully-fledged theories of nationalism, but as theoretical perspectives with a goal of stimulating further research on contemporary nationalism with different foci. First, we explore the reasons for the emergence and persistence of sub-state regionalism in its various forms as they have occurred throughout several surges of increased regional mobilization since the founding of what is today the EU. Against the background of the observation that many traditionally "secessionist" regions have supported the idea of European integration rather than continuing to demand sovereignty, we then discuss the importance of the regional level of governance within the European Union (EU) that has increased since the early 1990s. We also address some possible theoretical developments as a consequence of a growing importance of regional nationalist actors in the EU policy process. Second, we discuss the phenomenon of Euronationalism. We depart from the observation that the EU supports the idea of fluidity and hybridity and yet forges European collective identity, a contradictory endeavor of "unity in diversity." We explore the technologies of European nationalism and EU identity politics and discuss with the juxtaposition of European patriotism and European nationalism. Third, we deal with nationalism as one of the most powerful processes of boundary-building. With regard to the fact that the majority of scholars only mentions the relationship between nations and boundaries in passing, assuming a nearly "automatic" existence of boundaries, and does not see the need for any further examination, we show that all attempts at defining, "inventing," or reviving a nation imply a process of inclusion-exclusion—that is, the erection of boundaries between in-groups and out-groups. We investigate how the past Western legacy of destruction and self-destruction intersected with, and was accompanied by, a continuous stress on boundaries, and hence on exclusion and the creation of homogeneous identities as defined by these boundaries. Here, we propose solutions to overcome the legacy of conflict and violence in the supra-national projects like the European Union.

Our *third* aim is to enrich the theoretical debate with new empirical findings. We organize them around two questions relating both to the theoretical and empirical layer of the nationalism discourse. In part III, we pose the question of the old nationalism in Western Europe. This refers to the idea perpetuated by the civic-ethnic divide that Western European nationalism either tends to be more strongly civic or is more likely to be peaceful and integrating than the Eastern European variants of nationalism, which are in turn predisposed to violence, divisiveness, and fragmentation. However, we believe that it is not only an issue of the alleged specificity of Western nationalism, but also of the assessment of the current wave of nationalist sentiments in Western Europe. This wave of nationalist policies and discourses can be regarded either as a revival of latent nationalism suppressed in recent decades or as a new phenomenon only loosely linked to the modern nationalism of the nineteenth and twentieth century. In this context, we ask if such a new post-modern nationalism could be viewed, for instance, as a quest for certainty and collective ties dissolving in post-modern societies associated with fluidity and insecurity. Three chapters on Eastern Europe with regard to the question of new nationalism in Eastern Europe follow in part IV. Here, we try to explore if, first, the Eastern nationalism should continuously be seen in strong ethnic terms, second, the modernist paradigm positing that nationalism is closely associated with state-building or regime change processes still holds true. Hence, we ask if the post-Communist countries of Eastern Europe are more prone to nationalism (in whatever form) than their more stable counterparts in Western Europe, as believed by many scholars.

As far as our case studies are concerned, we turn both to in-depth single country cases and inter-country comparisons. In the section relating to Western Europe, the contributors discuss divergent cases of German, Italian, and Belgian nationalism. On the one hand, all these countries are founding members of the EU, which makes them good candidates for countries attempting to surpass their nationalist experiences. On the other hand, the origins of and motivations for their nationalism are different. Particularly revealing is the case of Germany, which according to some scholars adopted the ideology of constitutional patriotism, while trying to reduce the ethnic and exclusive core of its national ideology (until 1989). However, this begs the question of whether this type of civic nationalism was successfully disseminated within the population. Italy can be referred to as a "paradigmatic" case or "exemplar" of several simultaneous and concurrent dimensions of nationalism. The case of Belgium stands as an apparent example of the conflict between an "old" Flemish nationalism, with its modernist understandings of territorial authority, and an evidently post-modern EU. As far as the case studies in the section on Eastern Europe are concerned, we find that the overemphasis of scholars on a few well-known cases of nationalism in Eastern Europe (in particular the cases of Russia, Poland, Romania, and Hungary have received extensive attention in previous studies) has distorted analysts' view of the dynamics and characteristics of nationalism in the "East." That is the reason why this section includes some rare, but not idiosyncratic, examinations of nationalism at the fringes of Europe, such as Latvia and Bulgaria. In addition, we offer a comparative exploration of the Croatian and Serbian nationalism, which against the background of the violent forms of nationalism in the Balkan region is representative of a broader phenomenon and promises to be particularly informative. Moreover, the volume applies different methods of analysis of nationalism, such as the institutional approach (nationalist institutions and policies), the actor-centered approach (nationalist attitudes of political actors) as well as discourse analysis (structures and contents of nationalist discourses) and statistical analysis. By doing so, we cover both the qualitative and quantitative methods of social sciences.

The volume is a collection of studies by a multinational group of authors with backgrounds in Belgium, Bulgaria, Canada, Germany, Latvia, New Zealand, Poland, Spain, Ukraine, and the United States. This allows for a multi-aspect examination of nationalism in respect of different cultural perspectives, while maintaining a narrow focus on nationalism in Europe at the same time.

Part I
Questioning Conceptions of Nationalism

Chapter 2
Civic Nationalism and the Nation-State: Towards a Dynamic Model of Convergence

Taras Kuzio

This chapter argues that nationalism in the West and East has never been as divergent as scholars have argued. Indeed, the transformations that the East (Central-Eastern Europe and the three Baltic states) has undergone and its integration into NATO and the EU affirm that the convergence of Western and Eastern nationalism is based on a far narrower gulf than has been traditionally articulated by scholars. The ability of the East to fulfil the requirements of the Membership Action Plan for NATO membership and the Copenhagen Criteria for EU membership over two decades would also affirm that nationalism in the East was *never* fundamentally different to that found in the West. This chapter lays out the case that nationalism in the West and East is *not* radically different. Western nationalism emerged as a civic variant after two centuries of gestation, conflict and evolution. Eastern nationalism evolved into a civic variant during the course of the twentieth century, first under communism and secondly during the post-communist transition to a democratic-market economy. Both nationalisms—West and East—rapidly evolved in the second half of the twentieth century, especially during the 1960s in the West and in the 1990s in the East. The democratization of Eastern European post-communist states took place relatively quickly in the decade following the collapse of communism and the Soviet empire.[1]

North American and Western European nation-states matured into civic states only in the second half of the twentieth century. The West and East therefore evolved into civic states during the same century separated by only a few decades. The major difference between the West and East was that the arrival of a consolidated democracy in the West came after a journey that had begun in the late eighteenth century whereas the East transformed into civic states during a "big bang" following the collapse of communism. The East undertook its transition to a civic state at a faster pace than the West because of external pressure from the OSCE, globalization and the desire of the East to "return to Europe" through membership of the Council of Europe, NATO and the EU.

The arrival of a democratic civic state has been traditionally associated by scholars with greater pluralism. The majority of scholarly contributions in this field have discussed the greater inclusiveness of the civic state in a normative manner by arguing in favor of, or against, increased pluralism and multiculturalism.[2] Another group of scholars have critically responded to this claim by drawing on a wide variety of theoretical and comparative perspectives.[3] A growing body of revisionist work argues that the growth of pluralism within nation-states is part of a long-term trend that has been taking place since the late eighteenth century, a view that this chapter upholds.[4] This revisionist scholarship, which this chapter builds on, disagrees with the static model developed by Hans Kohn[5] that is still widely used by many scholars, policy makers, and journalists.[6] The chapter presents a dynamic theory of the convergence of nationalism in the West and East through a process of societal change over time, evolutionary in the case of the West over two centuries and revolutionary in the case of the East since the collapse of communism.

This chapter adds new conceptual theory to the relatively few scholars who have discussed the evolution of civic nationalism and the long-term forces that are driving North American and Western European nation-states to be more pluralistic and inclusive in how their communities are imagined. The chapter goes further by supporting a theory of the convergence of nationalism in the East and West.

The chapter analyzes the evolution of civic nationalism and movement toward greater pluralism and inclusiveness within nation-states in three areas—citizenship and the vote, gender, and immigration. These three categories of analysis are chosen for three reasons. First, citizenship and the vote are central as to how we define civic states and liberal democracies. In the West, citizenship and the right to vote evolved over two centuries from the late eighteenth to the late twentieth century with the last expansion of the right to vote in the 1960s when it was granted to native peoples. In the East, inclusive citizenship and the right to vote came automatically after the collapse of communism. Only two former Soviet republics—Estonia and Latvia—adopted exclusive citizenship and the right to vote policies. Yet, Estonia and Latvia's policies resembled those of Germany throughout the 1990s with all three states gradually moderating their exclusive citizenship rules to integrate non-indigenous minorities. A second category of analysis—gender—is included in this chapter because this field has traditionally been ignored in studies of nationalism. As Walby states, "Literature on nations and nationalism rarely addresses the question of gender . . ." and ". . . Most texts on nationalism do not take gender as a significant issue."[7] Gender rights, both the right to vote and the advancement of women, took place in the West and the East during the twentieth century. The West and East advanced the right to vote for women during the inter-war years. A third category of analysis—attitudes to immigration—primarily focuses on the West as the issue of immigration is not a policy concern, political problem or electoral liability in the East. Immigration is chosen as a category of analysis to highlight the evolving nature of contradictory attitudes in the West toward immigration as both a socio-economic asset and a threat to established national identities. The first arrivals of non-Anglo-Saxon, protestants to the U.S. took place in the 1840s with the immigration of Irish Catholics (Native Americans, Mexicans, and blacks were marginalized and not perceived to be part of the imagined American community). Irish Catholics were followed by different ethnic waves of immigrants to the U.S., Canada, Australia, and New Zealand and by immigration after World War II into Western Europe. Immigration has become an acute political and, in the case of Islamic terrorists, security issue in Western Europe in the last two decades[8] leading to most Western European states and Australia retreating from policies promoting multiculturalism to those promoting integration. Immigration was always a contentious issue in the settler societies of North America, Australia, and New Zealand, all of whom had restrictions on non-white immigration until the 1960s. Australia abandoned multiculturalism around the same time as Western Europe; New Zealand never adopted these policies. Canada remains the only Western liberal democracy still committed to multiculturalist policies and open immigration and the Canadian Conservative Party the only center-right party that does not regard multiculturalism and immigration as a threat to an established national identity.

The chapter is divided into two sections. The first discusses what I define as the "static" and "dynamic" models of nationalism and nation-states. The chapter argues that the dynamic model of the convergence of nationalism in the West and East best describes the evolution of Western nation-states since the late eighteenth century and the convergence of nationalism in the West and East in the twentieth century. The second section discusses three categories of analysis of civic nationalism in the West and East: citizenship and the vote, attitudes to gender, and policies on immigration.

1. Static and Dynamic Models of Nationalism

The Static Model of Nationalism

The framework developed by Kohn of a Western civic nationalism being different in origin, essence, and form to that of Eastern ethnic nationalism has traditionally been the standard framework used by scholars to understand nationalism. Kohn's static framework argued that Western states were civic from their inception in the late eighteenth century. Kohn believed that Western nationalism was inherently different because it evolved in conjunction with political rights and was therefore civic (i.e., democratic). This civic nationalism therefore owed more to territorial than to ethno-cultural factors. Western civic nationalism was also inclusive in permitting anybody within the given territory of a nation-state to become a citizen, regardless of their ethnicity, race, or gender. The civic nationalism that developed in Kohn's West was individualistic, liberal, rational, and cosmopolitan.

In contrast, Kohn defines Eastern nationalism as backward looking, prone to conflict, tribal, and irrational. Eastern nationalism was primitive because it focused its energy on building a new national identity and was inter-related to religion, language, and nationality. It lacked a "high culture" and therefore focused upon ethno-cultural issues.[9] By defining Eastern European nationalism in such a manner Kohn believed that it was inevitable that the East would tend toward creating authoritarian, culturally repressive, fascist, and autocratic states while the West would naturally establish liberal democratic states.

The alleged dichotomy between Western and Eastern nationalism was inevitable because of the backward socio-political and socio-economic level of development in the East. The East lacked a large bourgeois and was more closely associated with absolutist regimes. Eastern nationalism was also allegedly more prone to ethnic conflict because it inevitably had to resort to a greater degree of historical myth making. The boundaries of the nation-state did not coincide with ethnic groups and therefore there were a great number of demands for border changes along ethnographic lines. In contrast, the roots of Western nationalism lay in the age of enlightenment, liberty, the rule of law, and individualism. In the American and French revolutions individual liberty played a predominant role in mobilizing the revolutionaries. The American national idea, for example, was based on individual liberty and tolerance that overcame ethnic differences.[10]

Kohn did not see the expansion of Western empires necessarily as negating his dichotomy of two types of nationalism, Western civic and Eastern ethnic. If the West possessed a superior civilization and a civic (i.e., good in Kohn's definition) nationalism then contact with it would be inevitably beneficial to the colonies. "Through contact with the modern West, Asian civilizations and peoples were revitalized," Kohn argued. He pointed to England's liberal civilization that had allegedly, "infused a new spirit into Asia and later into Africa."[11] Such arguments can be obviously countered by historians and post-colonial theorists because they are highly questionable. The chapter does not have space to include a discussion and analysis of Western colonialism and the mistreatment and genocide of native peoples that accompanied the evolution of nation-states from the eighteenth to the twentieth century.[12] There is insufficient space to cover Western colonialism and territorial conflict in North and South America as a fourth category of analysis.

Dynamic Model and Theory of Convergence of Nationalism

The static Kohn framework of nationalism failed to take into account that nation-states have evolved over two centuries since the late eighteenth century. Kohn's framework mistakenly argued that nation-states in the West had *always* been civic, a view that could not include a dynamic framework that factored in long-term change. A dynamic model of convergence emphasizes the link between democratization and nation-building and discusses this within the context of an evolution of nation-states into more inclusive civic states in the West and East. In other words, a dynamic model of convergence offers an alternative to the static view of nation-states as inclusive and civic from their inception in the late eighteenth century. A dynamic model sees the arrival of the civic state as a twentieth century phenomenon in *both* the West and East and therefore posits an argument in favor of a theory of the convergence of nationalism in the West and East.

The nation-state has *always* been a complicated marriage of convenience between nationalist particularism and liberal universalism.[13] Traditional frameworks for discussing nationalism did not necessarily see this as a problem because Western nation-states were assumed to have *always* been civic in contrast to the allegedly ethnic basis of nation-states elsewhere in the world. When nationalism came to be seen as a negative term after World War II because of its close correlation to Nazism, the term "civic nationalism" was replaced by the less evocative "patriotism," although the theoretical or normative differences between them are unclear. One person's "patriotism" is, after all, a neighbor's "nationalism." As nation-states have become progressively more inclusive and pluralistic, nationalism has become increasingly buried deeper within Western public consciousness. Nationalism has not therefore disappeared with the arrival of greater inclusiveness and pluralism; it has merely become, in Billig's phrase, simply "banal."[14] Civic nationalism in the West has become an excepted, everyday part of life where if it is publicly raised, such as after the 9/11 terrorist attacks in the U.S., it is described as "patriotism." The "patriotism" of the Bush administration was traditionally seen as "nationalism" outside the U.S.,[15] including in Canada and Europe, and even more so in the Middle East.

A static view of nationalism, national identity, and society has been increasingly challenged by integrating these phenomena within a more dynamic framework. This has argued that in the early stages of nation-states, ethnic nationalism is stronger than the civic elements that are still in their early, embryonic stages of development. Over time, as democratization is consolidated, institutions are crafted, the rule of law is established, the right to vote is expanded, and minorities and immigrants receive greater rights, the proportionate relationship between nationalist particularist and liberal universalist factors moves from the former toward the latter; that is, the civic nature of the state widens and deepens. Democratic civic states as they emerged in the twentieth century did not therefore exist in the eighteenth and nineteenth centuries in the West or East.

Tension between nationalist particularism and liberal universalism will always be a constant feature of nation-states because of the lack of congruency between "cultural" and "political" nationalism.[16] "The durability of the nation-state is because it mediates between 'primordial bonds' and 'abstract, universal humanity,' it is open to strangers while remaining 'compact and contingent.'"[17] As long as nation-states continue to exist, this conflict between nationalist particularism and universal liberalism will be an integral component of the nation-state.[18] All nation-states are under-pinned by nationalism. The growth of rule of law and democratic institutions serves to constrain this nationalism within the confines of a democratic civic state. Since the 1990's evidence of the continued resilience of nationalism within European nation-states can be seen through the rise of ethnic and populist nationalism. France's National Front leader, Jean-Marie Le Pen, reached the final round of the 2003 French presidential elections.[19] Switzerland's largest political party, the Swiss Peoples Party, caused an international outcry over its openly racist election posters in the 2007 federal elections. Populist right anti-immigration parties are also popular in Denmark and Belgium. The European Parliament has three Political Groups who incorporate euro-skeptics, euro-separatists, populist-nationalist, anti-immigrant and fascist parties from western and Eastern Europe. Western European parties from the UK, Italy, and France dominate two of the three Political Groups: Independence/Democracy and Identity and Tradition and Sovereignty, while Polish parties dominate the Union for Europe of the Nations Group.[20]

The evolution of the civic element within nation-states, as seen in the expansion of the franchise and greater tolerance of cultural pluralism and inclusiveness, is a post-World War II phenomenon. The trend toward greater plurality did not necessarily mean that we were approaching the end of the nation-state, as many scholars have long predicted, in favor of the triumph of global universalism.[21] The nation-state has constantly changed and adapted since its inception in the late eighteenth century and will continue to remain with us for the long-term as it will always attract greater loyalty than that given to supra-national institutions or federations. The majority of EU members continue to oppose the transfer of their key powers in domestic economic, monetary, fiscal, and security policy to a supra-national EU.

Advances in democratization, inclusiveness, and plurality within nation-states have traditionally been associated with civic nationalism while intolerance, racism, and fascism have been linked to ethnic nationalism. Nevertheless, the boundaries between civic and ethnic nationalism and inclusive and exclusive nation-states are blurred.[22] *Both* types of nationalism, civic and ethnic, can be intolerant and tolerant. The ethno-cultural nationalism of minorities within empires, apartheid regimes, or even in civic nation-states can be purely defensive and benign. At other times, it can be intolerant and aggressive. France has long exhibited an intolerant attitude toward national minorities and immigrants who are meant to divest themselves of their linguistic and cultural background in favor of an official, state-sponsored French identity. The two main candidates in the 2007 French presidential elections, Conservative Nicolas Sarkozy and Socialist Ségolène Royal, used the nationalist card. Following his election, President Sarkozy established a new Ministry for Immigration and National Identity.

The center-right, populists, and fascists have found it most difficult to accept the evolution of nation-states since World War II. Nationality policies adopted by nation-states were never uniform, even in the civic West. Italy and Austria only began to create the foundations of a modern nation-state following the end of fascism after World War II. Italy only granted women the vote in 1945. In both countries, the fascist past still leaves a shadow over current politics, with former fascist and nationalist parties continuing to be electorally popular in Italy and Austria. Two populist right anti-immigration parties together received 29 % of the vote in the September 2008 Austrian elections after the Freedom Party jumped from 11 to 18 % of the vote and the Alliance for the Future of Austria—Jörg Haider's List increased its support from 4 to 11 %. Together they now command as much popular support as either of the two traditional large parties, the Social Democratic and center-right Peoples Party, who received 29 and 26 % respectively. After the collapse of the corrupt Christian Democratic Party in Italy its place was taken by a curious alliance of Italian nationalists, Forza Italia, regional separatists, Lega Nord and "post-fascists," Allianza Nationale, the former Italian Social Movement.[23] Italy has its most right-wing government since World War II. Spain and Portugal's fascist regimes lasted into the mid 1970s and only after a peaceful evolution in the former and a revolution in the latter did democratic nation-states emerge. Eire only emerged as a modern nation-state relatively recently after overcoming centuries of colonial rule.

Canada is also a recent addition to the Western family of nation-states, even though it became an autonomous dominion within the British Empire in 1867. Canadian citizenship, a separate flag and national anthem are all post-World War II creations. Until the 1960s the city of Toronto, Canada's largest metropolis, hosted the largest parades outside the British province of Ulster by rabidly anti-Catholic Orangemen celebrating Protestant Anglo-Saxon hegemony. In 1870, Canada had 900 Orange lodges.[24] Today, Toronto no longer hosts large Orange parades, is a multicultural city where half of the children do not have English as their first language and its largest parade is the annual June Gay Pride Week. As in Britain, Catholics and Protestants never mixed in pre-1960s Ontario society. Catholics in Ulster and cities on the British mainland, such as Glasgow, Manchester, and Liverpool, were disbarred from entering certain professions and the ruling elites until the last decades of the twentieth century. In certain cases these religious divides have ameliorated while in other cases they continue to exist in liberal democratic states.[25]

A key difference between civic and ethnic nationalism is that the latter is usually undertaken by insecure ethnic groups.[26] From a gender perspective, insecure "masculinist nationalism" grows where there is a heightened conflict with a domestic or external "Other."[27] After insecure ethnic groups achieve their aims and become hegemonic within their territories they can continue to remain intolerant of minorities, an example being the policies and attitudes of Francophone nationalists toward Anglophones, Jews, and immigrants following their election victory in Quebec in 1976. Quebec separatist Premier Jacques Parizeau blamed "the ethnics and the money" following the defeat of the 1995 separatist referendum in Quebec, a reference to new immigrants and Jews. After the victory of the "Quiet Revolution" in Quebec in the 1970s a majority of Montreal's long-standing Jewish population migrated from Quebec to Toronto, Ontario.[28] Toronto has since then replaced Montreal as Canada's business center.

Civic nationalism can be a type of nationalism that has evolved into a more liberal variant only after the ethnic group that espouses it has achieved its goal of hegemony within a state. Kaufmann traces the evolution of American nationalism in such a manner.[29] France is another example of the evolution of nationalism from an ethnic to a more civic variant. In both cases, American and French nationalism evolved into civic types in the second half of the twentieth century. Contemporary French civic nationalism was a minority viewpoint a century ago in France when Ernest Renan espoused it. Hefferman argues that, "The alternative, biological or social Darwinian interpretation probably commanded wider support amongst European intellectuals until the 1940s."[30] There was little support in the nineteenth century for writers such as Lord Action who called for cultural pluralism. In fact, Western political thought prior to World War II, "has shown little understanding or respect for the cultural diversity of mankind and has made scant allowance for it as a possible concern of government."[31]

The use of historical myths and nationalist historiography has been as commonplace in the West as in the East. The East may even have a better record than the West as most communist states did not utilize nationalist historiographies. Romania, Bulgaria, and Russia within the USSR were exceptions to this rule as communism had integrated with nationalism in these three cases. "Nationalistic history," of the kind used by France and Germany in their territorial disputes over Alsace-Lorraine, was commonplace throughout Western Europe and North America until the mid twentieth century.[32] Historical textbooks that legitimized empires, promoted ethnic superiority, patriotic prejudice, chauvinism, historical myths, and social Darwinism were commonplace in the West until the 1950s. Although nationalist historiography has declined into a minority viewpoint since the 1960s, "the patriotic ideals toward which those writers strove are still with us today, in certain school textbooks, and also in the popular press and comics."[33] Nationalist historiography has never completely gone away and often re-appears during elections, crises, wars, and international sports events.

2. Civic Nationalism and Nation-States: Three Categories of Analysis

Civic elements only came to dominate and overshadow ethnic particularism in Western and Eastern nation-states in the second half of the twentieth century. The growth of civic-political rights, let alone those pertaining to minority ethnic groups, has been a slow and very uneven process. As long as nation-states remain the primary manner in which populations are organized there will always be some elements of ethnic particularism within them as nation-states by their very nature are composed of civic and ethnic-cultural factors. The growth of the civic inclusiveness of Western and Eastern nation-states is discussed below in three categories of analysis—citizenship and the vote, gender, and immigration.

Citizenship and the Vote

Citizenship is important because it encompasses both a set of rights and demarcates "us" from "them." Citizenship not only confers a set of rights and obligations, but citizens acquire a new identity, are socialized into "civic virtues" and "become members of a political community with a particular territory and history."[34] Citizenship incorporates within itself historical baggage, myths, culture, language, codes of behavior, and institutional legacies. Citizenship and nationalism have been linked since the late eighteenth century because nation-states are bounded and incorporate political identities. Citizenship policies are regulated, formulated, and implemented within institutions, the rule of law, and political cultures of nation-states.

Unlike in the West, the granting of citizenship in post-communist Eastern Europe was less contentious. When communist regimes collapsed in 1989-1991 only two of the 27 states—Latvia and Estonia—introduced exclusive citizenship legislation. Their exclusive citizenship policies gradually evolved toward less restrictive criteria because of the influence of the OSCE, EU, and the Council of Europe. The remaining 25 post-communist states opted for the "zero option" whereby everybody resident on their territory automatically became citizens. This applied even in authoritarian regimes, such as those that emerged from the former Yugoslavia and Belarus. The record on citizenship in democratizing post-communist Eastern European states is in many ways better than that of the West, where citizenship was gradually made more inclusive over centuries to include women, minority religious groups, and racial and ethnic minorities.

European and North American nation-states have traditionally differed in their approaches to citizenship and their evolution toward greater civic inclusive states took place in the second half of the twentieth century. Citizenship, the vote, and immigration have been intricately linked. In the twentieth century, two waves of enlarging citizenship and the vote have taken place. In the inter-war era, women were granted citizenship and voting rights. In the second half of the twentieth century, the civic state widened its inclusiveness by incorporating indigenous peoples and, in most countries, immigrants. Australia was one of the last Western nation-states to grant citizenship and the vote to Aboriginals in 1967, only five years before Australia's adoption of multiculturalism, a policy which was itself downgraded to a policy of integration by the center-right Liberal Party in the 1990s.[35]

A majority of Western nation-states have evolved toward greater liberalized citizenship and immigration policies and moved away from assimilation to policies that promote the half-way house of integration over a largely discredited full-blown multiculturalism.[36] The 1981 UK Nationality Act was the exception that moved Britain from an over-inclusive nation-state to an identity based on blood and culture. Britain moved away from multiculturalism under a Labour government toward an emphasis on integration. After Germany was re-united in October 1990 it increasingly evolved in the 1990s from an ethnic definition of citizenship, which had been in place since the nineteenth century, to an inclusive definition. Prior to 1990 the ethno-cultural definition of "German" has been evoked because German nationalism emerged *after* a state was created and the state was not coterminous with the nation. Broadening the inclusiveness of the nation-state was only discussed in Germany from the 1980s but then implemented after 1999. The British and German country cases show how citizenship has been in a process of evolution. Germany now has more liberal citizenship tests than the U.S. But, unlike the U.S., Germany continues to place less emphasis on integration and remained hostile to immigration. Anti-immigration attitudes run highest in Western European EU members Germany, Austria, France, and Denmark that are the same countries that are most opposed to Turkish membership of the EU. Eastern European EU members support Turkish membership.

The U.S. evolved over the long-term toward greater civic inclusiveness. As Rogers M. Smith points out, "The U.S. is not an inherently and autonomous liberal democratic nation, as many glorifying histories would have it."[37] Race, gender, and class, "have always been such a defining feature of American life."[38] The U.S. evolved from a very narrow definition of the political community in 1790, when the U.S. Naturalization Act provided for citizenship to only white, protestant, wealthy men, toward greater civic inclusiveness 170 years later. Formal U.S. citizenship was only introduced in 1868 when black slaves were given the vote. The U.S. has engaged in discussions on immigration, citizenship, and their link to national identity with great frequency since the 1776 revolution.[39] This has resulted in, "clashing ideas about the foundation of American citizenship and nationality."[40]

U.S. citizenship has, "always expressed illiberal, undemocratic ascriptive myths of American civic identity; along with a variety of liberal and republican types, in logically inconsistent but politically effective combinations."[41] White supremacy could still be championed by those opposing slavery, full rights could be denied to those incorporated within conquered Spanish territories, Philippinos could be denied U.S. citizenship and there could be widespread fear of allowing the immigration of Jews and Catholics. The U.S. historical record on Native Indians, Mexicans, and blacks is very poor. At the same time, it has an exceptional record of integrating Jews and the U.S. has not experienced widespread anti-Semitism.[42] In 2007, the U.S. Congress rejected legislation to grant citizenship to millions of illegal immigrants, the majority of whom are Hispanics, even though the policy was supported by President George W. Bush.

In the U.S., as in most nation-states, citizenship legislation is "a product of ongoing contestation and compromise."[43] The dilemma of creating a political community that reflects the dominant ethno-cultural interests of the titular nation meant that this was in conflict with the civic ideals promoted by the U.S. This dilemma was only resolved as late as the 1960s when U.S. policy evolved toward combining *both* integration and cultural pluralism. Multiculturalism, U.S. elites believed, is likely to damage American national identity because it celebrates diversity, not unity. Meanwhile, policies of assimilation along the lines of the pre-1960s "melting pot" were no longer tenable. U.S. policies to integrate immigrants into Americans, while permitting them to celebrate their cultural background in the private domain, has been the dominant U.S. policy since the 1960s. The U.S. has continued to support integration while rejecting Canadian-style multiculturalism.

The U.S. has *always* remained concerned that if citizenship was granted to non- Anglo-Saxon ethnic groups they would not become sufficiently "American"; that is, their ethnic origins would determine if immigrants could assimilate into Americans. These views on citizenship and immigration changed in the 1960s in Europe and North America. In comparison to prior to the 1960s the culture, language, and history of immigrants is no longer vilified as inferior baggage only to be jettisoned at the earliest opportunity. Today, integration into American values and civic nationalism is not seen as contradicting the maintenance of pride in one's cultural heritage. Nevertheless, immigrants are still subjected to strong Americanizing pressures and taught "common core American values, a common U.S. history, and a common language."[44] This is what fundamentally differentiates the U.S. from its northern multicultural neighbor, Canada.

Pressures on new immigrants to become true Americans have led to new demands by those arriving from Asia and Latin America. They have denounced policies of integration as tantamount to continuing alleged "melting pot" policies that attempt to maintain white supremacy. Asians, blacks, and Hispanics have called for affirmative action and multicultural education that no longer ignores the contributions of blacks, Indians, Asians, and Hispanics to U.S., European, and World history. Such demands increase the fears of nativist Americans, such as Samuel Huntington, who warned of "The Hispanic Challenge."[45]

A major contrast between consolidated democracies in the West and democratizing states in post-communist Europe rests on the manner in which the vote has been introduced. In the West, the vote was only gradually introduced over the course of nearly 200 years, between the late eighteenth century and the second half of the twentieth century. Women, for example, were given the vote after World War I in *both* the West and the East. Women only obtained the vote between the 1920s-1970s in the West, with France only granting women the vote in 1944 and Switzerland as late as 1971. In France, women received the right to vote in 1944, fourteen years after Turkish women in Mustafa Kemal Atatürk's Turkey.[46] In Eastern Europe, the vote was granted to women in the inter-war period, then taken away from both gender groups in the communist era and granted to all citizens after the communist regimes disintegrated and their transitions to democracy began. The universal suffrage that took Western nation-states nearly two centuries to introduce came immediately to all sections of all post-communist states, with only two exceptions of exclusive citizenship and right to vote state policies, Latvia and Estonia.

Between the 1780s and the 1960s, the vote was gradually expanded in Europe and North America to include all social classes, religious groups, women, and aboriginal peoples. Even in two of the three countries that introduced multicultural policies—Canada and Australia—aboriginal peoples only obtained the vote in 1960 and 1967 respectively, a century later than in another settler nation, New Zealand, where multicultural policies have never been introduced.[47] In a large number of U.S. southern states, blacks were denied the vote until the 1960s through local racist Jim Crow policies.

Gender

The scholarly literature on nations and nationalism rarely addresses the gender question.[48] In Canada, for example, history textbooks dwelt exclusively on men when discussing the nation-building project.[49] Yet, women participate in the nation-building project in many different ways through membership of nationalist movements, biological reproduction, contributing to the ideological reproduction of collective culture and in the promotion of ethnic difference.[50]

Introducing gender issues into a dynamic theoretical framework of the convergence of nationalism will contribute toward our understanding of the role played by nationalism in nation-states. Nation-states could not be defined as civic if women were disbarred from voting. Even based upon the criteria of gender and the vote, nation-states traditionally defined as civic, such as France, the UK and the U.S., therefore only became civic and democratic after they granted women the vote in 1920, 1929, and 1944 respectively. Women obtained citizenship and the vote centuries or decades after men. In some cases, such as the American south, black women only enjoyed these rights many decades after white women had successfully achieved them.

Women were not only denied the vote between the conclusion of World War I and World War II, when 28 countries gave them the vote. They were also prevented from fully participating in politics, employment, and the social sphere until the great advances that came about as a consequence of societal changes in the 1960s. The advancement of women into traditional male employment preserves in Western and Eastern states remains an on-going struggle. Although the Labour Party under Prime Minister Tony Blair has greatly increased the proportionate number of women MPs, the Conservative Party remains dominated by middle class, white, male Anglo-Saxons. Multicultural Canada has a lower or similar proportion of women parliamentarians than the majority of post-communist states.[51]

In Britain, as in most European states, married women and men in the nineteenth century traditionally shared separate lives. Public life was reserved for men. Politics, education and culture were not reserved for women, a view promoted throughout European and North American nation-states until the 1950s. Cambridge University did not allow women to become full members until 1948 and many trade union and gentlemen clubs remained men only establishments until the last two decades of the twentieth century.[52]

The gradual expansion of women into politics, the media, and academia has contributed toward transforming the civic inclusiveness of nation-states.[53] Their advancement is felt to be a product of the "sixties revolution" that increased sexual freedom, women's rights, education, independence, and influence. Such advances for women also took place in the communist regimes of Eastern Europe where women, at least in legislation, were granted equal status to men. Women, in turn, in Western democracies are likely to be more cosmopolitan, less opposed to EU integration, supporters of the moderate wings of the Labour, Liberal, and Conservative parties, more supportive of policies to promote cultural pluralism toward racial and ethnic minorities and more open to change than their male counterparts.[54]

Women's greater support for policies that promote cultural pluralism does not necessarily translate into support for multiculturalism. Ethnic ghettoes in Muslim communities, for example, can lead to the continued denial of women's rights. Muslim men may see women's rights granted by the host nation-state as a threat to their continued hegemony over the Muslim community. Young Pakistani men have used Islam to justify violence and harassment against women, forced marriages, and to enforce a strict dress code and behavior. Multicultural policies in such situations can grant autonomy to men to create authoritarian environments for women by excluding "Western" (non-Islamic) rights. Asian women have a suicide rate in the UK three times the national average.[55]

Immigration

Post-communist states have not had to deal with the question of immigration, unlike Western Europe, North America, and Australia and New Zealand. Asylum seekers and immigrants from developing countries continue to look upon Eastern European states as transit routes to the more affluent West. They are also unlikely to seek employment as "guest workers" because employment opportunities are limited in post-communist countries. The attitude of the population in post-communist states to racial minorities and immigrants from developing countries is more likely to resemble that found in Western democratic states prior to the 1960s. Even in some of the democratically advanced post-communist states, such as the Czech Republic, the treatment of Roma continues to remain poor.

Western nation-states have adopted four policies to deal with greater immigration.[56] First, *differential exclusion* relates to policies where immigrants are excluded from full participation in the political, economic, and cultural life of society. Immigrants were typically only treated as "temporary" guest workers in Germany, Switzerland, Austria, Japan, and Belgium. Second, *rapid assimilation* was a policy that demanded immigrants to give up their culture and language in return for citizenship by assimilating into the majority titular nation's culture. This model was applied to some degree in all Western nation-states, at least until the 1960s. The UK, U.S., Australia, and Canada pursued these policies until the 1960s; France and the Canadian province of Quebec continue to uphold these policies of assimilation. The adoption of French culture and language in France and Quebec is viewed as an act of *civicisme* with little tolerance of cultural diversity and cultural pluralism.[57] Third, a policy of *gradual integration* was enacted as a moderate variant of *rapid assimilation*. Britain, for example, has adopted a mixture of both assimilation and pluralism, "without a clear overall objective."[58] Finally, there was a policy of *pluralism* where immigrants were accepted as ethnic communities granted equal rights with the "indigenous" or "titular" nation(s). The U.S. no longer adopts a negative view of cultural pluralism in the private domain. At the same time, it does little to promote the culture and language of ethnic groups. Australia, Canada, and Sweden, in contrast, encourage immigration and officially support ethnic groups through multicultural policies and short residencies of only two years for qualification for citizenship. A backlash against multiculturalism throughout the Western world has turned many countries toward policies that encourage integration, including in Australia.[59] Indeed, Canada remains the only bastion of continued faith in the policies of multiculturalism with the developed world's most liberal immigration policy. In this regard, Canada's Conservative Party stands out as unique in not being hostile to either immigration or multiculturalism.

The growth of Asian, Indian sub-continent, West Indian, and Hispanic immigration into European and North American nation-states since the 1960s has altered their ethnic make-up and increased cultural pluralism. The threat imposed by Asian immigration was perceived as sufficiently high for it to be fully banned in the U.S. and Canada until the 1950s. In the U.S. it was not until 1965 that all racial exclusions on immigration were fully removed.[60] The "White Australia" Policy introduced in 1901 aimed to keep out Asians and was only rescinded in 1966. Similar restrictions on non-white immigration existed until 1965 in the U.S., Canada until 1962-1967, and in New Zealand as late as 1986. Nativism, understood as hostility to immigration, "was a recurrent phenomenon in America, particularly during periods of economic and political crisis" as perhaps vividly seen in the film *Gangs of New York* where "Native Americans," as white, protestant settlers called themselves, clashed in the 1840s with the first non-protestants to immigrate to the U.S., Catholic Irish. Restrictions on immigration were in place in Western Europe until the de-colonization of their empires after World War II and characterized each wave of migration to the U.S. since the 1840s when the country was first opened up to non-protestant outsiders.[61]

There has been a gradual growth in the inclusiveness of the majority of Western nation-states, although more than often this was undertaken reluctantly by the states. Germany and Austria were the only two countries that adopted "differential exclusion" policies of immigration until the 1990s. In Germany the evolution toward a more inclusive society was clearly linked to greater security felt by its ruling elites after the unification of Germany in 1990. Of the defeated World War II powers, Western Germany was also the country that undertook the most in terms of overcoming its fascist past, especially in relation to other axis powers Japan, Austria, and Italy. German nationhood has cautiously evolved toward a more civic-territorial definition in the 1990s.[62] Japan, often described as a model democracy since 1945, does not permit immigration and continues to disbar half a million Koreans living in Japan, including those born in the country, from citizenship.

Britain has moved in the opposite direction to the majority of nation-states. The 1948 Nationality Act and 1962 Commonwealth Immigration Acts reflected an elite consensus among both the Conservative and Labour parties that was not hostile to immigration from the Commonwealth. This policy changed with the Margaret Thatcher government's 1981 British Nationality Act that moved toward a more ethnic policy of "racial group particularism." Prior to the 1981 Act, Britain had an over-inclusive definition of the civic nation as "citizenship universalism."[63] The 1981 Act reduced the possibilities for immigration and reflected the ascendancy of the "nationalist and anti-EU wing" within the Conservative Party. Conservative leaders William Hague, Ian Duncan-Smith, and Michael Howard continued in the Thatcher tradition with only David Cameron attempting to re-fashion a different "New Conservatism" following Tony Blair's example in transforming the center-left Labour Party into a centrist "New Labour" Party.

After 150 years of being barred from citizenship, Asians in the U.S. continue, "to be viewed as a group whose loyalty to America remains in doubt."[64] In World War II, 120,000 Japanese, including many U.S. citizens, were interned after they were collectively defined as a "fifth column." Such a collective designation of guilt was not directed against Germans living in America even though the U.S. was also at war with Germany. Ukrainians were interned in Canada in World War I and Italians were interned in Britain in World War II. Chinese, Japanese, and other Asians were seen as carriers of cultures that were allegedly incompatible with democratic systems and American (i.e., white Anglo-Saxon, protestant national identity) values. Asian "authoritarianism" and "non-European" values were contrasted with American democratic values.[65] Despite four decades of immigration and success in business and the professions in the U.S., only three out of 435 congressional representatives and two senators are Asians. A similar situation exists in most European democracies where there are few visible minorities in parliament.[66] In France, which has Europe's largest Muslim population and minorities account for 12 % of the population, only two of the 555 deputies to the lower house of parliament are from minority backgrounds.[67]

Immigration policies became more liberalized in Europe and North America in the 1960s; the exception was the UK which already had a liberal policy that changed toward increased restrictions. This evolution toward greater liberal immigration policies mirrored the transformation of Europe and North America into civic and inclusive nation-states. The evolution reversed a "two-hundred year tradition of increasingly 'ethnic' citizenship in Europe."[68] In the EU only Greece, Austria, and Luxembourg continue to deny citizenship rights to second-generation immigrants. While no longer demanding that immigrants should assimilate, the majority of Western nation-states do not provide official support for minority rights and only a minority ever introduced multicultural policies. The British Council on Racial Equality, which since October 2007 has been renamed the Equality and Human Rights Commission supports a culturally diverse Britain through integration. The middle ground of integration, while opposing multicultural policies rather than policies designed to promote assimilation, remains the most popular policy among nation-states because it attempts to reconcile the nation-state's unity with cultural diversity that has emerged since the 1960s. Integration is the most popular policy pursued by Western nation-states.

The majority of European nation-states adopted liberal immigration policies from the 1950s to the 1980s and immigration profoundly changed European and North American states. Until the 1950s three quarters of all Canadians could claim British or French backgrounds. By 1991, this had declined to only 40 %. The very fact that these nation-states became *de facto* more multi-ethnic made traditional assimilation policies untenable. These policies became untenable because assimilation into the dominant culture did not necessarily bring integration and acceptance into society, especially for non-Europeans, such as Northern African Muslims in France. Socio-economic marginalization and racism has made the allure of assimilation less tempting leading to calls for greater equality and cultural pluralism. In the U.S., the "American dream" has also not resolved the dilemma of extreme divisions based on class, race, and ethnicity.[69]

Liberal immigration policies came under attack from the populist and extreme right and center-right in the 1990s because of three factors. First, the perceived large numbers of immigrants were viewed to be too great in number for society and state institutions to accept.[70] This viewpoint became particularly resilient in countries such as The Netherlands and Britain into which the largest number of Eastern European immigrants arrived after the enlargement of the EU in 2004. Second, non-European immigrants were not viewed to be assimilating or even integrating into the host society. Third, the rise of Islamic terrorism, particularly of the homegrown variety in Britain, made societies nervous of the security threat posed by a minority of their Muslim populations. The resultant backlash has been tighter immigration controls, the incorporation of many extreme right anti-immigration policies into the platforms of the moderate center-right parties, as seen in the 2007 French elections, the rise of the populist right, and greater surveillance by intelligence agencies. The continued salience of ethnicity in Western European states could be readily seen in the electoral victories of populist and fascist parties in Italy, Austria, Belgium, Denmark, and the Netherlands.[71] In the European Parliament three populist and fascist political groups emerged in the 1990s and bring together 91 out of 786 MEPs.

Three decades of liberal immigration policies did not translate into general societal acceptance of immigrants, particularly those who arrived from outside Europe. Historical experience has shown that public acceptance of immigrants takes place over many decades.[72] The growth of Islamic fundamentalism and terrorism may lead to public reluctance to accept Muslims as co-citizens. This will be particularly the case in countries where homegrown Islamic terrorism has emerged, such as Britain and the Netherlands.

Conclusion

A static model of nationalism contrasting "Western civic nationalism" with that of the backward "ethnic nationalism" in the East ignores the evolution of European and North American states from the late eighteenth century, does not take into account their transformation into civic states only in the second half of the twentieth century. This chapter argues in favor of an alternative dynamic theory over time of the convergence of nationalism in the West and East. A dynamic model argues that nation-states only became inclusive and civic in the twentieth century, particularly during its second half. The transformation of Eastern European nationalism took place over the same time-frame. In the inter-war years Eastern European states granted women voting rights at the same time as Western Europe and North America. Women's rights and their societal advancement were simultaneously expanded under communism in Eastern Europe *and* during the "1960s revolution" in the West. In the second half of the twentieth century, nationalism in Eastern Europe transformed under communism with minor exceptions where nationalism merged with communism in Romania, Serbia within Yugoslavia, and in the Russian SFSR within the USSR. Eastern Europe's transition from communist totalitarianism to democratic market economies took place in the 1990s with the inducement of EU and NATO membership, the support of the U.S. and under the watchful eye of the OSCE and Council of Europe. Eastern Europe is no more prone than Western Europe to vote for populist or nationalist parties in national and European elections.

Citizenship and the franchise have traditionally developed in parallel. The major difference in the granting of citizenship and the franchise in the West and East has been the time factor. In the West, these rights were granted over the course of a two hundred year period that lasted from the late eighteenth to the second half of the twentieth centuries. The process was only completed in the 1960s when native peoples were given the vote in immigrant societies, such as Canada and Australia. In the case of Germany, its citizenship policies only became civic in the late 1990s. In the East the granting of citizenship and the vote took place immediately after the removal of communist regimes over a far shorter time frame in the 1990s.

Gender has been largely ignored in nationalism studies. Yet, nation-states could not be defined as civic if women were denied the vote, as they were until the First World War in Europe and North America. Both the West and East granted gender rights at the same time following World War I; France, the home of the 1789 democratic republican revolution, granted women the vote later than many Eastern European states and Turkey.[73] The West does not therefore have a better historical record on gender rights than the East and in the contemporary world women's proportional representation in North American and Western European parliaments is often lower than that found in Eastern European parliaments.

The tension between civic and cultural aspects of nation-states will continue to be an on-going problem because political parties in Europe have to fashion policies and react to the challenges of immigration, racism, and the new threat of Islamic fundamentalist terrorism. Immigration issues have been high on the agendas of European democracies, pushing the center-right to incorporate policies espoused by the populist or fascist right. The center-right and populist nationalist right have become the guardians of the traditional nation-state against immigration, multiculturalism, and a supra-national, federal EU. The politics of immigration has forced Western states to abandon assimilation policies, confront charges of racism and adapt. The nature in which European and North American states are in a constant process of evolution is provided by the turn away in the 1990s from multiculturalist and liberal immigration policies toward a strong emphasis on integration.[74] Multiculturalism has all but become a negative word in every Western democracy, except Canada.

Notes

1. Steven Levitsky and Lucan A. Way, "International Linkage and Democratization," *Journal of Democracy* 16, no. 3 (2005): 20-34; L. A. Way and S. Levitsky, "Linkage, Leverage, and the Post-Communist Divide," *East European Politics and Societies* 21, no. 1 (2007): 48-66; Antoanneta Dimitrova and Geoffrey Pridham, "International Actors and Democracy Promotion in Central and Eastern Europe: The Integration Model and Its Limits," *Democratization* 11, no. 5 (2004): 91-112; Marcin, Zaborowski, "Westernizing the East: External Influences in the Post-Communist Transformation of Eastern and Central Europe," *Journal of Communist Studies and Transition Politics* 21, no. 1 (2005): 16-32.

2. Will Kymlicka, *Multicultural Citizenship* (Oxford: Clarendon Press, 1996); John Rex, "The Concept of a Multicultural Society" in *The Ethnicity Reader: Nationalism, Multiculturalism and Migration,*ed. Montserrat Guibernau (Cambridge, Polity Press, 1997); 205-219; Jerzy J. Smolicz, "Tradition, Core Values and Intellectual Development in Plural Society," *Ethnic and Racial Studies* 11, no. 4 (1988): 387-410; J. J. Smolicz, "Nation-States and Globalization from a Multicultural Perspective: Signposts from Australia," *Na-*

tionalism and Ethnic Politics 4, no. 4 (1998): 1-18; James Forrest and Kevin Dunn, "Core Culture Hegemony and Multiculturalism," *Ethnicities* 6, no. 2 (2006): 203-230.

3. Yasmeen Abu-Laban and Daiva A. Stasiulis, "Ethnic Pluralism under Siege: Popular Partisan Opposition to Multiculturalism," *Canadian Public Policy* 18, no. 4 (1992): 365-386; Chandran Kukathas, "Are There Any Cultural Rights?," *Political Theory* 20, no. 1 (1992): 105-139; David G. Delafenetre, "Interculturalism, Multiculturalism and Transculturalism in Australia and Canada," *Nationalism and Ethnic Politics* 3, no. 1 (1997): 90-110; Katherine Fierlbeck, "The Ambivalent Potential of Cultural Identity," *Canadian Journal Political Science* 29, no. 1 (1996): 3-22; Mikael Hjerm, "Multiculturalism Reassessed," *Citizenship Studies* 4, no. 3 (2000): 357-381; Andre Lecours, "Theorizing Cultural Identities: Historical Institutionalism as a Challenge to Culturalists," *Canadian Journal of Political Science* 33, no. 3 (2000): 499-522; Raymond Aron, "Is Multinational Citizenship Possible?," *Social Research* 41, no. 4 (1974): 638-656; James W. Nickel, "The Value of Cultural Belonging: Expanding Kymlicka's Theory," *Dialogue* 33, no. 4 (1994): 635-642, Bhikhu Parekh, "Cultural Pluralism and the Limits of Diversity," *Alternatives* 20, no. 43 (1995): 431-457; and B. Parekh, "Dilemmas of a Multicultural Theory of Citizenship," *Constellations* 4, no. 1 (1997): 54-62.

4. Raymond Breton, "From Ethnic to Civic Nationalism: English Canada and Quebec," *Ethnic and Racial Studies* 2, no. 1 (1988): 85-102; Eric Foner, *The Story of American Freedom* (London and New York: W. W. Norton, 1998); Eric Kaufmann, "American Exceptionalism Reconsidered: Anglo-Saxon Ethnogenesis in the Universal Nation," *Journal of American Studies* 33, no. 3 (1999): 437-458; E. Kaufmann, "Liberal Ethnicity: Beyond Liberal Nationalism and Minority Rights," *Ethnic and Racial Studies* 23, no. 6 (2000): 1086-1119; E. Kaufmann, "Ethnic or Civic Nation? Theorizing the American Case," *Canadian Review of Studies in Nationalism* 27, nos. 1-2 (2000):133-155; Bernard Yack, "The Myth of the Civic Nation," *Critical Review* 10, nos. 1-2 (1996): 193-211; David Miller, *On Nationality* (Oxford: Clarendon Press, 1995); Taras Kuzio, "Nationalising States or Nation-building? A Critical Survey of the Theoretical Literature and Empirical Evidence," *Nations and Nationalism* 7, no. 2 (2001): 135-154; T. Kuzio, "The Myth of the Civic State: A Critical Survey of Hans Kohn's Framework for Understanding Nationalism," *Ethnic and Racial Studies* 25, no. 1 (2002): 20-39; and Rogers M. Smith, *Civic Ideals: Conflicting Visions of Citizenship in U.S. History* (New Haven, CT: Yale University Press, 1997).

5. Hans Kohn, "The Origins of English Nationalism," *Journal of the History of Ideas* 1, no. 1 (1940): 69-94; H. Kohn, *The Idea of Nationalism: A Study in Its Origins and Background* (New York, Macmillan, 1944); H. Kohn, *Nationalism: Its Meaning and History* (Malabar, FL: Krieger Publishers, 1982).

6. Michael Ignatieff, *Blood and Belonging: Journeys into the New Nationalism* (New York: Farrar, Strauss and Giroux, 1993); Jonathan Freedland, *Bring Home the Revolution: How Britain Can Live the American Dream* (London: Fourth Estate, 1998). For a critique of Ignatieff see W. Kymlicka, "Misunderstanding Nationalism," *Dissent* 42, no. 1 (1995): 130-137.

7. Sylvia Walby, "Woman and Nation" in *Mapping the Nation*, ed. Gopal Balakrishnan (London: Verso, 1996), 235.

8. "World Publics Welcome Global Trade—But Not Immigration," http://pewglobal.org/reports/display.php?ReportID=258 (10 Nov. 2007).

9. Ernest Gellner, *Nations and Nationalism* (Ithaca: NY: Cornell University Press, 1983); Anthony D. Smith, *Nations and Nationalism in a Global Era* (Cambridge: Polity Press, 1996), 77-83.

10. Kohn 1982, 64.

11. Kohn 1982, 84.

12. Walker Connor, "Nation-Building or Nation-Destroying," *World Politics* 24, no. 2 (1972): 319–55; Rogers Nichols, *Indians in the United States and Canada: A Comparative History* (Lincoln: University of Nebraska, 1998).

13. Margaret Canovan, *Nationhood and Political Theory* (Cheltenham: Edward Elgar, 1998); Michael Herzfeld, *Cultural Intimacy. Social Poetics in the Nation-State* (New York: Routledge, 1997).

14. Michael Billig, *Banal Nationalism* (London and Thousand Oaks: Sage Publications, 1996).

15. Andrew Kohut and Bruce Stokes, *America Against the World: How We Are Different and Why We Are Disliked* (New York: Henry Holt & Company, 2006). See also Anatoly Lieven, *America Right or Wrong. An Anatomy of American Nationalism* (Oxford: Oxford University Press, 2004).

16. John Breuilly, *Nationalism and the State* (Chicago: University of Chicago Press, 1993), 54-72.

17. David Scobey, "The Specter of Citizenship," *Citizenship Studies* 5, no. 1 (2001): 24.

18. Kauffman, *Ethnic and Racial Studies*, 2000, 1103.

19. Ineke van der Valk, "Political Discourse on Ethnic Minority Issues. A Comparison of the Right and the Extreme Right in the Netherlands and France (1990-1997)," *Ethnicities* 3, no. 2 (2003): 183-213.

20. "European Parliament Political Groups" http://www.europarl.europa.eu/groups/default_en.htm (3 Nov. 2007).

21. Mary Kaldor, "Cosmopolitanism Versus Nationalism: The New Divide?" in *Europe's New Nationalism. States and Minorities in Conflict*, ed. Richard Caplan and John Feffer (Oxford and New York: Oxford University Press, 1996), 42-58.

22. David Brown, "Are There Good and Bad Nationalisms?," *Nations and Nationalism* 5 no. 2 (1999): 281-302; D. Brown, *Contemporary Nationalism, Civic, Ethnocultural and Multicultural* (London: Routledge, 2000).

23. See the comparison of Italy's and Germany's political culture to that of the U.S. and UK in Gabriel A. Almond and Sidney Verba, *The Civic Culture: Political Attitudes and Democracy in Five Nations* (London: Sage, 1989).

24. Niall Ferguson, *Empire: How Britain Made the Modern World* (London: Penguin, 2003), 254.

25. Religious bigotry and sectarian violence in Glasgow, as exemplified in the "Catholic" Celtic and "Protestant" Rangers football teams, was the subject of a 2005 BBC Panorama documentary. "Scotland's secret shame" can be watched at http://news.bbc.co.uk/1/hi/programmes/panorama/4284023.stm (10 Sept. 2007).

26. Brown 1999, 298; Jack Snyder, *From Voting to Violence: Democratization and Nationalist Conflict* (New York: W. W. Norton, 2000), 75.

27. June Edmunds and Bryan S. Turner, "The Re-Invention of a National Identity? Women and 'Cosmopolitan' Englishness," *Ethnicities* 1, no. 1 (2001): 105.

28. John Dickinson and Brian Young, *A Short History of Quebec* (Montreal: McGill-Queens University Press, 2003).

29. Kaufmann, 1999, *Ethnic and Racial Studies*, 2000; Kaufmann, *Canadian Review of Studies in Nationalism*, 2000.

30. Michael Hefferman, "History, Geography and the French National Space: The Question of Alsace Lorraine, 1914-1918," *Space and Polity* 5, no. 1 (2001): 30.

31. Kenneth McRae, "The Plural Society and the Western Political Tradition," *Canadian Journal of Political Science* 12, no. 4 (1979): 685.

32. Daniel Francis, *National Dreams. Myth, Memory, and Canadian History* (Vancouver, Arsenal Pulp Press, 1997); Edwin Jones, *The English Nation: The Great Myth* (Stroud: Sutton Publishing, 2000); A. D. Smith, *Myths and Memories of the Nation* (Oxford: Oxford University Press, 1999); Lyn Spillman, *Nation and Commemoration: Creating National Identities in the United States and Australia* (Cambridge: Cambridge University Press, 1997).

33. Paul M. Kennedy, "The Decline in Nationalistic History in the West: 1900-1970," *Journal of Contemporary History* 8, no. 1 (1973): 87-88.

34. Bryan S. Turner, "Citizenship Studies: A General Theory," *Citizenship Studies* 1, no. 1 (1997), 9.

35. Lois Foster and David Stockley, "The Rise and Decline of Australian Multiculturalism, 1973-1988," *Politics* 23, no. 2 (1988): 1-10. See also T. Kuzio, "Can Western Multiculturalism Be Applied to the Post-Soviet States: A Critical Response to Kymlicka," *Journal of Contemporary European Politics* 13, no. 2 (2005): 217-232.

36. See Rogers Brubaker, "The Return of Assimilation. Changing Perspectives on Immigration and Its Sequels in France, Germany and the United States," *Ethnic and Racial Studies* 24, no. 4 (2001): 531-548; and Ellie Vasta, "From Ethnic Minorities to Ethnic Majority Policy: Multiculturalism and the Shift to Assimilation in the Netherlands," *Ethnic and Racial Studies* 30, no. 5 (2007): 713-740.

37. R. M. Smith 1997, 499.

38. R. M. Smith, "Citizenship and the Politics of People-Building," *Citizenship Studies* 5, no. 1 (2001): 87.

39. Dorothee Schneider, "Symbolic Citizenship: Nationalism and the Distant State. The United States Congress in the 1996 Debate on Immigration," *Citizenship Studies* 4, no. 3 (2000): 256.

40. Schneider 2000, 270. See also Leo R. Chavez, *Covering Immigration: Popular Images and the Politics of the Nation* (Berkeley: University of California Press, 2001).

41. R. M. Smith 1997, 470.

42. Seymour M. Lipset, *American Exceptionalism: A Double-Edged Sword* (New York: W. W. Norton, 1996).

43. R. M. Smith 1997, 472.

44. Foner 2001, 36.

45. Samuel Huntington, "The Hispanic Challenge" *Foreign Policy*, no. 141 (2004), 30-45.

46. Nergis Canefe, "Turkish Nationalism and Ethno-symbolic Analysis: The Rules of Exception," *Nations and Nationalism* 8, no. 2 (2002): 133-155.

47. James Forrest and Kevin Dunn, "Core Culture Hegemony and Multiculturalism," *Ethnicities* 6, no. 2 (2006): 203-230.

48. Walby 235 and Edmunds and Turner, 2001, 89-91.

49. Francis 1997, 108.

50. Walby 236-237.

51. "Women in National Parliaments," http://www.ipu.org/wmn-e/classif.htm (10 September 2007).

52. Jeremy Paxman, *The English: A Portrait of a People* (London: Penguin, 1999).

53. Edmunds and Turner.

54. Edmunds and Turner.

55. See Marie Macey, "Class, Gender and Religious Influence on Changing Patterns of Pakistani Muslim Male Violence in Bradford," *Ethnic and Racial Studies* 22, no. 5 (1999): 845-866.

56. Stephen Castles, "How Nation-States Respond to Immigration and Ethnic Division," *New Community* 21, no. 3 (1995): 298.

57. Max Silverman, "The French Republic Unveiled," *Ethnic and Racial Studies* 30, no. 4 (2007): 828-642; Elaine R. Thomas, "Keeping Identity at a Distance: Explaining France's New Legal Restrictions on the Islamic Headscarf, *Ethnic and Racial Studies* 29, no. 2 (2006): 237-259.

58. Castles 2001, 301.

59. "A lot done, a lot to do—the CRE's vision for an integrated Britain" http://www.equalityhumanrights.com/en/publicationsandresources/Pages/Recentpublications.aspx (7 November 2007).

60. Nancy Foner, "Immigrant Commitment to America, Then and Now: Myths and Realities," *Citizenship Studies* 5, no. 1 (2001): 27-40.

61. Scobey 2001, 18.

62. Ulrich K. Preuss, "Citizenship and the German Nation," *Citizenship Studies* 17, no. 1 (2003): 37-55.

63. Leti Volpp, "Obnoxious to Their Very Nature: Asian Americans and Constitutional Citizenship," *Citizenship Studies* 5, no. 1 (February 2001): 64. See also Randall Hansen, *Citizenship and Immigration in Post-War Britain* (Oxford: Oxford University Press, 2000).

64. Volpp 2001, 57.

65. Volpp 2001, 63 and 67.

66. Karen Bird, "The Political Representation of Visible Minorities in Electoral Democracies: A Comparison of France, Denmark and Canada," *Nationalism and Ethnic Politics* 11, no. 1 (January 2005): 425-465.

67. "Must the Rainbow Turn Monochrome in Parliament?," *The Economist*, 27 October 2007, 69.

68. Christian Joppke, "How Immigration Is Changing Citizenship: A Comparative View," *Ethnic and Racial Studies* 22, no. 4 (1999): 647.

69. Castles 1995, 302.

70. UK Minister of State for Culture, Media and Sport Margaret Hodge, "A Message to My Fellow Immigrants," *The Observer*, 20 May 2007, 21.

71. Ian Bruff, "The Netherlands, the Challenge of Lijst Pim Fortuyn, and the Third Way," *Politics* 23, no. 3 (2003): 156-162.

72. Chavez.

73. "A World Chronology of the Recognition of Women's Rights to Vote and to Stand for Election," http://www.ipu.org/wmn-e/suffrage.htm (5 September 2007).

74. Milne Seumas, "This Onslaught Risks Turning into a Racist Witch-hunt," *The Guardian*, 20 September 2007, 15.

Chapter 3
The Unbearable Lightness of British "Liberal Nationalism"

Enric Martínez-Herrera

Nationalism has had a bad intellectual reputation since World War II. Although it partially recovered during the decolonization struggles of the 1950-60s, the positive aura was soon dissipated again by ethnic conflict in many of the new and old states. The 1990s witnessed, however, a two-fold scenario of intellectual revisiting and debate on the subject. On the one hand, a racist revival in Western Europe and, overall, civil wars in former Yugoslavia revived fears about nationalism. On the other, a wave of political thought has postulated nationalism also has a human face. The aim of this study is to evaluate empirically some key theoretical assumptions about a hypothetical friendly side of nationalism and national identification. Some outstanding "liberal-nationalists" contend the existence of a number of positive elements in nationalism. Two alleged virtues often associated discursively with "good nationalism" are citizens' political confidence and support for the welfare state—the latter mediated through a perception of a national "common good" and "national solidarity." Unfortunately, there has been little systematic empirical evidence to support these claims, so this study tests them empirically as conventionally falsifiable scientific hypotheses.

The data examined here come from England and Scotland, as there the intellectual controversy on this subject is fairly lively and David Miller, one of the main proponents of these strands of thought, bears in mind British nationalism as a case in point.[1] The analysis begins by drawing hypotheses from the literature and differentiating the concepts of "nationalism" and "support for the political community." Then, the study goes on by developing a research design that enables us to test the causal hypotheses. The empirical analysis assesses the alleged effects of support for the political community by considering Britain as the reference political community in citizens' belief-systems. As a result, the theoretical claims are called into question.

A Human Face of Nationalism?

Atrocities perpetrated on behalf of national identification until the end of World War II period are well known. It is a history not only of the series of mass wars that occurred since the end of the nineteenth century—in which millions of men and women would die—but also a history of genocide, mass deportation, and other mass crimes committed in both wartime and peacetime. Knowledge is constantly growing regarding many other mass crimes committed on behalf of the nation or proto-national community since the Modern age. Nevertheless, the nationalism of the decolonization movements of the 1950-60s, primarily aimed at anti-imperialist emancipation and with a tendency to accept—initially at least—ethno-cultural diversity, gained again many sympathies. In fact, this would become an influential model for a number of minority ethno-nationalisms in the West. Yet more recent episodes of civil wars in multiethnic and multinational societies—especially those in former Yugoslavia, with large-scale ethnic cleansing and genocide—have dramatically increased suspicions about nationalism. Furthermore, both liberal and leftist observers show serious concern about xenophobia and different sorts of racist socio-political exclusion in the increasingly multiethnic post-industrial societies, as well as about the limits of citizenship for ethno-cultural minorities in polities ruled in nationalist manners.[2]

In sharp contrast, during the 1980-90s there was a significant theoretical revisiting of nationalism, looking back for some lost communitarian or republican ethical principia compatible with liberal values and institutions. From the viewpoint of "liberal-nationalists" such as Yael Tamir and David Miller, communitarian values might be necessary for the good performance of liberal democracy as well as for the survival of the welfare systems.[3] This theoretical production seeks to rescue the community by means of nationalism and national identification. As a matter of fact, the rediscovery of community has not only occurred in normative political theorizing, though. This move can be interpreted reading between the lines of a wider literature. Some of the most celebrated books of the 1990s in explanatory political science and sociology were about social trust and social capital, both concepts linked to that of cooperation.[4] However, the production of "liberal nationalist" has gone further still, seeking to rescue the community by means of nationalism and national identification.

Two specific common themes shared by numerous authors who sympathize with nationalism while maintaining some form of liberal stance are state legitimacy and welfarism—or "distributive justice," in Tamir's words. One or several of these concerns have caused several authors to turn their attention toward some supposedly beneficent properties of nationalism and national identification. "Liberal-nationalists," but also other authors who would prefer not to be qualified so, contend that nationalism is *necessary* for safeguarding citizens' support for their political systems and, more concretely, for the welfare state regimes.[5] In the following sections, I examine their theoretical assumptions and hypotheses and subsequently assess them empirically.

Nationalism and Political Confidence

The claim that nationalism facilitates commitment and loyalty toward the political system and to its authorities can be traced back, at the very least, to the French revolution,[6] and it would have a remarkable impact on almost every Western regime—be they republics or monarchies—during the second half of the nineteenth century. Rulers fostered national identification with the twofold aim of (1) counterbalancing the constant erosion of traditional guarantors of popular loyalty—such as dynastic legitimacy, divine ordination, historic right, or religious cohesion—and (2) transforming the former passive loyalty of subjects into more active participation in public affairs—particularly, mobilizing the population through conscripted armies in mass war.[7] To this day, the intellectual association between national identification and loyalty to political institutions and authority remains. For instance, recently a team of scholars asserted that "the state . . . requires the citizen to be loyal to it, to obey its rules, and, when required, to fight on its behalf. National identity is a necessary device for exacting the obedience of the citizen to the state. This does not need to be an oppressive feature, because people want to belong to the 'national community' from which they derive psychological, cultural and social benefits."[8]

The notion of loyalty to the state of course also has a second meaning, referring to the problem of states which have their national boundaries and loyalties challenged by alternative nationalisms. This is the case where minority nationalisms seek for either territorial political autonomy or, particularly, secession. Implications of this second theoretical issue have been widely studied in places such as Belgium, Canada, Spain, and the United Kingdom. Instead, the focus in this chapter is on the problem of political confidence.

Since the mid 1970s, the so-called "crisis of confidence" has been one major concern of empirical political science. A growing proportion of citizens tend to feel unsatisfied with political performance and to distrust government and, overall, political elites. Some authors assert that the crisis of confidence erodes in turn support for the political system,[9] whereas others dismiss such relationship, contending that despite the increasing political cynicism, citizens still support democracy,[10] or even more, that they actually push for a more democratic polyarchy.[11] Anyhow, lack of confidence in political authorities is supposed to reduce consent and compliance toward public decisions[12] and hence to diminish democratic institutions' performance,[13] and it is empirically related with protest activism and unconventional political action.[14]

Apparently related with the decline of political confidence is the weakening of social trust. Putnam has reported a decline of social capital in the United States and some authors might posit that interpersonal trust and political confidence are two sides of the same coin.[15] After all, if an individual distrusts other people—one might wonder—why should she trust public authorities and institutions?[16] However, recent empirical evidence shows that this direct relationship is fairly weak,[17] even statistically insignificant.[18] Even so, one still might suppose that political confidence has to do with more abstract considerations about the political system, rather than with everyday interpersonal trust.

The theoretical relationship between political confidence and general support for the political system has been stated by Almond and Verba and by Easton.[19] They contended that diffuse support for the political system provides a source of consent and compliance even if citizens are discontent with current institutional performance.[20] Since national identification makes, alongside support for the political regime, one of the basic pillars of diffuse support for a polity, one could envisage an empirical relationship between national identification and political confidence as well.[21] The hypothesis is, therefore, that the stronger citizens' support for the political community, the stronger their feelings of political confidence.

Nationalism and Support for the Welfare State

Looking at recent developments in political theory, nevertheless, the most common themes related with a friendly face of nationalism are national solidarity and social trust. The changes of the welfare state have drawn much attention in Western Europe, and a number of well-reputed authors have turned attention to nationalism as a possible remedy. Welfare state and nationalism would seem to influence each other in a reciprocal manner. On the one hand, the state has used the welfare system to gain loyalty and a sense of national solidarity from citizens.[22] On the other, however, it is often argued that social consent toward distributive and redistributive policies has one of its stronger bases in national identification, which is a product of nationalism. Of course, it has also been expected that support could flow from a universalistic sense of justice, but this alternative seems to be less in vogue these days.

Two main arguments hold the hypothesis that nationalism generates support for the welfare state. These arguments link both variables through two intermediate, compatible factors: mutual trust and a sense of national solidarity stemming from the ideas of "common good" and "mutual responsibility." Indeed, distributive and redistributive policies entail conflict, since some individuals or social sections must pay the costs of improving the situation of other individuals or sections. However, those policies, especially within the frame of a welfare system, often entail a coordination problem as well, insofar as most individuals and sections could be made better-off—especially in the long-run. Noticeably, though, many individuals or sections could still be tempted to escape the costs, thus leading to a problem of lack of cooperation.

As recalled above, from the 1980s much attention has been paid to the question of social trust and subsequently to that of social capital, encompassing it.[23] Many scholars contend that, for a citizen or a social section to contribute willingly to the provision of policies addressed to help other citizens or sections, there is a need for the former to *trust* that she would be reciprocated should the time arrive in which she needed help. At the scale of a large society, that trust is unlikely to be based on direct interpersonal relations between the individuals involved. Nonetheless, according to some authors, it could be made more likely to arise from the fact they know that they share identification with and loyalty to a common nation and its political institutions.[24] Hence national identification would increase the odds of mutual trust, which in turn would increase the likelihood of support for redistributive policies.[25]

The second general argument goes through the notions of common good and mutual responsibility. The analogy with the family that some authors put forward, can be a useful departure point, since it easily evokes both ideas, and it can be interpreted from either a strictly egoistic viewpoint or a less egoistic, perhaps even altruistic one.[26] However, different meanings of the term "common good" and a couple of different understandings of the welfare state must be considered altogether.[27] The first two meanings of the term "common good" as applied in relation to the welfare system are neatly individualistic and selfish. First, common good is seen as that which is good for all the members of, or a large majority in, a society. Here the welfare state is understood—and this meaning has also been applied in the argument of social trust above—as a "mutual insurance plan" where reciprocity is expected, and the fact that this plan exists is likely to benefit most members of the society.[28] Thus, nationalism helps coordinate individuals with a latent shared egoistic interest.

Second, the welfare system can be understood as a redistributive mechanism *tout court*, which only makes some sections of the society better off, whereas many sections and single members are unlikely to directly benefit. If the individual believes that she shares a "common interest," "common venture," "enterprise," or "project," even "common fate" with her nation fellow-members—as nationalism often induces individuals to perceive themselves—then she can still think in egoistic rational terms that she also benefits from her fellow nationals' improvement, since she is indirectly affected by their successes and failures.[29] Thus, "common good" is perceived by the selfish individual in terms of such interdependence—some degree of improvement of her fellow-nationals may also benefit herself.

In its third sense, the "common good" is no longer individualistic, but organicist instead. A society or nation is seen as an entity with its own autonomous life—independent to a degree from the individuals forming it—and the common good is referred to as the well-being of that thing. Since individuals can perceive a "sense of national interest," now the distributive and redistributive policies are intended to keep or improve the well-being of the social organism.[30] Selfish individuals' calculations are possible insofar as they believe that the welfare of the organism is also good for its cells—without denying that non-strictly egoistic sacrifices are possible too.

The analogy with the family also has the connotation that national identification, which is produced by nationalism, produces in turn a feeling of "mutual responsibility," a "fellow-feeling and mutual concern," or a "sense of bonding among the people working together."[31] The analogy is of a limited scope, since members of the nation do not know each other personally, nor do they share most daily life experiences. However, it is assumed that from the fact of identifying with the same social unit—the "nation"—individuals identify also with each other with comparable strength, and even more, they develop an affection for each other. This is indeed a much debatable assumption,[32] but it works to rhetorically legitimate the "distributive justice" understanding of the welfare state.[33] However, were it true, affection for fellow-nationals would inspire a sense of moral responsibility, obligation toward them, similar—though less intense—to the feelings within a Western ideal family. Therefore, from any of those arguments we should expect that the stronger the individual identifies with her political community, the more supportive she will be to redistributive policies.

Nationalism, National Identification and Support for the Political Community

Before examining these hypotheses, however, we need a clarification of what is meant by "liberal-nationalism" and "national identification" in this literature. To begin with, following from Gellner, it could be assumed that "nationalism" is a "principle of political legitimacy."[34] A principle that states that "the political and the national unit should be congruent," understanding the "national unit" as defined by ethno-cultural—e.g., religious and/or linguistic—markers. This principle gives rise to a wide array of phenomena under the label "nationalism," namely attitudes, doctrines, movements, and organizational patterns of the world. Second, Gellner emphasizes that the assumption of this principle has as a consequence a strong concern about the congruence in ethno-cultural traits between the rulers and the ruled. Therefore, one important dimension of nationalism as an attitude is a negative orientation toward any actor considered to be alien to the "nation" if that actor seeks to intervene in the political realm.

When Tamir and Miller refer to something they call "liberal nationalism" or "nationality," they seem to mean a different principle. This is because, albeit they praise a sense of belonging together, they would probably dislike that citizens mistrusted cultural minorities, foreigners, and other countries while being uncritical toward their own "nation." Rather than to nationalism as defined by Gellner, they seem to refer to a sense of "national identification," which others would willingly call "patriotism."[35] Actually, the concern with identification with the political unit is not new. There have been many studies on such identification before, especially in countries where it has been called into question, challenging the very basis of those political systems. Thus, the primary concern is about how much subjective support a political community enjoys, from which consent, loyalty, compliance, even solidarity are expected to flow.[36]

I propose to replace the concept of national identification by that of "support for the political community." For one thing, referring to "national" identification entails the flaw of not specifying whether we are referring to an ethno-culturally defined "nation" or to a widely understood political community.[37] To be certain, Miller seems to be clear enough that his "nationality" is culturally specific, but one could be prone to think that this is not Tamir's case.[38] By contrast, building upon Easton, I call "political community" to the population collectively ruled and represented by the structures of a political system, which does not need to be defined and delimited in ethno-cultural terms.[39] Moreover, this is a useful term because of its applicability to multilevel government as it refers to binding political structures, regardless of whether or not they fulfill the formal requirements of full sovereignty and are perceived as "nations."[40]

In most political systems, there is a "nesting" of political communities at various levels and even local councils and supranational governments need some social legitimacy. A legitimacy that, according to Easton, can be conceptualized as a source of long-term support, whose main expression would be self-identification with the political community.[41] I understand this identification as the self-recognition of its members with concepts and symbols that represent the abstract notion of such community as a whole. Yet the term "national identification" does not always cover that political feeling. For, on the one hand, this cannot be applied to all levels of government while, on the other, the political communities of states and other levels of government can enjoy the support of their populations without being generally regarded as "nations."[42] Further, there are polities assertively defined as "nations" that exclude, in one way or another, ethno-cultural minorities from the political realm.[43] Hence our primary concern ought to be about diffuse support for political communities, focusing on self-identification with them as its main attitudinal manifestation.

Identification with the general denomination of a political community may be insufficient evidence of political support for it, however, being necessary to accompany this identification with a desire of collective self-government. To distinguish the *political* community from other objects is not a straightforward task. Human beings tend to hold multiple identifications with various groups, especially in complex societies in which there are various criteria of social categorization.[44] However, a sole denomination may be used for referring to different things, so that survey respondents' identifications can be suspected of referring to rather vague denominations. To illustrate the point, this may happen when some individual identifies herself with "Scotland" *tout court*, without concretion about what exactly "Scotland" is considered to be. Inquiry on support for the political community ought to avoid eventual confusion because of a mere nominal agreement between the government structure of a society and other religious, linguistic, historical, or folkloric social sub-systems under the same name—often they correlate strongly, but this is not always the case. Hence close attention should be paid to individuals' wish of a degree of collective *self-government*, autonomy. This dimension entails the desire to retain or increase power for a specific level of government, and can be applied to different nested political communities, be they sub-state, state, or supra-state.

Method, Data, and Indicators

The testing of the hypothesis is conducted through classical (Ordinary Least Squares) multivariate regression analysis and the modeling includes various indexes measuring the different concepts involved.[45] The analysis falls into two steps. Concepts such as "support for the political community," "political confidence," and "support for the welfare state" are indirectly observable only, and scholars have not agreed on single indicators able to optimally operationalize them yet. Each of them can be better measured through various selected operational variables rather than only one. Thus, in the first place, indexes extracting the common meaning of each group of variables by means of principal component analysis were generated. In this study, a number of relevant items relating to the theoretical concepts were first selected from the dataset and subjected to exploratory factor analysis to determine their dimensionality and, hence, usefulness as a basis for the analysis. After achieving satisfactory results for the indices, the full causal models were tested.

The data analyzed are from the 1997 British General Election Study (BGES). This survey contains a richness of indicators intended to measure a so-called "British national sentiment" as well as attitudes around political confidence and support for the welfare state, and it is based on large numbers of respondents for both England and Scotland.[46] Let us introduce the observed variables. While there is no agreement in the literature on any indicators measuring validly either "nationalism," "national identification," nor "support for the political community," the survey includes a battery of questions intended to tap "British national sentiment" as a Likert scale, namely:[47]

BCITIZEN. I would rather be a citizen of Britain than of any other country in the world (reversed).

BTOGETHER. The government should do everything it can to keep all parts of Britain together in a single state (reversed).

BCOOPERATE. Britain should cooperate with other countries, even if it means giving up some independence.

BLEARN. Britain has a lot to learn from other countries in running its affairs.

BASHAMED. There are some things about Britain today that make me ashamed to be British.

Each question supplied closed answers of agreement on a scale ranging from one ("strongly agree") to five ("strongly disagree").[48] The answers to some items were rearranged (see the questions) so as the higher the score, the more pro British respondents express themselves.[49] As recognized by its designers, this question battery has some flaws in terms of both contents validity and internal reliability.[50] First, it does not fit very accurately to Gellner's concept of nationalism, in which congruence in ethno-cultural traits between the rulers and the ruled is a crucial concern, since this is not directly expressed in any of the items, while it includes some items that do not match a non-nationalist understanding of support for the political community. Second, they reported weak internal reliability in previous results. However, here it has been sought to make the best from the available items, classifying them around the concepts of "support for the political community" and "nationalism."

First, support for the British political community was operationalized through the items BCITIZEN and BTOGETHER, which should respectively tap identification with that community and support for its collective self-government—support for the unity of Britain.[51] This construct seems to be quite free of "nationalist excesses" while still tapping those two components. Moreover, as shown below, they are the most strongly correlated from within the question-battery set. Second, in order to isolate as much as possible this construct from nationalism interference, it was accompanied into the analyses by a second construct operating as a control variable. This construct was conceived as a proxy to British nationalism, composed of the three remaining items. Though they do not refer straightforwardly to ethno-cultural congruence between rulers and rulers, they are very close to illiberal nationalism, combining uncritical national pride and reluctance to any kind of "other countries" influence on British politics.[52]

Since survey research on "political confidence" has a longer tradition, its measurement benefits from a wide—though still incomplete—agreement, particularly on the basis of the standard provided by the pioneering National Election Study (NES) in the United States.[53] The British data set includes two items tapping political confidence:

GOVTRUST. How much do you trust British governments of any party to place the needs of the nation above the interests of their own political party?

MPsTRUST. And how much do you trust politicians of any party in Britain to tell the truth when they are in a tight corner?

Four possible answers were given for each question, ranging from "just about always" to "almost never," whose order was reversed so as the higher the score, the more politically confident the citizen manifests. The first item is intended to tap "trust in government." The second aims at measuring confidence in politicians as a group. None of them seems to be as much of a complete measure of support for any of both objects as the NES question battery for trust in government, but they can jointly reflect a good deal of the political confidence syndrome widely understood. It is worth to stress that both of them refer specifically to government and politicians at the British level.

The last theoretical construct refers to support for the welfare state. There is wide agreement that the main dimensions of that policy system are public health, public education, and, at the very least, a degree of income redistribution. Thus I selected the following questions:

Please use this card to say whether you think the government should or should not do the following things, or doesn't it matter either way?

PRIVEDU . . . get rid of private education in Britain?

RIDPOVERTY . . . spend more money to get rid of poverty?

PRIVMED . . . encourage the growth of private medicine?

MORENHS . . . put more money into the National Health Service?

SPENDEDU . . . spend more money on education?

Five possible answers were supplied for each, ranging from "definitely should" to "definitely should not." To these items I added:

REDISTRI. Income and wealth should be redistributed toward ordinary working people?

Five possible answers were given to this, ranging from "strongly agree" to "strongly disagree." Again, the answers to all six questions were arranged so as the higher the score, the stronger support for the welfare system is.

Finally, some control variables were included for avoiding eventual spurious relationships. Some basic socio-demographic variables were considered, namely: age, gender, number of years studying, and household income. Missing data (including DK/NA) in the three former variables were kept. The income variable was recoded to express the respondents' household income in British pounds.[54]

Two attitudinal and behavioral variables were also included as controls. First of all, a ten-point scale for left-right ideological self-placement was considered while examining support for the welfare state. Given the high number of DK/NA (30.0 % in England; 37.3 % in Scotland), these missing values were recoded as 5.22 in England and 4.98 in Scotland, in accordance with the means of the observed cases in each territory. Second, while examining political confidence, the memory of either having voted or not for the incumbent party in the previous general election was included as a control, as suggested by the literature on trust in government.[55] This was operationalized as a dummy that puts into the reference category (which scores 0) all those cases having not voted conservative—for whatever reason—in the 1992 general election.

Measurement Constructs

Before testing the theoretical causal relationships, the process of measurement of the theoretical variables is laid down. The construct measuring support for the political community is evaluated first. Table 3.1 presents the correlations between the five items tapping British national identification and nationalism. It shows that the correlations tend to be weak in both England—the strongest one is .28—and, particularly, in Scotland—the strongest is .23. This hardly comes as a surprise since Heath and his colleagues recognized that the items used in 1994 showed some problems of reliability.[56] Interestingly, moreover, the strongest correlation in both sub-samples comes out between BCITIZEN and BTOGETHER, i.e., the indicators operationalizing support for the political community.

An empirical distinction is expected between support for the political community and the proxy to nationalism, which should yield two different factors in the exploratory factor analysis. The factors have been rotated so that each of them best expresses the underlying dimensions to the survey items. The analysis comprises a comparison of England and Scotland, which can shed additional light on whether the items are capturing the same underlying concepts. Actually, there are no expectations that the measurement models of support for the political community "travel" well from one societal context to another. For according to the scientific literature, conflicts around political community perceptions are framed differently among Scots and English—sub-state self-governing is at stake among the former, whereas European supra-state integration is the prevailing issue among the latter. However, although two specific models make theoretical sense, it is still interesting to realize the differences.

The principal component analysis of the five items on nationalism and national identity yields two latent factors both in England and Scotland (with eigen values scoring above 1.0). Table 3.2 displays the standardized factor loadings of the selected indicators and the total variance of the data that is accounted for by the factors. The model accounts for a quite large proportion of variance in the data, which is also roughly the same across both historical nations (55 and 54 %, respectively). In turn, the magnitude of the correlations (or factor loadings) between the indicators and the factors can be interpreted as how well each of the factors represents the indicators. For one thing, the two indicators that are expected to represent support for the political community—i.e., identification with Great Britain (BCITIZEN) and preferences on keeping Britain's unity (BTOGETHER)—form a factor of their own in both England and Scotland. Second, two of the indicators that are expected to measure a different dimension, with

Table 3.1. Correlations, means, and standard deviations of the indicators of British national identification and nationalism in England and Scotland 1997.

	SCOTLAND				
ENGLAND	BLEARN	BCITIZEN	BASHAMED	BTOGETHER	BCOOPERATE
BLEARN		0.224	0.188	0.085	0.158
BCITIZEN	0.165		0.127	0.230	0.178
BASHAMED	0.169	0.162		0.122	0.075
BTOGETHER	0.101	0.285	0.078		0.013
BCOOPERATE	0.205	0.228	0.079	0.199	
ENGLAND	N	2413 after listwise deletion			
Mean	2.983	4.137	2.741	3.636	3.205
Std. Deviation	1.226	1.041	1.087	1.017	1.066
SCOTLAND	N	817 after listwise deletion			
Mean	2.898	4.058	2.720	3.243	3.106
Std. Deviation	1.389	0.963	1.042	1.156	1.025

Note: Entries below the diagonal refer to England; above the diagonal, to Scotland.

a more nationalist meaning, show strong correlations with a second factor across both territories. These indicators are uncritical national pride (BASHAMED) and closeness to learn from other countries (BLEARN).

However, the indicator of reluctance to any kind of "other countries" influence on British politics (BCOOPERATE) behaves differently across territories. Whilst it strongly correlates, as expected, with the proxy to British nationalism in Scotland, it correlates stronger with support for the British political community in England. This different pattern of correlations of the indicator makes sense as the sentence to which respondents show their degree of agreement/disagreement entails different shades of meaning. On the one hand, English respondents tend to pay more attention to the second part of the sentence—i.e., "giving up some independence." This can be seen as jeopardizing or, at least, undermining sovereignty of the political community, a notion that is at the center of the concept of support for the political community. On the other hand, Scottish respondents seem to be more sensible to the first part of the proposition, by placing more emphasis on their attitude toward other countries. In any case, these differences do not entail a major problem for the analysis. Since exploratory factor analysis captures the commonalities between variables without theoretical constraints, this observed variable (BCOOPERATE) is allowed to make part of the different factors in a different way across the two groups of respondents. Hence, it will make part of the index of nationalism in Scotland whilst it will primarily weigh as part of the index of support for the political community in England—although also having some weight on nationalism.

Table 3.2. Standardized factor loadings of selected items on support for the British political community and a British nationalism proxy in England and Scotland, 1997

	England		Scotland	
	SPC	Nat. Proxy	SPC	Nat. Proxy
Being GB citizen	**0.69**	0.24	**0.61**	0.41
To keep GB as single state	**0.79**	-0.15	**0.89**	-0.10
GB has a lot to learn from other countries	0.24	**0.70**	0.08	**0.73**
Ashamed to be GB	-0.01	**0.78**	0.26	**0.50**
To cooperate with other countries	**0.59**	0.26	-0.07	**0.68**
Total Variance Explained (%)	54.8		53.6	

Now the analysis turns to the examination of the measurement of the dependent factors. As shown in table 3.3, the means and standard deviations of the vari-

Table 3.3. Means, standard deviations, and correlations for the indicators of support for the welfare state and political confidence in England and Scotland, 1997

	SCOTLAND							
ENGLAND	PRIVEDU	RIDPOVERTY	PRIVMED	MORENHS	SPENDEDU	REDISTRI	GOVTRUST	MPsTRUST
PRIVEDU		0.179	0.224	0.137	0.090	0.343	-0.032	-0.081
RIDPOVERTY	0.212		0.082	0.260	0.311	0.376	0.048	-0.034
PRIVMED	0.243	0.101		0.102	0.016	0.137	-0.010	-0.100
MORENHS	0.158	0.313	0.137		0.605	0.189	-0.046	-0.078
SPENDEDU	0.099	0.286	0.055	0.539		0.222	-0.003	-0.039
REDISTRI	0.358	0.333	0.169	0.292	0.218		-0.038	-0.071
GOVTRUST	-0.055	0.013	-0.113	-0.069	-0.012	-0.074		0.387
MPsTRUST	-0.024	-0.019	-0.098	-0.055	-0.018	-0.065	0.416	
ENGLAND								
Mean	2.480	4.442	3.271	4.662	4.610	3.513	2.251	1.665
Std. Deviation	1.179	0.835	1.239	0.693	0.735	1.112	0.698	0.642
SCOTLAND								
Mean	2.951	4.596	3.421	4.721	4.655	3.830	2.214	1.663
Std. Deviation	1.176	0.679	1.223	0.613	0.697	1.035	0.663	0.658

Note: Entries below the diagonal refer to England; above the diagonal, to Scotland

Table 3.4. Standardized factor loadings of selected items on political confidence, support for the welfare state and support for increasing welfare spending. England and Scotland, 1997

	England			Scotland		
	Political Confidence	Support for Welfare State	Increase Public Spending	Political Confidence	Support for Welfare State	Increase Public Spending
Trust government	0.84			0.83		
Trust politicians	0.84			0.83		
Get rid of private education		0.79			0.79	
Encourage private medicine		0.61			0.55	
Income & wealth to be redistributed		0.73			0.74	
Spend more money against poverty			0.65			0.61
Put more money into NHS			0.83			0.84
Spend more on education			0.82			0.86
Total Variance Explained (%)	70.6	50.8	59.2	69.3	49.4	60.1

political confidence are about the same in England and Scotland, in ences that could be expected given the well-known opposition to the cabinets and a previous record of low satisfaction with the function- cracy in Scotland. Yet support for the welfare state was on the average stronger in Scotland. This might further enhance the interest to test the proposition about the influence of support for the political community on support for welfare state.

The construction of the indices of political confidence, generalized support for the welfare state and support for increasing public spending on welfare has been generated through three separate exploratory factor analyses. Table 3.4 presents the standardized factor loadings of the selected indicators and the total variance of the data that is accounted for by the factors. For one thing, the model accounts for a quite large proportion of variance in the data, which ranges between 49 (for support for the welfare state in Scotland) and 71 % (for political confidence in England). Second, the correlations (of factors loadings) between the indicators and their respective factors tend to be very strong, which gives an indication of a fairly good validity of the measures.

Regression Analysis

Once having established the measurement models of the theoretical concepts on the BGES dataset, the full causal model is evaluated. According to the theoretical hypotheses laid down above, statistically significant positive effects of support for the political community are predicted upon both political confidence and support for the welfare state. In addition, the models include a number of control variables. The inclusion of the proxy to British nationalism is useful as it helps to isolate the measurement of support for the political community from the interference of nationalism. This is because, as said above, although Miller and Tamir praise a sense of belonging together, they would probably dislike feelings of mistrust toward other countries while being uncritical toward one's own. In addition, given that both kinds of feelings often correlate—as they do in the British context—it is necessary both analytically and empirically to distinguish carefully between them. The models also specify other control variables with significant effects, namely citizens' self-placement on the left-right scale and household income, which are theoretically well-established predictors of support for the welfare state. Age, gender, education, and Conservative voting in 1992 (only considered for political confidence) are considered too.

Table 3.5 displays the findings of the analysis of the determinants of political confidence in England and Scotland. Support for the political community and the proxy of nationalism have different effects across both groups of respondents. In England, contrary to expectations, support for the political community does not have a statistically significant effect on political confidence,

Table 3.5. Regression estimates of selected variables on political confidence. England and Scotland, 1997

	England			Scotland		
	Coeff.	*Std. Error*	*St. Beta*	*Coeff.*	*Std. Error*	*St. Beta*
Support for the Political Community	0.028^{ns}	0.02	0.03	0.201^{***}	0.04	**0.20**
Nationalism Proxy	0.090^{***}	0.02	0.09	0.048^{ns}	0.04	0.05
Left-Right self-placement	0.014^{ns}	0.01	0.02	0.023^{ns}	0.02	0.04
Household income	0.000^{ns}	0.00	-0.02	0.000^{ns}	0.00	0.04
Terminal education age	0.014^{ns}	0.01	0.04	0.004^{ns}	0.02	0.01
Age	0.003^{**}	0.00	0.05	0.003^{ns}	0.00	0.04
Sex	0.031^{ns}	0.04	0.02	-0.013^{ns}	0.07	-0.01
Voted Conservative in 1992	0.141^{***}	0.05	0.07	-0.068^{ns}	0.10	-0.03
Constant	-0.501^{***}	0.19		-0.345^{ns}	0.32	
R^2	0.022			0.05		
Adj. R^2	0.02			0.04		
N	2413			817		

[illegible]ral nationalism that yields a statistically significant effect on it. [illegible], in England political confidence tends to increase with illiberal [illegible]alist attitudes, but the degree of identification with Britain and [illegible]bout its collective autonomy are irrelevant on this regard. This is [illegible]arly important result, as England seems to be the main empirical instance that inspires Miller's theory. Conversely, in Scotland support for the political community not only yields a statistically significant effect, but this is quite strong in magnitude. Paying attention to the standardized betas in the right column, this is the stronger—and single—determinant of political confidence in Scotland. Furthermore, age and conservative vote in 1992 also contribute to account for the dependent variable in England. Admittedly, this lends further empirical credence to Miller's claim, but the fact that this does not hold in England hinders any generalization attempt.

The results on generalized support for the welfare state are particularly relevant, as theoretical claims contend that feelings of national community produce predispositions to internal solidarity. The results in table 3.6 show that there is actually a statistically significant effect of support for the political community and the nationalism proxy on welfarism in England. Nevertheless, in the first place, the effects are not significant in Scotland. What is more, secondly, the statistical signification is backing the fact that the effects are negative in England. In other words, contrary to liberal-nationalist theoretical expectations, pro-welfare state attitudes tend to decrease in England as British nationalism and support for the British political community increase. Moreover, these effects are significant in spite of controlling the also significant effects of left-right identification, household income and other variables, which could be expected to produce a spurious association if they were not included—English people tend to be more nationalist as they are wealthier and more politically conservative. In other words, the negative effects of support for the political community and nationalism on support for the welfare state in England is independent of the effect of conservatism and wealth. Finally, although the finding does not produce any surprise, it is probably worth to highlight that it is citizens' self-placement on the left-right scale that has the strongest positive effect on backing the welfare system.

The distinction between diffuse support for the welfare state and specific support for increasing welfare spending throws additional light on the matter. The results in table 3.7 are quite similar to those in table 3.6. Again, there is a statistically significant effect of support for the political community and the nationalism proxy on welfarism in England, but the direction of the effect is, contrary to expectations, negative. One important difference is that here the results are the same for Scotland, which shows statistically negative effects for both independent variables on increasing welfare policies, too. Having said this, it is again citizens' self-placement on the left-right scale that yields the strongest positive effect on support for welfare policies.

Table 3.6. Regression estimates of selected variables on support for the welfare state. England and Scotland, 1997

	England			Scotland		
	Coeff.	*Std. Error*	*St. Beta*	*Coeff.*	*Std. Error*	*St. Beta*
Support for the Political Community	-0.098***	0.02	-0.10	-0.018 ns	0.04	-0.02
Nationalism Proxy	-0.129***	0.02	-0.13	-0.034 ns	0.04	-0.03
Left-Right self-placement	-0.177***	0.01	**-0.30**	-0.110***	0.02	**-0.17**
Household income	0.000***	0.00	**-0.19**	0.000 ns	0.00	-0.06
Terminal education age	-0.031***	0.01	-0.09	-0.024 ns	0.02	-0.06
Age	-0.003**	0.00	-0.05	-0.005**	0.00	-0.09
Sex	0.104***	0.04	0.05	0.224***	0.07	0.11
Constant	1.728***	0.17		0.928***	0.32	
R^2	0.19			0.06		
Adj. R^2	0.18			0.05		
N	2413			817		

Table 3.7. Regression estimates of selected variables on support for increasing spending on the welfare state. F Scotland, 1997

	England			Scotland		
	Coeff.	*Std. Error*	*St. Beta*	*Coeff.*	*Std. Error*	*St.*
Support for the Political Community	-0.027^{ns}	0.02	-0.03	-0.134***	0.04	-0.14
Nationalism Proxy	-0.091***	0.02	-0.09	-0.074**	0.03	-0.07
Left-Right self-placement	-0.122***	0.01	**-0.21**	-0.131***	0.02	**-0.20**
Household income	0.000***	0.00	-0.09	0.000***	0.00	**-0.18**
Terminal education age	-0.027***	0.01	-0.07	-0.050***	0.01	-0.13
Age	-0.005***	0.00	-0.09	-0.004^{ns}	0.00	-0.07
Sex	0.149***	0.04	0.07	0.151**	0.07	0.07
Constant	1.248***	0.18		1.719***	0.30	
R^2	0.09			0.14		
Adj. R^2	0.08			0.13		
N	2413			817		

To take stock of this section, therefore, the liberal-nationalist arguments under scrutiny are dramatically challenged by empirical evidence in Britain. Support for the British political community only has a positive significant effect on political confidence in Scotland, but it is irrelevant on this regard in England, where illiberal nationalist feelings show a comparable effect. In turn, concerning support for the welfare system, support for the political community and nationalism do not have significant effects on its generalized form in Scotland and, in all other instances, the effect is the opposite to that predicted by theory—in other words, the relationship is negative.

Discussion and Conclusions

Many hopes have been pinned on national identification since the nineteenth century, not only by ordinary citizens but also by political elites who have suffused their discourse with ubiquitous invocations to national feelings. During the 1990s a number of political theorists advanced a sophisticated and attractive combination of nationalism and liberalism. One of their most effective arguments was the suggestion that national identification—as a product of nationalism—helped secure or regain citizens' political confidence as well as their solidarity inclinations—in particular, their support for the welfare state. For they predict that citizens' support for the political community—as it seems preferable to call "national identification"—entails those two sorts of support. Since these syllogisms are widely extended but never proved, this study has empirically tested them as falsifiable scientific hypotheses.

Yet the findings are unbearably light to sustain either hypothesis. Support for the British political community only has a significant positive impact on political confidence in Scotland. As a matter of fact, it is British illiberal nationalism that has an impact on political confidence, but solely in England. As far as the support for the welfare schemes are concerned, the effects of both support for the political community and illiberal nationalism are either irrelevant or, in most instances, negative. Even if controlling by important variables as left-right identification and household income, citizens showing a greater reluctance toward any influence of other countries in British politics as well as holding an uncritical British pride, and citizens showing the stronger British identification and stronger wish to keep Great Britain united, tend to be the least supportive of welfarism. Therefore, the theory does not hold in Britain at large, and does only partially in Scotland.

In brief, this study has found that some inherently appealing and theoretically attractive liberal-nationalist arguments do not survive a proper empirical test even if applied to the British political community, which is typically portrayed as an instance of "civic nationalism."[57] Thus, one could expect that political communities that are considered to be less civic than Britain would have much more difficulty to pass the examination of liberal nationalist virtue. In consequence, perhaps liberal-nationalists should be more cautious in proclaiming the virtues of nationalism and national identification—or support for the political community—until they can accompany such claims with adequate evidence.

Notes

1. David Miller, *On Nationality* (Oxford: Clarendon Press, 1995) and "On Nationality," *Nations and Nationalism* 2 (1996): 409-21.

2. On citizenship and nationalist policies, see Rogers Brubaker, "Citizenship and Nationhood in France and Germany," *International Sociology* 5, no. 4 (1990): 379-407, and *Nationalism Reframed: Nationhood and the National Question in the New Europe* (Cambridge: Cambridge University, 1996); Will Kymlicka, *Multicultural Citizenship: A Liberal Theory of Minority Rights* (Oxford: Oxford Univ. Press, 1995); Bhikhu Parekh, "Being British," *Government and Opposition* 37, no. 3 (2002): 301-15; Christian Joppke, *Selecting by Origin: Ethnic Migration in the Liberal State* (Cambridge, MA: Harvard Univ. Press, 2005).

3. Yael Tamir, *Liberal Nationalism* (Princeton: Princeton Univ. Press, 1993).

4. Ronald Inglehart, *Cultural Shift in Advanced Industrial Society* (Princeton: Princeton Univ. Press, 1990); Robert D. Putnam, *Making Democracy Work: Civic Traditions in Modern Italy* (Princeton: Princeton Univ. Press, 1993).

5. Nevertheless, not all communitarian liberals subscribe to the nationalist agenda.

6. For a previous date, see Josep R. Llobera, *The God of Modernity: The Development of Nationalism in Western Europe* (Oxford: Berg Publishers, 1994).

7. Eric J. Hobsbawm, *Nations and Nationalism since 1780: Programme, Myth, Reality* [2nd ed.] (Cambridge: Cambridge Univ. Press, 1992).

8. Alice Brown, David McCrone, and Lindsay Paterson, *Politics and Society in Scotland* (London: Macmillan, 1998), 200.

9. See, for instance, Arthur Miller, "Political Issues and Trust in Government," *American Political Science Review* 68 (1974): 951-72; Paul A. Abramson, *Political Attitudes in America* (San Francisco: Freeman, 1983); Oscar W. Gabriel, *Cambio social y cultura politica: el caso de la República Federal de Alemania* (Barcelona: Gedisa, 1990).

10. Jack Citrin, "Comment: the Political Relevance of Trust in Government," *American Political Science Review* 68 (1974): 973-88; Oscar W. Gabriel, "Political Efficacy and Trust," in *The Impact of Values* [*Beliefs in Government*, Vol. 4], ed. Jan W. van Deth and Elinor Scarbrough (New York: Oxford Univ. Press, 1995), 357-389; José Ramón Montero, Richard Gunther, and Mariano Torcal, "Democracy in Spain: Legitimacy, Discontent, and Disaffection," *Studies in Comparative International Development* 32, no. 3 (1997): 124-60.

11. Inglehart (op. cit.); Russell J. Dalton, *Citizen Politics: Public Opinion and Political Parties in Advanced Industrial Democracies* (Chatham, NJ: Chatham House, 1996) [2nd ed.].

12. For instance, Richard Rose, "National Pride in Cross-national Perspective," *International Social Science Journal* 36 (1985): 85-96; and Miller (*op. cit.* 1995).

13. Susan J. Pharr, Robert D. Putnam, and Russell J. Dalton, "Introduction: What's Troubling the Trilateral Democracies?," in *Disaffected Democracies: What's Troubling the Trilateral Countries?*, ed. S. J. Pharr and R. D. Putnam (Princeton, NJ: Princeton Univ. Press, 2000), 3-27.

14. Kaase, Max. "Interpersonal Trust, Political Trust and Non-Institutionalised Political Participation in Western Europe," *West European Politics* 22, no. 3 (1999): 1-21.

15. Robert D. Putnam, "Bowling Alone: Declining Social Capital," *Journal of Democracy* 6 (1995): 65-78; cf. Miller (*op. cit.* 1995). However, apparently the decline of social capital is not occurring in Britain and the very claim of a decline in the U.S. is lively debated. See Peter Hall, "Social Capital in Britain," *British Journal of Political Science* 29 (1999): 417-61; Robert W. Jackman and Ross A. Miller, "Social Capital and Politics," *Annual Review of Political Science* 1 (1998): 47-73.

16. Cf. Putnam (*op. cit.* 1993) and Hall (*op. cit.*)

17. See Kaase (*op. cit.*); Kenneth Newton, "Social and Political Trust in Established Democracies," in *Critical Citizens: Global Support for Democratic Governance*, ed. P. Norris (Oxford: Oxford Univ. Press, 1999), 169-87; Kenneth Newton and Pippa Norris, "Confidence in Public Institutions: Faith, Culture or Performance?," in *Disaffected Democracies: What's Troubling the Trilateral Countries?* ed. S. J. Pharr and R. D. Putnam (Princeton, NJ: Princeton Univ. Press, 2000), 52-73.

18. William Mishler and Richard Rose, "What Are the Origins of Political Trust?: Testing Institutional and Cultural Theories in Post-Communist Societies," *Comparative Political Studies* 34, no. 1 (2001): 30-62. Newton and Norris (*op. cit.*) and Pharr and his colleagues (*op. cit.*), however, contend that the relationship is indirect, mediated by governmental performance.

19. Gabriel A. Almond and Sidney Verba, *The Civic Culture* (Princeton: Princeton Univ. Press, 1963); David Easton, "A Re-assessment of the Concept of Political Support." *British Journal of Political Science*, 5 (1975): 435-57.

20. See also Rose (*op. cit.*) and Charles Taylor, "Why Democracy Needs Patriotism," in *For Love of Country: Debating the Limits of Patriotism*, ed. M.C. Nussbaum and J. Cohen (Boston: Beacon Press, 1996), 119-21.

21. For the concept of diffuse support, see David Easton, *A Systems Analysis of Political Life* (New York: Wiley, 1965). Topf and his colleagues have offered some empirical evidence based on proxies, namely a positive bivariate relationship between national pride and general evaluations about the functioning of democracy in Britain and Germany. See Richard Topf, Peter Mohler, and Anthony F. Heath, "Pride in One's Country: Britain and West Germany," in *British Social Attitudes: Special International Report*, ed. R. Jowell, S. Witherspoon, and L. Brook (Aldershot: Gower, 1989), 132-133.

22. See Hobsbawm (*op. cit.*); Michael Keating, *Nations against the State. The New Politics of Nationalism in Quebec, Catalonia and Scotland* (Hampshire: Macmillan, 2001); Nicola McEwen, "State Welfare Nationalism: the Territorial Impact of Welfare State Development in Scotland," *Regional and Federal Studies* 12, no. 1 (2002): 66-90; Luis Moreno and Nicola McEwen, "Exploring the Territorial Politics of Welfare," *The Territorial Politics of Welfare*, ed. N. McEwen and L. Moreno (New York: Routledge, 2005), 1-40.

23. Inglehart (*op. cit.*); Putnam (*op. cit.*); Pahrr and Putnam (*op. cit.*)

24. Miller (*op. cit.*); Keating (*op. cit.*) and Parekh (*op. cit.*)

25. Unfortunately, no British survey includes any measure of interpersonal trust together with items similar to those analysed here, which prevents us from evaluating that intermediate causal mechanism.

26. See Keating (*op. cit.*) and Miller (*op. cit.* 1996).

27. For different meanings of "common good," see Robert Dahl, *Democracy and Its Critics* (New Haven: Yale Univ. Press, 1989); for two different views on the welfare state, see Keating (*op. cit.*)

28. See Keating (*op. cit.*)

29. See Keating (*op. cit.*); Tamir (*op. cit.*); and Taylor (*op. cit.*).

30. For the "sense of national interest," see Brown *et al.* (*op. cit.*)

31. See Keating (*op. cit.*), Taylor (*op. cit.*) and Parekh (*op. cit.*)

32. See Rogers Brubaker and Frederick Cooper, "Beyond 'Identity,'" *Theory and Society* 29, no. 1 (2000): 1-47; Arash Abizadeh, "Does Liberal Democracy Presuppose a Cultural Nation?," *American Political Science Review* 96, no. 3 (2002): 495-509.

33. See Tamir (*op. cit.*).

34. Ernest Gellner, *Nations and Nationalism* (Oxford: Blackwell, 1983).

35. For instance, Jürgen Habermas, "The European Nation-State: Its Achievements and Limits," in *Mapping the Nation*, ed. G. Balakrishnan (London: Verso, 1996), 281-94.

36. For the concept of subjective support of the political community, see Easton (*op. cit.*).

37. See Gellner (*op. cit.*).

38. For the same interpretation of Miller's book, see Abizadeh (*op. cit.*)

39. Cf. Easton (*op. cit.* 1965).

40. Enric Martínez-Herrera, "From Nation-Building to Building Identification with Political Communities: Consequences of Political Decentralization in Spain, the Basque Country, Catalonia and Galicia, 1978-2001," *European Journal of Political Research* 41, no. 4 (2002): 421-53.

41. Easton (*op. cit.* 1975).

42. Martínez-Herrera (*op. cit.*). As a case in point, despite the term "nation" being traditionally used for referring to England, Scotland, and Wales as much as Britain, its citizens' attitudes raise strong doubts about the alleged weakness of British identification, even in Scotland. However, it is plausible that the discursive and propagandistic handling of the category "nation" may help or hinder the development of this support.

43. Brubaker (*op. cit.* 1990, 1996); see also Kymlicka (*op. cit.*); Parekh (*op. cit.*).

44. Juan J. Linz, "Peripheries within the Periphery," in *Mobilization, Center-Periphery Structures and Nation-Building: A Volume in Commemoration of Stein Rokkan*, ed. P. Torsvik (Oslo: Universitetsforlaget, 1981), 335-389; David Laitin, "Political Culture and Political Preferences (Controversy with A. Wildavsky)," *American Political Science Review* 82, no. 2 (1988): 589-597; Hobsbawm (*op. cit.*).

45. For an analysis more sophisticated statistically, which is conducted through structural equation modeling, see Enric Martínez-Herrera, "Liberal-nationalist theory, political confidence and support for the welfare state. Evidence from Britain," *EUI Working Paper* SPS 2004/8 (Florence: European University Institute, 2004).

46. The data set includes a sampling boost for Scotland, thus making multivariate inferences for this territory statistically reliable. The number of productive interviews is 2,515 in England and 882 in Scotland. Unfortunately, the sub-sample for Wales is too small as to carry out multivariate analyses (n = 182). The standard weights for each sample were applied in the execution of the models as indicated by the CREST, "British Election Panel Study 1997-2002. 1997-1999 File. Note for Users" (London: CREST, 1999).

47. See Anthony Heath, Bridget Taylor, Lindsay Brook, and Alison Park, "British National Sentiment," *British Journal of Political Science* 29 (1999): 155-75.

48. The battery also included the item BCRITIC "People in Britain are too ready to criticise their country." However, many preliminary analyses showed its low validity and reliability, and that it seriously distorted the reliability and validity of the other nationalist items.

49. Missing cases (including the "Don't Knows") were given the mean value of the other cases. The number of missing values in most variables of both samples is quite small, not higher than 15%—the usual exception being left-right ideological self-placement. All the results shown draw from the weighted samples after missing value imputation with the

means of the productive cases. Missing values were kept only in some control variables (age, gender, and years studying). When introducing these controls, the few remaining missing values were deleted using the listwise procedure.

50. Heath et al. (*op. cit.*).

51. On a concurring appraisal of a similar International Social Survey question, see David McCrone and Paula Surridge. "National Identity and National Pride," in *British Social Attitudes, 15th report* (Aldershot: Ashgate, 1998), 1-17.

52. For other authors devising national pride as a proxy to nationalism, see Inglehart (*op. cit.*) and Mattei Dogan, "The Decline of Nationalisms within Western Europe," *Comparative Politics* 26, no. 3 (1994): 281-305. Moreover, Hobsbawm (*op. cit.*) and Heath and his colleagues (*op. cit.*) allude to an "external dimension" of nationalism, addressed against other countries.

53. Abramson (*op. cit.*).

54. Respondents were given the value of the mid-point of their income interval, except for the bottom and top categories, with values 2,000 and 46,000. Missing values were imputed a different mean in England (20320.68) and Scotland (17398.18).

55. See Citrin (*op. cit.*); Barbara Farah, Samuel H. Barnes, and Felix Heunks, "Political Dissatisfaction," in *Political Action: Mass Participation in Five Western Democracies*, ed. Samuel H. Barnes, Max Kaase et al. (Beverly Hills: Sage, 1979), 409-47; Gabriel (*op. cit.*).

56. Heath et al. (*op. cit.*), at fn. 10.

57. For instance, Liah Greenfeld, *Nationalism: Five Roads to Modernity* (Cambridge, MA: Harvard University, 1992).

Part II
Three Perspectives on Nationalism in Europe

Chapter 4
European Nationalism and European Identity

Ireneusz Paweł Karolewski

Nationalism and Collective Identity

In most of the publications on European nationalism one can find explorations of the nationalism of the European states. The bulk of the nationalism theory deals with nation-states for obvious reasons: nationalism was strongly associated with nation-building processes in particular in the nineteenth century in Europe. In this context, the European Union was viewed by many proponents of European integration as a circumvention of nationalism, rather than its rescue or repetition at a higher level. As long as the EU was a relatively loose organization of European nation-states focusing on economic integration, the issue of EU nationalism was not seriously debated. However, at the beginning of the 1990s, a progressive political institutionalization of the EU, in the sense of both a deepening (more majority decisions and new supranational institution-building) and an extension of the activity scope (including Home and Justice Affairs), ignited a debate on the collective identity of the EU.

In this chapter, I will focus on the issue of collective identity in the EU as a marker of European nationalism, since the strategy of European nationalism intends to construct collective identity in a way that emulates the integrative logic of national identity. It attempts therefore to generate a national sense of belonging in a non-nation-state environment. It is a particular case of identity politics, since most EU scholars negate the nation-state character of the EU, either by using neologisms such as mixed polity, consortio, condominio, and proto-federation[1] or by employing the rather vague term of the *sui generis* system for a lack of a precise description of the European polity.[2] Simultaneously, many advocates of collective identity in the EU require the fulfillment of one of the main characteristics of the continental nation-states, which is collective identity modeled after national identity. Collective identity appears to be central in both classical and contemporary discourses on nationalism. For instance, John Stuart Mill spoke of the feeling of nationality, describing specifically the object to which the feeling had to relate. "This feeling of nationality may have been generated by various causes. . . . But the strongest of all is identity of political antecedents; the possession of national history, and consequent community of recollections. . . . Free institutions are next to impossible in a country made up of different nationalities. Among a people without fellow-feeling, especially if they read and speak different languages, the united public opinion, necessary to the working of representative government, cannot exist."[3] In this sense, national identity as an essential feature of nationalism fulfils integrating functions regarding individuals in a society and establishes a national community, which is believed to be a necessary underpinning for any representative and majoritarian democracy. This theory of "benign nationalism" highlights the integrative and virtuous working of nationalism, rather than its destructive and vicious effects.

In the same vein, David Miller argues that even in contemporary democratic societies the bonds of collectivity are necessary.[4] Precisely nationalism is expected to generate them by producing social trust and obligations stemming from the feelings of relatedness. This argument is often applied to the conditions of the modern economy, which are regarded as requiring high levels of moral commitment in the form of mutual solidarity. Only against the background of a high level of social trust can democracy function in a sustainable manner, since redistributive measures cannot be otherwise justified. Furthermore, national identity is expected to deliver trust and motivation for citizens to participate and deliberate on public matters. By identifying with the community, individuals become receptacles of collective will. Therefore, the theory of "benign nationalism" presumes that the nation is not only the empirically most common form of a modern political community, but also implies a normative value of nations. The probably most pronounced argument in favor of nation and nationalism has been proposed by Liah Greenfeld, who associates the nation with popular sovereignty and equality, whereas nationalism becomes an engine of dignity provision for individuals in a modern society.[5] Therefore, national identity is viewed as conducive to individual enrichment in the moral and political sense. The collective bond of nationalism is supposed to deepen commitments and obligations between those who share it by providing an essential motivation behind civic commitments. For David Miller, the bonds of collectivity are drawn primarily from historical memory of the community, which fosters ancestral forms of political obligation. Since ancestors spilled their blood to build and defend the nation, citizens are believed to inherit an obligation to continue their work.[6]

Various versions of the arguments supporting nation-oriented EU-identity and nation-like EU-community can be found in the debate on European identity, in particular in the context of the democratic deficit of the European Union. The democratic deficit of the EU is believed to occur because majority decisions are not underpinned by a collective feeling of mutual trust and belonging to the same political community. At the same time, this diagnosis is often accompanied by skepticism about the EU being able to reproduce national identity at a higher level. For instance, Anthony D. Smith argues that the desire for European identity arises from the flawed assumption about the end of the nation-states, which are as naïve as they are unsubstantiated as they ignore both the perseverance of nation-states and the rootedness of national identities. Moreover, Europe lacks a common ethnic base with a reliable and visible set of common historical memories, myths, symbols, and values, since abstract allegiances lead to strong and stable identities.[7] A further skeptic, David Miller, rejects the idea of European nationalism on the grounds of lacking trust between European citizens. According to Miller, the EU must justify material redistribution beyond self-interest, which leads to obligations between compatriots. These obligations are justifiable only against the background of reciprocity and trust, which can be provided only by a national community, since it embodies continuity between generations and holds up virtues of the ancestors by encouraging citizens to live up to them. As the EU is unable to generate an equal level of trust and justify obligations, it suffers from a legitimacy deficit.[8]

This poses a dilemma for the application of nationalism by the EU. On the one hand, the EU might be in need of generating nation-like collective identity to establish acceptance for its decisions under the conditions of diversity and heterogeneity. On the other hand, the EU seems to lack the structural requirements (as a non-nation-state political system) for developing collective identity. The EU cannot suppress existing collective identities in the radical manner that the belligerent nationalism of the nineteenth and twentieth centuries did, since the major source of EU legitimacy still resides with the EU member-states. In addition, the nation-states of the EU not only possess significantly more bureaucratic and ideological resources than the EU to forge collective identities, but they can also draw on existing strong national attachments, which counteract European nationalism. Nevertheless, the EU applies identity technologies toward its citizens in an attempt to solve this dilemma. Bo Stråth remarked that the concept of European identity was already introduced at the EC Copenhagen summit in 1973 in order to instrumentally consolidate the EC, since the oil price crisis undermined the belief in the EC's political effectiveness.[9] In this sense, the political elites of the EU appear to be aware of the stabilizing effects of collective identity and attempt to generate it, albeit in a more subtle manner than the EU member states can do by reverting to nationalism. Therefore, the "nationalism light" of the EU uses either selected identity technologies of nationalism or uses them at a more subtle level, as the EU cannot exactly emulate nationalism regarding its strength, sacrificial appeal, and aggressiveness.[10]

The aim of this chapter is to explore the technologies of European nationalism and EU identity politics. I start by problematizing European identity under the conditions of fluidity and hybridity. In the next two sections, I will discuss the identity technologies of European nationalism by focusing on the manipulation of symbols by the EU and the generation of positive self-images of the EU. The final section will deal with the juxtaposition of European patriotism and European nationalism.

European Identity under the Conditions of Fluidity and Hybridity

The bulk of the contemporary literature on identity stresses fluidity and a dynamic reconstruction of identity. An example of that is the work of Zygmunt Bauman, in which individualization of identity is regarded as concomitant of "liquid" modernity, where the traditional collective identities lose their grip on individuals. The concept of liquid modernity suggests a rapidly changing social order that undermines all notions of durability. It implies a sense of "rootlessness" and fluidity of identity.[11]

Against this background, European identity tends to be conceptualized as a layer of multiple identities or as a component of a hybrid identity. Different layers or components of multiple identities can relate to each other in various configurations. As Matthias L. Maier and Thomas Risse argue, identities can be nested, crosscutting, or like marble cake. Nesting suggests some hierarchy between a people's sense of belonging and loyalties, whereby the EU forms the outer boundary and regions or nation-states constitute the core. In crosscutting identities, members of one identity group are also members of another identity group, even though conflictual relationships between the group identities are not excluded. In addition, in the marble cake model of multiple identities, various components of an individual's identity cannot be clearly separated, but rather blend into one another.[12] Depending on the salience of the situation, individuals change their identity layers.[13] In this sense, European identity only becomes activated when there is a context relating directly to the EU and the individual becomes mobilized as an EU citizen. However, it is frequently argued that the EU is likely to have relatively little salience in the everyday citizenship practice, since it regulates solely policy fields of secondary significance to the average citizen.[14]

In this perspective, European identity is unlikely to replace other attachments, particularly the national ones, and become a new supranational identity at a higher level. As the EU is characterized by cultural diversity, rather than unity, a cultural, societal, or political uniformization seems improbable. The fluidity, plurality, and multiplicity of collective identities of the EU can be conceptualized as "deep diversity," which denotes more than a mere cultural plurality. John Erik Fossum applies this term—first introduced by Charles Taylor—to describe the existence of cultural, national, and ethnic structures of a society which in turn bring about different collective goals.[15] These different collective goals are acknowledged by society and political authorities as legitimate, and are regarded as a wishful and legitimate state not subject to assimilating, acculturating and other homogenization policies.[16] In this view, the collective identity of European citizens disintegrates into diverse belongings to separate groups which, depending on the context, lay political claims of public recognition and attempt to extract public resources as a result of these claims. Diverse social identities become politicized and depoliticized, increasing the contextual and fragmented character of the European identity. The demarcation lines between groups are contextual and situational, as individuals belong to overlapping groups and exhibit a multitude of social roles and identities. Therefore, it remains questionable whether the EU is able to construct a nation-like integrative meta-identity providing a sort of primary identity framework of reference, able to transcend all other social identities.

Besides features of deep diversity, the hybridity of collective identities in Europe is becoming a dominant aspect of the identity discourse in the EU. The notion of hybridity puts emphasis on the fusion of identities (rather than engendering a meta-identity), which is viewed as a consequence of the increasingly intertwined and multicultural nature of modern societies. This is primarily a result of the large-scale migration within the EU as well as from outside Europe into the EU.[17] The expansion of European borders and the consequent transnationalization of the European societies are expected to foster not only cultural diversity, but also cultural hybridity.[18] In this view, hybrid identities correspond to the institutional hybridity of the EU itself. As identities in the EU are likely to become increasingly multiple and hybrid, a sense of belonging to a particular territory or a community can be upheld alongside a simultaneous attachment to supranational collectivities such as the EU.[19] The socio-cultural dimension of the EU matches the notion of transnational syncretism[20], whereas the EU promotes "the unity in diversity" by respecting the national identities of the member states. Therefore, the debate dichotomizing national and European identities is rejected by the proponents of multiplicity and fluidity in collective identities. In this perspective, not only are the citizens capable of having multi-layered and fluid identities, but these tend also to be inclusive and nested, rather than mutually exclusive. In this vein, Gary Marks analyzes multiple identities along two dimensions: intensity of attachment to a particular territorial community, and exclusive versus multiple attachments across territorial levels. With the example of Catalonia, he shows that identity is not a zero-sum game, and that European identity may very well coexist with strong regional and national identities, even though this co-existence is not context-dependent.[21] Marks suggests that attachments can be mutually inclusive: attachment at one territorial level is associated with greater rather than less attachment at other levels. Additionally, an individual with a relatively high attachment to any one of these territorial levels is likely to have a relatively high attachment to other levels. Nonetheless, a more conflictual relationship between national, regional, and European identity may also develop. In cases of conflict or salience of conflictual issues, the primary or core identity is activated, since individuals tend to reduce the cognitive complexity of social reality.

In a similar vein, Daniel Fuss and Marita A. Grosser highlight the hybridity of European identity by relating the construction of European identity to specifically European social interactions: European identity cannot develop unless individuals participate in social interactions related to the EU or Europe.[22] Consequently, there are at least two conditions for the development of European identity. Firstly, as Europe has to be salient in social interactions of individuals, citizens with only local and national horizons are unlikely to develop European identity. Secondly, European identity (as any other social identity) requires "raw material" such as contacts with foreigners or a command of foreign languages. However, this raw material is unequally distributed within the population. Therefore, individuals develop European identity to differing extents. This conception of European identity purports an abstract feeling of belonging, but not necessarily in the emotional sense. Fuss and Grosser demonstrate in the empirical study that European identity, as an abstract category, is a lower priority (in contrast to national identity). However, dual focus identification on the nation and on Europe appears to be a dominant feature of collective identity among Europeans.

The perspective on European identity highlighting fluidity and hybridity draws heavily on the concept of salience which activates one or the other layer of multiple collective identities. However, this perspective does not explain what would happen when the salient context triggers not one but several identities, thus bringing them into conflict. One possibility is for the citizen to commit to one dominant group identification and subordinate all other affiliations, precisely as the notion of "chronic identity" presupposes.[23] This would imply that either national or European identity will have to take the upper hand. Consequently, citizens would identify with their fellow Europeans, mostly to the extent that European identity converges with national identity, equalizing European nationalism with the nationalism of a given member state.

A second possibility would include ascribing different group identities to different domains, whereby segregated multiple identities would not be mobilized simultaneously. European identity would therefore be adopted in the political context, for instance in relations between the EU and the United States, and ethnic identity would be maintained in the cultural domain. A third case would cover a situation in which identities can be neither subordinated to one "chronic identity" nor segregated. When two identities become salient at the same time, one can use the inclusive strategy of extending the in-group category to all members of the conflicting identity groups. For instance, when a German national identifies both with Europe and Germany and finds it conflictive, he might consider being German as a category of Europeanness, thus assuming an overlapping between Germany and Europe. In other words, every German would be European by definition. The alternative strategy would include a conjunction, in which the in-group is perceived as the intersection of several categories. For instance, only Western Germans would perceive themselves as genuine Europeans, since the EU was the part of their social reality for the last fifty years, as opposed to the Eastern Germans. In this case, only Western German identity would overlap with the European identity, thus excluding the other Germans. While the additive strategy would increase the inclusiveness of an individual's collective identity, the conjunctive approach would narrow it down.[24]

The perspective highlighting fluid and hybrid collective identity centers on the individual strategies of coping with the complexity and multiplicity of identity. As citizens can change their collective identity at will, heterogeneous societies can be confronted with changing and fragmenting patterns of identity formation, rather than with the development of a resilient, stable, and overarching collective identity for a political community. However, this perspective neglects the political aspects of identity technologies employed by the political authorities, which attempt to stimulate collective identity either by gluing particular identities (hybridization) or by engendering meta-identity.[25] Whereas fluidity and hybridity of collective identity make a development of European nationalism undetermined, identity technologies aim in a top-down manner at collective identity as a subject of identity politics. In this view, citizens are "receivers" of collective identity, whose orientation is constructed by the political authorities. The following two chapters focus on the identity technologies applied by the EU, in particular on the manipulation of symbols and the construction of positive self-images.

The EU Identity and the Manipulation of Symbols

The fluidity and hybridity of collective identities in the EU on the one hand and still-strong national identities on the other limit the EU's ability for identity construction. Against this background, there are two scenarios for the EU. Firstly, the EU can induce a "soft" collective identity by promoting fluid and fragmented identity in an attempt to weaken national bonds in the member states. The European Union seems to be one of the most important factors responsible for the increasing relevance of regionalism in Europe. The EU supports projects and finance initiatives at the regional level and stimulates an intermediary level of political decision-making by offering to the regions numerous European programs and cooperation initiatives which support regional identities. As the EU increasingly becomes a political point of crystallization for regional policies and interest representation, institutions of national identity formation are circumvented, even if not entirely weakened.[26] Secondly, in a skeptical view the EU might fail to establish any sense of broad collective identity at all. European cultural and political diversity is therefore viewed as undermining a solid sense of collective self and of social belonging. For instance, Gerard Delanty suggests that the EU cannot rest on any culturally stable grounds similar to a common language, a shared history, religion, an educational system, and mass media. Even if skeptical, Delanty's position stresses the significance of cultural symbols for the construction and stability of European identity.[27] These cultural symbols are expected to pave the way for an emergence of collective identity based not only on the dichotomy of Europeanness and non-Europeanness, but also on identification allowing for a more "thick" collective identity, resembling culturalist conceptions of nationalism.

Against this background, some authors believe that the EU practices manipulation of cultural symbols pertaining to collective identity. One of the cases of the EU's manipulation of cultural symbols is the introduction of the common currency in the EU.[28] The establishment of the tangible symbol of the Euro and its iconography raises the salience of Europeanness without the necessity of homogenizing the European cultural diversity, since the Euro allows for different iconographic connotations. Simultaneously, a common currency establishes a degree of commonality and therefore fosters new identity content.[29] This common currency is compatible with the fluid and hybrid nature of European identities since it is open to multiple interpretations, at the same time endowing the citizen with something to identify with, without surrendering their own subjective vision of the European "community." This trend toward abstraction is also visible with regard to other collective symbols such as flags and anthems.[30] In the same vein, Thomas Risse stresses the significance of the Euro for the development of the collective identity in the European Union. Since money generally fulfils a role of a relevant symbolic marker in the processes of community building, the Euro is essential for the creation of collective European identity. Risse argues that the Euro has a substantial impact on citizens' identification with the EU and Europe, as the common currency enhances the "realness" of Europe by providing a tangible link from the European level to the daily lives of the citizens.[31] Consequently, the EU attempts to use cultural symbols which are tangible but still sufficiently abstract. Symbols that are too abstract are likely to be ignored by individuals as lacking any connection to their daily social practices. However, tangibility cannot turn into suppression of meaning, since it can become associated with cultural hegemony, rather than common identity. Therefore, there is no unique writing or pronunciation of the common currency, as Greece and Bulgaria for instance use their national alphabets and pronunciation. In this respect, despite a vernacular diversity of the Euro, common currency acts as an "identity signifier."

Further cases of manipulation of cultural symbols pertain to the EU's cultural policy. This includes symbolic initiatives such as the "European Cities of Culture," with the goal of raising the visibility and identifiablity of the EU. The EU increasingly promotes commonality symbols, while attempting to respect the realm of national cultures.[32] Thus, the EU tries to enhance its salience via symbolic diffusion into the everyday life of citizens, but without relinquishing the symbolic ambiguity. This ambiguity does not however entail confusion, but rather is to be viewed as a response to the European cultural fluidity and hybridity. Consequently, as Sassatelli suggests, the EU's manipulation of symbols recalls Durkheimian analysis of the totem, which is a part of the symbol it represents.[33] The EU's totem-like symbolism serves as a tool for constructing a community in the specific context of the EU's multiple identities.

In contrast to the aggregated view of cultural policy, Michael Bruter examines separate symbols and items pertaining to collective identity in Europe. According to his qualitative analysis of focus-group discussions in France, the UK and the Netherlands, he argues that the majority of the participants' perceptions of Europe and their self-assessment of their European identity referred to predominantly "civic" images, whereas only a minority perceived the EU in "cultural" terms. This classical vocabulary of ethnic (or cultural) and civic nationalism suggests that the images of Europe are not distant from the categories used in the nationalism research. The images of "cultural" Europe by the participants were associated with peace, harmony, the disappearing of historical divisions, and cooperation between similar people. In contrast, the images of "civic' Europe were linked to borderless-ness, circulation of citizens, and prosperity.[34] In his further study, Bruter confirms his preliminary conclusions about civic and cultural images with regard to the symbols. He highlights that the EU imitates nation-states by delivering proper national symbols in order to stimulate a European political community. These include—besides Euro notes and coins—a flag, an anthem, a national day, and until recently an attempt to introduce a constitution.[35] As a result, the EU manipulates cultural symbols to construct European mass identity by mimicking technologies of national identity. In addition, Bruter argues that political communication affects collective identities of citizens with regard to both components of identity; both the mass media and political authorities have the power to induce or to inhibit the formation of European identity through the construction and usage of symbols. However, the particular role of symbols in the development of collective identities seems to be particularly instructive for the technology of collective identity, since symbols apparently have more impact on the cultural component of collective identities, rather than on the civic one. This could suggest that a more intense construction and application of symbols could stimulate a thicker and more stable identity in the EU.[36]

Furthermore, one could argue that attempts to personify the EU, for instance through the establishment of an office of Foreign Minister or President (as envisaged by the draft Constitutional Treaty), point in the same direction as the manipulation of symbols.[37] Personification techniques are frequently used by the nation-state elites to stimulate collective identity and hence loyalty. Since nation-states or political systems in general are abstract entities, they necessitate a more concrete embodiment for mass population to conceive of them and develop shared identity. This embodiment can occur as personification, in which a polity becomes associated with the most salient figure in the political system. Recent studies in political psychology confirm the hypothesis that personification of political systems facilitates "stronger" attitudes and hence may be decisive in the formation of collective identities. As opposed to personification, embodying the political system as a parliamentary institution is likely to produce weaker attitudes, which leads to the conclusion that a widespread practice of personification of the political system has robust and potentially far-reaching attitudinal consequences.[38] For the EU, it could mean that the proposals made in the draft Constitutional Treaty (integrated to a large extent into the Lisbon Treaty) implying personification techniques would be more effective in terms of collective identity than public visibility of the European Parliament.

In sum, the EU applies a mixed strategy of identity construction. On the one hand, it attempts to preserve and even to promote cultural diversity to weaken the national bonds within the member-states. In this respect, it employs a balanced and "soft" strategy combining tangibility with abstraction of identity symbols. On the other hand, it uses more traditional technologies borrowed from nationalism, both from its civic and cultural versions. In addition, the EU seems to apply personification techniques, well known from the context of the nation-state.

Positive Self-images of the EU as "Identity Markers"

The social identity theory posits that individuals develop collective identity as they acquire a positive image from membership in a social group. The motivation for positive social identity is created by comparing oneself favorably to the outgroup.[39] Consequently, if one identifies with a negatively valued group, the self-stereotyping will have a negative impact on one's current level of self-esteem. Since the underlying motivation for membership in groups is the enhancement of self-esteem, psychological gains are achieved only through identification with a favorably evaluated group.[40] Therefore, a production and diffusion of positive self-images can be an efficient instrument of generation of collective identity without the necessity to recourse to symbols of commonality. This is also the case with the EU.

The first type of positive imaginary tools used to describe the EU substantive identity is cosmopolitan Europe.[41] One of the most fervent proponents of cosmopolitan Europe is Jürgen Habermas, who believes that the European Union can be based on a collective identity stemming from a set of abstract universalistic principles such as human rights, but evolves and thickens into the European constitutional patriotism, which is expected to replace the ethnic bonds of European nations.[42] Since the EU should represent a "post-national constellation," European citizens, induced by the process of European constitution-making, are expected to develop a sense of loyalty and solidarity "among strangers" with regard to each other by abstracting from their particular identities. This cosmopolitan Europe is also associated with a constitution rather than a state, and is anchored in a shared culture of universal and liberal values.[43] Even though we deal in this case with a relatively open and inclusive identity, the cosmopolitan self-image of Europe shows normative boundaries, which distinguish Europe for instance from the United States. Jürgen Habermas regards the historical and institutional peculiarities of Europe (such as secularization, the priority of the state over the market, the primacy of social solidarity over achievement, skepticism concerning technology, awareness of the paradoxes of progress, rejection of the law of the stronger, and the commitment to peace as a consequence of the historical experience of loss)[44] as an appropriate boundary-mechanism.

Other scholars also base collective identity in Europe on its constitutional distinctiveness where the United States remains the major object of differentiation, while Europe maintains both cosmopolitan and particularistic features.[45] In accordance with Habermas, Wojciech Sadurski offers a set of constitutional identity distinctions between the EU and the United States which, politically perpetuated, could construct and strengthen European identity. The main feature of European constitutional identity which distinguishes it from the United States points to a much more favorable conception of the state, which is treated not only as the source of threats but also as an ethical institution for the creation of justice and protection of citizens against misfortunes stemming from the inequalities and irrationalities of the market.[46] A further fundamental difference would pertain to minority rights, since European constitutional identity exhibits less faith in the positive effects of individualistic liberal principles, particularly when the societal diversity is associated with anti-minority prejudices and discrimination. In contrast, American constitutionalism is regarded as hostile to minority rights, since it is based on the liberal approach to the American immigrant society, where the main concern of new minorities is to enjoy the same rights as the older population, whereas European minorities' main concern is to enjoy special group rights as structurally disadvantaged minorities. Moreover, there is a crucial difference between American and European constitutionalism with regard to the secularity of the state. Since in the United States the constitutional doctrine protects a far-reaching separation of state and religion, many practices of European states (such as tax-collecting by the German state for the Church or favoring certain churches as in the case of the Church of England) would be deemed unconstitutional. Nevertheless, the political culture in Europe is less tolerant of frequent references to God and religion in the public discourse, which is apparently a feature of the American political culture.[47] These differences are expected to function as a "difference engine," thus fostering European common identity and simultaneously being ingrained in universalistic principles.[48]

Beyond the differences to the United States, the cosmopolitan image of the EU is expected to rest on the EU's transformed concept of power politics, according to which the EU exports the rule of law, democracy, and human rights worldwide. Erik Oddvar Eriksen argues that the criteria for the EU's missionary activities can be derived from cosmopolitanism, suggesting that the EU subordinates its external policies to the constraints of a higher ranking law. In this perspective, the EU is regarded as different from (and morally superior to) the interest-maximizing actors in international politics, as it is able to act out of a sense of justice or duty pertaining mainly to human rights. Consequently, infringements of human rights become sanctioned, whereby the EU increasingly fulfils the role of the forerunner of the new ethical international order.[49] Not only does the EU project its cosmopolitan image outside, but also attempts to enhance the positive image consistency between the externally projected and the internally applied standards. The EU Charter of Fundamental Rights is believed to be the indicator of these attempts. Both approaches to constructing a positive image (either via differentiation from the United States or its missionary cosmopolitism) reflect universalistic codes of collective identity, which are based on a transcendental interpretation of its community values and an ethical supremacy vis-à-vis others.

A further positive image of the EU discussed in the debate pertains to the notion of the EU as a civilian power.[50] This issue has aroused considerable interest in recent years, since it seemingly gives the EU an additional feature to distinguish it from other global powers, such as the United States. The notion of civilian power refers to the methods of international politics rather than the substance.[51] The EU is believed to pursue post-national or ethical interests by using methods of normative change rather than use of force. According to this self-image, the civilian power Europe acts primarily in tune with ideas and values, and not military or economic strength. In this sense, the EU's actions are believed to be more humanitarian and civilizing, which echoes the debate on the EU as a post-Westphalian political system. In this perspective, the EU's external policies result from the "post-modern," "post-sovereign," and "post-national" nature of the political system of the European Union.[52] One of the tenets of civilian power Europe is believed to be multiculturalism, which is a form of self-binding by law. Seen from this angle, the EU's objective is not to maximize its selfish interests, but to promote the development of an international society according to rule-based international order of multilateral institutionalism. The EU therefore fosters the power of international institutions and regional organizations which allow for an extensive coordination and cooperation of actors in international politics. The goal is the creation of institutionalized and global governance capable of solving global and regional collective problems. As opposed to the U.S., which defines its civilizing mission more internally, EU member states revert to deliberative and institutionalized cooperation mechanisms among themselves.[53] Consequently, even in an uncertain political environment, member states are likely to remain attached to deliberation and cooperation, which is an indicator of a basic trust between the member states.[54] In this sense, trust among nations is expected to play an important role in the European identity, as opposed to the anarchy of brute power outside the EU.[55]

The third self-image of European identity is the EU as a normative power, which is directly linked to the cosmopolitan and civilizing image. Here, the EU stresses its progressive stance in promoting and implementing human rights and environmental policies, and by so doing it asserts its leading role and depicts the U.S. as a laggard. In other words, the EU promotes its positive image as the forerunner in advocating human rights worldwide and in the fight against climate change, thus claiming its moral supremacy.[56] Simultaneously, the EU represents the policies and concerns of the United States as illegitimate, as they are constrained by national boundaries and over-attached to the state sovereignty as well as to the economic and/or security interests.[57] Consequently, the EU uses the vanguard-laggard dichotomy in order to describe its own identity in contrast to the U.S. In this case, the EU uses differentiation techniques associated with the construction of inferiority of the others with the aim of establishing and perpetuating its own positive image.[58] The image of the EU as a normative power is applied among other things to its ability to transform border conflicts and to promote selfless environmental politics. Since borders are socially constructed institutions, they rely on discursive processes of constructing a shared understanding among participants. Normative power in Europe is expected to be capable of bringing about conflict transformation through the desecuritization of conflicts.[59]

It is still difficult to assess how effective the positive self-images of the EU as "identity markers" will be and whether the EU can develop a consistent set of identity politics based on images of normative superiority. Robert Falkner argues that the EU's policies, especially in the field of environmental protection, do not simply result from normative orientation but from domestic economic conflicts. For example, in the debate on genetically modified (GM) food, the EU offered international leadership only after strong anti-GM sentiments appeared among the public. Prior to this, the EU attached little importance to the bio-safety talks. However, even after the EU claimed international leadership in that field, it sought to export its own domestic regulatory model, which would ensure that international rules would not damage the EU's economic interests in medical biotechnology.[60]

European Patriotism or European Nationalism?

Regardless of the methods of creating collective identity in the EU, there is a debate on the necessary strength of European identity leading directly to the notion of European nationalism. Some authors would like to reproduce the strength and resilience of the national bond in the EU by establishing a sort of European nationalism. The concept of constitutional patriotism proposed for the EU by Jürgen Habermas can be interpreted as a form of civic nationalism for the EU, as being grounded on a devotion to liberal and democratic principles of a European political community.[61] Even if constitutional patriotism rests on cosmopolitan values, it requires a contextualization with regard to a specific territory and a concrete community and thus supersedes pre-political identities of citizens such as the ethnical or the national ones. In this view, not only could European constitutional patriotism supersede collective identities of nation-states, but it could also induce a European identity based on rational moral and political bonds.[62]

Nonetheless, constitutional patriotism does not have to be interpreted as circumventing nationalism, but rather as close to the notion of civic nationalism, since both concepts exhibit communitarian features.[63] It remains controversial whether Habermas himself is a proponent of constitutional patriotism or rather an advocate of civic nationalism, as he speaks of supportive political culture which would stabilize the allegiance to the legal principles of a political community.[64] According to this reading, Habermas' constitutional patriotism would still be nationalism. Craig Calhoun argues that constitutional patriotism should be supplemented by a stronger approach to social solidarity, which would include creation and reproduction of social institutions and reconfiguration of social relations, as it is too weak to generate sustainable collective identity.[65] Consequently, he proposes a European form of civic nationalism that embraces both constitutionalism and social solidarity. However, it implies that the more constitutional patriotism shifts away from civic nationalism, the less collective and cohesive identity it can create. Whenever the cosmopolitan element in constitutional patriotism becomes dominating, it will lead to more inclusiveness, but it will also entail weaker collective bonds. In the same vein, Philippe Schmitter and Michael W. Bauer argue in favor of expanding social citizenship in the European Union, which would entail stronger and more numerous redistributive measures in the EU.[66] This would shift the EU again in the direction of a welfare state with national character. Schmitter and Bauer want to enhance the visibility of the EU by bringing it closer to European citizens and thus to make it a part of their everyday lives.

Beyond the problem of the "thickness" of European nationalism, there are some other methodological dilemmas voiced for instance by Rogers Brubaker in his studies on nationalism. Brubaker questions the dichotomy between civic and ethnic nationalism on methodological and normative grounds. Regarding the criteria of "thickness," civic nationalism does not have to be distinct from its ethnic variant, as civic communities are a culmination of a long past of common endeavors, sacrifice and devotion, which are stabilized by institutions, customs, historical memories, and common values. In this sense, even civic nationalism or constitutional patriotism are not entirely chosen, but are also given, since they are incapable of generating collective identity without the backup of the common culture and collective memory.[67] In addition, the normative assumption of civic nationalism as being inclusive, since it is based on citizenship and not on ascriptive features or descent, is questioned by Brubaker. He argues that civic nationalism is also exclusive, but differently exclusive than ethnic nationalism. Civic and ethnic nationalism manage the access to the nation differently, but they are both devices of social closure and exclusion.[68] The exclusionary aspects of the European Union are currently apparent, even without the internal bonds denoted as civic nationalism.[69]

For instance, Anita Böcker and Tetty Havinga argue that statistics on asylum applications in the EU have been deliberately used in the debates on refugee and asylum policies in a highly selective manner to justify restrictive measures. Consequently, even with its dedication to cosmopolitism and civility, the EU establishes and uses mechanisms of social closure and exclusion.[70] In addition, Peo Hansen argues that the concept of European identity envisaged by the European Community has given the citizen/non-citizen of the EU categories increasingly ethno-cultural underpinning, with implications for the European identity. As a result of ethno-cultural articulation, European citizenship became an instrument of exclusion toward the EU's non-white and non-Christian populations, thus fostering a collective identity in essentialist terms.[71] In other words, we could argue that the European integration with its inclusive developments strongly relied on the continued exclusion of outsiders, which renders the EU by no means a post-Westphalian polity, but rather territorial and replicating the identity-making mechanisms of the nation-state.[72] Even though the EU is perceived as endorsing multi-cultural values and attitudes, we could argue in accordance with Brubaker that civic and multicultural European identity (in the sense of European nationalism) could be associated with intolerance toward non-members. Laurent Licata and Olivier Klein argue that even the mere creation of the status of "Citizen of the Union" in Maastricht may promote intolerance toward resident foreigners, thus questioning the normative validity of collective identity. In this case, a paradoxical situation could emerge, as citizens' degree of tolerance toward foreigners would contradict the values propagated by the EU.[73]

In contrast, for Habermas it is neither possible nor desirable to melt national identities of the member states down into a European nation.[74] Therefore, a new form of (post-conventional and post-national) identity is supposed to rest on a community other than the nation-state (even if it boils down to civic nationalism at the European level). For this purpose, a shared political and social space (for instance in the form of European civil society) should be promoted in order to generate new emotional attachments (or redirect emotional energy of national identities toward the EU) which would lie at the heart of European identity. Others argue that European identity cannot be easily produced, as most Europeans are still strongly attached to their nations.[75] For instance, Mathieu Deflem and Fred C. Pampel suggest that European citizens' concern with the interests of their own countries implies the persistence of national identity at the expense of post-national identity. They conclude that there exists a myth of post-national identity which does not reflect the reality of the European Union.[76]

Beyond the debate on European nationalism in terms of civic and ethnic categories, there is a turn toward a narrative understanding of European identity in which nationalism becomes intertwined with Europeanism, as the EU interlocks both the political sphere of the nation-state and the European Union. In this perspective, even nations are not "given," but constructed in discourse which establishes both uniqueness of the self and the differences toward the outer world.[77] In this vein, Andrzej Marcin Suszycki argues that the sense of European identity can be found in political actors' discursive commitment to the fundamental values of the EU such as solidarity, parity, and equality between member states, which echoes European constitutional patriotism.[78] Discursive narratives reveal actors' reasoning and motives with regard to the historically developed identities.[79] Against this background, European identity can be understood as a set of narratives by which political actors regard themselves profoundly and enduringly as constituents of the EU as a political entity. The commitment to the EU can be discovered by examining arguments used to justify the transfer of main nation-state functions onto the European level. The mere support for the sovereignty transfer does not denote the sense of European identity, as their support (particularly of the political decision-makers) could be motivated by national interests, for example to enhance the efficiency of political decisions, to stimulate economic growth, or to guarantee external and legal security.[80] In this case, actors are inclined to maintain or improve nation-state functions via the European Union, but do not exhibit any commitments to the European values. In this perspective, the values of solidarity, equality, and parity take into account other member states. According to Suszycki, this would have implications for European identity. First, we deal with contextualized European identity, since both political actors and citizens can develop commitment to European values to a different degree depending on the political issue at hand. Consequently, European identity could be viewed as an issue-dependent phenomenon, rather than a territorial or holistic concept. Second, Suszycki postulates a decoupling of support for the EU and European identity. This is because the support for EU institutions (and so for the transfer of sovereignty) may occur on the basis of national narrative—in other words, in the name of nationalism. Conversely, actors rejecting sovereignty transfer onto the European level can exhibit stronger European identity than its advocates.

Conclusions

From the perspective of theories of nationalism, there are two implications for the collective identity in the post-national context. First, we might identify national identity as historically non-coincidental. In this case, national identity cannot be replaced or superseded at the post-national level. Although there might be collective identities beyond the nation-state, they will never assume a resilience and durability comparable to the national identity. In this perspective, the nation-state represents the end of history in terms of nationalism. Second, there might be post-national identities with similar strengths and stability as national identity. However, the construction of such an identity would need to follow the same path of state-building as nation-states. In other words, we would deal here with a new nation-state at a higher level, which would spawn a European nation. The development of a European nation would occur to the detriment of national identities, which would be diluted in the process. In addition, a European nation will be associated with European nationalism, involving its sinister side in forms of discrimination and even oppression, mostly with regard to non-European minorities. Even if European nationalism exhibited a weaker discriminatory potential than its nation-state protoplast, it would be based on exclusion and boundary-making.

Notwithstanding the controversies on the possibility and necessity of European identity as European nationalism, the mainstream debate argues that the emergence of a collective European identity is central for the viability of the EU. It is expected to compensate for the lack of direct interactions among citizens, thus creating a symbolic illusion of unity in a space without social interaction. However, the concept of European nationalism is linked to technologies of collective identity departing from the analytical and methodological template of the nation-state. Therefore, European nationalism, precisely because it has no certain roots, is associated with a danger or even a necessity of the EU elites engaging in propaganda actions and strategic socialization with the aim of changing the attitudes of European citizens, even if it occurs in a more subtle form of "nationalism light." Manipulation of symbols and generation of positive self-images are methods thereof. When we consider that state nationalism developed in Europe largely under non-democratic circumstances of elite-driven mobilization, it could imply that any European nationalism (as an ideology of the EU and identity technology practiced by the EU) would shift the focus within European citizenship more strongly from active citizen toward compliant subject, which would be disastrous for the democratic deficit of the EU and the EU's legitimacy problems.

Notes

1. Phillipe C. Schmitter, "Representations and the Future Euro-Polity," *Staatswissenschaften und Staatspraxis* 3, no. 3 (1992): 379-405; Markus Jachtenfuchs et al., "Which Europe?: Conflicting Models of Legitimate European Political Order," *European Journal of International Relations* 4, no. 4 (1998): 409-45.

2. Markus Jachtenfuchs, "Die Europäische Union: ein Gebilde sui generis?," in *Projekt Europa im Übergang? Probleme, Modelle und Strategien des Regierens in der Europäischen Union*, ed. Klaus-Dieter Wolf (Baden-Baden: Nomos, 1997), 15-35.

3. John Stuart Mill, "Considerations on Representative Government," in *Utilitarism, on Liberty, Considerations on Representative Government*, ed. Geraint Williams (London: J.M. Dent, 2002 [1861]), 188-410, esp. 391f.

4. David Miller, *On Nationality* (Oxford: Oxford University Press, 1995).

5. Liah Greenfeld, "Is Nation Unavoidable? Is Nation Unavoidable Today?" in *Nation and National Identity: The European Experience in Perspective*, ed. Hanspeter Kriesi et al. (Zürich: Verlag Rüegger, 1999), 37-54; cf. also Paul Gilbert, "Ethics or Nationalism," *Journal of Applied Philosophy* 19, no. 2 (2002): 185-187.

6. David Miller, *Citizenship and National Identity* (Cambridge: Polity Press, 2000), 29.

7. Anthony D. Smith, "A Europe of Nations. Or the Nation of Europe?," *Journal of Peace Research* 30, no. 2 (1993): 129-135; Anthony D. Smith, *Nations and Nationalism in a Global Era* (Cambridge: Polity Press, 1995), esp. chapters 5 and 6.

8. David Miller, *On Nationality* (Oxford: Oxford University Press, 1995), 36.

9. Bo Stråth, "A European Identity: To the Historical Limits of a Concept," *European Journal of Social Theory* 5, no. 4 (2002): 387-401.

10. Cf. Ireneusz Paweł Karolewski, "Regionalism, Nationalism, and European Integration," in *Nationalism and European Integration: The Need for New Theoretical and Empirical Insights*, ed. Ireneusz Paweł Karolewski and Andrzej Marcin Suszycki (New York: Continuum, 2007), 9-32.

11. Cf. Zygmunt Bauman, "Identity in the Globalizing World," *Social Anthropology* 9, no. 2 (2001): 121-129; Zygmunt Bauman, *Liquid Modernity* (Cambridge: Polity Press, 2000).

12. Matthias L. Maier and Thomas Risse, eds., *Europeanization, Collective Identities and Public Discourses, Final Report,* Robert Schuman Centre for Advanced Studies, European University Institute, Florence; cf. also Juan Díez Medrano and Paula Gutiérrez, "Nested Identities: National and European Identity in Spain," *Ethnic and Racial Studies* 24, no. 5 (2001): 753-778.

13. See also the typology proposed by Bettina Westle, who distinguishes between a competition model, a concordance model and a sandwich model of collective identity in the EU. Bettina Westle, "Europäische Identifikation im Spannungsfeld regionaler und nationaler Identitäten: Theoretische Überlegungen und empirische Befunde," *Politische Vierteljahresschrift* 44, no. 4 (2003): 453-482; Bettina Westle, "Europäische Identität und europäische Demokratie," *WeltTrends* 15, no. 54 (2007): 69-83.

14. Cf. Andrew Moravcsik, "What Can We Learn from the Collapse of the European Constitutional Project?," *Politische Vierteljahresschrift* 47, no. 2 (2006): 219-241.

15. For an empirical estimate of European diversity see Dieter Fuchs and Hans-Dieter Klingemann, "Eastward Enlargement of the European Union and the Identity of Europe," *West European Politics* 25, no. 2 (2002): 19-54.

16. John Erik Fossum, *Still a Union of Deep Diversity? The Convention and the Constitution for Europe*, Arena Working Paper 21/03 (Arena: University of Oslo, 2003); John Erik Fossum, "The European Union: In Search of an Identity," *European Journal of Political Theory* 2, no. 3 (2003): 319-340; Charles Taylor, *Reconciling the Solitudes: Essays on Canadian Federalism* (Montreal: McGill-Queen's University Press, 1993); Charles Taylor, *Sources of the Self: The Making of Modern Identity* (Cambridge: Harvard University Press, 1989), esp. 25.

17. Cf. Christian Joppke, "How Immigration Is Changing Citizenship: A Comparative View," *Ethnic and Racial Studies* 22, no. 4 (1999): 629-652. However, for a thesis that increasing immigration is associated with a reassertion of national identity see Eleonore Kofman, "Citizenship, Migration and the Reassertion of National Identity," *Citizenship Studies* 9, no. 5 (2005): 453-467.

18. Cf. Steven Vertovec, "Transnationalism and Identity," *Journal of Ethnic and Migration Studies* 27, no. 4 (2001): 573-582; Adrian Favell and Randall Hansen, "Markets Against Politics: Migrations, EU Enlargement and the Idea of Europe," *Journal of Ethnic and Migration Studies* 28, no. 4 (2002): 581-601; José Itzigsohn, "Immigration and the Boundaries of Citizenship: The Institutions of Immigrants' Political Transnationalism," *International Migration Review* 34, no. 4 (2000): 1126-1154.

19. Ayse S. Çaglar, "Hyphenated Identities and the Limits of Culture: Some Methodological Queries," in *The Politics of Multiculturalism in the New Europe: Racism, Identity, Community*, ed. Pnina Werbner and Tariq Modood (London: Zed Books, 1997), 169-185; Martin Kohli, "The Battlegrounds of European Identity," *European Societies* 2, no. 2 (2000): 113-137, esp. 130ff.

20. Thomas Faist, "Transnationalisation in International Migration: Implications for the Study of Citizenship and Culture," *Ethnic and Racial Studies* 23, no. 2 (2000): 189-222, esp. 214; Elizabeth Meehan, "Europeanization and Citizenship of the European Union," *Yearbook of European Studies* 14 (2000): 157-177; Christian Joppke, "Transformation of Citizenship: Status, Rights, Identity," *Citizenship Studies* 11, no. 1 (2007): 37-48, esp. 38.

21. Gary Marks, "Territorial Identities in the European Union," in Jeffrey Anderson, *Regional Integration and Democracy* (New York: Rowman & Littlefield, 1999), 69–91.

22. Daniel Fuss and Marita A. Grosser, "What Makes Young Europeans Feel European?: Results from a Cross-Cultural Research Project," in *European Identity: Theoretical Perspectives and Empirical Insights*, ed. Ireneusz P. Karolewski and Viktoria Kaina, (Muenster: Lit, 2006), 209-241.

23. Cf. Steven J. Sherman and David L. Hamilton and Amy C. Lewis, "Perceived Entitativity and the Social Identity Value of Group Memberships," in *Social Identity and Social Cognition*, ed. Dominic Abrams and Michael Hogg (Oxford: Blackwell, 1999), 80-110.

24. Marilynn B. Brewer, "The Many Faces of Social Identity: Implications for Political Psychology," *Political Psychology* 22, no. 1 (2001): 115-125, esp. 121.

25. Cf. Lars-Erik Cederman, "Nationalism and Bounded Integration: What It Would Take to Construct a European Demos," *European Journal of International Relations* 7, no. 2 (2001): 139-174, esp. 144.

26. Ireneusz Paweł Karolewski, "Regionalism, Nationalism, and European Integration," in *Nationalism and European Integration: The Need for New Theoretical and Empirical Insights*, ed. Ireneusz Paweł Karolewski and Andrzej Marcin Suszycki (New York: Continuum, 2007), 9-32, esp. 20.

27. Gerard Delanty, *Citizenship in a Global Age: Society, Culture, Politics* (Buckingham: Open University Press, 2000), 114 ff; cf. also Gerard Delanty, *Inventing Europe: Idea, Identity, Reality* (London: Palgrave, 1995).

28. Cf. Eva Jonas et al., "Currencies as Cultural Symbols: an Existential Psychological Perspective on Reactions of Germans towards the Euro," *Journal of Economic Psychology* 26, no. 1 (2005): 129-146.

29. Jacques E. C. Hymans, "The Changing Color of Money: European Currency Iconography and Collective Identity," *European Journal of International Relations* 10, no. 1 (2004): 5-31, cf. also Thomas Risse et al., "To Euro or Not to Euro?: The EMU and Identity Politics in the European Union," *European Journal of International Relations* 5, no. 2 (1999): 147-187.

30. Cf. Karen A. Cerulo, *Identity Designs: The Sights and Sounds of a Nation* (New Brunswick: Rutgers University Press, 1995).

31. Thomas Risse, "The Euro between National and European Identity," *Journal of European Public Policy* 10, no. 4 (2003): 487-505.

32. Monica Sassatelli, "Imagined Europe: The Shaping of a European Cultural Identity through EU Cultural Policy," *European Journal of Social Theory* 5, no. 4 (2002): 435-451.

33. Monica Sassatelli, *ibid.*, 446; Emile Durkheim, *The Elementary Forms of the Religious Life,* translated by J.W. Swain (New York: Collier, 1961).

34. Michael Bruter, "On What Citizens Mean by Feeling European: Perceptions of News, Symbols and Borderless-ness," *Journal of Ethnic and Migration Studies* 30, no. 1 (2004): 21-39.

35. Cf. also Caryl Clark, "Forging Identity: Beethoven's Ode as European Anthem," *Critical Inquiry* 23, no. 4 (1997): 789-807.

36. Michael Bruter, "Winning Hearts and Minds for Europe: The Impact of News and Symbols on Civic and Cultural European Identity," *Comparative Political Studies* 36, no. 10 (2003): 1148-1179; Michael Bruter, *Citizens of Europe? The Emergence of a Mass European Identity* (Basingstoke: Palgrave, 2005).

37. Cf. Spyros Blavoukos et al., "A President for the European Union: A New Actor in Town?," *Journal of Common Market Studies* 45, no. 2 (2007): 231-252.

38. Kathleen M. McGraw and Thomas M. Dolan, "Personifying the State: Consequences for Attitude Formation," *Political Psychology* 28, no. 3 (2007): 299-327.

39. Rupert Brown, "Social Identity Theory: Past Achievements, Current Problems and Future Challenges," *European Journal of Social Psychology* 30, no. 6 (2000): 745-778.

40. Cf. Riia Luhtanen and Jennifer Crocker, "A Collective Self-Esteem Scale: Self-Evaluation of One's Social Identity," *Personality and Social Psychology Bulletin* 18, no. 3 (1992): 302-318.

41. Cf. Ulrich Beck and Edgar Grande, "Cosmopolitanism: Europe's Way Out of Crisis," *European Journal of Social Theory* 10, no. 1 (2007): 67-85.

42. Cf. Jürgen Habermas, "Making Sense of the EU: Towards a Cosmopolitan Europe," *Journal of Democracy* 14, no. 4 (2003): 86-100; Heidrun Friese and Peter Wagner, "The Nascent Political Philosophy of European Polity," *Journal of Political Philosophy* 10, no. 3 (2002): 341-364.

43. Cf. Omid Payrow Shabani, "Constitutional Patriotism as a Model of Postnational Political Association: The Case of the EU," *Philosophy and Social Criticism* 32, no. 6 (2006): 699-718; Justine Lacroix, "For a European Constitutional Patriotism," *Political Studies* 50, no. 5 (2002): 944-958.

44. Jürgen Habermas and Jacques Derrida, "February 15, or What Binds Europeans Together: A Plea for a Common Foreign Policy, Beginning in the Core of Europe," *Constellations* 10, no. 3 (2003): 291-297.

45. Wojciech Sadurski, *European Constitutional Identity?*, EUI Working Papers, Law No. 2006/33, 9ff; Michel Rosenfeld, "American Constitutionalism Confronts Denninger's New Constitutional Paradigm," *Constellations* 7, no. 4 (2002): 529-548.

46. Wojciech Sadurski, *European Constitutional Identity?*, 13ff. For a view on European constitutionalism as "responsible and inclusive" see Jo Shaw, "Process, Responsibility and Inclusion in the EU Constitutionalism," *European Law Journal* 9, no. 1 (2003): 45-68; Jo Shaw, "Postnational Constitutionalism in the European Union," *Journal of European Public Policy* 6, no. 4 (1999): 579-597.

47. Wojciech Sadurski, *European Constitutional Identity?*, 19f.

48. Cf. Judith Squires, "Liberal Constitutionalism, Identity and Difference," in *Constitutionalism in Transformation: European and Theoretical Perspectives,* ed. Richard Bellamy and Dario Castiglione (Oxford: Blackwell, 1996): 208-222.

49. Erik Oddvar Eriksen, "The EU—a Cosmopolitan Polity?," *Journal of European Public Policy* 13, no. 2 (2006): 252-269.

50. Cf. Björn Hettne, and Fredrik Söderbaum, "Civilian Power of Soft Imperialism? The EU as a Global Actor and the Role of Interregionalism," *European Foreign Affairs Review* 10, no. 4 (2005): 535–552.

51. A review of the debate is offered by Jan Orbie, "Civilian Power Europe: Review of the Original and Current Debates," *Cooperation and Conflict* 41, no. 1 (2006): 123-128.

52. Cf. Karen E. Smith, "The European Union: A Distinctive Actor in International Relations," *Brown Journal of World Affairs* 9, no. 2 (2003): 103-113; Christian Freres,

"The European Union as a Global Civilian Power: Development Cooperation in EU-Latin American Relations," *Journal of Interamerican Studies and World Affairs* 42, no. 2 (2000): 63-85.

53. However, it is increasingly argued that there is nothing altruistic about the EU's external policies. For instance, Sandra Lavenex demonstrates that the "Europeanization" of some policy fields such as immigration control does not necessarily follow merely humanitarian considerations, since the shift "outwards" can be regarded as a strategy to increase the autonomy of national ministers toward political, normative and institutional constraints on national policy-making. Cf. for instance Sandra Lavenex, "Shifting Up and Out: The Foreign Policy of Immigration Control," *West European Politics* 29, no. 2 (2006): 329-350.

54. Jennifer Mitzen, "Anchoring Europe's Civilizing Identity: Habits, Capabilities and Ontological Security," *Journal of European Public Policy* 13, no. 2 (2006): 270-285; Federica Bicchi, "Our Size Fits All: Normative Power Europe and the Mediterranean," *Journal of European Public Policy* 12, no. 2 (2006): 286-303.

55. Cf. Andreas Føllesdal, "Union Citizenship: Unpacking the Beast of Burden," *Law and Philosophy* 20, no. 3 (2001): 313-343; Jonathan Mercer, "Anarchy and Identity," *International Organization* 49, no. 2 (1995): 229-251.

56. Cf. Adrian Hyde-Price, "Normative Power Europe: A Realist Critique," *Journal of European Public Policy* 13, no. 2 (2006): 217-234.

57. Sibylle Scheipers and Daniela Sicurelli, "Normative Power Europe: A Credible Utopia?," *Journal of Common Market Studies* 45, no. 2 (2007): 435-457; Ian Manners, "Normative Power Europe Reconsidered: Beyond the Crossroads," *Journal of European Public Policy* 13, no. 2 (2006): 182-199.

58. Ian Manners and Richard Whitman, "The Difference Engine: Constructing and Representing the International Identity of the European Union," *Journal of European Public Policy* 10, no. 3 (2003): 380-404; Thomas Diez, "Constructing the Self and Changing Others: Reconsidering Normative Power Europe," *Millennium: Journal of International Studies* 33, no. 3 (2005): 613–636.

59. Ole Wæver, "European Security Identities," *Journal of Common Market Studies* 34, no. 1 (1996): 103-132; Tuomas Forsberg, "Explaining Territorial Disputes: From Power Politics to Normative Reasons," *Journal of Peace Research* 33, no. 4 (1996): 433-449.

60. Robert Falkner, "The Political Economy of Normative Power Europe: EU Environmental Leadership in International Biotechnology Regulation," *Journal of European Public Policy* 14, no. 4 (2007): 507-526.

61. Cf. Patchen Markell, "Contesting Consensus: Rereading Habermas on the Public Sphere," *Constellations* 3, no. 3 (1997): 377-400.

62. Patchen Markell, "Making Affect Safe for Democracy: On Constitutional Patriotism?," *Political Theory* 28, no. 1 (2000): 38-63, esp. 39.

63. Cf. Justine Lacroix, "For a European Constitutional Patriotism," *Political Studies* 50, no. 5 (2002): 944-958, esp. p. 945ff; Richard Bellamy and Dario Castiglione, "Lacroix's European Constitutional Patriotism: A Response," *Political Studies* 52, no. 1 (2004): 187-193.

64. Justine Lacroix, "For a European Constitutional Patriotism," p. 955.

65. Craig Calhoun, "Constitutional Patriotism and the Public Sphere: Interests, Identity, and Solidarity in the Integration of Europe," *International Journal of Politics, Culture and Society* 18, no. 3-4 (2005): 257-280.

66. Philippe C. Schmitter and Michael W. Bauer, "A (Modest) Proposal for Expanding Social Citizenship in the European Union," *Journal of European Social Policy* 11, no. 1 (2001): 55-65.

67. Rogers Brubaker, "The Manichean Myth: Rethinking the Distinction between Civic and Ethnic Nationalism," in *Nation and National Identity: The European Experience in Perspective,* ed. Hanspeter Kriesi et al. (Zürich: Rüegger, 1999), 55-71, esp. 62.

68. Ibidem, p. 65.

69. Cf. Theodora Kostakopoulou, "The Protective Union: Change and Continuity in Migration Law and Policy in Post-Amsterdam Europe," *Journal of Common Market Studies* 38, no. 3 (2000): 497-518.

70. Anita Böcker and Tetty Havinga, "Asylum Applications in the European Union: Patterns and Trends and the Effects of Policy Measures," *Journal of Refugee Studies* 11, no. 3 (1998): 245-266.

71. Peo Hansen, "European Citizenship, or Where Neoliberalism Meets Ethno-Culturalism," *European Societies* 2, no. 2 (2000): 139-165.

72. Else Kveinen, "Citizenship in a Post-Westphalian Community: Beyond External Exclusion?," *Citizenship Studies* 6, no. 1 (2002): 21-35.

73. Laurent Licata and Olivier Klein, "Does European Citizenship Breed Xenophobia? European Identification as a Predictor of Intolerance towards Immigrants," *Journal of Community and Applied Social Psychology* 12, no. 5 (2002): 323-337.

74. Cf. Dominique Schnapper, "Citizenship and National Identity in Europe," *Nations and Nationalism* 8, no. 1 (2002): 1-14.

75. Patchen Markell, "Making Affect Safe for Democracy: On Constitutional Patriotism?," *Political Theory* 28, no. 1 (2000): 38-63, esp. 39.

76. Mathieu Deflem and Fred C. Pampel, "The Myth of Postnational Identity: Popular Support for European Unification," *Social Forces* 75, no. 1 (1996): 119-143.

77. Cf. Rudolf De Cillia et al., "The Discursive Construction of National Identities," *Discourse & Society* 10, no. 2 (1999): 149-173.

78. Andrzej Marcin Suszycki, "European Identity in Sweden," in *European Identity: Theoretical Perspectives and Empirical Insights*, ed. Ireneusz P. Karolewski and Viktoria Kaina, (Muenster: Lit, 2006), 179-207.

79. Cf. Thomas Diez, "Europe as a Discursive Battleground: Discourse Analysis and European Integration Studies," *Cooperation and Conflict* 31, no. 1 (2001): 5-38; Thomas Diez, "Speaking Europe: the Politics of Integration Discourse," *Journal of European Public Policy* 6, no. 4 (1999): 598-613.

80. Cf. Andrew Moravcsik, "Preference and Power in the European Community: A Liberal Intergovernmentalist Approach," *Journal of Common Market Studies* 31, no. 4 (1993): 473–524; Andrew Moravcsik, *The Choice for Europe: Social Purpose and State Power from Messina to Maastricht* (Ithaca: Cornell University Press, 1998).

Chapter 5

Globalization and Nationalism in Europe: Demolishing Walls and Building Boundaries

Daniele Conversi

The modern era was probably born with the enclosure acts emanated by the United Kingdom Parliament (1750-1860 ca.), which bounded open fields and shattered the rights of citizens to access common lands.[1] Since then, the medieval sense of collective responsibility changed forever and the people began dissociating themselves from the land as a shared resource (indeed, the original "commonwealth"). Great swaths of common land were slowly reduced to private property. Enclosures marked the end of the right of land use, particularly of the commons, from which a great number of peasants fully depended. The modern proletariat was being born. Urbanization and the decline of rural culture were thus associated to this series of parliamentary acts of confiscation, more than to industrialization per se, since many impoverished and dispossessed peasants had no other options than migrating to the cities. Here they provided cheap labor for a rapidly expanding and all-devouring capitalist class. The birth of early modernity was thus associated with a process of annexation and boundary-building. The seizure of territory remained its main scope, involving sweeping expropriation of property from its erstwhile usufructuaries. Since then, the modern era has been characterized by a frenetic rush to size and classify, which nourished an obsession with boundary-building.

Nationalism is one of the most powerful processes of boundary-building. All attempts at defining, "inventing," or reviving a nation imply a process of inclusion-exclusion, that is, the erection of boundaries between in-groups and out-groups. However, this remains an under-stated assumption in much of sociopolitical literature: The majority of scholars mention the relationship between nations and boundaries *en passant*, nearly accidentally, assuming that they are there, without needing further elaboration. Only recently the changing role and dynamics of ethno-national boundaries has been conceptualized and elaborated in such a way as to make the process more understandable. This chapter sets to explore theoretically and comparatively the linkage between violence, nationalism, and boundary-making. It stresses the importance of culture and inter-generational cultural transmission as an inclusive, more permeable, boundary-related strategy that should be compatible with cosmopolitan ideals, as well as with supra-national projects like the European Union.

One of the scopes of this chapter is to investigate how the past Western legacy of destruction and self-destruction intersected with, and was accompanied by, a continuous stress on boundaries, hence on exclusion and the creation of homogeneous identities as defined by these boundaries. The chapter finally concludes with some comments on how to overcome this legacy of conflict and pain in the multinational, multicultural, and multi-confessional project of European unification.

Boundary Theories across Disciplines

First emerged in anthropology as an analytical tool for investigating ethnic group interaction, "boundary theories" have inexorably moved toward a focus on ethnic conflicts and nationalism as processes of boundary-creation and maintenance. This shift from anthropology to sociology and politics has brought a new stress on the oppositional character of boundaries: boundaries function as ethnic identifiers establishing who is situated at either side of the boundary.[2] Boundaries exist not only to enclose and delimit, but also to clarify and highlight who "the other" is. In this way the "self" or in-group is defined primarily by constant comparison with the "other."

Before the era of nationalism, oppositional boundedness was associated with *ethnocentrism*, which Claude Lévi-Strauss and other anthropologists identified as a universal feature of ethnic groups across the world. The essence of ethnocentrism is oppositional, with strong hierarchical components, in an evaluative sense. Lévi-Strauss confirmed its linkage with racism, as it often implies a rejection of ethnic, sometimes cultural, differences. For Lévi-Strauss, the most desirable method to overcome racism and ethnocentrism is the knowledge and appreciation, indeed the enjoyment, of different cultures.[3] Ethnocentrists typically regard ethnic differences as imperfections, deviations, even anomalies. In general, the us/them dichotomy is extendable to all sorts of groups, as it remains a key attribute of groupness. Thus, the logic of opposition between groups reinforces boundaries that are not necessarily ethnic.[4]

Boundaries theories have developed within several disciplines.[5] First of all, they have encountered a naturally fertile ground within *political geography*, since boundaries constitute the raw material of this discipline.[6] The trend has touched briefly upon *international relations theory* with the *"Minnesota School" of Identities, Borders, Orders"* (the "IBO triad") and its attempt to re-conceptualize the discipline's ethno-territorial epistemology within a constructivist methodology. These authors have influenced the debate on national identities as part of a wider "cultural" and "sociological turn" in international relations. More recently, *sociological theory* has also begun to embrace boundary approaches, with the promising adoption of a processual and interactionist angle in the study of ethnic violence.[7]

Some authors have reached quite innovative conclusions, emphasizing how a stress on boundaries and violence can indeed flourish around a lack of actual cultural differences. For these authors, cultural differences can be better interpreted as "denied resemblance."[8] Against common sense interpretations, the political implication of such assessment is that inter-group similarity and cultural assimilation are *not* conductive to stability or peaceful coexistence. Groups remain groups, even when concealed by a lack of cultural distinction. The breakup of Yugoslavia provides an experience *in vitro* of the impact of violence and cultural similarity on boundary-building.[9]

Nationalism has often been "launched" as a binding enterprise in situations of cultural assimilation: for instance, the goal of the oppositional ideology shaped by the founder of Basque nationalism, Sabino de Arana, was to maintain, re-create, and reinforce the boundary between Basques and non-Basques.[10] In subsequent forms of radical Basque nationalism, ideological contrasts, cultural differences, and political pluralism have been superseded through the boundary-building effect of violence.[11]

More generally, a focus on boundaries can be applied to all forms of nationalism. Nationalism remains at heart a process of boundary-building aimed at inclusion/exclusion, even though the rhetoric may be one of "national security," that is, of boundary-maintenance, rather than boundary-construction. Ties of ethnic kinship across state boundaries around the world mean that ethnic boundaries are often more important and long-lasting than official state boundaries. Ethnic kins in neighboring states can harbor separatist desires spurring domestic secessionist and irredentist movements. Neo-liberal globalization has also interacted with the persistence of ethnic ties, contributing to destabilizing many regions across the world.

Boundaries versus Content

In anthropology, Frederick Barth first elaborated the concept of *ethnic boundary* in the introduction of an edited collection in 1969.[12] Accordingly, ethnic identities do not derive from intrinsic features but emerge from, and are reasserted in, encounters, transactions, and oppositions between groups. The crucible of ethnic identities are the "boundaries" which specific aggregates of people establish for different purposes, or simply result from human interaction. Barth focused on the subjective, self-experienced dimension, rather than on objective traits as perceived by the outsiders: *ethnic boundaries* describe the perception of ethnic identity and its limits, whereas *ethnic contents* define its substance, that is, the group's culture. Because ethnic boundaries are directly linked to subjective self-perception, they are particularly relevant to the study of identity formation. Thus, culture can change while ethnic boundaries remain unaffected. A person's or group's identity is grounded on its boundary, rather than its content. Historical records can testify to such discontinuity, i.e., that cultural elements (content) can vary considerably throughout the centuries, even in cases in which the homeland's name or the ethnonym have persisted.

A more promising direction should try to determine how, and in what ways, cultural elements can influence socio-political behavior, including the construction and maintenance of ethnic identities. Departing from Barth's original emphasis, I argue that the role of the boundary should be analyzed in relation to its content. "Content" in this acceptation will be taken to mean whatever is enclosed in a boundary: while the boundary represents the subjective perception of ethnicity, separating in-group from out-group, the content is instead the tangible and objective repertoire. It provides a cornucopia of human skills, whose heritage can enrich the cultural experience of ethnic belonging. While boundary relates to psychology, content relates to culture; the latter is visible, the former invisible: you may certainly feel ethnic boundaries, but you cannot often see them.

The next sections investigate the relationship between boundaries, content, and political violence. First, the term "ethnic boundary" needs to be related to the study of ethnogenesis and nationalism. Secondly, the relativist usage of boundaries as infinitely malleable and situationally adaptable ephemera is questioned. Finally, the ethnic boundary is functionally related to the rise of ethnic violence, while violence is related to cultural assimilation, or lack of cultural contents. The case of former Yugoslavia will illustrate the use of violence as a tool of boundary-building. The concluding remarks emphasize that a stress on boundaries, rather than content, is normally an indicator of deep feelings of threat and insecurity leading to, or resulting from, violence.

Ethnic Identity versus "Ethnic" Culture

The anti-objectivist turn in anthropology was an attack on reification, the idea that it was possible to identify externally the existence of ethnic groups independently from the perceptions of the individuals who made them up. In classical anthropology, it was quite normal to catalog and itemize all sorts of groups from the viewpoint of the scholar, producing inventories, lists, indexes, charts, and, in particular, colorful ethno-linguistic maps with neatly demarcated borders. Groups were classified on the basis of external clues, characteristics, marks, peculiarities and traits. As in other social sciences, *pre*-Barthian anthropology tended to focus on alleged *objective* traits, assuming the importance of discrete cultural features as criteria for establishing group identity. Barth stressed instead that groups could maintain a sense of separateness, while their observable markers or diachritica can change or even become invisible. "Invisibility" may conceal a heightened sense of "us"-ness, moreover with the seeds of aggravated ethnic assertiveness. As a corollary, cultural assimilation does not automatically lead to integration. On the contrary, the two may well be incompatible.

Nationalist propaganda is often keen to point out that identity can be dormant and ready to be stirred and aroused by some national awakener. In fact, ethnicity has resisted state-making and nation-building. More recently, the failure to notice the persistence of ethnic identity has represented one of the major blunders in political science and practice since the end of the Cold War.[13] Modernization theories, particularly Karl Deutsch's "social mobilization" paradigm, have dominated American political science since the 1950s.[14] They exemplified yet another academic failure, the incapacity or refusal to see the persistence of ethnic boundaries ensuing sustained modernizing and assimilationist efforts by state elites. Indeed, the study of ethnic boundaries should also be seen as the study of identity *persistence*: It should help us to understand why ethnicities have resisted overwriting premature necrologies.

The issue of persistence is central to theories of nationalism as a whole. The recurring question is: why are ethnic boundaries thoroughly maintained despite all-pervasive changes, including cultural impoverishment and sometimes total assimilation? Anthony D. Smith's *ethno-symbolism* explains the persistence of ethnic identities by focusing on the importance of myths. [15] Myths have an exceptional capacity to convey a sense of belonging and continuity through successive generations. They articulate the distinction between in-group and out-groups, therefore playing an essential function in boundary maintenance, even in the absence of promptly visible ethnic markers. Myths do not require cultural diachritica as a condition *sine qua non*, but they need to be ritually anchored on, and revived by, the use of symbols.[16] The latter need not to be particularly distinctive. Indeed, modern nationalist symbols are often mere replicas and copy-cats, mutually aping each other. Most "national" flags are banal imitations of the French *tricoloeur* with few references to pre-modern indigenous traditions. Likewise, most armies and paramilitaries wear the same set of uniforms, with only minimal identificational details. A large number of national anthems appear to be shamelessly mimicked from each other, with only nominal and superficial connection to local folk tradition and popular culture. Other anthems are brazenly imported from abroad—including the U.S.' "Star-Spangled Banner," originally a popular cockney drinking song.

According to the ethnosymbolist school, none of these icons could attract any meaningful attention if a mythical framework did not sustain them.[17] Similar modern inventions have a parasitical relationship with the ethno-symbolic landscape underneath them. As argued by Donald Horowitz, "group boundaries must be underpinned by a suitable apparatus of myth and legend, which cannot be generated spontaneously."[18] Ethnosymbolism postulates a historical continuity between ethnic and national identity: common myths, historical memories, and common culture are shared by both premodern *ethnies* and modern nations. But how are nations different from ethnies? The difference lies in the nation's association with a more modern political organization, the state, based on territorial legality. Myths and memories have an important function in assuring the solidarity of the members toward the group. Yet, they should be distinguished from the more complex, pluralistic, and rich cultural heritage that is carried across generations within local communities or national groups.

The confusion between appearance and substance has beset scholarly accomplishments for quite a long time. I have argued that at the roots of much of this disarray lie in an underlying confusion between culture and ethnicity.[19] Barth's distinction between ethnic *boundaries* and ethnic *contents* can be simplified by considering the parallel distinction between *subjective* feelings and *objective* data, between *ethnicity* and *culture*. Ethnic boundaries are related to identity, whereas ethnic contents are related to culture. *Culture* can in turn be considered as the common pool and repository from which groups can draw on to maintain, root and embed their identity. Hence we need to appraise and evaluate the relation between the two. Their diverging configurations relate to different levels, degrees and quantities of "content" (from rich cultural production to simple cultural maintenance, mere survival in the forms of relics and antiquarianism, and finally to virtual assimilation into the dominant culture).

In both social science and political praxis, the terms ethnicity and culture are often confused—sometimes deliberately so. By *ethnicity*, we normally refer to a belief in putative descent (that is, a belief in something which may or may not be real). Ethnicity is thus similar to race, in that they both refer to descent.[20] While ethnic descent is conjectural and suppository, racial descent acquires a biological determinant. Both are based on speculation and myth—even though early this century pseudo-science came to the fore to uphold the latter. Thus, ethnicity is a perception of commonality and belonging supported by a myth of common ancestry. As Walker Connor has stressed, what matters here is the *subjective* and psychological quality of this perception, rather than its objective and hardly testable "substance."[21]

As previously mentioned (and as shall be reiterated in the following sections), *culture* means here an open project. You can become a member of a culture by learning its norms, traditions, and codes, then sharing what you have learned by participating in cultural events. Even though the contractual element may be inconspicuous (a person raised in a particular culture can familiarize earlier and more fully with it), there is an implicit give-and-take inference: "I belong to this culture insofar as I can share its benefits while contributing to its maintenance and development." However, culture is necessarily based on continuity, being passed through generations. Because of this, it is often confused with ethnicity. But its exclusivist association with a single ethnic group is a relatively modern one.

The confusion between ethnicity and culture is helped by the fact that the latter's usage is quite new: in fact, the term "ethnicity" only appeared in English during the late 1950s. Yet a more important reason for this confusion may be that cultural continuity is stressed at the expense of cultural innovation: "ethnicity" is a highly conservative, unadventurous concept. Its inborn conservatism is visible as it sacrifices a group's outstretching and creative power together with its capacity for development beyond rigid ethnic parameters.

Cultures need to be defended through creative endeavors, active policies, temporal accommodation, environmental adaptation, as well as by enhanced inter-generational communication. A culture is either expanding or contracting, that is, it cannot remain static. For a non-dominant culture, this is of vital importance. Its existence is perpetually questioned and in balance. It needs incessant efforts to be maintained, cherished, and cultivated. Moreover, in order to survive, a culture must also have an assimilative power, a capacity to integrate newcomers and attract possible members or practitioners. All cultures must have an assimilative core to live on and endure. Assimilation means just that a member from another cultural group is allowed to become an in-member by simply adopting and sharing its basic elements. Therefore, assimilation is not an exclusive prerequisite of dominant cultures. Small cultures need to assimilate newcomers, too, in order to endure, persist, and live to tell the tale. In the pre-industrial era, scattered communities were not totally isolated and normally allowed a limited number of "outsiders" to join in and share their fruits on the implicit (or explicit) basic covenant that cardinal traditions, core values, and key symbols had to be treasured and enhanced.

To resume, *culture* and *ethnicity* should be kept firmly distinct particularly when we are dealing with political issues. Yet, in the modern world this has *not* usually been the case. Why so? The main answer can be found in the advent of nationalism as the key legitimizing principle of the modern state.[22] Ernest Gellner's definition of nationalism as a political precept which holds that the rulers should belong to the same ethnic (i.e., national) group as the ruled means in practice that the modern state has to become ethnicized.[23] Indeed, the prototypical modern nation-state is the *exclusive* domain of a single dominant ethnic group. The doctrine of ethnic exclusivism is thus in-built in the national principle, at least if this is left to run its course unchecked.

In other words, the modern state tended to become ethnically, culturally, and linguistically "purified." On the one hand, the modern state cannot be linguistically neutral; perhaps no functioning institution can ever be so. On the other hand, it *can* at least be ethnically neutral. Yet, Gellner's definition of nationalism implied precisely the contrary, namely that mass mobilization created by modernity, industrialization, and urbanization demands that the state needs to become ethnicized. This again stems from a conceptual overlap between culture, language, and ethnicity (with language seen perhaps as the *trait d'union* between the former and the latter). To claim that all education has to be performed in a single language does not mean that it cannot allow for some flexibility in other cultural spheres. With typical Herderian zest, Gellner instead conflates language and culture as if they were nearly synonymous, and then merges this combined amalgamation into an even broader usage of the concepts of nation and ethnicity.[24]

This section has stressed how the crucial distinctions between language, culture, and ethnicity must be related to the study of the subjectivity and the persistence of national feelings. The next step will be to relate the "content" of ethnicity to nationalism in general and to different types of ethnic mobilization as paramount processes of boundary-building.

Nationalism as Boundary-Building

The idea of nationalism is founded on the premise that there are persistent and coherent groups of people and that their differences are natural or self-evident. The collective "self" needs to be delimited by specific territorial and ethnic boundaries. Thus, nationalism actually works as a process of boundary maintenance or, often, just boundary creation. The erection of barriers in place of existing porousness and fluidity is attempted by political leaders who wish to promote an ideology of egalitarian, yet exclusive, legitimacy, according to which each self-defined "nation" has the right to its own state and to be governed by in-group members.[25] We shall start by noting that such a goal is impossible to achieve until the leaders are able to establish who is a member and what differentiates an in-group from an out-group. In other words, the elites' preemptive task is to decide which are the criteria of membership. In order for their project to succeed, they have to draw a sharp distinction between *us* and *them*. This is the prerequisite without which, not only can we not have nations, but we also cannot generally have cohesive groups.

It follows that the study of nationalism is the study of how elites strive to defend, strengthen, or even construct this sense of distinctiveness.[26] Since distinctiveness is unattainable without some distinguished "other(s)," it follows that oppositional dynamics are what give tenor and substance to groupness, particularly to ethnic and national identities. The point of contact between different others, the domain, imaginary or real, where in-group and out-group meet and face each other is called *boundary*. The main question remains: who needs to use, raise, or safeguard the boundary?

Ethnic boundaries have acquired a newly fixed essence with the advent of the nation-state. In antiquity, power was established more through personal liaisons or extra-territorial institutions, such as the Church. With modernity, political power becomes exercised not only upon a strictly defined and bounded space, but only and exclusively upon that space. The new relationship between power and territory is unmitigated: the state exercises power over its entire territorial extent and over every single individual who lives or transits therein. The very concept of sovereignty is based on this preclusive relationship. Sovereignty, territoriality and the rise of the modern nation-state are all intrinsically related to the establishment of boundaries and frontiers.

Yet, recent trends have contributed to tempering the modern territorial vision of power. An extra-territorial notion has instead emerged as a hallmark of post-modernity. Perhaps the most crucial facet of this change is the role of culture and information. A key power of the state lay in its control of the flow of information through compulsory education, universities, and the media. By selecting and sieving information, it was then possible to "build-up" nations, a project which entailed homogenizing peoples—or at least coveting such a goal. Information is power. Wherever the state could control the flow of information, it could justify its exclusive, unchallenged monopoly over the means of violence—hence its legitimacy.

The ongoing technological revolution has begun to erode this prerogative. The spread of the printing press has first worked as a bounding contraption preparing for the advent of modern nationalism through the creation of "empty homogeneous time."[27] The key role of the press was associated with the spread of literacy, which in turn received the greatest support with the advent of the modern state and its sustained effort of mass public instruction.[28] This kind of monopoly began to be infringed upon with the advent of non-literacy related mass media, namely radio and TV. Their boundless character could still be kept in check through the combined alliance of language (mutual unintelligibility) and power (state regulation and control of the media).

Even before WWII it was possible to listen to foreign radio waves across borders. But this had a minor impact upon the homogenizing trend of the nation-state and rarely infringed upon the territorial concept of power. Given their one-way character, mass-media were easily controlled by the state. Competing foreign broadcasts could easily be branded as "enemy propaganda." Significantly, the popular spread of *two-way* communication tools, from the telephone and the fax to email and other information technology, has made censorship less practical and difficult to implement, although a nightmare scenario would include a direct control of critical web content under the pretext of "protecting" global security. The post-9/11 "war on terror" has greatly eroded these basic freedoms, perhaps beyond repair. In the past, totalitarian systems made a large use of one-way top-down communication tools like the radio and the television, preferring them over two-ways media. For instance, in former Communist Europe the use of the telephone was limited to a selected few. As we know, the Internet revolution has allowed written, spoken, and visual information to be instantly spread throughout the globe in potentially infinite directions. Its impact has been extra-territorial, not bound to any particular space, and conceivably limitless. Of course, no "virtual" community can ever replace the density and effectiveness of daily face-to-face interaction and it would be insane to suggest that it may replace it. The trend is to both atomize and globalize society: we are now more alone and more interconnected with alone others. Unfortunately, all crises advancements in communication have historically produced a delayed response or concern in the social sciences. The concept of boundary has been slowly *de-territorialized* or enlarged to encompass non-geographical factors. Ethnic boundaries have become a popular item of study also because their fixedness is not absolute, contrary to political-administrative borders. The boundedness we normally invoke when referring to the nation-state is relative to spatial and territorial borders. But the fixedness of state frontiers is in sharp contrast with the adaptability and ductility of ethnic boundaries. As the latter involve a subjective dimension, they are not easily objectified or "put on the map." They are not easily perceived from the outside despite the use of markers and symbols to signal them. For this reason, the concept has gained ground among post-modernists who view the very vessel of modernization, the nation-state, "collapsing" before their eyes.

Cultural Assimilation: From Europe to the Westernizing World

Thomas H. Eriksen has observed that "groups may actually become more similar at the same time that boundaries are strengthened."[29] He considers boundary maintenance through endogamy and assimilation to explain the ways in which ethnic boundaries can persist notwithstanding cultural communication and demographic flows across the boundary. But how are boundaries strengthened in situations of cultural fluidity, assimilation, and hybridization? How do boundaries work when cultural differences have vanished or are hardly visible, though they may not appear irrelevant to the beholders?

In order to reply to these questions, we need to add another variable: External factors can propel the erection of particularly high, often insurmountable, ethnic barriers. The most powerful factor is possibly violent aggression, in the forms of war, state repression, or grassroots counter-violence. I have argued that internal factors related to cultural contents rarely play a role. When cultural distinctiveness disappears or vanishes due to policies of cultural assimilation or guided "modernization," its vacuum is likely to be filled by violence. In such cases, violence can override more peaceful cultural endeavors as avenues of mass mobilization. The twentieth century European experience of wars and genocide has taught us that rigid identities have been molded in continuing or periodic conflict.

Why has inter-state and ethnic violence subsided in postwar Europe? One of the possible reasons is relevant here: the falling perception of collective threat. The rise of violence has often been associated with a lack of security concerning the future and self-preservation of a group—sometimes independently from the actual threat.[30] A sense of impending menace, vulnerability, and defenselessness is connected with cultural assimilation, in at least one powerful way: cultural homogenization or de-differentiation is perceived as the ultimate threat to a group's or a culture's very existence. The response to the menace can either be a reassertion of cultural values, or, failing the cultural option, a path of confrontation and heightened conflict. This has occurred, for instance, in periods of decolonization and empire breakup, precisely when boundaries have been reshuffled, superimposed, or weakened. Donald Horowitz maintains that "a common source of cultural movements is concern about potential shifts in group boundaries. The colonial period was filled with such movements. The form they took was largely a response to the direction of boundary change underway, to growing differentiation and assimilation. An ethnic group fragmented into subgroups that threatened to overtake the larger group identity might react by reinforcing elements of common culture and common ancestry, suppressing, for example, differences in dialect or stressing descent from a single ancestor."[31]

A stress on uniformity, common ancestry, and homogenization is also one of the root causes of the rise of fascism in many countries. In particular, post-unification Italy's and Germany's effort to build "efficient," unified nation-states upon a patchwork of former independent states, linguistic isoglosses, economic systems, and cultural lifestyles could only be achieved by violent, authoritarian means and by mass mobilization. The more fragmented was the territory to be transformed into a single common nation, the more the stress on unity was necessary.[32] Indeed, the entire unitarist rhetoric of fascist movements served precisely the purpose of concealing the internal fragmentation of their constituencies. This reasoning can also be applied to the emergence of radical nationalism in areas strongly assimilated into the dominant culture and hence internally fragmented, such as in the Basque Country.[33]

It is, however, the common background of threat perceived by minorities which elicits new boundary reinforcement, through either violence or culture: "The cultural revivals that emerged in response reflected an awareness of the danger of a fading group identity. They tended to emphasize the history of separateness and even hostility between the groups. Memories of insult were recalled. Languages were "purified" of words that derived from the language of the neighboring group. Religious practices were cleansed in the name of returning to some former state of orthodoxy that may or may not have existed. Group identity was thus infused with a new or revived cultural content that served to demarcate the lines between groups more clearly, thereby reducing the ease with which individuals could cross group boundaries. Movements that went furthest in asserting the distinctiveness of groups believed to be in danger of assimilation ultimately become strongly separatist."[34]

Violence as a boundary-reinforcing factor normally results in eminently *subjective* behavior. But this does not result in an increase of cultural *differen-*

tiae per se, nor in an upsurge of creative endeavors. On the other hand, Barth has argued that "cultural variation may be an *effect* and not a *cause* of boundaries."[35] The direct and shared experience of state-led violence against individuals *qua* members of a group or followers of a faith has a particularly powerful ethnogenetic impact. The "object" of violence turns her/himself into the "subject" of his/her own history, destiny, and identity. But, born out of aggression, this rise of ethnic awareness is not often matched by a parallel rise in cultural-maintaining activities. Despite claim to the contrary, culture and violence remain ultimately incompatible.

Yugoslavia: War-Making, Ethnogenesis and Boundary-Building

The archetypal case of systematic use of violence to separate, dissect, and dichotomize formerly unified and interacting groups can be found in the events leading to the breakup of Yugoslavia. Elsewhere, I argued that Yugoslavia's breakup developed from within the center (Belgrade), before reaching the periphery.[36] According to the 1981 census, Serbs were a minority in former Yugoslavia (35%).[37] Thanks to its firm grip on the media, the regime could easily spread a sense of threat among Serbs strewn in mixed areas, particularly in Croatia and Bosnia.[38]

The most long-lasting effect of state violence was the change in *ethnonyms* (self-definition). Notably, this included the names of languages spoken in the theaters of war: Until 1989 Croatia, Serbia, Bosnia, and Montenegro shared a common Serbo-Croat language.[39] Both international linguists and local political leaders defined Serbo-Croat as a single unified language.[40] Supported by grammars, dictionaries, and broader linguistic consensus, it was sanctioned that the regional variants of Serbo-Croat were far too similar to grant them separate status. However, both Croats and Serbian "dialectologists" and linguists slowly began to challenge the official vision since the 1960s. But their ethnicist ideas did not achieve legitimacy until the outbreak of war.[41] Ensuing years of prolonged war and mass murder, few Croats, Bosnians, and Serbs dared to claim that they still spoke "Serbo-Croat." Average Bosnians had experienced horrific glimpses of murder, rape, abduction, dislocation, "domicide," and the destruction of their belonging within their inner circle of family and friends. All this was carried out in the name of Serbian and, to a lesser extent, Croatian (hence, Serbo-Croat?) ethnic purity. For this reason it became disturbing and inappropriate to refer to their language as Serbo-Croat. The consequence was the formation of a novel language, Bosniak, or Bosnian. New grammars, dictionaries, and literary works sprang up in Bosniak, with a relatively new terminology, distinguished, for instance, by the preference for Turkic loan-words instead of alleged "Serbianisms" and "Croatianisms."[42] Although a Bosnian-

English dictionary has been available since 1996, it was initially classed in Western library shelves under the "Serbo-Croatian dictionaries" section, since the term Bosnian (or Bosniak) was still relatively unheard-of.[43] The war led to a capillary search of linguistic distinctiveness in villages controlled by opposing armies. Tone Bringa mentions the local philologists' rediscovery of an "old Bosnian vocabulary which was common currency in villages and among older Muslims, but, before the war, was perceived as archaic by the urban, educated elites."[44] The process is so subliminally widespread that one does not have to be a nationalist—and make a stand of Bosnianness—in order to speak Bosniak. It became a rampant trend, even though the average Bosnian has never been a nationalist, and even though most Bosnians would have been happy to continue speaking Serbo-Croat, as until 1989 most were happy to belong to Yugoslavia. This externally induced drive toward separation also led to a deeper divergence between Croatian and Serbian.

Further along the line, great efforts have been devoted to the creation of a standard Montenegrin language, as a result of the wishes of several Montenegrins not to be identified with Serbia, but also for historical reasons, as most inhabitants of Montenegro (*Crna Gora*) proudly maintained the memory of independent statehood.[45] Those who began by learning Serbo-Croat found later to be rewarded by the acquisition of four languages, killing four birds with one stone: Serbian, Croatian, Bosniak, and Montenegrin, the differences between them remaining minimal. But for a long while it will be difficult to cross boundaries, as the utterance of a wrong expression, the murmur of an old-fashioned expression, may turn potential friends into instant outsiders, immediately to be located beyond the borders of one or the other community. On the Serbian side, attempts to purify the language of the Bosnian Serbs by replacing it with the Belgrade norm predated similar Bosnian and Montenegrin attempts.[46]

Externally imposed violence on peaceful co-existing groups has in many cases led to unprecedented impenetrability of borders. In particular, it resulted in a new stress on endogamy.[47] In Bosnia's erstwhile ethnically mixed areas, including Sarajevo, a dramatic drop in inter-ethnic marriages testifies to this endogamic shift. The collapse of mutual trust as a direct consequence of violence and boundary-rising has led to a sudden decline of exogamy.

The Yugoslav case illustrates the mechanisms which made possible to create impenetrable barriers where none existed before. It also helps to clarify the distinction between ethnic content and ethnic boundaries in the oppositional construction of ethnic identities. In Bosnia, Turkey, and elsewhere, ethnogenesis has been related to state violence, rather than culture and continuity. This is not intended to propose that no sense of identity existed before the eruption of violence, but simply that fence-raising may be a quite independent process from objective cultural differentiae. Ethnic identities have the power to survive over long periods of time at a latent, dormant stage only to be "re-awakened" by the dark prince of nationalist violence. Through violence new boundaries are superimposed on a situation of previous fluidity, characterized by a lack of core values, elite assimilation, secularization, and widespread insecurity over a group's survival.

Assimilation, Homogenization, and Violence

Modernity's deepening cycle of homogenization has often related to the spread of war and ethnic cleansing.[48] In the process, hitherto permeable boundaries were transformed into insurmountable barriers. Walls of homogeneity have been imposed around entire communities by human agents and chains of events related to their decisions and actions. The resulting homogeneity has in turn created the conditions for new dilemmas when culturally assimilated elites reacted by generating new identities, trying to build a sense of separateness with the scarce human "material" they could find.

Many studies of nationalism have focused on the initial assimilation of proto-nationalist leaders.[49] It is well known that "ethnic" leaders have been frequently reared in highly assimilated milieus. Donald Horowitz stresses that contrary movements of "dissimilation" are "often begun by group members who are furthest along in the individual assimilation process," a fact that pushes them in the direction of "an explosive and violent assertion of group separateness."[50] Most of these movements ended up stressing violent confrontation, rather than cultural revival—given the fact that in those particular, often extreme, circumstances and having been robbed of their culture, violence became the only possible glue for their constituencies. We have seen the same mechanism at work and dramatically amplified in former Yugoslavia, where the war pitted against each other elites who originally shared virtually everything, from language to secularism, even atheism.

Liah Greenfeld has noted that nationalism as an ideology often arises as a response to inter-ethnic competition, which set the basis for the resentment of intellectuals suffering dislocation as their cultural markets shrink. Borrowing the concept of *ressentiment* from Friedrich Nietzsche's *On the Genealogy of Morals,* Greenfeld identifies this sense of frustration as a result of pressures toward assimilation and conformity ensuing cross-cultural contact, particularly while facing a powerful outspreading West. For instance, resentment emerged among eighteenth century Russian elites as a result of the increasing contacts with a wealthier, technologically superior West. The fear of losing the indigenous culture and the resulting feeling of inferiority and humiliation were among the major sources for the onset of Russian ethnic nationalism.[51] Other "ideological diffusionists," such as Elie Kedourie, claimed that once the model of the nation-state was created, it was promptly adopted by other "awakening" proto-national elites in a self-degrading imitation effort.[52] The latter admired and wanted to emulate the foreign model of national development. But copying and imitation resulted in debasement and humiliation, continually striving to prove that one's own group was not less capable than its rivals in conforming to the ideal model. Nationalist intellectuals were, and are, typically obsessed with their self-image and the image of their country. At any possible encounter, the propensity is to heighten one's Western credentials, while tending to "orientalize" one's most immediate neighbors. This has historically resulted in an inner dilemma between striving for assimilation into the wider West and avoiding the humiliation connected with it.[53] While speaking in the name of an ancient community, nationalism's implicit Janus-faced schizophrenia further contributes to modern uprootedness. Indeed, Gellner argued that "the rhetoric of nationalism is inversely related to its social reality: it speaks of *Gemeinschaft*, and is rooted in a semantically and often phonetically standardized *Gesellschaft*."[54]

In order to grasp the relationship between assimilation and the making and remaking of boundaries, we have to analyze its long-term influence, its repercussion and imprint on ethnic identity. A help in this direction may come from immigration studies and related social science literature. Yet, we shall also have to maintain that cultural loss in non-immigrant contexts often results in a rekindled stress on boundaries as a replacement or surrogate of contents.

The concept of *symbolic ethnicity* has been used by Herbert J. Gans to define those instances of group identity largely emptied of cultural content: highly assimilated groups can display a variety of forms of allegiance to their ethnic heritage, from the use of "ethnic" symbols to the participation in ethnic festivals or militancy in "ethnic" causes.[55] This situational, "lazy" and opportunistic form of group membership implies a personal identification with the ethnic background, but avoids the commitment derived from participating in formal or informal cultural organizations and it does not require practicing the ethnic culture, particularly language. Therefore, it is an example where ethnic boundaries remain, while ethnic contents have largely disappeared. We should again note here that highly assimilated diaspora groups of the "symbolic ethnicity" type, are often behind the financing of extreme co-nationalist groups, where the use of violence, state repression, and terrorism against historical enemies can become legitimated.[56] Some known cases are Serbian, Greek, and Croatian lobbies, Palestinian radicals and the Zionist far-right, as well as various Basque, Armenian, Tamil, Sikh, and Irish liberation fronts, and many other diaspora-sponsored organizations. Gans' kindred concept of *symbolic religiosity* refers to "the consumption of religious symbols, apart from regular participation in a religious culture and in religious affiliations—other than for purely secular purposes."[57]

The idea that apparently trivial elements like a piece of cloth on a mast or a humdrum anthem may command emotional attachment has been observed since the emergence of nationalism. This phenomenon has been identified by both psychologists and social psychologists. Sigmund Freud used the term "narcissism of small differences," remarking that "it is precisely communities with adjoining territories, and related to each other in other ways as well, who are engaged in constant feuds and in ridiculing each other."[58] Freud's approach reminds us that nationalism and ethnic conflicts are not based on objective differences, but on a principle of inclusion and exclusion. Thus, "it is always possible to bind together a considerable number of people in love, so long as there are other people left over to receive manifestation of their aggressiveness."[59] Freud intuitively identified the difference between perceived and tangible distinctions as one between subjective perceptions of groupness and objective cultural features.[60]

To sum up, a reductive use of the concepts of boundaries as opposed to content risks trivializing the study of inter-ethnic relations. In particular, it risks obfuscating the dynamic relationship between ethnic identities, cultural contents, and boundaries maintenance.

Boundary-Making and European Unification

What are the implications of boundary theories for the current process of European integration? Can they be useful to implement specific policy action? Can they help us to anticipate troubles ahead and avoid them? The most important single lesson to be extrapolated is: when traditional boundaries are eroded and collapse, new ones always emerge to replace the old ones. In periods of dramatic socio-cultural change, new boundaries are likely to become more impermeable and higher than previous ones. Throughout the twentieth century, this has been the European experience. In an era of aggressive globalization and free-market expansionism, there is little evidence that this trend is going to abate. Cosmopolitanism and universalism are likely reactions to the erection of new boundaries, which in turn are a reaction to the collapse of previous ones. Cosmopolitanism can potentially be an antidote to the dangers of extreme nationalism, state patriotism, and other forms of boundary-building.[61] However, in order to be so, it must be strictly dissociated from alien phenomena like imperialism, globalization, nationalism, patriotism and elitist individualism.

Boundary theories have at least an immediate implication regarding the perverse effects of globalization: Globalization has brought about an unprecedented destruction of traditional boundaries accompanied by the simultaneous rise of particularistic ideologies. These include such a diverse array of positions and choices as communitarianism, xenophobia, nationalism, patriotism, fundamentalism, feminism, and even opportunistic varieties of multiculturalism. In other words, the spread of group-specific, particularistic ideologies has accompanied the onslaught of globalization. Fragmentation and division have not been accompanied by "deep pluralism," or by a consistent, full-range respect for cultural diversity. Globalization has mostly meant homogenization and thus has led to the global erosion of both national and local cultures—as well as the natural environment. Globalization itself has become an ideology which, like past totalitarian forms of nation-building, has stressed the need to unify.[62] Like fascism and communism, its ideologues have rhetorically defended the need to "indigenize" their creed and respect local cultures. Some have even argued that globalization has actually contributed to the safeguard and respect of local cultures: The spurious term "*glocalization*" has been skillfully crafted to defend the idea that globalization is actually compatible with local cultures and ways of life. However, the opposite is true: for large minorities and perhaps for many ordinary people globalization has meant uniformity, specifically in the formal aspect of Americanization.[63]

European integration may be related to broader visions of a post-ethnic Europe.[64] However, this has been made impossible by two crucial factors: on the one hand, the persistence of ethnically based forms of nationalism;[65] on the other hand, the superimposition of uniform cultural patterns emanating principally from the U.S. This has made mutual inter-communication between European countries and individuals harder, if not impossible. More specifically, Americanization is working against inter-cultural dialogue since its consumerist ephemera have partly replaced a century-old shared European communication space. For instance, the production and free circulation of, say, French, British, Russian, Italian, and Spanish movies and music has been hampered, curtailed, and clamped down by imposed import quotas for American products which have monopolized the totality of European markets. Everywhere, the indigenous film and music industry has been struggling to survive, even where it had to confront few rivals, as in Russia and Serbia.[66] This reduced share of European cultural space has per force serious implications for the future development of a European civil society.[67] Along with territorial and spatially identifiable borders, less visible, more subtle boundaries mark both inter-personal and inter-ethnic relations. These have been the subjects of much cross-disciplinary research. Despite their frequent invisibility, ethnic boundaries are clearly perceived by in-group members, as well as by those groups with which in-group members usually interact. They can be all-pervasive and crosscutting, orientating behavior and action, while manifesting themselves in the life of every individual.

Neither tied to administrative-political notions, nor to clearly discernible geographical spaces, ethnic boundaries have assumed new meanings through, and beyond, *de-territorialization*. An older generation of conservative scholars saw boundaries, notably state boundaries, as static and forever given. Since at least their anthropological conceptualization by Frederick Barth, ethnic boundaries have begun to denote ethnic identities and collective self-perceptions. Therefore, their empirical identification by outsiders has become more problematic. In general, the idea of porousness and permeability of ethnic boundaries has proliferated in all social sciences.

As the new field of study of nationalism emerged in the early 1980s, approaches began to proliferate to explain the "unexpected" revival of national sentiments. Because the failure of conservative political and social sciences highlighted incapacity to detect the persistence of ethnicity, studies explaining the reasons of ethnic *persistence* have attracted more interest and showed a more robust explanatory power. In fact, erstwhile "modernization theory" had proven unable to detect the embers of ethnonational vitality under the ashes of modernization. Led by the state and encouraged by the military, cultural assimilation and homogenization advanced dramatically in the twentieth century.[68] Local cultures ("ethnic contents") associated with specific non-dominant ethnic groups were declining as a consequence of the state's attempts at "homologation." But, contrary to the aspirations of authoritarian politicians and state-makers, the increasing invisibility of culture and the disappearance of cultural contents, were not reflected in a parallel decline of their symbolic significance and political potential. On the contrary, the persistence, indeed the regeneration, of ethnic boundaries, became fiercer, more intensified, and aggravated by perception of a vital threat against the group's cultural continuity.[69]

A more comprehensive understanding of ethnic conflicts can be achieved by considering the role played by *internal* variables, that is, ethnic contents and culture, or more specifically "core values," which are directly related to how the in-group is defined (I stress the *role* of internal variables, rather than internal variables *per se*). This focus should be accompanied by an attention to the role of *external* agents, like state policies and political violence, on the formation of ethnic boundaries. In particular, a scrutiny of the mutual relationship between internal variables and external agents may help to formulate a typology of ethnic conflicts as depending on the role of what lies on both sides of the boundary. Content and culture can be identified as *internal* variables, not directly related to the dynamics of ethnic conflict. Boundaries and identities can instead be identified as *external* variables, that is, elements which are based on their transactional, relational character with "the other." External variables are those more directly correlated to the rise of violence and external agents are directly involved in this process. A major problem in the study of ethnic boundaries is the alleged "malleability" of the concept. But this relativist vision of infinite ductility betrays its limits by evoking that very sense of insecurity that inevitably results in the strengthening of old boundaries—and even the rise of new ones. Michael Billig has defined this quotidian, reiterating, nearly ritual character of nationhood as the practice of "*banal nationalism*."[70] Boundaries are not necessarily *loci* of conflict: Miroslav Hroch's seminal study showed that nationalist movements in Europe were *not* most popular in ethnic boundary zones but instead flourished in centers of expanding communication networks.[71]

A related problem is the difficult empirical grounding and "measurability" of boundaries. The only way to "measure" their weight and endurance would be to focus on the intensity of identities and "us/them" feelings. This can be done in several ways: synchronically, with the use of surveys, large-scale questionnaires, voting patterns, and other statistical data, as well as with qualitative data or more belatedly with the recourse to media reporting on the magnitude of ethnic conflicts once they have started. Diachronically and on a more *longue durée* basis, by studying the evolution of shifting identities in political practice. The most suitable way of empirically grounding boundaries on practice is to relate them to content. By emphasizing their relationship with cultural content one can more easily estimate the boundaries' salience and shifting importance, without falling into the trap of reification. The subjective character of boundaries is precisely emphasized by referring to their inner relationships with what they enclose and contain. It is this relationship which provides evidence of something which would otherwise remain obscure to the external observer or analyst.

Ethnic violence often occurs when there are few cultural "markers" accessible to differentiate between groups. When groups in conflict share too many elements of the same culture, difficulties in their self-definition may emerge. The leaders of a non-dominant, subordinated group have then to create new contexts and "fabricate" new options in order to emphasize group identity and re-define ethnic boundaries. One of these options, the use of violence as a means of boundary-building, has been chosen by leaders in some of the cases analyzed here. The main rationale of many threatened groups is the defense of a boundary, particularly an ethnic boundary, from what is subjectively perceived as external aggression: The boundary is reinforced by focusing negatively on what lies "outside" and opposing it positively to what is "inside."[72] For instance, David Campbell theorized the oppositional nature of U.S. foreign policy, arguing that, while the Cold War discourse was based on a narrative of the American self constructed in opposition to the "other," such narrative did not change despite the end of the cold war. U.S. foreign policy makers began immediately to concoct and single out new targets of enmity, primarily political Islam or specific pariah states, thus justifying new military build-ups in front of U.S. public opinion. Indeed, the perception of the "other" as an unfathomable danger is central to the construction of American identity. In general, the perception of threat can be either fabricated or authentic, but a "patriotic" control over the mass media and state bureaucracy makes it possible for murderers to be painted as "victims."

As Horowitz points out, "the violent character of these responses to the feared loss of group distinctiveness is a powerful point in the case against assimilationist policies of nation-building."[73] For smaller stateless groups the experience of threat can of course be overwhelming, but lacking a grasp on the mass media, their response is delayed. At the same time, the loss of cultural identity as a consequence of assimilationist policies makes radicalization more likely. In general, multiculturalism, federalism, and the promotion of all forms of cultural pluralism have great healing powers for building civic peace, by assuaging the sense of mutual threat which is at the core of violent strife.[74] If cultural autonomy can enshrine the protection of minority rights, the legal limits of self-determination rights can be reassessed within the parameters of both EU integration and globalization.[75]

In our examples, groups in contact share the ethnic boundary while cultural contents span the boundary. The boundary created by violence replaces the missing boundary that was, or could have been, created by culture. Emptied, cleared, voided boundaries are more insecure than boundaries that protect a rich cultural content. Empty boundaries can easily be filled by violence to replace the cultural hiatus. Hence, paradoxically, communities where ethnic borders entirely circumscribe the diffusion of cultural contents are deemed to be safer places for an ethnic group to exist. This, of course, does not insinuate a rejection of multiculturalism; quite the contrary, it makes it all the more vital and imperative. When boundaries are culturally defined (rather than merely identificationally so), culture can work as an inter-generational bridge, restraining violent deviations, keeping radical fringes at bay, reassuring members of the group's continuity, lessening intergenerational gaps, filling the life of cultural communities with everyday meaning, and, finally, contributing to their mutual contacts, coexistence, and persistence. In short, it is not the permanence of ethnic boundaries as such which matters, but rather the need to fill them with significant cultural content.

As global homogenization amalgamate, blend, and intermingle cultures, behaviors, tastes, appearances in a planetary melting pot, as contents tend to evaporate and disappear, boundaries risk becoming unprecedentedly reinforced.[76] The sweeping spread of reactive nationalism, statism, ethnic cleansing, and separatism testifies to the prevalence of this drift. This trend can only be rectified by restoring attention to the importance of culture and content, of creativity and continuity. In general, a stress on boundaries, rather than content, always indicates some deep insecurity. The need to raise boundaries, while forgetting the content they are supposed to defend, should be enough to alarm us about the rise of some deeply seated sense of vulnerability and fear. Violence may well be a logical finale of this parallel stress on boundaries and abdication of culture. This may be particularly true when all efforts to reinforce cultural specificity are discarded—often in the name of culture's alleged inefficacy in terms of granting a group's identity and survival.

In conclusion, boundaries and boundary theories are relevant to current European trends and patterns of integration.[77] Their relationships to more traditional forms of nationalism should be kept in mind, together with the widespread, universal sense of threat unleashed by globalization.

Notes

1. Jeremy Rifkin, *The European Dream: How Europe's Vision of the Future Is Quietly Eclipsing the American Dream* (Cambridge: Polity Press, 2004); and Jeremy Rifkin, *The End of Work: The Decline of the Global Labor Force and the Dawn of the Post-Market Era* (New York: G.P. Putnam's Sons, 1995).

2. Andreas Wimmer and Conrad Schetter, "Ethnic Violence," in *International Handbook of Violence Research*, ed. Wilhelm Heitmeyer and John Hagan (Dodrecht: Kluwer, 2003).

3. Claude Lévi-Strauss, *Race et histoire* (Paris: Gonthier, 1967).

4. On the importance of myths of descent in the formation of ethnonational identities, see Anthony D. Smith, *Nations and Nationalism in a Global Era* (Cambridge: Polity Press, 1995); Anthony D. Smith, *National Identity* (Hammondsworth: Penguin, 1991).

5. See Thomas M. Wilson and Hastings Donnan, eds., *Border Identities: Nation and State at International Frontiers* (Cambridge: Cambridge University Press, 1998).

6. See John Agnew, ed., *Political Geography: A Reader* (London/New York: Edward Arnold, 1997); Martin Jones, *An Introduction to Political Geography: Space, Place and Politics* (London: Routledge, 2004); Anssi Paasi, "Bounded Spaces in the Mobile World: Deconstructing Regional Identity," *Tijdschrift voor Economische en Sociale Geografie*, 93, no. 2 (2002): 137-148; Anssi Paasi, "Place and Region: Regional Worlds and Words," *Progress in Human Geography* 26, no. 6 (2004): 802-811.

7. Rob Shields, "Boundary-Thinking in Theories of the Present: The Virtuality of Reflexive Modernization," *European Journal of Social Theory* 9, no. 2 (2006): 223-237.

8. Simon Harrison, "The Politics of Resemblance: Ethnicity, Trademarks, Head-Hunting," *The Journal of the Royal Anthropological Institute* 8, no. 2 (2002): 211- 232; Simon Harrison, *Fracturing Resemblances. Identity and Mimetic Conflict in Melanesia and the West* (Oxford: Berghahn, 2006).

9. Sharyl Cross and Pauline Komnenich, "Ethnonational Identity, Security and the Implosion of Yugoslavia: The Case of Montenegro and the Relationship with Serbia," *Nationalities Papers* 33, no. 1 (2005): 1-27; Thomas Cushman, "Anthropology and Genocide in the Balkans: An Analysis of Conceptual Practices of Power," *Anthropological Theory*, 4, no. 1 (2004): 5-28; Cathie Carmichael, "The Violent Destruction of Community during the Century of Genocide," *European History Quarterly* 35, no. 3 (2005): 395-403; Denisa Kostovicova, "Republika Srpska and Its Boundaries in Bosnian Serb Geographical Narratives in the Post-Dayton Period," *Space and Polity* 8, no. 3 (2004): 267-287.

10. William A. Douglass, "Sabino's Sin: Racism and the Founding of Basque Nationalism," in *Ethnonationalism in the Contemporary World*, ed. Daniele Conversi (London: Routledge, 2004), 95–112.

11. Daniele Conversi, *The Basques, the Catalans, and Spain: Alternative Routes to Nationalist Mobilization* (London: Hurst/Reno: University of Nevada Press, 1997).

12. Frederick Barth, "Introduction," in *Ethnic Groups and Boundaries: The Social Organization of Culture Difference*, ed. Frederick Barth (London: Allen & Unwin, 1969).

13. Walker Connor, *Ethnonationalism: The Quest for Understanding* (Princeton: Princeton University Press, 1994) (especially ch. 4: "Terminological Chaos," 89-117); Orest Subtelny, "American Sovietology's Greatest Blunder: The Marginalization of the Nationality Issue," *Nationalities Papers* 22, no. 1 (1994): 141-55. On the inglorious end of "Soviet Studies," see Patrick Cockburn, *Getting Russia Wrong: The End of Kremlinology* (London: Verso, 1989).

14. Karl Wolfgang Deutsch, *Nationalism and Social Communication: An Inquiry into the Foundations of Nationality* (New York: Wiley, 1953).

15. See in particular Anthony D. Smith, *Nationalism and Modernism: A Critical Survey of Recent Theories of Nations and Nationalism* (London: Routledge, 1998).

16. On the relationship between symbols and boundaries, see Anthony P. Cohen, ed., *Symbolising Boundaries: Identity and Diversity in British Cultures* (Manchester: Manchester University Press, 1986).

17. Athena S. Leoussi and Steven Grosby, eds., *Nationalism and Ethnosymbolism: History, Culture and Ethnicity in the Formation of Nations* (Edinburgh: Edinburgh University Press, 2006).

18. Donald L. Horowitz, *Ethnic Groups in Conflict* (Berkeley: University of California Press, 1985), ch. 2: "A Family Resemblance", 70.

19. Steve Fenton, *Ethnicity* (Cambridge: Polity Press, 2003).

20. Steve Fenton and Stephen May, "Ethnicity, Nation and 'Race': Connections and Disjunctures," in *Ethnonational Identities*, Steve Fenton and Stephen May (New York: Palgrave Macmillan, 2002), 1-20.

21. Walker Connor, *Ethnonationalism: The Quest for Understanding* (Princeton: Princeton University Press, 1994), particularly, ch. 8, 195-209.

22. For a Weberian reading of the concept of "legitimacy" as applied to nationalism and for the essential relationship between the two, see Walker Connor, "Nationalism and Political Illegitimacy," in *Ethnonationalism in the Contemporary World*, ed. Daniele Conversi (London: Routledge, 2004), 201-228.

23. Ernest Gellner, *Nations and Nationalism* (Oxford: Blackwell, 1983), 1.

24. Daniele Conversi, "Homogenisation, Nationalism and War: Should We Still Read Ernest Gellner?," *Nations and Nationalism* 13, no. 3 (2007): 371-394.

25. Daniele Conversi, "Reassessing Theories of Nationalism: Nationalism as Boundary Maintenance and Creation," *Nationalism and Ethnic Politics* 1, no. 1 (1995): 73-85.

26. For a more nuanced view, see Joseph M. Whitmeyer, "Elites and Popular Nationalism," *British Journal of Sociology* 53, no. 3 (2002): 321–341.

27. Benedict Anderson, *Imagined Communities: Reflections on the Origin and Spread of Nationalism* (London: Verso, 1983).

28. Ernest Gellner, *op. cit.*

29. Thomas Hylland Eriksen, *Ethnicity and Nationalism: Anthropological Perspectives* (London: Pluto Press, 1993), 8. However, Eriksen partly rejects Barth's view of ethnic groups as mere "categories of ascription and identification," returning in part to a definition of ethnic groups as "culture-bearing" units.

30. On the centrality of this feeling of threat in the rise of mutually exclusive nationalisms in East-Central Europe, see Istvan Bibo, "The Distress of Small European Nations," in *Democracy, Revolution, Self-Determination: Selected Writings,* Istvan Bibo (Boulder: Social Science Monographs/Highland Lakes: Atlantic Research Publications, 1991).

31. Horowitz, *op. cit.*, 70.

32. Daniele Conversi, "Democracy, Nationalism and Culture: The Limits of Liberal Mono-Culturalism," *Sociology Compass* 2, no. 1 (2008): 156-182.

33. See Daniele Conversi, *The Basques, the Catalans, and Spain: Alternative Routes to Nationalist Mobilization* (London: Hurst/ Reno: University of Nevada Press, 1997), particularly ch. 9 ("The Roots of Violence"); Cynthia L. Irvin, *Militant Nationalism: Between Movement and Party in Ireland and the Basque Country* (Minneapolis : University of Minnesota Press, 1999).

34. Horowitz, *op. cit.*, 72.

35. Cited by Eriksen, *op. cit.*, 39. [emphasis in the original].

36. Daniele Conversi, "The Dissolution of Yugoslavia: Secession by the Centre?," in *The Territorial Management of Ethnic Conflicts,* ed. John Coakley (London: Frank Cass, 2003), 264-292; Daniele Conversi, "Central Secession: Towards a New Analytical Concept? The Case of Former Yugoslavia," *Journal of Ethnic and Migration Studies* 26, no. 2 (2000): 333-356; Daniele Conversi, "Reconsidering the Breakup of Yugoslavia: The International Relations of Central Secession," *Nationalities Papers* 35, no. 5 (2007): 961-967.

37. Gale Stokes, "From Nation to Minority: Serbs in Croatia and Bosnia at the Outbreak of the Yugoslav Wars," *Problems of Post-Communism* 52, no. 6 (2005): 3–20.

38. On the role of the Serbian media and, in particular, Belgrade TV, see Mark Thompson, *Forging War: The Media in Serbia, Croatia and Bosnia-Herzegovina* (London: Article 19, 1994). For the broader scenario, see Brad K. Blitz, ed., *War and Change in*

the Balkans: Nationalism, Conflict and Cooperation (Cambridge: Cambridge University Press, 2006); Anzulovic Branimir, *Heavenly Serbia: From Myth to Genocide* (New York: New York University Press/London: Hurst, 1999); Brad K. Blitz, "Refugee Returns, Civic Differentiation, and Minority Rights in Croatia 1991-2004," *Journal of Refugee Studies* 18, no. 3 (2005): 362-386; Valerie Bunce, *Subversive Institutions* (Cambridge: Cambridge University Press, 1999).

39. For a broader view of the Yugoslav meltdown, see Sabrina P. Ramet, *Balkan Babel: The Disintegration of Yugoslavia from the Death of Tito to the Insurrection in Kosovo* (Boulder: Westview Press, 1999); Sabrina P. Ramet, "Views from Inside: Memoirs concerning the Yugoslav Breakup and War," *Slavic Review* 61, no. 3 (2002): 558-580; Sabrina P. Ramet, "For a Charm of Powerful Trouble, Like a Hell-broth Boil and Bubble: Theories about the Roots of the Yugoslav Troubles," *Nationalities Papers* 32, no. 4 (2004): 341-362; Sabrina P. Ramet, "A Theory about the Causes of the Yugoslav Meltdown: The Serbian National Awakening as a Revitalization Movement," *Nationalities Papers* 32, no. 4 (2004): 765–779; and Brad K. Blitz, ed., *War and Change in the Balkans. Nationalism, Conflict and Cooperation* (Cambridge: Cambridge University Press, 2006).

40. See, for instance, George L. Campbell, *Compendium of the World's Language* (London: Routledge, 1991), vol. 2, 1220.

41. Robert D. Greenberg, "The Politics of Dialects among Serbs, Croats and Muslims in the Former Yugoslavia," *East European Politics and Society* 10, no. 3 (1996): 393-415.

42. See Alija Isakovic, *Rjecnik bosanskoga jezika: karakteristicna leksika* (Dictionary of the Bosnian Language: Characteristic Words) (Sarajevo: Bosanska knjiga, 1995), 2nd ed.; 1st ed. published as *Rjecnik karakteristicne leksike u bosanskome jeziku* (Dictionary of Characteristic Words of the Bosnian Language) (Wuppertal: Bambi, 1993).

43. Nikolina S. Uzicanin, *Bosnian-English, English-Bosnian Dictionary* (New York: Hippocrene Books, 1996). See Tom Gallagher, *The Balkans After the Cold War: From Tyranny to Tragedy* (London/New York: Routledge, 2003).

44. Tone Bringa, *Being Muslim the Bosnian Way: Identity and Community in a Central Bosnian Village* (Princeton: Princeton University Press, 1995), XVIII. Bringa uses the term "Bosnian language" when referring to the protagonists of her anthropological fieldwork. See Tom Gallagher, *op. cit.*

45. Sharyl Cross and Pauline Komnenich, *op. cit.*, and Tom Gallagher, "Identity in Flux, Destination Uncertain: Montenegro During and After the Yugoslav Wars," *International Journal of Politics, Culture, and Society* 17, no. 1 (2003): 53-71; Milan Popovic, "Europe versus Europe," *Montenegrin Mirror*, February 2001, [http://www.ndc.cg.yu/eng/DOCUMENTS/mnmirror/Europe%20versus%20Europe.htm, last accessed: 7 January 2003].

46. See Robert D. Greenberg. "The Politics of Dialects among Serbs, Croats and Muslims in the Former Yugoslavia," *East European Politics and Society* 10, no. 3 (1996): 393-415.

47. Horowitz, *op. cit.*, 74.

48. Daniele Conversi, "We Are All 'Equals!' Militarism, Homogenization and 'Egalitarianism' in Nationalist State-Building (1789-1945)," *Ethnic and Racial Studies* 31, no 1 (2008): 1286-1314.

49. See for instance Miroslav Hroch, *Social Preconditions of National Revival in Europe : A Comparative Analysis of the Social Composition of Patriotic Groups among the Smaller European Nations* (Cambridge /New York: Cambridge University Press, 1985). For the Basque case, see Daniele Conversi, *The Basques, the Catalans, and Spain: Alternative Routes to Nationalist Mobilization* (London: Hurst, 1997, American edition, Reno:

University of Nevada Press), 44-79. For Finland, see Risto Alapuro, "The Intelligentsia, the State and the Nation," in *Finland: People, Nation, State,* ed. Max Engman and David Kirby (London: Hurst and Company, 1987), 148-151.

50. Horowitz, *op. cit.*, 72.

51. See Liah Greenfeld, *Nationalism: Five Roads to Modernity* (Cambridge, MA: Harvard University Press, 1992).

52. Elie Kedourie, *Nationalism* (London: Hutchinson, 1993).

53. On the opposition between assimilationist, traditionalist, and reformist intellectuals, see Anthony D. Smith, *National Identity* (Harmondsworth: Penguin/ Reno: University of Nevada Press, 1991).

54. Ernest Gellner, *Conditions of Liberty: Civil Society and Its Rivals* (New York: Allen Lane/Penguin Press, 1994), 107.

55. Herbert J. Gans, "Symbolic Ethnicity: the Future of Ethnic Groups and Cultures in America," *Ethnic and Racial Studies* 2, no 1 (1979): 1-20.

56. See Benedict Anderson, *Long-Distance Nationalism: World Capitalism and the Rise of Identity Politics. The Wertheim Lecture* (Amsterdam: Centre for Asian Studies, 1992).

57. Herbert J. Gans, "Symbolic Ethnicity and Symbolic Religiosity: Towards a Comparison of Ethnic and Religious Acculturation," *Ethnic and Racial Studies* 17, no. 4 (1994): 577-592.

58. Sigmund Freud, *Civilization and Its Discontents* (New York: J. Cape & H. Smith, 1930), reprinted as *Civilization, Society and Religion* (Hammondsworth: Penguin, 1991), 305. Freud also applied the concept to the study of anti-semitism, in his *Moses and Monotheism* (New York: A. A. Knopf), vol. 13, 335. See also his *Group Psychology and the Analysis of the Ego* (London/ Vienna: The International Psychoanalytical Press, 1922), 131.

59. Sigmund Freud, *Civilization, Society and Religion,* 305.

60. Probably the most articulated subjectivist approach to nationalism is in Connor's collection of essays: Walker Connor, *Ethnonationalism: The Quest for Understanding* (Princeton: Princeton University Press, 1994).

61. Eric Kaufmann, "The Rise of Cosmopolitanism in the 20th-century West: A Comparative-historical Perspective on the United States and European Union," *Global Society* 17, no. 4 (2004): 359–383; Daniele Conversi, "Cosmopolitanism and Nationalism," in *Encyclopaedia of Nationalism,* ed. Anthony D. Smith and Athena Leoussi (Oxford: Transaction Books, 2000), 34-39.

62. On globalization as an ideology, see Manfred B. Steger, "Ideologies of Globalization," *Journal of Political Ideologies* 10, no. 1 (2005): 11–30.

63. Daniele Conversi, "Americanization and the Planetary Spread of Ethnic Conflict: The Globalization Trap," in *Planet Agora*, January 2004 (http://www.planetagora.org/english/theme4_suj2_note.html); and Daniele Conversi, "Globalization and Ethnic Conflict," in *Handbook of Globalization Studies*, ed. Bryan Turner (London: Routledge, 2009).

64. Marco Martiniello, "Towards a Post-Ethnic Europe," *Patterns of Prejudice* 35, no. 1 (2001): 59-68.

65. Anthony D. Smith, *National Identity* (Harmondsworth: Penguin/Reno: University of Nevada Press, 1991); Anthony D. Smith, *Nationalism in a Global Era* (Cambridge: Polity Press, 1996); Anthony D. Smith, *Nationalism and Modernism: A Critical Survey of Recent Theories of Nations and Nationalism* (London: Routledge, 1998); Anthony D. Smith, *Myths and Memories of the Nation* (Oxford: Oxford University Press); Anthony D. Smith, *The Nation in History* (Cambridge: Polity Press, 2000).

66. See Benjamin R. Barber, *Jihad vs. McWorld* (New York: Ballantine Books, 1996).

67. See Graham Pollock, "Civil Society Theory and Euro-Nationalism," *Studies in Social & Political Thought* 4 (2001); Carlo Ruzza, *Europe and Civil Society: Movement Coalitions and European Governance* (Manchester: Manchester University Press, 2004).

68. Daniele Conversi. "Homogenisation, Nationalism and War"; id., "We Are All Equals!"

69. For the Basque case, see Daniele Conversi, *The Basques, the Catalans, and Spain: Alternative Routes to Nationalist Mobilization* (London: Hurst/ Reno: University of Nevada Press, 1997).

70. Michael Billig. *Banal Nationalism* (London: Sage, 1995).

71. Miroslav Hroch, *The Social Preconditions of National Revival in Europe* (Cambridge: Cambridge University Press, 1985); Miroslav Hroch, "From National Movement to the Fully-formed Nation: The Nation-building Process in Europe," in *Mapping the Nation,* ed. Gopal Balakrishnan (New York and London: Verso, 1996), 78-97.

72. David Campbell, *Writing Security: United States Foreign Policy and the Politics of Identity* (Minneapolis: University of Minnesota Press, 1998), rev. ed.

73. Horowitz, *op. cit.*, 73.

74. John Coakley, "The Challenge," in *The Territorial Management of Ethnic Conflicts,* ed. John Coakley (London: Frank Cass, 2003); Yash Ghai, ed., *Autonomy and Ethnicity. Negotiating Competing Claims in Multi-Ethnic States* (Cambridge: Cambridge University Press, 2000); Will Kymlicka and Alan Patten, eds., *Language Rights and Political Theory* (Oxford: Oxford University Press, 2003); Dennis Austin and Michael O'Neill, *Democracy and Cultural Diversity* (Oxford: Oxford University Press, 2000).

75. Steven C. Roach, *Cultural Autonomy, Minority Rights, and Globalization* (Aldershot: Ashgate Publishing, 2005).

76. A similar thesis on a global scale has been put forward in Benjamin R. Barber, *Jihad vs. McWorld* (New York: Ballantine Books, 1996), see in particular 88-99 and 169-183.

77. See Anssi Paasi, "Europe as a Social Process and Discourse: Considerations of Place, Boundaries and Identity," *European Urban and Regional Studies* 8, no. 1 (2001): 7-28.

Chapter 6
Theorizing Regional Minority Nationalism

Anna M. Olsson

"The regional question, like the poor, is always with us and has been on the political agenda since the formation of the nation-state."[1]

Introduction: Making Sense of Regional Minority Nationalism

The idea of a "Europe of the regions" stems from the 1960s, but the importance of the regional level of governance within the European Union (EU) has increased since the early 1990s, when the regions were given a consulting role in the decision making process through the creation of the Committee of the Regions.[2] In addition, it has been observed that many traditionally protectionist regions have lessened their focus on sovereignty and instead embraced the idea of European integration. An obvious consequence of this growing importance of the regions is an increased scholarly interest in regional minority nationalism, and the purpose of this chapter is to explore and synthesize the literature on the role of regions and regionalism in the EU since its inception in the 1950s. First, I will summarize various existing attempts to conceptualize regions and regionalism, placing the focus of this chapter—sub-state regionalism[3]—in its proper context. Second, I will summarize and organize the theories of the emergence and persistence of sub-state regionalism in its various forms as they have occurred throughout several surges of increased regional mobilization since the founding of what is the EU today. Finally, I will address some possible theoretical developments as a consequence of a growing importance of regional actors in the EU policy process.

Conceptualizing Regions and Regionalism

A review of the massive literature on regions and regionalism reveals that a conceptualization and definition of what constitutes a "region" is not only a difficult, but, as one scholar contends, "a hazardous and, it could be argued, futile task."[4] The definitional problem is particularly difficult in the study of regions, where competing concepts from disciplines as diverse as law, political science, geography, history, and economics often clash. Coombes criticizes regionalism for failing to distinguish between phenomena as diverse as separatism, irredentism, and decentralization.[5] Likewise, Hebbert recognizes the contradictory nature of regionalism as a phenomenon that can be either centralist or peripheral; modern or traditional; left or right; and separatist or loyalist.[6] To add to the confusion, the term may refer to territorialities and phenomena at vastly different levels, ranging from economically driven definitions of regions as trading blocs formed by states in a certain geographic area, to definitions utilized by geographers and political scientists of regions as more or less formal spatial units at different levels across and within the boundaries of states.[7] It appears that more recent scholarly work has become more accepting of the diverse nature of regions and regionalism, however, as the multidisciplinarity that formerly was seen as a hindrance to the generation of theory on regions and regionalism is increasingly viewed as a necessity.[8]

Recently, political geographers in particular appear to be more comfortable with the dual notion of regionalism at different scales, and regional scholars within political science are increasingly adopting similar notions of regionalism.[9] The longstanding negligence of territory and geography within political science can largely be explained by the positivist tradition of the behavioral era, during which geography was seen as an obstacle for the testing of generalizable hypotheses, "as the recognition of geography implies uniqueness rather than universality."[10] In the realm of integration theory, the conceptual confusion regarding the meaning of region and regionalism can be viewed as both a result of and a reason for the lack of theories explaining the most recent eruption of territorial politics at the regional level, as traditional integration theory has tended to treat territorial cleavages as the result of conflicting *state* interests.[11] Both the lack of theory and the fact that the regions in Europe have had such different experiences has surely contributed to the abundance of case studies of territorial politics in single member states, or across a few regions, and to the lack of studies of comparative territorial politics.[12] Increasingly, however, scholars have come to the conclusion that it is not possible, or desirable, to construct a single theory explaining all cases, but that more comparative analysis can help in the development of partial theories, and therefore, definitions of "region" vary depending on the particular problem under investigation.[13]

Spatial Levels of Regionness

One of the most immediate distinctions that must be made when attempting to conceptualize regionalism is that between micro and macro regionalism, and it should be stated at this point that the remainder of this chapter will focus on the former.[14] As indicated above, regionalism in the field of economics, and to some extent in the field of international relations, tends to refer to the formation of large trading blocs created by groups of states, or the "process that leads to patterns of cooperation, integration, complementarity and convergence within a particular cross-national geographical space."[15] This type of regions is referred to as macro regions, world-regions, global regions, or international regions.[16] Whereas earlier works on macro-regionalism tended to limit their analysis to regionalism as a supranational phenomenon, recent works have attempted to link micro and macro regionalism as two connected, but different, phenomena which need to be understood within the same analytical framework.[17] In this context, micro regions most often refer to territorial units below the level of the state, or "between the 'national' and 'local' level"[18] but also to smaller *transnational* regions below the level of the macro-region, which are sometimes referred to as meso-regions.[19] Others use the term meso-regionalism or meso-government as a collective term for all sorts of units and governance between the local and the national level, whether or not they constitute regional political units or cross-regional movements, arguably "to avoid the value-laden discussion about what constitutes a region."[20] Finally, yet others prefer to avoid the confusion caused by the inclusion of any reference to nationalism entirely (such as in international, transnational, and subnational), and refer to sub-state regions as "subcentral territorial units."[21] For a similar reason, as some regions indeed could just as well be referred to as nations, I have chosen to use the term sub-state regions, rather than subnational regions, despite the fact that the latter is a more common term in the literature.

Varieties of Sub-State Regionalism

Once the distinction between different spatial levels of regionalism—such as that between macro- and micro-regions—has been established, a great deal of variation in scholarly definitions of the kind of regions that are the primary focus in this chapter—sub-state regions—remains. As will be shown in a later section of this chapter examining the development of theories attempting to explain the emergence of sub-state regionalism, it is a phenomenon that has emerged, disappeared, and reemerged throughout European history, and depending on its nature and context, it has been described by a plethora of different terms and definitions. In fact, one scholar argues that regions are so multifaceted that the term "almost escapes descriptive definition."[22] Peter Lynch lists the varieties "sub-state nationalism, regionalism, ethnonationalism, new nationalisms, ethnic separatism, and stateless nationalism," but is careful to point out that the terms partially refer to quite different phenomena, once again adding to the conceptual confusion discussed above.[23] Lynch argues that the linguistic and conceptual vagueness of minority nationalism and regionalism springs from two facts: (1) the economic, social, and political forces which drive minority nationalism have very different effects across the many cases of the phenomenon; and (2) one of the central tenets of minority nationalism is the demand for self-determination, but "this demand does not always mean the establishment of a separate nation-state . . . [but rather that] minority nationalism and regionalism are varied because of a self-determination which is pluralistic enough to allow relatively similar national and regional movements to support diverse constitutional solutions such as independence, federalism, Home Rule, devolution, cultural autonomy and . . . European Union."[24]

In an attempt to clarify the conceptual confusion, Lynch classifies minority nationalisms along three different dimensions of the phenomenon: goals, ideology, and strategies. When discussing goals, he refers exclusively to the agendas of minority nationalist parties, using Rokkan and Urwin's seven escalating goals of autonomy—separatism/irredentism, confederalism, federalism, regional autonomy, regionalism, peripheral protest, and peripheral identity-building—as a measure.[25] It is evident that this narrow focus is a bit dated, as several alternative regional goals have been identified since Lynch wrote his piece, along with other types of actors beside regionalist political parties. These will be examined in greater depth below. When discussing the ideological dimension of regionalism, Lynch tries—unsuccessfully—to apply minority nationalism to a left/right measure. Again, because Lynch restricts his analysis to regionalist political parties, the ideological position of the cases he mentions is largely contingent on the domestic political pattern in each state, and other analyses show that regionalism as a political movement at one time or another has been linked to just about every ideology.[26] Finally, when discussing regional strategies, he discusses the different types of mobilization used by different minority nationalist parties and movements along the violent/non-violent dimension, and along the party/non-party/cross-party dimension.[27] Again this proves to be somewhat dated, as regionalist movements have greatly extended their repertoire of strategies since the mid-1990s.

Another basic way to distinguish different types of sub-state regionalism that is commonly used in the literature, and that is built around the strategies of regionalism, is differentiating between top-down regionalism, emphasizing "politics from above," which refers to regional policies initiated by states, and bottom-up regionalism, emphasizing "politics from below," which refers to regional political and economic mobilization.[28] Some scholars prefer to limit the term "regionalism" to the latter phenomenon, while top-down regional strategies are referred to as "regionalization."[29]

Other scholars, such as Michael Keating and John Loughlin, pursue a broader conceptual classification that transcends Lynch's more narrowly defined politicized regionalism. Keating differentiates among three types of regions, while arguing that "the constitution of territorial systems varies greatly, depending on the coincidence of the various senses of region, and on political leadership and mobilization, as well as institutional structures."[30] The three types of regions, which vary along these three dimensions, include the following: (1) *historic nationalities*, or minority nationalist regions, characterized by a strong sense of culture and linguistic or historic identity, their own civil institutions and networks, with or without national pretensions (the former including examples such as Scotland, Catalonia, Brittany, and Flanders, and the latter including examples such as Sicily, Sardinia, Alsace, and Bavaria); (2) *institutional regions*, characterized by the use of institutions to build a political space and an effective system of action (examples include the German *Länder* and the stronger Italian regions); and (3) *administrative regions*, which lack a sense of common identity and which do not correspond to regions in the other two senses, and where regions are more or less recent artificial creations for administrative purposes (examples include regions in the Scandinavian countries, the weaker Italian regions, and regions in Ireland and Portugal).[31]

Loughlin uses a similar typology, although he splits the administrative category into economic regions, referring to territories defined according to economic activities, and administrative/planning regions, referring to territories defined for purposes of administration, economic planning, or the gathering of statistics.[32] A more useful contribution, which is particularly important for the study of regions in the EU, is the mentioning of the NUTS (Nomenclature des Unités Territoriales Statistiques), which is the way in which the European Commission defines regions.[33] It should be kept in mind, however, that this category, created by simply adopting the regional units of the member states, encompasses all the other categories of sub-state regions in the EU under a single concept.

A similar but even more parsimonious classification is pursued by Montserrat Guibernau, who simply distinguishes between what he refers to as "nations without states" (corresponding to Keating's historic nationalities) and "regions defined purely upon economic criteria."[34] The political and economic role of sub-state regions in the EU has increased over time, however, and the variation in the relative influence among what Guibernau calls economic regions is increasing, depending on their level of institutionalization. Therefore, Keating's regional typology is more useful and will form the structure for the remainder of this account of varieties of sub-state regionalism. Not surprisingly, a proportionally large number of scholarly studies on sub-state regionalism in Europe have focused on minority nationalist regions, a smaller proportion on institutional regions, and very few have focused on purely administrative regions. In the last decade, however, an increasing politicization of *all* regions in Europe, evident through the increasing influence of regions in the policy process of the EU, and through the concurrent drastic increase in the number of regional information offices in Brussels, has begun to change this pattern.[35]

Any discussion of the first category of sub-state regions—minority nationalist regions—ought to incorporate definitions of both components of the term. Although no internationally agreed-upon, precise definition exists of what constitutes a minority, or more specifically a national minority, most definitions describe it in terms of "a numerical minority that combines objective criteria, such as specific cultural characteristics distinct from the majority of the population and subjective criteria, such as a collective sense of community."[36] Combinations of such objective and subjective criteria are also evident in definitions attempted in international law, but developing from a very basic definition, such as the one attempted in 1949 by the United Nations (UN): that "minority" has come to refer to a particular kind of community, and especially to a national or similar community that differs from the predominant group in the state.[37] In a subsequent report, UN Special Rapporteur Francesco Capotorti provided a narrower definition of minority, as "a group, numerically inferior to the rest of the population of a State, in a non-dominant position, whose members—being nationals of the State—possess ethnic, religious or linguistic characteristics differing from those of the rest of the population and show, if only implicitly, a sense of solidarity, directed towards preserving their culture, traditions, religion or language."[38] Since this chapter specifically applies to minorities in Europe, it may be worth mentioning a few definitions that stem from the European context. First, the Organization for Security and Co-operation in Europe (OSCE), while reluctant to directly define the term to avoid definitional debates, made use of an unofficial list of criteria for the meaning of minorities as (1) being recognizably distinct from the dominant national group in the state; (2) usually possessing differences in ethnicity, religion, or language; and (3) wanting to maintain and develop their own distinct identities.[39] The Council of Europe (COE), on the other hand, provided a much more precise definition in a 1993 addition to the European Convention on Human Rights, stating that the expression "national minority" refers to persons in a state who:

> a. reside on the territory of that state and are citizens thereof; b. maintain longstanding, firm, and lasting ties with that state; c. display distinctive ethnic, cultural, religious, or linguistic characteristics; d. are sufficiently representative, although smaller in number than the rest of the population of that state or of a region of that state; and e. are motivated by a concern to preserve together that which constitutes their common identity, including their culture, their traditions, their religion or their language.[40]

The COE's European Charter for Regional or Minority Languages used similar criteria to define what is meant by a minority language, referring to those languages as "(i) traditionally used within a given territory of a State by nationals of that State who form a group numerically smaller than the rest of the State's population; and (ii) different from the official language(s) of that state; it does not include either dialects of the official language(s) of the State or the languages of migrants."[41] Although these definitions are quite precise, the most recent ones in particular, some confusion still persists in academia regarding what constitutes a national minority. Sasse points at the common distinction between "old" and "new" minorities in the policy debates; the former referring to historical, or traditional minorities, and the latter referring to recent immigrants, although she also critiques this distinction for ignoring the grey area between the two categories.[42] Although others point at the useful differentiation between national minorities, which can be defined as minority groups that see themselves as living on their ancestral territory, and immigrants, which are defined as minority groups that have arrived from distant countries and thus have a remote homeland, it is important to remember that some groups, such as Russians in the Baltic states, cannot easily be put in either category, but belong to both.[43]

The second component of the term minority nationalism that needs some elaboration is nationalism, which has been described as "one of the most powerful political forces of the modern age,"[44] and is consequently one of the most researched phenomena within comparative politics, although terms like "nation" and "nation-state" have consistently been misused and are often ill defined both within and outside of academia.[45] Therefore, a careful definition of what constitutes minority nationalism is essential. A good starting point is a basic definition of nationalism, such as "a doctrine of self-determination."[46] Kymlicka and Straehle then succinctly differentiate among *state nationalism*, which is defined as nationalist movements conducted by states that "have adopted various 'nation-building' policies aimed at giving citizens a common national language, identity and culture," and *minority nationalism*, where "ethnocultural minorities within a larger state have mobilized to demand a state of their own."[47] Keating similarly defines minority nationalism as an antithesis of state nationalism, involving "the denial of exclusive claims on the part of the state nationalism and the assertion of national rights of self determination for groups within it."[48]

There is little agreement, however, over whether minority nationalism per definition must include a claim to statehood, but with the decreasing role of the Westphalian state and the transfer of state sovereignty to the EU, this pattern has begun to change.[49] Whereas Keating, along with several other scholars, admits that minority nationalism does not necessarily need to be separatist in this new context, others still choose to avoid any contention by replacing the term minority nationalism with regionalism in cases where the political goal is anything less than secession.[50] Although it is important to keep in mind the great diversity among different cases of regionalism and minority nationalism, in the West there is a trend toward accommodating minority nationalism through some form of territorial autonomy, thus deeming the quest for statehood replete.[51] Also, one of the most prevalent differences between what has been labeled "old regionalism" and "new regionalism" at the sub-state level is that the former was characterized by protectionism, separatism, and sometimes violence, whereas the latter is characterized by a diminished focus on sovereignty, breaking the traditional linkage between regionalism and protectionism.[52]

Two ideal types have often been recognized in the literature on nationalism: (1) *ethnic nationalism*, characterized by an ascriptive, or given, membership in the national community; and (2) *civic nationalism*, characterized by a voluntary membership in the national community.[53] Keating initiated a corresponding distinction between ethnic and civic minority nationalism, two categories which largely correspond to the above-mentioned historic nationalities and institutional regions, as well as to the common distinction between political and cultural nationalism, and which have been used to conceptualize minority nationalism in subsequent scholarship.[54] Throughout his scholarship, and throughout the deepening of European integration, Keating has compared ethnic and civic minority nationalism, and increasingly found a predominance of the latter kind, ultimately coining the term *new minority nationalisms*, also called regional minority nationalisms, defining these as "post-nation-state in inspiration, addressing a world in which sovereignty has ceased to be absolute and power is dispersed."[55] In his more recent work, he makes the interesting observation that minority nationalist demands have been framed in exactly the same way as those made by the states themselves, moving "from an ethnic particularism to a broader civic nationalism, invoking liberal democratic norms and often embracing the new international order."[56]

The second category of sub-state regions—institutional regions—is much easier to define, although disagreements among scholars exist here as well. Different from the first category, this type of regions excludes any regions with a strong sense of culture and identity, but typically includes regions that have an established position and a large amount of autonomy within their state.[57] Typically this category includes regions in federal states that are not historic nationalities, but increasingly, scholars use a more relaxed definition of how much institutionalism is sufficient, and rather than including just purely federal regions also include decentralized and devolved regions such as the ones in Spain and the United Kingdom.[58] Essentially, a definition stating that regions are institutional if they "possess democratically elected councils or assemblies who in turn choose an executive accountable to the electorate"[59] is flexible in that it allows for institutional change, but may exclude regions that have quite a lot of political autonomy, while including regions that rather belong in the administrative category. Institutional regions are sometimes referred to as *strong regions*—an attribute that they have won through their evidently privileged position within the policy process of the EU, and which has been reinforced by such events as the formation of groups such as RegLeg (The Conference of Presidents of Regions with Legislative Power) and CALRE (The Conference of Presidents of European Legislative Assemblies).[60] A final way to frame institutional regions is in the context of regions as a level of government. With the increasing importance of regions within the governance system of the EU scholars have examined the role of regions within this structure, with different conclusions. Whereas some prefer to give the regional level an increasingly important role, as an integrated part of the larger European system of multi-layered governance, others contend that as long as the asymmetries in the level of influence are so large among EU regions, there is no such thing as a regional level of governance.[61]

Finally, the third type of sub-state regions defined by Keating—administrative regions—is the least researched of all. The probable cause for this is the fact that such regions lack any sense of common identity, being more or less artificially created in order to carry out the tasks of the state. In the last 20 years, however, they have become a more interesting object of study, as regions have increasingly been presented as production systems, due to functional change in economic development, with a new role as competitors in the European and global marketplace.[62] In addition, subnational mobilization in the European arena is increasingly seen as an alternative form of representation (or an alternative way to aggregate interests) in the EU, beside the usual form of representation through state executives and non-elected European institutions.[63] Although institutional and historical regions have an obvious advantage over administrative regions in this realm, this subnational mobilization has accelerated to a point where virtually all regions in the EU have opened an office in Brussels, and this is likely to generate a greater research interest in the near future.[64]

A different approach to conceptualizing regions that allows for more dynamic is pursued by proponents of a constructivist view of the phenomenon as a process involving four stages of institutionalization: "(1) assumption of territorial shape, (2) development of conceptual shape; (3) development of institutions; and (4) establishment as part of the regional system and regional consciousness of the society concerned."[65] According to this model, which is clearly influenced by political geographers, EU scholars anticipate that regions will become a more and more vital part of the EU policy process.[66] In line with this notion, multi-level governance theorists like Gary Marks and Liesbet Hooghe argue that "European integration is a polity creating process in which authority and policy-making influence are shared across multiple levels of government—subnational, national and supranational."[67] Similarly, Kohler-Koch argues that the EU has helped institutionalize a new style of politics that emphasizes decentralization and joint problem-solving in multi-level policy-networks instead of hierarchical relationships where the state rules "from above."[68]

In this type of multi-level policy networks, yet another type of sub-state regions, that was not part of Keating's typology, has emerged and grown immensely just in the past decade—*cross-member state regions*.[69] These include different types, such as transnational polycentric regions (for example the Øresund region), noncontiguous or virtual regions (such as Ultra-Peripheral Regions), and transborder regions (such as the Germany-Czech Republic-Poland border area). These new types of regional groupings stand in contrast to the formal administrative regions of Europe, and scholars suggest that a new type of regionalism is emerging, which they call "unbounded regionalism," and which moves away from the standard conception of the region being based around "either functional metropolitan areas or culturally and administratively distinct provincial regions."[70] Such regions are often created for economic reasons, such as in the case of global economic competitiveness, and have little or nothing to do with regional culture or identity—they are "'imaginary spaces' envisioned by politicians."[71] Moreover, they argue that these "mega-regions" were consciously delineated to grate against existing nation-state boundaries, as an attempt to contribute to the frictionless mobility of labor and capital across the EU.[72]

Explaining the Emergence and Maintenance of Regional Minority Nationalism

Theories about the emergence and maintenance of sub-state regionalism and regional minority nationalism have been as diverse and abundant as the attempts to conceptualize the notion of the region, even more so as it is a phenomenon that has emerged, disappeared, and reemerged throughout European history, and depending on its nature and context, a number of theories have been suggested. A first basic distinction that is commonly made in scholarly reviews of the literature on theories of regionalism and minority nationalism is the distinction between old and new sub-state regionalism.[73] Whereas old regionalisms are often described as traditionalist and cultivating separatism, new regionalisms seek entirely other ways to increased autonomy than through secession. Christiansen contends that these key changes from old to new regionalism, "from exclusion to inclusion, from a national focus to a European focus, from a backward-looking and primordial to a future-oriented and associational discourse, are a break with centuries of political practice in most regions."[74]

Corresponding to the distinction between old and new regionalism, and based on various and changing understandings of regionalism and regional questions over time, John Loughlin divides the phenomenon into three distinct periods, characterized by different modes of regionalism.[75] First, from 1945-1975, the period of the growth of the Welfare State in Europe, regions were viewed within the context of reducing the disparities between stronger and weaker territories, achieved by the policy instrument regional policy, initiated and implemented by the nation-state. This is referred to as *assisted regionalism*, and corresponds to early theories attempting to explain the resurgence of regional nationalism as a result of political, economic, and cultural differences between the center and the peripheries within states.[76] Second, during the 1980s and 1990s, national regionalist policies were abolished, motivated by neo-liberal reforms, while regional authorities were forced to adopt strategies that reached beyond their own states, encouraging what is referred to as *competitive regionalism*, corresponding to political economy explanations of the resurgence of regionalism. Overlapping with this period, however, through the decreased role of national governments as policy actors and the increased role of the EU as such, concepts such as subsidiarity and partnership encouraged the development of *collaborative regionalism*, corresponding to a plethora of political theories of regionalism. This process, according to Loughlin, is what set the stage for the most recent mobilization of sub-state regions.[77]

Early Theories of Regionalism

Most scholars studying regionalism and minority nationalism would probably agree that these movements pose a significant challenge to the existing nation-state order and that the most fundamental reason for this is that they "challenge the assumed coincidence between politically significant identities and political boundaries."[78] In the course of the development of the modern state system in Europe, social theorists developed an expectation that the modernization of society would eventually lead to homogenized nation-states with convergent economies.[79] From the middle of the nineteenth century until the years following the Second World War, theories of modernization and political development predicted that industrialization would be accompanied by the disappearance of conflicts based on ethnic or cultural divisions.[80] Similarly, the diffusionist theory of social integration predicted that the culture and values of the core community of states would gradually diffuse throughout the peripheral communities to produce territorial homogeneity.[81] In the realm of economic theory, neo-classical economists expected less developed and peripheral regions within national economies to be able to exploit their comparative advantages of low cost to attract investment, thus producing a convergence in living standards.[82]

As mentioned above, the longstanding negligence of territory and geography within political science can largely be explained by the positivist tradition of the behavioral era of American political science, and this was yet another hindrance for the development of the study of territorial politics until the 1960s.[83] Both the resurgence of regionalist and minority nationalist movements in Western Europe and Canada in the 1960s and the evident economic disparities among regions within European states challenged the modernization theorist and diffusionist predictions, and following this a number of works emerged that tried to explain this discrepancy.[84] Liesbet Hooghe identifies four strands of theories that attempt this: (1) development models; (2) center-periphery-models; (3) uneven development theories; and (4) competition theories.[85] In addition to these, (5) post-materialism can be added as a fifth category.[86]

First, with his *social communications theory*, Karl W. Deutsch suggested that the precarious territorial balance in a state is disturbed if social mobilization resulting from economic development grows faster than the assimilation to the dominant culture.[87] The solution that he presented, which would prevent the development of alternative identities and movements in the periphery and thus eliminate the threat to the integrity of the state, was a modernity-induced increase in social communications among diverse communities.[88] Second, Rokkan and Urwin's *center-periphery model* posits a division within nation-states between privileged locations, or centers, and peripheries, or "those geographical locations at the furthest distance from the centre but still within the territory controlled by the latter."[89] They identify two necessary conditions for the emergence of regional nationalism: (1) that regions must have considerable power in at least one of the dimensions economy, culture or politics; and (2) that the center must try to impose a state-building policy that does not adjust sufficiently to the power structures in the peripheral regions.[90] Minority nationalism can thus be explained as a manifestation of the tensions between centre and periphery, or as "the politicisation of peripheral predicaments."[91]

Third, and somewhat related, *uneven development theories* contend that regional nationalism is linked to the struggle of a people to free itself from structures of oppression. One example is Tom Nairn's Marxist interpretation of nationalism as a bourgeois phenomenon in the peripheries that changes imperialist relationships by mobilizing the peripheral masses.[92] Another argument that—although different—belongs to the same theoretical strand is Michael Hechter's internal colonialism argument, which states that the existence of minority nationalist movements is a result of central capitalist control over commerce and political life in the periphery, leaving the residents of the latter with the options of joining the core, or seeking to defend the periphery.[93] Minority nationalism is ultimately stimulated by "an awareness of persisting regional underdevelopment,"[94] and ultimately results when the support for the promotion of peripheral interests has reached a sufficient level.[95] Fourth, *competition theories*, inspired by early social movement theory, emphasize the importance of a power struggle for limited resources along with the relative ease with which social movements emerge and break up. Building on Tilly's resource mobilization theory, the main contribution of this rationalist (or instrumentalist) approach is its rejection of ethnicity as an inherent source of conflict, instead suggesting that ethnicity is just one of many tools used by competing groups to define their allies and enemies.[96] Finally, early accounts of *postmaterialist theory* offered an explanation to the resurgence of regionalist minority nationalism as follows: "a decline in the importance of issues that reflect the stratification system of industrial society, ideology, ethnicity, life-style, and so on may assume greater importance. Class politics may decline in favor of status or cultural or 'ideal' politics."[97] In other words, the reasons for the upsurge of minority nationalism in the postindustrial state is that greater economic security enables people to satisfy "higher order needs" such as identity, and to leave class conflict and ideology behind.[98]

Theories Explaining the New Regionalism

One factor which affects the relationship between political territory and identities, and regional political mobilization stands out in particular in the transition from old to new regionalism: European integration.[99] The role of an ever increasing integration of European states for the resurgence of regionalism and the mobilization of regional actors since the late 1980s cannot be emphasized enough, and it appears as a crucial element in nearly all theories attempting to explain the wave of regional and minority nationalist movements that emerged since then.[100] The notion of a "Europe of the Regions," the idea of which dates as far back as the 1920s, resurged first in the 1960s as a way to promote a federal Europe, and then in the late 1980s following the EU structural fund reforms.[101] It is the most recent surge that has been the focus of a large literature on what has been labeled the new regionalism. Whereas some accounts of the new regionalism focus more narrowly on specific theoretical explanations, such as social movement theory or political economy, or on certain types of regionalism, such as the identity politics of minority nationalism, other scholars have attempted more general explanations of the re-emergence of regionalism, drawing on different existing theoretical strands. One such example is the analysis of the emerging pattern of regional representation in Brussels up until the mid 1990s, conducted by Marks et al. using a multilevel governance perspective of the EU.[102] Another example of a more generalizing theory is what I will refer to as the *bypass-theory of regionalism*, with roots in early integration theory and more recently elaborated extensively in the scholarship of Michael Keating.[103]

The surge of theories attempting to explain regionalism as a result of European integration in the late 1980s can undoubtedly not only be attributed to the changing intensity of European integration and the following resurgence of regional mobilization at the time, but also to the failure to explain this mobilization by the two main approaches to theorizing European integration since its infancy—intergovernmentalist or state-centric and neo-functionalist theories. Whereas the former attributes special importance to the state and to inter-state bargaining, while the latter considers institutional evolution as the main driving force behind European integration, neither ascribes a strong role for the regions in the EU governance system.[104] It is therefore not surprising that one of the main contenders for an alternative theory of European integration in its current form—the multilevel governance (MLG) approach—attempts to move away from this dichotomy, and sees the region as one of its corner stones.[105]

These theorists conceptualize the EU as a single, multi-level polity, where "subnational and national governments are not simply differentiated layers of decision-making, but institutions of interest aggregation based on different constituencies with potentially conflicting interests and identities,"[106] and it is characterized by the interaction of political actors across these levels.

To explain the emerging pattern of regional representation in the form of the growing number of information offices in Brussels up until the mid 1990s, Marks et al. test several hypotheses. First, they hypothesize that regional governments that have potential access to more resources at the European level, measured as the amount of structural funding allocated to the regions, are more likely to open an office in Brussels.[107] Since no regional governments from the poorest EU member states—which are typically the recipients of the largest amounts of funding—were represented in Brussels at the time of their investigation, they do not, as could be expected, find any evidence supporting this hypothesis. A second hypothesis is based on the resource mobilization theory that the availability of resources, here measured as subnational revenue, facilitates social movement activity.[108] The findings suggest that the contrast between well-funded and poorly funded regions lies rather in the size than in the existence of a regional office in Brussels. Whereas they find little or no support for economic explanations for the establishment of regional offices in Brussels, Marks et al. emphasize two strong findings regarding political explanations in their analysis. First, they find that the subnational governments with the most extensive political role, or the greatest autonomy within their respective domestic political systems, are the most likely to open an office in Brussels, because they are more affected by decisions that are made there. Second, Marks et al. find a strong correlation between regional representation in Brussels and regional distinctiveness, measured as the strength of regional identity vis-à-vis national identity across regions, explained by the simple fact that these regions have political demands which conflict with those of their national governments. In fact, at the time of the investigation, almost all regions that were ethnically, culturally, or linguistically distinct from their respective national societies had offices in Brussels.[109] It is clear from the analysis that the multilevel governance approach is very useful as a new way of describing the current governance structure of the EU, by taking all the political actors which are evidently part of this process into account. The approach is less useful, however, as has been argued above, for understanding the reasons behind the increased role of regions in the EU today, mostly because of the vast variation in both the goals and strategies of regions to mobilize politically. One important contribution of the work of the multilevel governance proponents for the study of the new regionalism, however, was that attention was drawn to the mobilization of new types of regions that were not stateless nations.[110] On the other hand, it has been criticized for neglecting the intra-state environment of sub-national actors, which plays an important role as a catalyst for sub-national mobilization.[111]

Michael Keating early emphasized the mutual reinforcement of the two processes of European integration and regional devolution as "twin challenges to the nation-state in western Europe"[112] and as a key to understanding the resurgence of regionalism in the post-War era. This process, also referred to as constantly resurging "crises of territorial representation,"[113] facing states each time a regionalist wave occurs, can be formulated in terms of a bypass-theory of regionalism, according to which regions increasingly seek to bypass their central governments to achieve their policy goals at the EU level by forging direct links with the EU.[114] The theory has its roots in the early functionalist theory of European integration, arguing that functional linkages would increasingly bypass the nation-state, but differently from these early non-statist theorists, Keating admits that the state still has a great deal of power.[115] Furthermore, just like Keating emphasized the duality of the processes of European integration and devolution, the process is often described as a mutual one, where "regional interests have sought channels of influence into Europe, while the European Union has itself sought to use regions in pursuit of its own policy objectives."[116] A number of scholars have adopted this notion of a regional-EU bypass strategy in their own work, and it has often been used as an explanation for the somewhat paradox phenomenon of traditionally protectionist minority nationalist regions becoming among the strongest supporters of European integration.[117] Keating explains this transformation, which can also be viewed as part of the transformation from old to new regionalism, as a reaction beginning in the mid-1980s, where regions moved from "oppos[ing] European integration fearing a further loss of democratic control, more remote government and the triumph of market principles" to seeing Europe "as a source of material support for economic development" and using Europe "as a framework for the international projection of the regions, and even as a source of support for minority cultures and languages threatened within large states."[118]

The bypass-theory of regionalism has not been accepted without criticism, however, and as is usually the case with theories and hypotheses aiming for universalism, the main critique—which also has policy implications—is that the key determinants for subnational mobilization in Brussels can be found within each member state, and that the opportunities and constraints of mobilization are thus bound to be unequal across member states.[119] Jeffery's main point of critique is—similar to his critique of the multilevel governance approach—that the bypass-theory tends to overstate regional capacities to reach *beyond* the nation-state, ignoring the fact that a lot of their renewed influence is actually carried out *through* the nation-state.[120] Liesbet Hooghe counters this critique by arguing that "subnational units do not need member states to have access to the European arena. In fact, regional authorities in particular are important additional channels to tie newly mobilized interests to Europe."[121] Not surprisingly Hooghe—being one of the main proponents of the multilevel governance view—points out that regions constitute a governmental level as important as the national, European, and local levels, and reinforces the bypass-theory by arguing that "supranational institutions must nurture constituencies and therefore need to exploit any potential counterweight to national power. They are likely to encourage a pluralist setting, which would be open not only to bureaucrats or political executives, but also to regionalist movements, subnational interest groups, local action groups, and other alternative sources of interest aggregation."[122] Finally, she concludes that the democratic representativeness of the EU suffers from a bias in subnational representation, as "the subnational actors most likely to be involved are a privileged subset."[123] Similarly, Marks et al. argue that "regional mobilization does not empower regional governments in general, but only a select subset of them,"[124] and Arter argues that the bypass route is used not by all regions, but mainly by those which are peripheral, and which have little access to the central government of their states.[125]

A type of explanation for the new regionalist wave of mobilization that utilized a political economy perspective was particularly common in the early phase of the internal market following the Single European Act (SEA), perhaps thanks to the very economic nature—and the limitation to the economic sphere—of the European Community at the time. Scholars pointed on one hand at the effects of the reformed structural funds, and on the other hand at the new economic incentives facing the regions within the single market.[126] Whereas earlier theories on the relative economic deprivation of some regions over others, such as the center-periphery model, focused on economic differences within states, European integration, and particularly the introduction of a regional cohesion policy, shifted the focus of reducing the gap between levels of development away from the member states and to the regions.[127] A common argument is that the regional policy, and the economic incentives it has created for the regions, has in fact given rise to a number of new regional areas "by putting the regional question on the agenda and giving it important subsidies"[128] which in turn has resulted in the mobilization of new regional actors. Other scholars point at the different incentives facing different regions, arguing that statistical analyses—such as that conducted by Marks et al.—that fail to control for the many differences among regions are bound to produce unreliable findings, as regions benefit differently from the new economic opportunities provided by the EU.[129] In short, whereas poor regions benefited from changes in the Structural Funds, better-off regions benefited from the economic advantages of the Single Market.[130] Another effect of European integration that has contributed considerably to the change from old regionalist protectionism to new regionalist openness is the fact that "free trade potentially lowers the economic costs of separation . . ., a factor which . . . has led nationalist movements to abandon protectionism in favor of autonomy within the free-trade regime."[131]

Another type of political economy argument has been proposed by scholars promoting globalization as the major cause of regionalism, such as Kenichi Ohmae, who while following a functionalist logic argues that it is sub-state regions that form the basic building-blocks of the new global economy.[132] Ohmae's coining of the term "region state," defined as "medium size economic units, not political ones, oriented toward the global economy, and willing to attract foreign investment to improve the quality of life of their people"[133] has been criticized, however, particularly from scholars studying minority nationalism, for being economically reductionist, acultural, and ahistorical.[134] A different argument for explaining the increased importance of regions as a direct result of the effects of globalization is that "the fact that it is at the regional and local levels that the impact of change is felt has helped create new coalitions of territorial defense and increased the political salience of regions."[135] In his more recent work, Keating has increasingly moved beyond the realm of European integration as a key cause of regionalism, and elaborated on the importance of the effects of globalization for regional economies, arguing that "the context for the new regionalism is not merely, as in the past, the nation state; it is the continental, and even global economy."[136] Regions face entirely different challenges in this new context, as they are forced to compete with each other in a fiercer economic climate than within the protected sphere of the state. In fact, Keating identifies arguments such as Ohmae's—that globalization, and the borderless world that it produces will render the notion of territory meaningless—as a contemporary variation of the old modernization argument discussed above.[137] Rather than undermining minority nationalism, the process of globalization is seen as explaining its strength, exemplified by but not limited to the growth of "an international regime that places minority rights ahead of state sovereignty."[138]

Yet another way of understanding sub-state regional mobilization is in terms of social movements. Following the works of social movement scholars such as Tilly and Tarrow, who early argued that what we know as the social movement emerged in response to the modern state, it is not surprising that many scholars studying regionalism adopted these types of explanations.[139] Although few scholars explicitly use a social movement framework when explaining the resurgence of regionalism, many use concepts from the social movement literature, such as in the argument that the EU provides the regions with a new political opportunity structure.[140] More recent social movement theory contends, however, that political opportunities are just the beginning of what has been labeled "social movement cycles," and although the EU has continuously provided the regions with such opportunity structures, it takes both mobilization of resources, and the framing of issues and identities to actually constitute a social movement.[141] Evidence suggesting that the regions with the most institutionalized domestic structures along with the regions with the strongest distinct identities are the ones most likely to mobilize in Brussels, clearly supports a conclusion that social movement theory applies to regional movements.[142]

Finally, any theory attempting to explain the emergence and maintenance of regionalism in general, and regional minority nationalism in particular, must involve a discussion of the role of identity and identity formation. In fact, it is at the intersection of the concepts of territory and identity that most accounts of regional minority nationalism start, and it is where the two do not perfectly coincide—which is rarely the case—that regional minority nationalism is likely to mobilize.[143] Due to space constraints, I will not review the vast literature on ethnic and national identity in this context, but will rather confine this section to a brief summary. Theories about the origins and shaping of ethnic and national identities vary enormously, but most scholarly accounts can be placed along the primordialist-constructivist-instrumentalist continuum.[144] On the one side of the continuum, primordialism, or "Simmering Cauldron" theory, attempts to explain the resurgence of minority nationalism by arguing that the powerful state and the international order of the Cold War suppressed ancient ethnic sentiments and identities that erupted as soon as the lid was taken off.[145] On the other side of the continuum, instrumentalists argue that ethnic and national identities are fabricated by political elites in order to take advantage of changing international conditions.[146] Most accounts of regional identity in Europe fall somewhere between these two extremes, using a constructivist perspective, seeing ethnic and national identity not as a given, but as something constructed, that once created is rather enduring.[147]

Keating sees a parallel between regional identity and national identity in that both often rest upon "imagined communities"[148] rather than lived experience, since their scale—different from local identities—requires citizens "to relate to people whom they only know at second hand, through the media, political parties or broader social institutions."[149] European integration, he argues, facilitates the construction of alternative identities, "both by weakening the prestige of the established states, and by providing opportunities for regional leaders to project their regions and themselves in the international and European arenas."[150] Similarly, Lynch discusses the role of the EU as an external support system for minority nationalist identities, that does not threaten these identities in the same way nation-state identities do, as "Europe is essentially seen as pluralist and multilingual, with no uniform cultural or linguistic agenda to put across, in contrast to individual nation-states."[151] More recently, it has been argued that "the hegemony of national identities is being eroded, and being replaced by more complex multiple identities."[152]

Conclusion: The Increasing Importance of Sub-State Regionalism in the EU

Paradoxically, by the early 2000s, the concept of a "Europe of the Regions" was largely seen as discredited by scholars of European regionalism, while the level of regional mobilization in Europe continued to grow exponentially.[153] In a recent book chapter Loughlin argues that the setting up of the Committee of the Regions (CoR) in 1994 seems to have somewhat deflated the mobilization of sub-state regions, and finds evidence for this in the absence of regional questions in both the Amsterdam and the Nice treaties.[154] Others pointed to the danger of regional disappointment already a year after the introduction of the CoR, largely due to the limitation of CoR competencies to advisory powers; to the fact that members are appointed and not elected; and to the internal division of the CoR through the representation of both local and regional authorities.[155] The debate surrounding the Treaty Establishing a Constitution for Europe has given new momentum to the regions, however, resulting in yet another surge of regional mobilization. In 2005, Keating identified three key processes explaining this surge: "the new debate on a European constitution and the challenge of democratizing the EU; the Commission's need to reduce its administrative overload while improving efficiency; and the rise of strong regions within several member states."[156] Many of the demands put forward by the regions in the Convention on the Future of Europe were rejected for inclusion in the final constitutional document, however, and the resulting draft treaty was described as a "robustly statist"[157] vision of the EU. At the same time, however, the number of regional information offices in Brussels has continued to increase drastically, doubling in size from 140 in 1995 to 280 in 2008.[158] It thus appears likely that the regions, whether or not they are granted any greater political influence through direct incorporation in the EU decision-making process in the near future, will continue to attempt influencing this process in alternative ways.

The recent resurgence of regional actors in the governance system of the EU is an apparent contradiction to scholarly pessimism regarding the role of regions, and this clearly indicates a need for more research attempting to explain this surge, designed to develop and test theories of regionalism that span across disciplines. In particular, there is a need for more comparative analyses of regions, which control for cross-state variation among regions while attempting to explain phenomena such as the increased mobilization of regional offices in Brussels; the growing regional identities in merely administrative regions; and the variation in support for European integration at the regional level. In particular, any theoretical development would require scholars to move beyond a narrow focus on official regional actors, such as those appointed to the Committee of the Regions, to a perspective that takes unofficial representatives, such as regional lobbyists, as well as actors at all other levels—from elites to grassroots—into consideration. A promising possible theoretical development that would do this would be the development of a theory of regional mobilization that builds on the framework of the various aspects of social movement theory.

Notes

1. John Loughlin, "The Regional Question, Subsidiarity and the Future of Europe," in *The Role of Regions and Sub-National Actors in Europe*, ed. Stephen Weatherill and Ulf Bernitz (Oxford: Hart Publishing, 2005), 157.

2. Council and Commission of the European Communities, *Treaty on European Union*, 1992.

3. I will use the term "sub-state regionalism," rather than the more common term "subnational regionalism," simply to avoid unnecessary confusion with nationalism at the regional level.

4. Thomas Christiansen, "Reconstructing European Space: From Territorial Politics to Multilevel Governance," in *Reflective Approaches to European Governance*, ed. Knud Erik Jørgensen (London: Macmillan, 1997), 53.

5. David Coombes, "Europe and the Regions," in *National Identities: The Constitution of the United Kingdom*, ed. Bernard Crick (Oxford: Political Quarterly/Blackwell, 1991), 134-50.

6. Michael Hebbert, "Regionalism: A Reform Concept and Its Application to Spain," *Environment and Planning. C, Government and Policy* 5, no. 3 (1987): 239-50.

7. Peter Schmitt-Egner, "The Concept of 'Region': Theoretical and Methodological Notes on Its Reconstruction," *Journal of European Integration* 24, no. 3 (2002): 179-200;

Marie-Claude Smouts, "The Region as the New Imagined Community?" in *Regions in Europe*, ed. Patrick Le Galès and Christian Lequesne (New York: Routledge, 1998), 30-38; Andrea Witt, "The Utility of Regionalism for Comparative Research on Governance: A Political Science Perspective," in *Regionalism in the Age of Globalism. Volume 1: Concepts of Regionalism*, ed. Lothar Hönnighausen, et al. (Madison, WI: University of Wisconsin-Madison, 2005), 47-66.

8. Schmitt-Egner, "The Concept of 'Region.'"

9. Michael Keating, "Europe, the State and the Nation," in *European Integration and the Nationalities Question*, ed. John McGarry and Michael Keating (New York: Routledge, 2006), 23-34; Virginie Mamadouh, "The Regions in Brussels: Subnational Actors in the Supranational Arena," *Tijdschrift voor Economische en Sociale Geografie* 92, no. 4 (2001): 478-87; Robert Ostergren, "Concepts of Region: A Geographical Perspective," in *Regionalism in the Age of Globalism. Volume 1: Concepts of Regionalism*, ed. Lothar Hönnighausen, et al. (Madison, WI: University of Wisconsin-Madison, 2005), 1-14.

10. Lawrence J. Sharpe, "The West European State: The Territorial Dimension," in *Tensions in the Territorial Politics of Western Europe*, ed. R.A.W. Rhodes and Vincent Wright (London: Frank Cass, 1987), 149.

11. Christiansen, "Reconstructing European Space," Michael Keating, *State and Regional Nationalism: Territorial Politics and the European State* (New York: Harvester Wheatsheaf, 1988).

12. Scott L. Greer, *Territory, Democracy and Justice: Regionalism and Federalism in Western Democracies* (New York: Palgrave Macmillan, 2006); Björn Hettne, "Beyond the 'New' Regionalism," *New Political Economy* 10, no. 4 (2005): 543-71.

13. Hettne, "Beyond the 'New' Regionalism"; Michael Keating, "Europeanism and Regionalism," in *The European Union and the Regions*, ed. Barry Jones and Michael Keating (Oxford: Clarendon Press, 1995), 1-22.

14. The "Levels of Regionness" discussed here explicitly refer to the spatial levels ranging from sub-state to supranational regions, and should not be confused with Hettne's conceptualization of "five levels of regionness," which refer to the gradual development of supranational regions. For a more detailed account of this notion, see Björn Hettne, "Globalization and the New Regionalism: The Second Great Transformation," in *Globalism and the New Regionalism*, ed. Björn Hettne, Andreas Inotai, and Osvaldo Sunkel (New York: St. Martin's Press, 1999), 1-25; Björn Hettne, "The New Regionalism: Implications for Development and Peace," in *The New Regionalism—Implications for Global Development and International Security*, ed. Björn Hettne and Andreas Inotai (Helsinki: UNU World Institute for Development Economics Research, 1994), 1-50; Björn Hettne and Fredrik Söderbaum, "Theorising the Rise of Regionness," *New Political Economy* 5, no. 3 (2000): 457-72.

15. Hettne and Söderbaum, "Theorising the Rise of Regionness," 458.

16. Hettne, "Beyond the 'New' Regionalism"; John Loughlin, "Representing Regions in Europe: The Committee of the Regions," in *The Regional Dimension of the European Union. Towards a Third Level in Europe?*, ed. Charlie Jeffery (London: Frank Cass, 1997), 147-65; Schmitt-Egner, "The Concept of 'Region.'"

17. Hettne and Söderbaum, "Theorising the Rise of Regionness."

18. Hettne, "Beyond the 'New' Regionalism," 557.

19. Hettne and Söderbaum, "Theorising the Rise of Regionness"; Lawrence J. Sharpe, *The Rise of Mesogovernment in Europe* (London: Sage, 1993).

20. Michael Keating and Nicola McEwen, "Introduction: Devolution and Public Policy in Comparative Perspective," *Regional & Federal Studies* 15, no. 4 (2005): 420.

21. Christiansen, "Reconstructing European Space," 51.

22. Michael Keating, *The New Regionalism in Western Europe: Territorial Restructuring and Political Change* (Cheltenham: Edward Elgar, 1998), 79.

23. Peter Lynch, *Minority Nationalism and European Integration* (Cardiff: University of Wales Press, 1996), 4.

24. Peter Lynch, *Minority Nationalism.*

25. Peter Lynch, *Minority Nationalism*, Stein Rokkan and Derek W. Urwin, *Economy, Territory, Identity: Politics of West European Peripheries* (London: Sage, 1983).

26. Keating, *The New Regionalism.*

27. Lynch, *Minority Nationalism.*

28. Christiansen, "Reconstructing European Space"; Keating, "Europeanism and Regionalism"; Michael Keating, *Regions and Regionalism in Europe* (Northhampton, MA: Edward Elgar, 2004).

29. Christiansen, "Reconstructing European Space"; Colin H. Williams, "Territory, Identity and Language," in *The Political Economy of Regionalism*, ed. Michael Keating and John Loughlin (London: Frank Cass, 1997), 112-38; Witt, "The Utility of Regionalism."

30. Keating, *The New Regionalism*, 109.

31. Keating, *The New Regionalism.*

32. Loughlin, "Representing Regions in Europe."

33. Loughlin, "Representing Regions in Europe."

34. M. Montserrat Guibernau, *Nations without States: Political Communities in a Global Age* (Cambridge: Polity, 1999), 173.

35. Committee of the Regions of the European Union, "Associations/Bureaux de Répresentation Regionale et Communale à Bruxelles: Repertoire," (Bruxelles: Comite des Regions de'l Union Europeenne, 2008); Liesbet Hooghe, "Subnational Mobilisation in the European Union," in *The Crisis of Representation in Europe*, ed. Jack Hayward (London: Frank Cass, 1995), 175-98; Keating, *The New Regionalism*; Michael Keating and Liesbet Hooghe, "Bypassing the Nation-State? Regions and the EU Policy Process," in *European Union. Power and Policy-Making*, ed. Jeremy Richardson (New York: Routledge, 2001), 239-56; Peter Lynch, "Organising for a Europe of the Regions: The European Free Alliance-DPPE and Political Representation in the European Union" (paper presented at the European Union Studies Association Biennial Conference, Montreal, Canada, May 2007), Mamadouh, "The Regions in Brussels."

36. Gwendolyn Sasse, "Securitization or Securing Rights? Exploring the Conceptual Foundations of Policies Towards Minorities and Migrants in Europe," *Journal of Common Market Studies* 43, no. 4 (2005), 675.

37. United Nations, *Definition and Classification of Minorities*, memorandum submitted by the Secretary-General, E/CN.4/Sub.2/85, 27. Dec. 1949.

38. United Nations, *Study on the Rights of Persons belonging to Ethnic, Religious and Linguistic Minorities*, UN Document E/CN.4/Sub.2/384/Add. 1-7 (1977).

39. Jennifer Jackson Preece, *National Minorities and the European Nation-States System* (Oxford: Clarendon Press, 1998).

40. Council of Europe, *Parliamentary Assembly Recommendation 1201 and Additional Protocol on the Rights of National Minorities to the European Convention on Human Rights*, Section 1, Article 1 (1993).

41. Council of Europe, *European Charter for Regional and Minority Languages* (1992), Article 1(a).

42. Sasse, "Securitization or Securing Rights?"

43. John McGarry, Michael Keating, and Margaret Moore, "Introduction: European Integration and the Nationalities Question," in *European Integration and the Nationalities Question*, ed. John McGarry and Michael Keating (New York: Routledge, 2006), 1-20.

44. Michael Keating, *Nations against the State: The New Politics of Nationalism in Quebec, Catalonia, and Scotland* (New York: St. Martin's Press, 1996), 1.

45. For an overview, see Walker Connor, "A Nation Is a Nation, Is a State, Is an Ethnic Group, Is a . . .," in *Nationalism*, ed. John Hutchinson and Anthony D. Smith (New York: Oxford University Press, 1996), 36-46.

46. Keating, *Nations against the State*, 1.

47. Will Kymlicka and Christine Straehle, "Cosmopolitanism, Nation-States, and Minority Nationalism: A Critical Review of Recent Literature," *European Journal of Philosophy* 7, no. 1 (1999), 66.

48. Keating, *Nations against the State*, 18.

49. Keating, "Europe, the State," Keating, *Nations against the State*; Michael Watson, ed., *Contemporary Minority Nationalism* (London; New York: Routledge, 1990).

50. Keating, "Europe, the State"; Keating, *Nations against the State*; Watson, *Contemporary Minority Nationalism.*

51. Will Kymlicka, "Justice and Security in the Accommodation of Minority Nationalism," in *Ethnicity, Nationalism, and Minority Rights*, ed. Stephen May, Tariq Modood, and Judith Squires (New York: Cambridge University Press, 2004), 144-75.

52. Keating, *Nations against the State*; Keating, *The New Regionalism*; Lynch, *Minority Nationalism*; Witt, "The Utility of Regionalism."

53. Liah Greenfeld, *Nationalism: Five Roads to Modernity* (Cambridge, MA: Harvard University Press, 1992); Keating, *Nations against the State*; Anthony D. Smith, *National Identity* (London: Penguin Books, 1991).

54. Rogers Brubaker, *Ethnicity without Groups* (Cambridge: Harvard University Press, 2004); Keating, *Nations against the State*; Saul Newman, "Nationalism in Postindustrial Societies: Why States Still Matter," *Comparative Politics* 33, no. 1 (2000): 21-41.

55. Keating, *Nations against the State*, 53.

56. McGarry, Keating, and Moore, "Introduction: European Integration," 7.

57. Keating, *The New Regionalism.*

58. Udo Bullmann, "Germany: Federalism under Strain," in *Subnational Democracy in the European Union: Challenges and Opportunities*, ed. John Loughlin (New York: Oxford University Press, 2001), 83-116; Greer, *Territory, Democracy*; Michael Keating and John P. Loughlin, *The Political Economy of Regionalism* (London: Frank Cass, 1997); Loughlin, "The Regional Question."

59. Keating and Loughlin, *The Political Economy of Regionalism*, 4.

60. Angela K. Bourne, "Introduction: The Domestic Politics of Regionalism and European Integration," *Perspectives of European Politics and Society* 4, no. 3 (2003): 347-62; Hooghe, "Subnational Mobilisation"; Gary Marks et al., "Competencies, Cracks, and Conflicts: Regional Mobilization in the European Union," *Comparative Political Studies* 29, no. 2 (1996): 164-92; Hendrik Vos, Tine Boucké, and Carl Devos, "The Condition Sine Qua Non of the Added Value of Regions in the EU: Upper-Level Representation as the Fundamental Precondition," *Journal of European Integration* 24, no. 3 (2002): 201-18.

61. Udo Bullmann, "The Politics of the Third Level," in *The Regional Dimension of the European Union. Towards a Third Level in Europe?* ed. Charlie Jeffery (Portland, OR: Frank Cass, 1997), 3-19; Hooghe, "Subnational Mobilisation"; Keating, "Europe, the State"; Keating, "Europeanism and Regionalism"; Gary Marks, "Structural Policy in the European Com-

munity," in *Europolitics, Institutions and Policymaking in the 'New' European Community*, ed. Alberta Sbragia (Washington, DC: The Brookings Institution, 1992), 191-224.

62. Michael Keating, "Regions and the Convention on the Future of Europe," in *Mobilizing Politics and Society? The EU Convention's Impact on Southern Europe*, ed. Sonia Lucarelli and Claudio M. Radaelli (New York: Routledge, 2005), 192-207.

63. Hooghe, "Subnational Mobilisation."

64. Committee of the Regions of the European Union, "Associations/Bureaux"; Mamadouh, "The Regions in Brussels."

65. Ansi Paasi, "The Institutionalization of Regions: A Theoretical Framework for Understanding the Emergence of Regions and the Constitution of Regional Identity," *Fennia* 164, no. 1 (1986): 121.

66. Christiansen, "Reconstructing European Space"; Schmitt-Egner, "The Concept of 'Region.'"

67. Gary Marks, Liesbet Hooghe, and Kermit Blank, "European Integration from the 1980s: State Centric v. Multi-Level Governance," *Journal of Common Market Studies* 34, no. 3 (1996), 342.

68. Beate Kohler-Koch, "Catching up with Change: The Transformation of Governance in the European Union," *Journal of European Public Policy* 3, no. 3 (1996): 359-80.

69. Iain Deas and Alex Lord, "From a New Regionalism to an Unusual Regionalism? The Emergence of Non-Standard Regional Spaces and Lessons for the Territorial Reorganisation of the State," *Urban Studies* 43, no. 10 (2006): 1847-77.

70. Deas and Lord, "From a New Regionalism," 1865.

71. Deas and Lord, "From a New Regionalism," 1856.

72. Deas and Lord, "From a New Regionalism."

73. Keating, *Nations against the State*; Ostergren, "Concepts of Region"; Schmitt-Egner, "The Concept of 'Region.'"

74. Christiansen, "Reconstructing European Space," 66.

75. Loughlin, "The Regional Question."

76. Karl W. Deutsch, *Nationalism and Social Communication: An Enquiry into the Foundations of Nationality*, 2nd ed. (Cambridge, MA: MIT Press, 1966); Michael Hechter, *Internal Colonialism: The Celtic Fringe in British National Development, 1536-1966* (London: Routledge & Kegan Paul, 1975); Tom Nairn, *The Break-up of Britain: Crisis and Neo-Nationalism* (London: NLB, 1977); Rokkan and Urwin, *Economy, Territory.*

77. Loughlin, "The Regional Question."

78. McGarry, Keating, and Moore, "Introduction: European Integration," 3.

79. Ralph Dahrendorf, "Preserving Prosperity," *New Statesman and Society* 13, no. 29 (1995); 36-40; Eric J. Hobsbawm, *Nations and Nationalism since 1780: Programme, Myth, Reality* (New York: Cambridge University Press, 1990); Keating, "Europeanism and Regionalism."

80. Anthony H. Birch, "Minority Nationalist Movements and Theories of Political Integration," *World Politics* 30, no. 3 (1978), 325-44; Keating, *Nations against the State.*

81. Birch, "Minority Nationalist Movements."

82. Keating, "Europeanism and Regionalism."

83. Dylan Griffiths, *Thatcherism and Territorial Politics: A Welsh Case Study* (Aldershot: Avebury, 1996).

84. Griffiths, *Thatcherism and Territorial Politics*, Keating, *Nations against the State.*

85. Liesbet Hooghe, "Nationalist Movements and Social Factors: A Theoretical Perspective," in *Social Origins of Nationalist Movements: The Contemporary West European Experience*, ed. John Coakley (London: Sage, 1992), 21-44.

86. Griffiths, *Thatcherism and Territorial Politics*.

87. Deutsch, *Nationalism and Social Communication*.

88. Deutsch, *Nationalism and Social Communication*.

89. Rokkan and Urwin, *Economy, Territory*, 2.

90. Rokkan and Urwin, *Economy, Territory*.

91. Rokkan and Urwin, *Economy, Territory*, 118.

92. Nairn, *The Break-up of Britain*.

93. Hechter, *Internal Colonialism*.

94. Hechter, *Internal Colonialism*, 310.

95. John Coakley, "The Social Origins of Nationalist Movements and Explanations of Nationalism: A Review," in *The Social Origins of Nationalist Movements: The Contemporary West European Experience*, ed. John Coakley (London: Sage, 1992), 1-20; Hechter, *Internal Colonialism*.

96. François Nielsen, "Toward a Theory of Ethnic Solidarity in Modern Societies," *American Sociological Review* 50 (1985): 133-49; Susan Olzak, "Contemporary Ethnic Mobilization," *Annual Review of Sociology* 9 (1983): 355-74; Charles Tilly, *From Mobilization to Revolution* (Reading: Addison-Wesley, 1978).

97. Ronald Inglehart, *The Silent Revolution* (Princeton, NJ: Princeton University Press, 1977), 13.

98. Vernon Bogdanor, *Devolution* (Oxford: Oxford University Press, 1979).

99. Michael Keating, "Is There a Regional Level of Government in Europe?" in *Regions in Europe*, ed. Patrick Le Gales and Christian Lequesne (New York: Routledge, 1998), 11-29; Keating, *The New Regionalism*; Loughlin, "The Regional Question," Ostergren, "Concepts of Region."

100. Keating, "Is There a Regional Level"; Keating, *The New Regionalism*; Loughlin, "The Regional Question"; Ostergren, "Concepts of Region."

101. Maurice Dumhamel, *Le federalisme international et la reveil des nationalités* (Rennes: Editions du Parti Autonomiste Breton, 1928); Yann Fouere, *L'Europe aux cent drapeux* (Paris: Presse d'Europe, 1968); Lynch, "Organising for a Europe."

102. Marks et al., "Competencies, Cracks, and Conflicts."

103. Ernst Haas, *The Uniting of Europe* (Stanford, CA: Stanford University Press, 1958); Michael Keating, "Minority Nationalism and the State: The European Case," in *Contemporary Minority Nationalism*, ed. Michael Watson (New York: Routledge, 1990), 174-94; Keating, *The New Regionalism*; Keating and Hooghe, "Bypassing the Nation-State?"

104. Hooghe, "Subnational Mobilisation."

105. Charlie Jeffery, *The Regional Dimension of the European Union: Towards a Third Level in Europe?* (London; Portland, OR: Frank Cass, 1997); Charlie Jeffery, "Sub-National Mobilization and European Integration: Does It Make Any Difference?," *Journal of Common Market Studies* 38, no. 1 (2000): 1-23, Keating, "Regions and the Convention"; Marks, Hooghe, and Blank, "European Integration"; Marks et al., "Competencies, Cracks, and Conflicts."

106. Marks et al., "Competencies, Cracks, and Conflicts," 169.

107. Marks et al., "Competencies, Cracks, and Conflicts."

108. Marks et al., "Competencies, Cracks, and Conflicts."

109. Marks et al., "Competencies, Cracks, and Conflicts."

110. Greer, *Territory, Democracy*.

111. Jeffery, "Sub-National Mobilization and European Integration."

112. Keating, "Europeanism and Regionalism," 1.

113. Keating, "Is There a Regional Level," 15.

114. William M. Downs, "Regionalism in the European Union: Key Concepts and Project Overview," *Journal of European Integration* 24, no. 3 (2002): 171-77; Keating, "Europeanism and Regionalism," Keating, "Minority Nationalism and the State"; Keating and Hooghe, "Bypassing the Nation-State?"; Stephen Weatherill, "The Challenge of the Regional Dimension in the European Union," in *The Role of Regions and Sub-National Actors in Europe*, ed. Stephen Weatherill and Ulf Bernitz (Portland, OR: Hart Publishing, 2005), 1-31.

115. Haas, *The Uniting of Europe*, Keating, "Europeanism and Regionalism."

116. Keating, *The New Regionalism*, 164.

117. Downs, "Regionalism in the European Union," Frederik Fleurke and Rolf Willemse, "The European Union and the Autonomy of Sub-National Authorities: Towards an Analysis of Constraints and Opportunities in Sub-National Decision-Making," *Regional & Federal Studies* 16, no. 1 (2006): 83-98; Anna M. Olsson, "Regional Minority Nationalist Attitudes Towards European Integration," in *Nationalism and European Integration*, ed. I. P. Karolewski and A. M. Suszycki (London: Continuum, 2007), 52-66; Roland Sturm and Juergen Dieringer, "The Europeanization of Regions in Eastern and Western Europe: Theoretical Perspectives," *Regional & Federal Studies* 15, no. 3 (2005): 279-94.

118. Keating, *The New Regionalism*, 163.

119. Hooghe, "Subnational Mobilisation"; Jeffery, "Sub-National Mobilization and European Integration"; Marks et al., "Competencies, Cracks, and Conflicts"; Vos, Boucké, and Devos, "The Condition Sine Qua Non."

120. Jeffery, "Sub-National Mobilization and European Integration."

121. Hooghe, "Subnational Mobilisation," 178.

122. Hooghe, "Subnational Mobilisation," 178.

123. Hooghe, "Subnational Mobilisation," 192.

124. Marks et al., "Competencies, Cracks, and Conflicts," 63.

125. David Arter, "Regionalization in the European Peripheries: The Cases of Northern Norway and Finnish Lapland," *Regional & Federal Studies* 11, no. 2 (2001): 94-114.

126. Guibernau, *Nations without States*; Keating, "Is There a Regional Level"; Smouts, "The Region."

127. Smouts, "The Region."

128. Smouts, "The Region," 37.

129. Guibernau, *Nations without States*, Marks et al., "Competencies, Cracks, and Conflicts."

130. Guibernau, *Nations without States*.

131. Keating, "Europeanism and Regionalism," 7.

132. Kenichi Ohmae, *The End of the Nation State; the Rise of Regional Economies* (New York: Free Press, 1995).

133. Ohmae, *The End of the Nation State*, 89.

134. Guibernau, *Nations without States*; Michael Keating, "European Integration and the Nationalities Question," *Politics & Society* 32, no. 3 (2004): 367-88.

135. Keating, "Europeanism and Regionalism," 3.

136. Michael Keating, "The Political Economy of Regionalism," in *The Political Economy of Regionalism*, ed. Michael Keating and John Loughlin (Portland, OR: Frank Cass, 1997), 25.

137. Keating, *Nations against the State*; Michael Keating and John McGarry, *Minority Nationalism and the Changing International Order* (Oxford; New York: Oxford University Press, 2001).

138. Keating and McGarry, *Minority Nationalism and the Changing*, 8.

139. Sidney Tarrow, *Power in Movement: Social Movements, Collective Action, and Politics* (New York: Cambridge University Press, 1994); Tilly, *From Mobilization to Revolution*.

140. Bullmann, "The Politics of the Third Level"; Fleurke and Willemse, "The European Union and the Autonomy"; Keating, "Is There a Regional Level," Gary Marks and Doug McAdam, "Social Movements and the Changing Structure of Political Opportunity in the European Union," in *Governance in the European Union*, ed. Gary Marks, et al. (London: Sage, 1996), 95-120; Doug McAdam, "Conceptual Origins, Current Problems, and Future Directions," in *Comparative Perspectives on Social Movements—Political Opportunities, Mobilizing Structures, and Cultural Framings*, ed. Doug McAdam, John D. McCarthy, and Mayer N. Zald (New York: Cambridge University Press, 1996), 1-26; Tilly, *From Mobilization to Revolution*.

141. Hooghe, "Nationalist Movements"; Marks and McAdam, "Social Movements and the Changing Structure"; Tarrow, *Power in Movement*.

142. Guibernau, *Nations without States*; Hooghe, "Nationalist Movements"; Marks and McAdam, "Social Movements and the Changing Structure."

143. Guibernau, *Nations without States*; Hooghe, "Nationalist Movements"; Marks and McAdam, "Social Movements and the Changing Structure"; John McGarry and Michael Keating, *European Integration and the Nationalities Question* (London: Routledge, 2006).

144. James D. Fearon and David D. Laitin, "Violence and the Social Construction of Ethnic Identity," *International Organization* 54, no. 4 (2000): 845-77; Henry Hale, "Explaining Ethnicity," *Comparative Political Studies* 37, no. 4 (2004): 458-85.

145. Daniel Patrick Moynihan, *Pandaemonium: Ethnicity in International Politics* (Oxford: Oxford University Press, 1993).

146. Paul Brass, "Elite Competition and the Origins of Ethnic Nationalism," in *Nationalism in Europe: Past and Present*, ed. Justo G. Beramendi, Ramón Máiz, and Xosé M. Núñez (Santiago de Compostela: University of Santiago de Compostela, 1994), 111-26.

147. Hale, "Explaining Ethnicity."

148. Benedict Anderson, *Imagined Communities: Reflections on the Origin and Spread of Nationalism* (London: Verso, 1983).

149. Keating, *The New Regionalism*, 87.

150. Keating, *The New Regionalism*, 87-88.

151. Lynch, *Minority Nationalism*, 16.

152. Keating and McGarry, *Minority Nationalism and the Changing*, 4.

153. Lynch, "Organising for a Europe"; Carolyn Moore, "A Europe of the Regions vs. The Regions in Europe: Reflections on Regional Engagement in Brussels" (paper presented at the European Union Studies Association Biennial Conference, Montreal, Canada, May 2007).

154. Loughlin, "The Regional Question."

155. Thomas Christiansen, "Second Thoughts on Europe's 'Third Level': The European Union's Committee of the Regions," *Publius* 26, no. 1 (1996): 93-116; Hooghe, "Subnational Mobilisation."

156. Keating, "Regions and the Convention," 193.

157. Neil MacCormick, "The European Constitutional Convention and the Stateless Nations," *International Relations* 18, no. 3 (2004), 342.

158. Committee of the Regions of the European Union, "Associations/Bureaux"; Mamadouh, "The Regions in Brussels"; Moore, "A Europe of the Regions."

Part III
Old Nationalism in Western Europe?

Chapter 7
"Back to the Future" with Vlaams Belang? Flemish Nationalism as a Modernizing Project in a Post-Modern European Union

Janet Laible

Events of the past two decades suggest that nationalism as a mode of political mobilization hardly seems to be in retreat in Europe and Eurasia. The creation of nearly two dozen newly independent states, the on-going—and at times violent—manifestations of separatism in numerous states, including the established capitalist democracies of Western Europe, and the prevalence of extremist right-wing sentiment among numerous European electorates testify to the apparent attractiveness of nationalist ideology in a variety of guises and to its continuing salience in shaping political behavior. At the close of the twentieth century, Rogers Brubaker noted that it was tempting to conclude that the "future displayed recently by Europe to the world looks distressingly like the past," and that in the former Communist world in particular, European history seemed to be "moving *back* to the nation-state."[1]

Yet regardless of the tenacity (or resurgence) of nationalism in contemporary Europe, a range of current literatures expresses doubt that European nationalist movements can be characterized in the same terms as those located at previous points in history. In these perspectives, social and economic developments in the European context—specifically, the twin forces of globalization and European integration—have subverted traditional understandings and possibilities of nationalism as a political project, by undermining the validity of the modern or Weberian state as the goal of nationalist mobilization and by creating a new post-modern European space in which the congruence of territory, identity, citizenship, and political power is increasingly questioned. Drawing on both liberal and Marxist intellectual traditions, these skeptical arguments challenge the relevance of political mobilization dedicated to securing statehood and territorial sovereignty for national, minority, or ethnic communities, suggesting that the possibilities for nationalist political expression in modern Europe have shifted dramatically from those available to nationalists in the past.

If these arguments are valid, what are the consequences for nationalist movements that continue to seek statehood? Can claims to territorial sovereignty based on "national" authority be accommodated in the contemporary European order, and what does this suggest about the extent to which nationalists in Europe assert different claims than did nationalisms of previous eras? In this paper, I focus on the case of the Flemish separatist party Vlaams Belang[2] to explore the political logic of a party that seeks to create an independent state in Flanders, in a historical era and geographical context that are argued to militate against the possibility of such an outcome. The party has attracted considerable attention because of its advocacy of an extreme right-wing ideology, with one academic observer arguing that the party's vision of Flemish society resembles the organic solidarism embraced by proto-fascist Flemish movements of the 1930s.[3] However, the core of the party platform since its creation in 1979 has been a dedication to Flemish statehood, and constitutional issues remain central to party politics: independence for Flanders remains the top priority in party election manifestoes, framing the rest of the party agenda.[4] For the past decade and a half, Vlaams Belang has denounced what it refers to as "Maastricht-Europe," by which it means an EU with increasingly supranational institutions and deepening regulatory functions. Instead, party officials articulate a vision of the EU in which Flanders as an ethnic state would interact with sovereign equals in a minimal confederation to sustain commitments to a common market, to shared "European" cultural norms, and to an intergovernmental security partnership.

This paper is a descriptive work that maps the parameters of a political conflict. I explore two conflicting logics about sovereignty and political space, embodied in the practices of the European Union and the arguments of Vlaams Belang as two poles representing different ideologies about how power should be exercised over territory. I argue that at the heart of the Vlaams Belang political agenda is the desire to reappropriate space and sovereignty for a Flemish nation-state in an effort that recalls the modernizing ideals of earlier nationalists, a political vision that cannot be reconciled with the post-modern articulations of European integration. To assess the conflict between a "modernizing" Vlaams Belang and a purportedly post-modern EU, I focus on problems of political territory for Vlaams Belang, in particular on the party's understandings of EU citizenship and the freedom of movement accorded as a fundamental freedom of the EU. While right-wing ideology may underpin the party's commitment to modernity, the key points of contention between the party and the terrain of European integration lie not in the policy solutions popularly linked to the extreme right, for example, in the areas of immigration, crime, and social policy, but in the deeper commitment of the party to modernist understandings of territorial authority, from which many of its policy positions derive.

I begin by describing the characteristics of what some commentators have called the post-modern architecture of the European Union. I follow this with a brief consideration of the history and policies of Vlaams Belang, with a focus on the party's understanding of territorial authority as one that mirrors nationalist territorial agendas of earlier centuries. I then sketch the tensions between this vision and that of an integrating Europe by concentrating on the party's responses to European citizenship and to freedom of movement for EU citizens, before concluding with suggestions that the party's "back to the future" nationalist politics are unlikely to be reconcilable with even the minimalist, intergovernmental vision of the EU espoused by Vlaams Belang members.

The Post-Modern European Polity and the Problem of Separatist Politics

The existence and electoral success of avowedly separatist parties in a number of EU member states, including the United Kingdom, Belgium and Spain, imply that party activists as well as some European voting publics remain convinced of the value of creating new independent national states. Yet literature on European integration suggests that the fundamental task of separatist nationalism—the assertion of sovereign control over territory with the achievement of independent statehood—is increasingly an impossibility, as the authority of states is diffused to European, sub-state, and transnational political actors. While states remain "indispensable structures" for negotiating power and identity in Europe, the territoriality of the state "becomes more and more abstract"[5] and therefore the project of separatism in the contemporary era becomes less viable.

While the vocabulary of post-modernity is controversial, I use it here to evoke an understanding of statehood in the European Union that appears radically different than the ideology and practice of territorial authority under the so-called modern, Westphalian, or Weberian state. The modern state evokes a historically unique set of claims to territorial sovereignty, including claims to final authority with no superior jurisdiction and to "exclusive authority over a fixed territorial space."[6] Despite on-going debates about the degree and quality of sovereignty that EU member states retain, as early as the 1960s the adjudication of the Treaty of Rome by the European Court of Justice and the growing authority of supranational[7] institutions were pointing to the capacity of European actors and decision-making processes to undermine the ideology and the empirical manifestations of the modern state.[8] With the creation of the single market in the 1980s, a consensus was emerging that the supranational authority of European institutions was imposing a unique set of constraints on the actions of purportedly sovereign states. The Single European

Market was established with the intention of promoting the "four freedoms" across the European Community—the free movement of goods, services, capital, and people—which by themselves implied a radical reconceptualization of authority over territory. By removing barriers to the movement of workers across the Community and introducing a new dimension of European governance in the areas of economic citizenship and immigration, economic integration challenged a long-asserted instrument of the protection of state territorial sovereignty, the ability of states to regulate population flows across their respective borders.[9]

The "multi-level governance" approach to European integration also offers a critical perspective on the integrity of state territory in the EU, arguing that central state actors have surrendered their monopoly on influencing the content of European policy, and thus on claims of ultimate jurisdiction over their respective territories. The foregrounding in particular of regional, or substate, actors in the EU since the Single European Act of 1987 has contributed to an attack "from below" on the traditional central state monopolization of access to the international arena and has challenged domestic territorial control by the state. Regional actors have developed their capacity as lobbyists in Brussels in order to influence policy outcomes; they have engaged European Commission officials directly to build and implement regional development funding priorities; and they have been legally empowered by the Maastricht Treaty to play a formal role in EU legislation in the consultative Committee of the Regions and to stand in, when agreed by their respective governments, for national ministers in votes of the Council of Ministers. Thus states share authority over the policies that are implemented on their territories and populations with European, regional and local actors, a transformation that directly challenges the traditional role of central state governments as gatekeepers between domestic interests and the European domain of politics.[10]

While these arguments do not imply the end of the states as privileged and dominant actors in the EU, this reconceptualization of state power in the EU offers a view of sovereignty as increasingly diffuse and ambiguous in its territorial locus. Efforts to reevaluate the qualities of statehood in the European Union have led some theorists to use the term *post-modern* to characterize the nature of political authority over territory in the EU. In contrast to the Weberian modern state ideal-type, with its congruence of hierarchical authority and territory, a post-modern state or polity "corresponds to emerging forms of governance that are fractured, decentered and often lacking in clear spatial (geographical) as well as functional (issue area) lines of authority."[11] Although globalization has stimulated the production of these forms of governance everywhere, the crumbling of modern state forms and the emergence of post-modern forms have been most marked under the conditions of European integration, with the EU representing the site where the "unbundling of territory" to dispersed political authorities, the "rearticulation of international space," and the "decoupling" of territorial boundaries and domestic political authority has gone the furthest.[12] In this perspective, the relationship between territory and power in the contemporary EU is as much post-modern as "pre-modern": it hints at similarities with medieval Europe, in which individuals were subject to multiple and often overlapping and non-territorially based forms of authority.[13]

Furthermore, such "unbundlings" and "decouplings" are reflected not only in the distribution of policy-making capacities in Europe but in the new spatial possibilities for a range of social and economic transactions. Although the literature cannot be explored in detail here, scholarship on the impact of European integration—and globalization—on capital has asserted the extent to which capitalism has helped to produce, and has benefited from, these new articulations of power and space.[14] Yet capital is not uniquely empowered by European integration (or globalization). The post-modernity of the European polity is also suggested by the creation of a European political space in which the practices of citizenship can occur outside the boundaries of the member states. The multi-level governance perspective outlined above indicates some dimensions of this space (i.e., the production of new relationships among local, regional, and other sub-state political actors and European institutions) that challenge sovereign state control over territory. However, a new European political space has also been created legally: European integration, treaties, and secondary legislation have restructured long-assumed linkages between citizenship and statehood. European citizenship as established by the Treaty on European Union remains contingent upon legal citizenship granted by a member state, but it has also been "reterritorialized," to allow EU citizens the right to live and work in any member state, and to vote in local and European elections, regardless of their country of origin.[15] Contrasting this type of citizenship with that once understood as the norm in modern states, where territorial sovereignty was coterminous with citizenship rights and nationality, and where the internal sovereignty of states implied sole authority to grant citizenship and its concomitant rights, Riva Kastoryano has argued, "the practice of [European] citizenship gives rise to a multiplicity of interests as well as multiple kinds of belonging and allegiance within the European framework, detached from an entity that is exclusively national and territorial, separating therefore citizenship from nationality."[16]

The transformation of state sovereignty in the EU and the dispersion of political authority away from the domain of the central state pose challenges to the basic motivations of separatists. Many separatist movements base their claims for independence on arguments that their "national" constituents have suffered from inappropriate economic, social, or cultural policies executed by unresponsive central state governments, and that only governance by co-nationals will restore the dignity and authority of the nation; separate statehood thus will restore control over relevant policy jurisdictions to the aggrieved nation. Ernest Gellner's influential formulation of nationalism as a political principle that "holds that the political and national unit should be congruent" indicated that the relevant political unit of concern was the modern state: building on Max Weber's definition of the state ("that agency within society which possesses the monopoly of legitimate violence"), Gellner added that "the state is the specialization and concentration of order maintenance." The modern state emerges as the crux of the nationalist principle because it establishes clear territorial boundaries; Gellner noted, "If there is no state, one obviously cannot ask whether or not its boundaries are congruent with the limits of nations."[17]

Yet European integration has denuded states of a variety of policy jurisdictions that nationalists claim ought to be in the hands of their co-nationals, and blurs the relationship between political authority and territorial boundaries. Some observers conclude that European integration therefore has fundamentally altered the strategic calculations of separatists and that both the ability of nationalists to achieve "independence" and the very desires of nationalists to do so have been undermined.[18] The new European environment offers possibilities for the expression of national identity that do not require the institutional framework of statehood, including possibilities for the mobilization of "national" communities with national claims around existing regional (substate) territories, obviating the need for independent statehood.[19]

More radical materialist interpretations of nationalism also indicate that the era of "true" nationalism has passed from the historical stage, regardless of the claims of purported nationalists themselves. Eric Hobsbawm acknowledged the likely perpetuation of nationality based politics, but argued that any political party that sought to create a state in the European Union was "in practice abandoning the classical aim of such movements, which is to establish independent or sovereign states."[20] Nor could any such nationalisms be understood to possess the socially progressive motives and goals as nationalisms of an earlier era, i.e., "extend[ing] the scale of human social, political and cultural units," because contemporary European separatisms instead sought to limit the scale of human communities. Instead, self-identified nationalist movements in the industrialized west are usually bourgeois regional interests that draw on the rhetoric and imagery of nationalism to legitimize themselves.[21]

With contemporary European transformations of political space and power, the goal that once seemed to define the separatist project becomes suspect. Separatism itself becomes increasingly difficult to conceptualize in a post-modern European polity, with its practices of multi-level governance and non-territorially constructed understandings of citizenship. Furthermore, viewing independent statehood as a means to secure the authority to address specific policy goals seems equally archaic: the "authority" achieved with independence will immediately be subject to contestation by European, substate, and transnational political actors.

Vlaams Belang and Claims for Modern Statehood

Even as the post-modern tendencies of the European polity grow increasingly pronounced, European Union member states continue to incubate separatist movements that demand "modern" states, movements that assert claims for sovereign authority over bounded territories and national populations. Vlaams Belang seeks an independent Flemish state that appears to epitomize modern statehood; although the party platform envisions an independent Flanders located in the European Union, the party rejects what it refers to as a "Maastricht-Europe" with supranational tendencies, instead advocating a European Union that is confederal and based on intergovernmental cooperation among sovereign states.

In the post-war period, Flemish nationalism initially emerged as a movement containing a variety of potentially, and ultimately overtly, conflicting tendencies, in particular over defining the contours of the Flemish nation and over the institutional structures that would best protect its interests. The Volksunie (People's Union) was founded in 1954 to advance the political goals of the Flemish Movement, which had been working since the nineteenth century to win legal recognition and support for the Dutch language in Belgium. Language rights were at the core of the Volksunie agenda, but by the 1960s its platform came to focus on federalism and on social and economic development for Flanders as key underpinnings for the health of the language community. In 1978, the party was invited to participate in drafting proposals for the first round of significant devolution of power to the Belgian regions, but disputes emerged within the Volksunie over political compromises with French language interests, in particular over the status of Brussels and voting rights for French speakers in the Flemish periphery of the city. Outraged Flemish nationalists demanding the protection of Dutch speakers in the capital and of the 1963 linguistic border within the Belgian state defected from the Volksunie to form two new Flemish nationalist parties, the Vlaams-Nationale Partij (VNP) and the Vlaamse Volkspartij (VVP—Flemish People's Party). These joined in a coalition to compete in the 1978 elections as the Vlaams Blok, which was formally established to replace the VNP and the VVP in 1979.

Despite popular impressions of the party, the Vlaams Blok did not initially embrace a right wing agenda: it was founded to continue the struggle for radical constitutional reform (i.e., independence for Flanders) as the sole means for protecting the Flemish community, and this was the dominant theme for the party in its early years. The Blok platform did include a number of substantive policy goals that, as they became more dominant on its agenda with respect to constitutional questions, would shift it toward the far right: the party argued for respect for the family and for life "under all its forms" (that is, it opposed abortion), the expulsion of migrant workers, amnesty for Nazi collaborators, and economic liberalism.[22]

Only in the mid-1980s with the political rise of new, younger members did the party turn decisively toward the right and shift its election focus to immigration issues, a move that drove out some of its more prominent constitutional nationalists who believed that the party needed to retain its focus on independent statehood. The success of Jean-Marie Le Pen's National Front in the French communal elections of March 1983 also provided an impetus for the Blok to turn its attention to immigrant issues in Flanders. Recognizing the potential for success from campaigning on immigrant questions, Blok leaders took their long-standing interest in defining the Flemish nation along linguistic and cultural lines and turned this into a comprehensive immigration policy for Flanders. Along with its turn toward anti-immigrant policies, the Blok was embracing common themes of the extreme-right in Western Europe, calling for the defense of European culture, strong government, and opposition to Marxism, while situating its demands for Flemish independence in the context of a Europe of ethnically based states. Much of the party program is now devoted to issues other than the constitutional one: the return of immigrants and political refugees is part of a platform that also includes an emphasis on Catholic family life and values, action against crime and drugs, rejecting the Maastricht Treaty-based European Union, and an end to political corruption.

Similar to voters for many extreme-right parties, voters for Vlaams Belang/Blok are largely motivated by questions about immigration: concerns about immigration have proven more important in the party's electoral support than concerns about the economy or political corruption.[23] However, the party does draw support from a constituency that is dissatisfied with the political system by positioning itself in opposition to a purportedly corrupt political establishment, a tactic that has also underpinned the electoral success of other right-wing parties.[24] Vlaams Belang, as the party was renamed after the Belgian Supreme Court banned the Blok as a racist organization in 2004, continues to place "an independent Flanders" at the beginning of its electoral program, but its anti-immigration and anti-foreigner policies have proven important vote-winning policies and it has firmly established itself on the extreme right of the political spectrum.[25]

The general elections of 1991 represented the electoral breakthrough of the Vlaams Blok: the party won 10.3% of the Flemish vote and won 12 seats out of 122 Dutch community seats in the Belgian Chamber of Deputies, eclipsing for the first time the Volksunie (9.3%) in share of the Flemish vote (all parties in Belgium organize only on a regional, not state-wide, basis). Never again would the more politically centrist and socially progressive Volksunie come close to matching the support for the Blok at either the regional or federal level in Belgium. By the end of the twentieth century, the Vlaams Blok had claimed a place as an established party in Belgium, drawing increasing shares of votes and seats at every federal and regional election, and drawing not insubstantial public funds as an electoral organization. But in a result that shocked many Belgians, the newly reconstituted Vlaams Belang won the second largest share of the vote in the Flemish regional elections in June 2004, as well as the second largest number of seats, 32 out of 124 seats in the Flemish Parliament.[26] With the municipal elections of October 2006, Vlaams Belang's showing slipped slightly, as it polled only 20% in Flanders, compared to its share of 24% of the Flemish vote in the 2004 regional elections. However, the party remains strong enough to force other parties in many municipalities, including Antwerp, into awkward coalitions (what are locally described as *cordons sanitaires* against

Vlaams Belang), and in the Belgian elections of 2007, its share of the Flemish vote increased to 19.2%, its highest level ever at a federal election.

Vlaams Belang and the Ethnic State in Europe

The relationship between the Vlaams Blok, and more recently Vlaams Belang, and the integrating European polity has always defied easy description. Unlike parties of the far-right in other countries, such as the Front National of Jean-Marie Le Pen in France, or even the moderate right "Euro-skeptics" in the United Kingdom who abandoned the Conservative Party to form the UK Independence Party, Vlaams Belang has never argued in favor of leaving the European Union. Whether speaking of the current Belgian state or their proposed independent Flemish state, Vlaams Belang leaders claim that Flanders belongs at the heart of the European Union; although they reject the current form that the European Union takes, dismissively referred to as "Maastricht-Europe" in party literature, they envision a radically refashioned European polity that can accommodate their interests in an independent, ethnically Flemish state.

The idea of a Flemish ethnic state underpins Vlaams Belang's understanding of territorial authority and consequently produces the main points of tension between the party's view of sovereignty and the post-modern articulations of the European polity. The Vlaams Belang conception of the ethnic nation forms the basis of its vision of statehood. The party presents a solidaristic view of society based on ethnicity: membership in the nation is based on blood, or Flemish descent, not language (a strategy by which the party can claim that the French speakers of Brussels, if descended from Flemings, are actually Flemish), and cannot be acquired from birth in Flemish territory or by marriage.[27] The 1990 party program described *volksnationalisme* as "based on the ethnic community being a naturally occurring entity whose cultural, material, ethical and intellectual interests need to be preserved." These interests must be protected not solely by the creation of ethnic states (discussed below), but by a vanguard elite within the ethnic group.[28] The party distinguishes between the "ethnically committed" and "non-ethnically committed" Flemish: the former are the elite, with "higher moral values such as a perception of responsibility, self-sacrifice, social justice, solidarity and tolerance"; the latter, the masses, need to be shown the "right path."[29]

Yet the defense of the ethnic nation is not articulated as a form of racism by the party; instead, the ethnic community is presented as the key to human self-fulfillment. An article in the official party paper notes: "[O]utside of the group [one] can neither exist nor even grow up and live. It is natural groups like the family, the ethnic community, which in their turn, like man himself, are equal and different."[30] Within such communities, the party argues that there will be little of the conflict that plagues contemporary (multicultural) societies. Social problems such as crime and drug addiction emerge when individuals are "deracinated" from their respective cultures. Hence the problems that the party attributes to immigrants in Flanders are the fault not of immigrants themselves, but of the politicians who want them to integrate. The party does not excuse foreigners who commit crimes but notes, "The Vlaams Blok does not here reach backward toward simple racial 'explanations'. . . crimes [go] together with the cultural uprooting of which foreigners are the victim," arguing that foreigners are "alienated from their original culture."[31]

The commitment to an ethnic understanding of the *demos*, in Flanders and as a universal principle, and to ethnic self-governance, thus has clear implications for the type of polity the party aspires to create and for the type of political system the party hopes will emerge at the European level. The legitimate polity is that which is coterminous with the ethnic nation; only this way can social order be maintained and the culture of the national group be protected. It is therefore apparent that certain forms of political governance must be ruled out: federalism or other power-sharing devices by which one ethnic group would govern another, or in which ethnicity would not be the organizing principle, are unacceptable, whether at the European or at the domestic level. The proclaimed artificiality of Belgium itself, and the mixing of ethnic populations—even European ethnicities—in a single state is thus a primary focus of Vlaams Belang concern. These populations must be "unmixed" to protect each group's identity, and only with the construction of separate states in which each ethnic group governs itself will each be able to live in accordance with its particular cultural interests.[32]

Just as Belgium is artificial because it seeks to regulate the relations of different so-called peoples within a single political entity, the legitimate political order of Europe can only be one that is based on the ethnic state. For Vlaams Belang, there can be no distinction between a "Europe of the states" and a "Europe of the peoples" to achieve political justice. This vision of the basis of the EU also has implications for the structure that Europe ought to take: the party sees Europe as a "union of nations" with a common culture and history, each of which also possessed a separate identity that needed to be preserved. Thus a Europe of the Peoples would be a loose confederation involving cooperation among ethnic states that would work to resolve common problems but that would retain their respective identities.[33] The EU is, in this formulation, an arena for political cooperation among ethnic states, but it is *only* an arena. It cannot, or should not, be endowed with capabilities or autonomy that might interfere with the ability of national states to protect their respective identities. Confederation thus represents the best means of ensuring that nations can cooperate and still survive as cultural entities, and the components of this confederation must remain uniquely sovereign with regard to their respective cultural groups.

The Meanings of "Freedom of Movement" in the EU: Vlaams Belang's "Modern" Response to Post-Modern Europe

For Vlaams Belang, territorial authority must enable citizens to express the interests and values of their ethnic group, and the territory over which authority is exercised must be bounded and patrolled (metaphorically or literally) to prevent the mixing of ethnic groups: borders, space, and ethnic authority are viewed as necessarily *unambiguously* congruent. Recalling Spruyt's above-quoted understanding of the modern sovereign state, in Vlaams Belang's understanding of Europe, ethnic community leaders must claim "final authority" and be subject to no higher source of jurisdiction (i.e., from outside the ethnic community), and the political structures in which ethnic self-governance occurs must allow for "exclusive authority over fixed territorial space." Transgressions of territorial authority are therefore also understood as transgressions of the community.

However, this interpretation of sovereignty inherently conflicts with EU understandings of citizenship, including the guarantee of freedom of movement within EU member states for work or residency, and the Maastricht Treaty's introduction of an EU citizenship that explicitly recasts the relationship between citizenship rights and country of origin. The rise of immigration politics on the Vlaams Blok agenda in the 1980s and 1990s occurred in tandem with the extension of European citizenship rights, turning the question of freedom of movement within the European Union into a lightning rod for party concerns about threats to the Flemish ethnic nation and for antipathy toward European integration.

The Vlaams Blok/Belang reaction to European citizenship provisions in the Maastricht Treaty demonstrates party concerns about both Flemish mis-representation by the Belgian state in European institutions (and by what the party referred to as "non-ethnically committed Flemings" in the Belgian federal state), and the construction of a European polity in which neither ethnicity nor territory will serve as boundaries of a political community. In the aftermath of the signing of the Maastricht Treaty in 1991, party leaders blamed the creation of an ethnically destructive treaty on the failure of Flanders to have a voice in EU affairs as an independent state and on Belgian officials' inability and unwillingness to recognize Flemish interests. According to Vlaams Belang, Belgian politicians failed to protect Flemish cultural rights by agreeing to a treaty that would enable French language interests to make gains at the expense of Dutch speakers in the Dutch linguistic region. The provisions of the Maastricht Treaty necessitated amending the Treaty of the EEC; these revisions of what became the Treaty Establishing the European Community included the establishment of European Union citizenship, which would be conferred on everyone holding citizenship in an EU member state. Among the practical rights associated with EU citizenship was the right to vote and be a candidate in European Parliament and local elections anywhere in the Union, with a few caveats, regardless of one's national citizenship. This right alarmed many Flemish nationalists, who were particularly concerned that the areas of Flemish Brabant closest to Brussels would lose their Dutch-speaking character as EU citizens moving into the area would be more likely to speak French than Dutch, would seek official accommodation within the Dutch region for their French language rights (e.g., for the education of their children), and would use their voting rights to support French-speaking candidates. The Vlaams Blok denounced the Belgian leadership that had acquiesced to these electoral rights for EU citizens: along with other Flemish politicians, the Blok demanded a delay in the enactment of voting provisions that it argued clearly indicated the lack of regard that the Belgian state—and the European Union—had for Flemish identity.[34]

The situation in Flemish Brabant offered a microcosm to illustrate what Vlaams Belang feared would be the general fate of ethnic Flemish. The "struggle" between European ethnic groups, however, was only one element of the party's argument that breaking the linkages among territory, identity, and political sovereignty would prove disastrous for all ethnic groups, not only for the Flemish. Freedom of movement within the EU, in particular by non-Europeans, remains the core of party criticisms of the "unbundling" of sovereignty in the European polity. The Schengen Agreement and the elimination of passport controls among most EU member states have been a particular target of Vlaams Belang anger, and party members of the European Parliament (MEPs) have devoted considerable time in European Parliament sessions to criticisms of Schengen. Party MEPs have argued that cultural identities are endangered by European policies that either promote immigration or do not serve the goal of repatriating non-European foreigners. However party activists frame this as a problem for all ethnic or cultural groups, not just the Flemish: multiculturalism contributes to social friction, with migrants who cannot assimilate becoming "uprooted" and alienated from their respective cultures, and potentially tempted into criminal or anti-social behavior.[35] Vlaams Belang MEPs thus regard European citizenship and freedom of movement within the EU as threatening to exclusive ethnic identity and to states' capacity to regulate the boundaries of ethnic communities. In a European Parliament plenary session on European citizenship, then-president of the Vlaams Blok Karel Dillen described a healthy state as both an ethnic one and one that could control its borders and protect its citizens' social and cultural interests. In contrast, European citizenship was an "artificial laboratory fertilization" that would produce "a political, intellectual, cultural and national freak," and that would lead to a "final extinction, the destruction of all national identity, of all national characteristics. Anyone who loves and serves his people and fatherland rejects out of hand the idea of a European citizenship."[36]

The responsibility for Vlaams Belang members to stop immigration and to deport immigrants thus emerges from a belief that "ethnically committed" Flemings must defend their cultural and social identity, and that this action serves the greater moral good of native and immigrant populations: Vlaams Belang activists focus on defining their actions and beliefs as "pro-migrant" in this respect.[37] The Schengen Accord and voting rights deriving from EU citizenship thus challenge fundamental aspects of Vlaams Belang philosophy and the party's understanding of political morality, directly weakening the capacity of states to govern in a variety of areas with policy implications for culture and identity. Schengen abolished checks at most internal EU borders, allowing for increased population mixing by diverse ethnic groups with potentially dangerous social consequences, and the participation in local and European-level electoral contests by non-members of native ethnic communities threatened the ethnic identity of *all* communities affected.

Is Vlaams Belang's "Modern" Flemish State Possible?

Vlaams Belang ideology and rhetoric have changed little in the past decade: immigration politics and defense of the Flemish nation remain salient in party literature, framed by the larger project of Flemish independence. The party is in many respects an anomaly among contemporary European nationalist movements because other parties, including Catalan, Irish, and moderate Flemish nationalists, have gracefully acquiesced to the transformations of European political space, transforming themselves from independence-seeking parties to movements that seek to use regional platforms to pursue cultural, economic, and political goals. Some nationalist parties, including parties on the left of the ideological spectrum such as the Scottish National Party and Plaid Cymru in Wales, retain old arguments in favor of separate statehood or have produced new arguments for statehood in the wake of the changing European environment. But even these parties seek some accommodation with the European polity, casting themselves as committed European citizens and accepting, if not enthusiastically promoting, the increasing supranationalism of the EU.[38]

Vlaams Belang has a vision of a minimal European Union, a confederation in which modern states based on ethnic identities are the dominant political actors, and in which the transnational and supranational challenges to state sovereignty are limited or, ideally, non-existent. Regardless of how other states would or would not adapt the party's vision of the ethnic state, is there any understanding of a European "Union" or even a "community" that would accommodate this vision? Even the European Coal and Steel Community, with its limited policy scope, entrenched veto for all member states, and minimally supranational institutions, was created with recognition by its member states that other post-war coal and steel arrangements had failed in part due to a lack of supranational authority. The complexity of the contemporary European Union suggests that membership must involve some "unbundling" of sovereign state authority, if only to ensure a level playing field for citizens participating in the common market.

The Vlaams Belang view of statehood appears similar to the view that nationalists asserting independence from wobbly empires and feudal monarchs have historically espoused: Ernest Gellner would likely recognize the project of radical Flemish separatism as one that embodies his principle of nationalism, the effort to make the national and political units congruent. However—whether or not one adopts the vocabulary of post-modernity to describe the contexts created by the European Union—true "independence" may no longer be possible, given the multiple challenges to territorial sovereignty engendered by European, substate, and global forces. And despite Vlaams Belang's adoption of a political program that echoes the agendas of separatists of an earlier era, the party's choice of situating an independent Flanders in an integrating Europe does suggest that its vision is not simply an attempt to go "back to the future" with sovereign statehood. Party rhetoric emphasizes territorial sovereignty for the ethnic Flemish community, but party strategy admits to the value of a collective European approach to defending Flemish values and interests: the Vlaams Belang constitutional program thus possesses an element of internal contradiction that situates it neither fully in the "past" of nationalism nor in the pro-integrationist "present" of many other Western European nationalisms. Perhaps this contradiction offers an opportunity for those who oppose the extreme right to call attention to the ultimate impossibility of the Vlaams Belang's vision of constructing a sovereign ethno-national Flemish state in modern Europe. Or perhaps the main task of Vlaams Belang, if it wishes to be successful, is therefore not simply to win independence for Flanders, but to recast popular understandings of what the EU itself should look like.

Notes

1. Rogers Brubaker, *Nationalism Reframed: Nationhood and the National Question in the New Europe* (Cambridge: Cambridge University Press, 1996), 2.

2. Formerly known as the Vlaams Blok, Vlaams Belang (Flemish Interest) emerged in 2004 after the Blok was officially banned in Belgium.

3. Marc Swyngedouw, "The Extreme Right in Belgium: Of a Non-existent Front National and an Omnipresent Vlaams Blok," in *The New Politics of the Right*, ed. Hans-Georg Betz and Stefan Immerfall (New York: St. Martin's Press, 1998), 59-76.

4. See Vlaams Belang, *Toekomstplan voor Vlaanderen: Verkiezingsprogramma 10 juni 2007* (Brussels: Vlaams Belang, 2007).

5. Riva Kastoryano, "Europe: Space, Territory and Identity," in *European Responses to Globalization: Resistance, Adaptation and Alternatives*, ed. Janet Laible and Henri J. Barkey (Amsterdam: Elsevier JAI Press, 2006), 103.

6. Hendrik Spruyt, *The Sovereign State and Its Competitors* (Princeton: Princeton University Press, 1994), 34. The modern or Westphalian state also represents one of three "forms of state" or "conceptually possible expressions of political authority organized at the national and transnational levels" described by James Caporaso: an idealized model, its properties include political institutions with an internal monopoly of legitimate violence. Caporaso emphasizes that different state forms should be thought of as embedded in particular historical and geographical contexts, not "reified and thought of as eternal fixtures of politics." James A. Caporaso, "The European Union and Forms of State: Westphalian, Regulatory or Post Modern?" *Journal of Common Market Studies* 34, no. 1 (1996): 31, 35.

7. Supranationalism implies autonomous political authority above the state, "with powers of coercion that are independent of the state." John McCormick, *Understanding the European Union* (New York: Palgrave Macmillan, 2005), 5.

8. Standard case law in this area includes: *Van Gend en Loos v. Nederlandse Administratie der Belastingen* (case 26/62 [1963]); *Costa v. ENEL* (case 6/64 [1964]); and later cases including *Simmenthal v. Commission* (case 92/78 [1978]). For discussion see Neill Nugent, *The Government and Politics of the European Union* (Durham, NC: Duke University Press, 2003).

9. Saskia Sassen, *Losing Control? Sovereignty in an Age of Globalization* (New York: Columbia University Press, 1995).

10. See Sonia Mazey and Jeremy Richardson, eds., *Lobbying in the European Community* (Oxford: Oxford University Press, 1993); Harvey Armstrong, "The Role and Evolution of European Community Regional Policy," in *The European Union and the Regions*, ed. Barry Jones and Michael Keating (Oxford: Clarendon Press, 1995), 23-62; and Gary Marks, Liesbet Hooghe, and Kermit Blank, "European Integration From the 1980s: State-Centric versus Multi-level Governance," *Journal of Common Market Studies* 19, no. 2 (1996), 249-78.

11. Caporaso, "Forms of State," 35.

12. See John Gerard Ruggie, "Territoriality and Beyond: Problematizing Modernity in International Relations," *International Organization* 47, no. 1 (1993): 139-74; and James Caporaso, "Changes in the Westphalian Order: Territory, Public Authority and Sovereignty," *International Studies Review* 2, no. 2 (2000): 1-28.

13. See Spruyt, *The Sovereign State*.

14. Caporaso argues that instead of viewing the Single Market as a mechanism by which capital has escaped the state, we should understand that "the state has created new transnational spaces for capital" in the EU; Caporaso, "Forms of State," 47. This perspective echoes Marxist proposals that late capitalism exists not in the bounded spaces of the territorial state but in a postmodern "hyperspace." See the discussion in Ruggie, "Territoriality and Beyond," 146.

15. The situation of the twelve most recently admitted member states thus represents an anomaly: the terms of accession allow each member of the EU-15 to impose restrictions on the freedom of movement (including residency and work) for citizens of member states admitted in 2004 until 2011 (although several of the EU-15 states have opted not to do so), with additional restrictions on Bulgarian and Romanian citizens.

16. Kastoryano, "Europe: Space, Territory and Identity," 99.

17. Ernest Gellner, *Nations and Nationalism* (Ithaca: Cornell University Press, 1983), 1-5.

18. See Derek W. Urwin, *The Community of Europe: A History of European Integration Since 1945* (New York: Longman, Inc., 1991), 246; and Gary Marks and Doug McAdam, "Social Movements and the Changing Structure of Political Opportunity in the European Union," *West European Politics* 19, no. 2 (1996): 266.

19. See Michael Keating, *Plurinational Democracy: Stateless Nations in a Post-Sovereignty Era* (Oxford: Oxford University Press, 2001).

20. Eric Hobsbawm, *Nations and Nationalism Since 1780* (Cambridge: Cambridge University Press, 1992), 185.

21. Eric Hobsbawm, "Ethnicity and Nationalism in Europe Today," in *Mapping the Nation*, ed. Gopal Balakrishnan (London: Verso, 1996), 257; and Hobsbawm, *Nations and Nationalism Since 1780*, 178.

22. Serge Govaert, "Flanders' Radical Nationalism: How and Why the Vlaams Blok Ascended," *New Community* 21, no. 4 (1996): 538.

23. See Elisabeth Ivarsflaten, "What Unites Right-Wing Populists in Western Europe? Re-examining Grievance Mobilization Models in Seven Successful Cases," *Comparative Political Studies* 41, no. 1 (January 2008): 3-23.

24. An analysis of the 1995 Belgian federal elections concluded that anti-immigrant attitudes and regionalism distinguished Vlaams Blok voters from those of the other main Flemish parties, but that Vlaams Blok voters were also more dissatisfied with politics than were voters from these other parties. See Elisabeth Ivarsflaten, "The Populist Centre-Authoritarian

Challenge: A Revised Account of the Radical Right's Success in Western Europe," (Oxford: Nuffield College Working Paper 2002-W25, 2002). See also Terri E. Givens, *Voting Radical Right in Western Europe* (Cambridge: Cambridge University Press, 2005).

25. Elisabeth Carter includes the Vlaams Blok in a sub-category of right-wing extremist parties that she refers to as "authoritarian xenophobic parties," defined as radically xenophobic, culturist, and seeking reforms of the current political system that would result in less democracy and pluralism, and greater intervention by the state. This sub-category also includes the FPÖ of Austria, the Republikaner of Germany, and the Front National of France. See Elisabeth Carter, *The Extreme Right in Western Europe* (Manchester: Manchester University Press, 2005), 51.

26. See William Fraeys, "Les elections legislatives du 18 mai 2003," *Res Publica* 45, no. 2/3 (2003): 379-99 and <http://polling2004.Belgium.be/en/vla/seat_etop.html> (28 November 2004).

27. Some party activists do argue that migrants can integrate into Flemish culture; however others suggest that a significant foreign population will remain a threat to the Flemish ethnic group. See for example the interviews in Hans De Witte, "Extreme Right-wing Activism in the Flemish Part of Belgium: Manifestation of Racism or Nationalism?" in *Extreme Right Activists in Europe: Through the Magnifying Glass*, ed. Bert Klandermans and Nonna Mayer (London: Routledge, 2006), 127-50.

28. See Cas Mudde, *The Ideology of the Extreme Right* (Manchester: Manchester University Press, 2000), 96.

29. Swyngedouw, "The Extreme Right in Belgium," 63.

30. *Vlaams Blok* 7/83, quoted in Cas Mudde, *The Ideology of the Extreme Right*, 99.

31. Vlaams Blok, *Nu afrekenen! Verkiezingsprogramma 1995* (Brussels: Vlaams Blok, 1995), 69.

32. See De Witte, "Extreme Right-wing Activism"; and Janet Laible, *Separatism and Sovereignty in the New Europe: Party Politics and the Meanings of Statehood in a Supranational Context* (New York: Palgrave Macmillan, 2008).

33. Interviews with former party president in the Belgian Chamber of Deputies, Gerolf Annemans, and Flemish Parliament member Karim Van Overmeire, conducted by the author in Brussels, Belgium; February 1996. Similar perspectives are articulated by a range of Vlaams Blok/Belang party activists in De Witte, "Extreme Right-wing Activism."

34. The comments of the late Karel Dillen, former party leader and member of the European Parliament, on EU citizenship and voting rights illustrate the dimensions of Vlaams Blok concerns about these rights. See *Annex: Official Journal of the European Communities* (Luxembourg: Office for Official Publications of the European Communities, 1993), 3-437: 161.

35. Examples of activists' opinions on this issue are offered in De Witte, "Extreme Right-wing Activism," 143-44.

36. *Annex: Official Journal of the European Communities* (Luxembourg: Office for Official Publications of the European Communities, 1991), 3-411: 97.

37. See De Witte, "Extreme Right-wing Activism," 144.

38. See Laible, *Separatism and Sovereignty in the New Europe*.

Chapter 8
National Pride and Prejudice: The Case of Germany

Hilary B. Bergsieker

"I am proud to be German." (Laurenz Meyer, Christian Democratic Union, 2000)
"Meyer not only looks but also thinks like a skinhead." (Jürgen Trittin, Green Party, 2001)[1]

In early 2001, German Environmental Minister Trittin alleged that Secretary-General Meyer's expression of pride to be German aligned him with neo-Nazi thugs who voice national pride as an identity marker. These comments ignited a heated national debate over the relationship between German national pride and prejudice. This debate, which informed the current investigation, underscores the culturally specific and contested nature of German national pride and nationalism.

Focus on Germany and Theoretical Approach

This empirical work examines national pride and nationalism in contemporary Germany using an approach focused on two generational cohorts. The investigation aims to (a) document demographic variation in constructs related to national pride and nationalism, (b) identify aspects of national identity that predict national pride and symbolic nationalism, and (c) test the relationship between national pride, symbolic nationalism, and outgroup derogation in the form of ethnocentrism. Relative to younger Germans, older Germans reported higher levels of national pride, identity strength and positivity, cultural preference, and symbolic nationalism. Identity strength and positivity mediated the pride difference between cohorts. Among the young, national pride was rarer but strongly predicted anti-outgroup attitudes, consistent with social identity theory (SIT),[2] suggesting that, in a context where national identity is contested, asserting "pride to be German" may sound patriotic but in fact verges on prejudice.

German national pride and nationalism are of particular interest not because of their prevalence or extremity relative to other nations, but because of their distinctive historical and social context. Cross-national studies consistently show that in the latter part of the twentieth century Germans have reported less national pride than citizens of other countries.[3] Germany occupies a unique position in twentieth-century history as instigator of two world wars and massive genocide, a legacy that has made German national pride and nationalism highly controversial in recent decades. Post-Nazi era *Vergangenheitsbewaltigung*, or "coming to terms with the past," a term and concept specific to Germany's language and society,[4] reflects a collective effort to disavow nationalism and adopt a critical perspective on German history and national identity. Atonement for national wrongdoing has occurred elsewhere—reparations for internees, memorials to the oppressed, "truth and reconciliation" proceedings—but its long-standing cultural emphasis makes Germany an especially compelling site to investigate national pride and nationalism.

In examining national pride and nationalism, the current work adopts an etic-emic approach similar to that advocated by Minoru Karasawa.[5] This work synthesizes etic, or global, theory from political and social psychology (e.g., the patriotism vs. nationalism distinction) with the emic, or particular, contextual elements (e.g., *Vergangenheitsbewaltigung*) emphasized in cultural psychology. Rather than presume cross-national consistency in levels, components, and correlates of national pride, this research focuses on variations in the particular, potentially negative national identity of Germans who lived through the Nazi era or were born decades later. Whereas much prior work has explored East-West contrasts, the current research intentionally emphasizes generational cohort, highlighting a comparison across time rather than place.

Supporting an emic (contextual) perspective, national pride differs quantitatively and qualitatively across contexts. For instance, it correlates with commitment to national heritage in Japan;[6] regard for civil liberties in the United States;[7] and social dominance orientation among U.S. whites but not ethnic minorities.[8] Even the item "I am proud to be [my nationality]" often used to assess national pride[9] may indicate nationalistic attitudes in a German context.[10]

National identity acquires added significance for national pride in the context of SIT. The basic SIT postulates are that (a) individuals strive to maintain a positive social identity; (b) a positive social identity requires perceiving the ingroup as positively differentiated from relevant outgroups; and (c) when a social identity is unsatisfactory, people seek to join a more positively distinct group or to make their existing group more positively distinct.[11] From the outset, SIT aimed to describe real-world groups, including national groups.[12]

Many definitions of national identity have been proposed. These conceptions include subjective knowledge of one's formal or desired nationality;[13] a nation-related emotion ranging between positive and negative poles;[14] high salience or significance of national affiliation in one's overall identity;[15] shared ideology surrounding a nation's values, goals, and character;[16] or a continuum ranging from national consciousness to extreme nationalism.[17] Thomas Blank suggests that national identity "varies on a positive-negative continuum, which stretches from a negative identity (in the sense of an explicit contra-identity) to a positive identity with a nation" with indifference at the midpoint.[18] The present research conceptualizes "national identity" as a multifaceted affiliation with one's nation, with "identity positivity" indicating its valence, and "identity strength" indicating its extremity.

According to SIT, identity positivity and strength should be interchangeable, because when a group identity ceases to be adequately positive, group members will either diminish their attachment to the group or seek to positively distinguish the group. German public discourse, however, suggests that one could feel strongly, saliently German yet experience ambivalence or even shame with respect to that identity. Some Germans report experiencing ambivalence between pride and shame,[19] feeling "torn between shame for the crimes of the Nazi period and pride in German culture."[20] Others construe pride and shame in German identity as mutually exclusive, precluding ambivalence.[21] In this view, expressing pride to be German implies renouncing shame in German history or Auschwitz.[22]

An emic or discourse-derived approach thus highlights a potential contrast between concepts of pride's antipode in Germany versus other nations. Elsewhere, researchers often construe absence of pride as indifference, using items such as: "It is not that important for a citizen to develop a patriotic attitude";[23] "It is not constructive for one to develop an emotional attachment to his/her country";[24] and "I feel no differently about the place I grew up than any other place."[25] In Germany, however, the implicit question may be one of pride versus shame, not pride versus indifference, as reflected in the survey question "Are you proud or ashamed of German culture?"[26] The present research empirically examines whether shame is opposed versus orthogonal to pride.

Notably, happiness to be German, unlike pride, is not presumed in this discourse to negate shame or reflect nationalism. Sources ranging from Johannes Rau, president of Germany during the debate, to a citizen who quipped "I'm glad not to be proud!" cite the appropriateness of happiness but not pride to be German.[27]

Outgroup Derogation: Patriotism, Nationalism, and Ethnocentrism

Early SIT work highlighted arbitrary experimental groups' tendency to favor the ingroup over the outgroup in allocating resources,[28] implying that if even such groups discriminate, real-world groups with long histories of contact and comparison should display robust pro-ingroup, anti-outgroup biases. A pro-German identity, for example, would require negative comparisons with and bias toward non-Germans.

Evidence connecting ingroup identification with outgroup derogation comes from a meta-analysis that found an average correlation magnitude of .23, $p <$ .001, between identification and pro-ingroup bias across 15 studies.[29] Other studies, however, suggest a positive-negative asymmetry, finding greater pro-ingroup bias in distributing positive outcomes than anti-outgroup bias in allocating negative outcomes.[30] Several studies challenge the predicted link between ingroup identification and outgroup derogation. Identification may not entail derogation when comparisons are made to abstract standards (an autonomous orientation) rather than other groups (a relational orientation).[31] Ingroup identification and bias appear correlated for collectivists with relational orientations, but not for individualists with autonomous orientations.[32] When British and German participants were led to positively evaluate their nation relative to other nations, the past, or a freely chosen standard, identification correlated significantly with bias only for those induced to make cross-national comparisons.[33]

If "pro-ingroup" and "anti-outgroup" attitudes are separable, so, too, might be patriotic and nationalistic national pride. For example, President Rau asserted that "a patriot is someone who loves his or her own country [whereas] a nationalist is someone who hates the countries of others."[34] Social scientists have theorized a similar dichotomy at least since Randolf Bourne contrasted "military" versus "civic" patriotism in 1919[35] and Floyd Allport distinguished between a "nationalistic fallacy" and a patriotic "notion of America as something great" in 1927.[36] More recent research has frequently aimed to distinguish patriotism from intergroup discrimination, including racism, ethnocentrism, and nationalism.[37] In a German context, researchers have contrasted ethnic, economic nationalism with democratic, constitutional patriotism.[38]

Kosterman and Feshbach's model[39] of patriotism, nationalism, and internationalism as three distinct constructs has found support in the United States,[40] Israel,[41] Japan,[42] as well as Great Britain and Germany.[43] Similarly, "blind" patriotism appears to correspond to nationalism and perceived foreign threat, whereas "constructive patriotism" is associated with political involvement.[44] This cumulative evidence suggests a distinction between love of country and hatred of foreigners.

Differentiating between positive ingroup evaluation and negative outgroup attitudes does not establish whether German national pride is more patriotic or nationalistic. Some, seeing German national pride as benign, claim that Germans are less proud than other Europeans due to Germany's splintered history before 1871 and after 1945, not a repudiation of its nationalist past.[45] To differentiate national pride from nationalism, these researchers cite a 1986 forced-choice survey in which 70% of German participants agreed that "National pride is a good trait, which has nothing to do with hostile attitudes toward other nations," 18% were undecided, and only 12% agreed that "National pride is something bad. National pride and hostility toward other nations go hand in hand." Empirical findings from nearly 400 former West Germans, however, indicate strong ties between national pride and nationalism.[46] Endorsing the statement "I am proud to be German" correlated positively with xenophobia, anti-Semitism, exclusion of immigrants, and trivialization of Nazism.

Moreover, holistic national pride in Germany may not equal the sum of its constituent parts. Former Chancellor Gerhard Schröder, for instance, eschewed pride to be German but expressed pride in "Germans' achievements and democratic culture."[47] Blank distinguishes between "diffuse" national pride and "specific" dimensional pride in "collective goods," such as German athletic or military achievements, political prominence, history, democracy, and tolerance toward foreigners.[48] This dimensional pride approach[49] yielded relatively distinct clusters of "nationalistic" and "patriotic" pride in Russia, Austria, the United States, Great Britain, Italy, and Germany.[50]

Dimensional pride can border on nationalism for national symbols—such as the anthem and military—that are historically problematic. Symbols perceived as nationalistic can evoke powerful negative responses, such as the suicide of a Japanese principal after the instatement of the Japanese anthem and flag at graduation ceremonies.[51] Teachers protested that such symbols evoked "the wartime image of the Japanese Empire,"[52] and analogous claims can be made for the anthem "Deutschland über alles." Endorsing such symbols is thus thought to reflect nationalistic attitudes. In the present research, symbolic nationalism and ethnocentrism serve as the key indices of anti-outgroup prejudice.

Predictions

In prior studies, national pride and dimensional pride correlated positively with age.[53] Age may reflect different experiences with a nation's historical, political, and social developments, as well as international encounters enabled by economic, technical, and political advances.[54] Germans raised after the war may have a very different relationship to Nazism relative to older Germans who lived through it. Consistent with previous studies, older people were predicted to report higher levels of national pride and "pro-German" attitudes, including happiness to be German, relative to the young. Lower overall levels of disidentification were expected among the older cohort, who had decided not to emigrate after the war and spent numerous decades in Germany. Predictions for shame were unclear: Older Germans experienced the Nazi era more directly, but might have psychologically distanced themselves from it to maintain a positive identity. This study aims to identify factors—cultural preferences, identity strength and positivity, or progressive values—that contribute to generational differences.

Gender and regional differences, while not the primary focus, could also cause variation in German national pride and shame. Patriotism correlates positively, at least for white Americans, with social dominance orientation,[55] which is more prevalent among men than women.[56] West German public discourse stressed responsibility for Nazi atrocities, whereas East German authorities portrayed their nation as an "anti-fascist state" long opposed to Nazism. Following reunification, Daniel Goldhagen's *Hitler's Willing Executioners*,[57] Martin Walser's criticism of "instrumental" mentions of Auschwitz,[58] and other events have sparked national discussions of Germans' relationship to the past, but former East Germans might nevertheless feel less responsibility or shame. Studies focused on East-West differences have yielded inconclusive findings.[59]

Consistent with SIT, identity positivity was predicted to correlate positively with identity strength. Both the strength and positivity of Germans' national identity were hypothesized to strongly influence their levels of pride, happiness, and shame. Identity positivity was expected to positively predict both national pride (some researchers consider the two interchangeable)[60] and happiness to be German, while negatively predicting shame.

Similarly, national pride was expected to correlate positively with happiness to be German and negatively with shame to be German and desire for a non-German identity (disidentification), consistent with SIT's implication that strongly held social identities should be positive. Otherwise, weak correlations between identity strength, national pride, and shame could indicate ambivalence or even reflect a "contra-identity."[61] Given descriptions of happiness to be German as more appropriate than pride, proud Germans were predicted to be happy, but not necessarily the reverse. Identity positivity and strength were expected to mediate the relationship between cohort and pride, such that older and younger Germans with comparably strong and positive German identities would express comparable pride.

With respect to the disputed relationship of national pride to patriotism, symbolic nationalism, and ethnocentrism, this research was exploratory. The positive correlations observed in 1993 between national pride and nationalism[62] could have declined, after the Holocaust receded another decade into the past, or increased, following increases in right-extremist violence. Of interest for SIT is the relationship of national pride and identity positivity to symbolic nationalism or ethnocentrism. A positive association between the former and the latter would bolster SIT's claim that positive ingroup identity leads to outgroup derogation, whereas the absence of a link would indicate a positive national identity that did not entail anti-outgroup bias.

Method

Between June 2001 and September 2002, German participants completed a questionnaire assessing national pride, dimensional pride, cultural preferences, progressive values, identity positivity, identity strength, symbolic nationalism, and ethnocentrism. The study employed an intergenerational approach, excluding individuals born after 1946 and before 1976. This cohort-based selection method involved comparing two age groups separated by three decades, making shifts in attitudes across generations easier to detect. This research was conducted in six German federal states. The cities Cologne, Hanover, Landshut, Berlin, Rostock, and Dresden were selected to ensure political, ethnic, geographic, religious, and economic diversity in the sample.

Approximately 850 people participated, 737 of whom satisfied the study eligibility criteria, after excluding from analysis non-citizens, minors, people born between 1947 and 1975, and two participants who answered fewer than 10% of the survey items. Women represented 57% of the overall sample and 72% of the older cohort; 1% did not indicate gender. (According to the International Data Base of the U.S. Census Bureau, from 2000 to 2003 roughly 71% of Germans over 75 years old were female, and 80% of the older study participants were over 75.) The older cohort made up 18% of the sample, with a mean birth year of 1920; the younger cohort made up 82%, with a mean birth year of 1982. At the time of data collection, 78% of participants lived in the former FRG ("Westerners") and 22% in the former GDR ("Easterners"). Of the 42% who indicated their religious affiliation, 62% were Protestant, 28% Catholic, 4% Muslim, and less than 1% Jewish; 49% were not religious. Most (55%) of the participants did not provide occupational status, though 10% listed blue-collar jobs and 35% listed white-collar ones. Only 6% reported belonging to a political party.

The study questionnaire and a cover letter asking permission to conduct research on the premises were faxed or mailed to every high school (with grade levels old enough to include non-minors) and retirement home listed in the yellow pages for each city. In cities where all schools required a governmental research license, the survey was distributed at youth centers or dormitories. The overall institutional compliance rate was about 30%. All aspects of the research were conducted in German.

Despite attempts to recruit a representative sample, some limitations emerged. The majority of younger participants came from college preparatory schools or universities, as opposed to vocational schools that end before students reach the age of majority (required for participation). Approximately 11% of the younger cohort were vocational school students training for blue-collar careers (e.g., bank tellers, seamstresses, salesclerks, mechanics), and an additional 2% were educationally diverse young people recruited from youth centers.

Self-selection concerns among the older group were twofold. Whereas in schools the survey was distributed broadly and most students completed it, in retirement homes research liaisons often ascertained in advance which residents were willing or able to participate in a "national consciousness" study. Most non-participants lacked the mental or physical resources to take part, but a few stated reluctance to revisit the Nazi period. The second selection factor is historical:

Those who chose to remain in post-war Germany may have different attitudes toward and understandings of their national identity relative to their counterparts who emigrated.

Demographic questions asked for year and region of birth and upbringing, citizenship status and duration, gender, as well as political and religious activity and affiliation. The questionnaire format exactly replicated Kawasara's national identity scale:[63] Participants rated 33 declarative sentences on 5-point Likert scales[64] from 1 (*strongly disagree*) to 5 (*strongly agree*), with 3 (*neutral*) as the midpoint. To reduce response biases, survey items were counterbalanced and conceptually similar items were not consecutive. Study materials were translated into German by a native speaker and back-translated for accuracy.

The questionnaire incorporated several items from the patriotism-nationalism literature, such as "I am proud to be German," the standard etic measure of national pride. Items assessing affective responses to the national anthem or a critical stance toward German culture and history were added to explore the connections between national pride and symbolic nationalism or critical patriotism.[65] To assess cultural identification, seven items assessing cultural pride, cultural activities, and social affiliations were adapted from the General Ethnicity Questionnaire,[66] which has revealed a strong correlation for American-born Chinese between pride in and identification with a given culture.

Two German media public opinion polls also contributed items. The former adopted a "collective goods" approach[67] exploring dimensional pride in the German economy, military, arts, culture, reunification, and athletics.[68] The latter defined specific affective attitudes toward national identity: pride, happiness, or shame in being German, or indifference to patriotism.[69] Press coverage of the pride debate also contributed emic material concerning the distinction between pride in Germany versus a German identity, acceptance of foreigners, past- versus future-orientation of thoughts about Germany, and worry over Anglicization of German language and culture.

Results

The following steps were used to analyze the data. A principal components analysis was conducted to identify the scale's factor structure and latent dimensions (see table 8.1).[70] After the emergent factors had been evaluated and interpreted, several theoretically significant item clusters were assessed. Scores on eleven outcomes of interest were analyzed using three-way univariate analysis of variance (ANOVA) with a 2 (cohort: old, young) × 2 (gender: male, female) × 2 (region: East, West) design. Only significant effects are reported, with means and standard error for cohort and gender displayed in table 8.2.[71] Finally, linear regressions (see table 8.3) and mediation analyses were conducted to test the predictions of SIT.

The questionnaire demonstrated good internal reliability (α = .88) for the overall sample, and remained acceptably high across demographic subgroups. A varimax-rotated principal component analysis was performed on all items except national pride, happiness, shame, and disidentification, which were excluded so that their relationships with emergent factors could be examined subsequently.[72] This three-factor structure (see table 8.1) was confirmed in a follow-up analysis using a randomly selected subsample with no more than 40 participants per cohort per city. Individuals' scores on a given factor were computed by averaging their responses on all items that loaded primarily on that factor.

Table 8.1. Dimensional pride (DP), cultural preference (CP), and progressive orientation (PO) item loadings

Survey items with factor loadings	DP	CP	PO
I am proud of the technical achievements of the Germans (e.g., German cars).	.74		
It should be more acceptable to express pride in Germany.	.70		
I am proud of the German economy and the German Mark.	.69		
I am proud of the achievements of the German military.	.60		
I am proud of German culture.	.57	.48	
I like to hear the German national anthem.	.54	.46	
I do not care how successful German athletes are (e.g., the soccer team).	-.52		
German culture has had a positive impact on my life.	.51	.36	
I think that many foreigners have an undeservedly negative view of Germany.	.49		
I feel closer to Europeans than to Germans.	-.47		.39
I think more about Germany's future than Germany's past.	.39		
I listen mostly to music with German lyrics.		.72	
I prefer to travel in Germany than abroad (ignoring financial considerations).		.71	
I prefer to watch movies from foreign countries.		-.65	

Continued on next page

Survey items with factor loadings	DP	CP	PO
I would be happy to emigrate to another country.		-.63	
I would prefer a foreign lifestyle to the German lifestyle.	-.44	-.55	
My world outlook is German.	.46	.52	
I prefer to read books by German authors.		.50	
I am worried about the Anglicization of the German language and culture.		.49	
I believe that German history is of vital importance for modern Germany.			.58
I think immigrants and resident foreigners enrich the German culture.			.55
I esteem German writers and artists highly.		.39	.51
I criticize German culture and history more than that of other countries.			.50
I am pleased with the German reunification.			.48
It is substantially different to be proud of Germany versus being German.			.43

The first factor, dubbed "dimensional pride," included all items related to pride in specific aspects of Germany—such as technology, economy, military, culture—as well as support for expressing German national pride. Dimensional pride was strongly correlated with national pride, $r(717) = .72$, and happiness to be German, $r(714) = .64$, $ps < .001$. Older people expressed greater dimensional pride than younger people, $F(1, 717) = 40.03$, $p < .001$, as did men relative to women, $F(1, 717) = 10.45$, $p = .001$.

The second factor, "cultural preference," comprised a range of preferences for living in Germany and for German cultural products—such as German books, films, travel, and "lifestyle"—over non-German ones. Older people reported higher levels of German cultural preference than younger people, $F(1,717) = 424.22$, $p < .001$, as did Easterners ($M = 3.35$, $SEM = .06$) relative to Westerners ($M = 3.12$, $SEM = .04$), $F(1, 717) = 9.85$, $p = .002$.

The third factor is less reliable ($\alpha = .50$) but resembles "constructive patriotism" as operationalized by Blank (2003). The name "progressive orientation" attempts to reflect the more liberal positions this factor incorporates: emphasizing the relevance of German history, respecting German artistic and literary accomplishments, supporting German reunification, regarding Germany's history and culture critically, endorsing immigration, and differentiating pride in Germany versus in being German. Older people reported a more "progressive" orientation than younger people, $F(1, 717) = 45.56$, $p < .001$. A significant cohort × re-

Table 8.2. Estimated marginal means (with standard error) of principle variables by cohort and gender

	Pre-1947			Post-1975			Total		
Measure	Male	Female	Total	Male	Female	Total	Male	Female	Total
Dimensional pride	3.64	3.55	3.59[a]	3.32	2.91	3.11[a]	3.48[b]	3.23b	3.35
	(.11)	(.07)	(.07)	(.06)	(.05)	(.04)	(.06)	(.04)	(.04)
Cultural preference	3.93	4.00	3.96[a]	2.57	2.44	2.51[a]	3.25	3.22	3.24
	(.11)	(.07)	(.06)	(.05)	(.05)	(.03)	(.06)	(.04)	(.04)
Progressive orientation	3.92	3.99	3.96[a]	3.45	3.53	3.49[a]	3.69	3.76	3.72
	(.10)	(.06)	(.06)	(.05)	(.04)	(.03)	(.06)	(.04)	(.03)
National pride	3.89[c]	4.18[c]	4.04[a]	3.36	2.93	3.15[a]	3.63	3.55	3.59
	(.21)	(.13)	(.12)	(.10)	(.09)	(.07)	(.12)	(.08)	(.07)
Happiness	3.65[c]	4.20[c]	3.93[a]	3.53	3.04	3.29[a]	3.59	3.62	3.61
	(.18)	(.12)	(.11)	(.09)	(.08)	(.06)	(.10)	(.07)	(.06)
Shame	1.77	2.48	2.13[a]	2.23	2.73	2.48[a]	2.00[b]	2.61b	2.30
	(.23)	(.15)	(.14)	(.11)	(.10)	(.08)	(.13)	(.09)	(.08)
Disidentification	1.90	1.64	1.77[a]	2.36	2.72	2.54[a]	2.13	2.18	2.15
	(.22)	(.14)	(.13)	(.10)	(.09)	(.07)	(.12)	(.08)	(.07)
Identity strength	3.91	3.98	3.94[a]	3.31	3.09	3.20[a]	3.61	3.54	3.57
	(.13)	(.08)	(.08)	(.06)	(.06)	(.04)	(.07)	(.05)	(.04)
Identity positivity	4.06[c]	4.06[c]	4.06[a]	3.37[c]	3.00[c]	3.18[a]	3.71[b]	3.53b	3.62
	(.13)	(.08)	(.07)	(.06)	(.05)	(.04)	(.07)	(.05)	(.04)
Symbolic nationalism	3.68	3.67	3.68[a]	2.83	2.54	2.69[a]	3.26	3.11	3.18
	(.16)	(.10)	(.09)	(.07)	(.07)	(.05)	(.09)	(.06)	(.05)
Ethnocentrism	2.93	2.51	2.72	2.69	2.52	2.60	2.81[b]	2.51b	2.66
	(.21)	(.13)	(.12)	(.10)	(.09)	(.06)	(.11)	(.08)	(.07)
Sample size (n)	37	94	134	264	332	603	301	426	737

Note: Superscripts indicate [a]cohort effects, [b]gender effects, and [c]cohort-by-gender interactions that attained significance ($p < .05$)

gion interaction, $F(1, 717) = 4.49$, $p = .034$, revealed that older Easterners ($M = 3.94$, $SEM = .09$) and older Westerners ($M = 3.97$, $SEM = .08$) did not differ, but younger Easterners ($M = 3.62$, $SEM = .06$) were more progressive than younger Westerners ($M = 3.36$, $SEM = .03$).

Further analyses revealed that cultural preference correlated strongly with dimensional pride, $r(735) = .56$, $p < .001$, and weakly with progressive orientation, $r(735) = .18$, $p < .001$. Interestingly, the relationship between dimensional pride and progressive orientation differed by cohort, $F(1, 733) = 11.45$, $p = .001$, according to tests of interaction in regression.[73] For older Germans, greater dimensional pride predicted a more progressive orientation, $r(132) = .23$, $p < .01$, whereas for younger Germans this relationship was reversed, $r(601) = -.10$, $p < .05$.

Cohort × gender × region ANOVAs were used to analyze the extent to which participants felt proud, happy, ashamed, or reluctant to be German, as indicated by agreement with the following statements:

Overall, I am proud to be German. (pride)

I am happy to be German. (happiness)

Sometimes I am embarrassed/ashamed to be German. (shame)

Sometimes I would like to have another nationality. (disidentification)

Each measure was regressed on all three components of national identity: dimensional pride, cultural preference, and progressive orientation (see table 8.3 for standardized betas). Older people reported feeling more proud to be German than the young, $F(1, 701) = 40.40$, $p < .001$. A gender × cohort interaction, $F(1, 701) = 6.60$, $p = .01$, revealed that older women expressed more national pride than older men, whereas younger women were less proud than younger men. Dimensional pride and cultural preference positively predicted national pride for both cohorts: For older Germans they were equivalently predictive, but for younger Germans dimensional pride was over three times more predictive than cultural preference.

A similar pattern emerged for happiness to be German. Older Germans reported feeling happier to be German than the young, $F(1, 698) = 26.52$, $p < .001$, again with older women happier than older men, but younger women less happy than younger men, reflecting a gender × cohort interaction, $F(1, 698) = 17.43$, $p < .001$. Again, dimensional pride and cultural preference (but not progressive orientation) positively predicted happiness for both cohorts, although the effect of cultural preference was marginal for older Germans.

Older people reported feeling less shame to be German than younger people, $F(1, 702) = 5.09$, $p = .024$, as did men relative to women, $F(1, 702) = 15.24$, $p < .001$. For both cohorts shame was positively predicted by progressive orientation and negatively by dimensional pride, and cultural preference negatively predicted shame for the young. Younger people reported more desire not to be German than older people, $F(1, 701) = 27.70$, $p < .001$. Older men wished to disidentify as German marginally more than older women, whereas younger women wished to disidentify marginally more than younger men, reflecting a marginally significant gender × cohort interaction, $F(1, 701) = 4.60$, $p = .03$, with alpha (.025)

Table 8.3. Regression coefficients for dimensional pride, cultural preference, and progressive orientation as predictors of national pride, happiness, shame, and disidentification by cohort

Variables		Pre-1947 cohort				Post-1975 cohort			
Dependent	Independent	*B*	*SE B*	β	R^2	*B*	*SE B*	β	R^2
National pride	Dimensional pride	0.66	0.16	.35***	.36***	1.09	0.06	.64***	.55***
	Cultural preference	0.59	0.14	.35***		0.32	0.07	.16***	
	Progressive orientation	-0.13	0.15	-.07		-0.09	0.05	-.05†	
Happiness	Dimensional pride	0.76	0.16	.43***	.29***	0.81	0.06	.52***	.43***
	Cultural preference	0.26	0.14	.16†		0.38	0.07	.21***	
	Progressive orientation	0.12	0.16	.06		0.08	0.06	.05	
Shame	Dimensional pride	-0.83	0.25	-.33**	.21***	-0.69	0.08	-.36***	.49***
	Cultural preference	-0.33	0.21	-.15		-0.28	0.10	-.13**	
	Progressive orientation	0.68	0.23	.25**		0.35	0.08	.16***	
Disidentification	Dimensional pride	-0.52	0.20	-.25*	.16***	-0.57	0.07	-.31***	.58***
	Cultural preference	-0.34	0.18	-.19†		-0.69	0.08	-.33***	
	Progressive orientation	0.35	0.19	.16†		0.18	0.07	.09**	

Notes: Including higher-order interaction terms did not improve the fit of the regression models.

†$p < .10$; *$p < .05$; **$p < .01$; ***$p < .001$

reduced due to heterogeneity of variance. For both cohorts disidentification was negatively predicted by dimensional pride and cultural preference, but positively predicted by progressive orientation, although the last two effects were marginal for the older cohort.

Summing up, the cumulative effect of cohort was clear: Relative to younger Germans, older Germans expressed more national pride and happiness, combined with less shame and disidentification concerning their German identity. The positive affective attitudes—national pride and happiness—were strongly intercorrelated, $r(703) = .66, p < .001$, and the negative attitudes—shame and disidentification—were as well, $r(706) = .45, p < .001$. Little evidence suggested ambivalence between the positive and negative attitudes: They were negatively correlated relative to one another, with *r*s ranging from -.38 to -.51 and all *p*s < .001.[74] Reflecting a tight coupling of "pro-German" attitudes, only 9.5% of participants professed happiness without also expressing national pride, whereas 57.9% reported equivalent happiness and pride.

Although identity strength and identity positivity did not emerge as extracted factors from the principal components analysis, they remain theoretically important from a SIT perspective. Identity strength and positivity indices were created by averaging each participant's responses on items selected beforehand for their conceptual relevance to each construct. The identity strength index showed acceptable reliability ($\alpha = .63$) and comprised four items,[75] with "(R)" denoting reverse-coding:

I feel closer to Europeans than to Germans. (R)
Sometimes I wish I had another nationality. (R)
My world outlook is German.
I am familiar with German cultural practices and customs.

Older people reported identifying more strongly as German than younger people, $F(1, 719) = 71.48, p < .001$, and identity strength correlated positively with national pride, $r(717) = .63$.

The identity positivity composite also showed acceptable reliability ($\alpha = .65$) and consisted of five items:

German culture has had a positive impact on my life.
Sometimes I am embarrassed/ashamed to be German. (R)
I am happy to be German.
I would be happy to emigrate to another country. (R)
I think that many foreigners have an undeservedly negative view of Germany.

Older people expressed a more positive German identity than the young, $F(1, 719) = 109.14, p < .001$, and as did men relative to women, $F(1, 719) = 4.76$, $p = .029$. Younger men reported more positivity than younger women, whereas older men and women did not differ, reflecting a gender × cohort interaction, $F(1, 719) = 4.69, p = .031$. Identity positivity correlated positively with national pride, $r(717) = .66, p < .001$, and identity strength, $r(735) = .70$, *p*s < .001.

To examine whether other variables might mediate the observed cohort difference in national pride, national pride was regressed on cohort (dummy coded: 0 = old, 1 = young), identity strength, and identity positivity, following standard procedures for assessing mediation.[76] Including identity strength and positivity, with respective ßs of .32 and .44, $ps < .001$, caused cohort to become a non-significant predictor of national pride (dropping from $ß = -.29$, $p < .001$, to $ß < .01$, $p > .9$). As individual mediators, identity positivity fully mediated the effect of cohort, Sobel's $z = 10.25$, $p < .001$, reducing it to non-significance, whereas identity strength partially mediated the cohort effect, Sobel's $z = 8.81$, $p < .001$, with cohort remaining significant ($ß = -.08$, $p = .008$). In sum, identifying strongly as German appears to entail identifying positively, consistent with SIT, and identity positivity largely accounted for the cohort difference in national pride.

To explore SIT's most controversial prediction, namely, that a positive ingroup identity requires optimal distinctiveness (achieved by comparing the ingroup favorably to outgroups), subtle measures of symbolic nationalism and ethnocentrism were included in the questionnaire.

Symbolic nationalism was assessed using the following three-item composite, with acceptable reliability ($\alpha = .68$):

I like to hear the German national anthem.

I am proud of the achievements of the German military.

I would prefer a foreign lifestyle to the German lifestyle. (R)

Although these items might seem short on face validity, prior findings suggests a connection to nationalism: Pride in the German military, for instance, correlated with xenophobia, anti-Semitism, and trivialization of the Nazi past.[77] While some defend the national anthem on aesthetic grounds, most of those who object to "Deutschland über alles" cite its nationalist ties.

For the current sample, only cohort revealed significant differences, $F(1, 717) = 90.47$, $p < .001$, with older Germans expressing more symbolic nationalism than younger Germans. For the young, symbolic nationalism correlated significantly not only with national pride, $r(594) = .66$; happiness, $r(588) = .54$; shame, $r(592) = -.42$; and disidentification, $r(594) = -.52$; but also with identity strength, $r(601) = .64$, and identity positivity, $r(601) = .63$, all $ps < .001$. Notably, for the older cohort these correlations were substantially weaker.

Ethnocentrism (or xenophobia) was measured with a reverse-coded item designed to minimize reactance: "I think the immigrants and resident foreigners enrich the German culture" (see reverse-coded means in table 8.2). No difference for cohort emerged, $F(1, 700) < 1$. Men reported more ethnocentrism than women, $F(1, 700) = 4.61$, $p = .032$, although this effect was stronger among Easterners than Westerners, $F(1, 700) = 7.27$, $p = .007$. Older Eastern men (who reported the most ethnocentrism) and older Eastern women (who reported the least) drove this effect, as shown by a significant 3-way interaction $F(1, 700) = 6.43$, $p = .011$.

Ethnocentrism correlated positively with symbolic nationalism, $r(596) = .40$, $p < .001$, and national pride, $r(589) = .30$, $p < .001$, for the younger cohort, but not the older cohort, $r(117) = .08$, $p = .392$, and $r(109) = .10$, $p = .292$, respectively. Similarly, for the young several items and indices showed significant correlations with ethnocentrism: happiness, $r(584) = .23$, identity strength, $r(596) = .34$, identity positivity, $r(596) = .32$, and shame, $r(588) = -.29$, all *ps* < .001. In the older cohort, by contrast, significant correlations emerged for only identity positivity $r(117) = .18$, $p = .047$, and shame $r(117) = -.23$, $p = .015$.

To test the prediction derived from SIT that maintaining a positive ingroup identity entails preferring the ingroup over the outgroup, symbolic nationalism and ethnocentrism were each regressed on identity positivity and national pride. For both older and younger Germans, national pride partially mediated the strong positive relationship between identity positivity and symbolic nationalism, respective Sobel's *zs* = 2.05 and 9.91, $p = .041$ and $p < .001$, but positivity remained a significant predictor of nationalism (for older and younger Germans respective ßs = .44 and .35, *ps* < .001). A parallel analysis replacing identity positivity with happiness to be German as a predictor of symbolic nationalism also showed partial mediation for national pride within both cohorts.

Identity positivity significantly predicted ethnocentrism only within the younger cohort, and remained significant (ß = .22, $p < .001$) even with national pride partially mediating this relationship, Sobel's $z = 2.98$, $p = .003$. National pride did fully mediate the effect of happiness in predicting ethnocentrism, which dropped from ß = .23, $p < .001$, to ß = .06, $p = .225$, Sobel's $z = 4.94$, $p < .001$, but the former identity positivity analysis provides a more stringent test of the hypothesis that ingroup-positivity leads to outgroup-derogation. Identity positivity encompassed more items and explained twice as much variance in ethnocentrism ($R^2 = .10$) as happiness ($R^2 = .05$).[78]

Discussion

Returning to the starting predictions, most of the hypotheses were supported. National pride, nationalism, and other attitudes toward being German did show substantial demographic variation, and these differences were largely confined to cohort, rather than gender or region.[79] Relative to the young, older people reported more "pro-German" attitudes, scoring higher on national pride, happiness, dimensional pride, cultural preference, "progressive" orientation, identity positivity, identity strength, and symbolic nationalism; and lower on shame and desire to disidentify.

Women expressed more shame and less identity positivity, dimensional pride, and ethnocentrism on average than men. Several variables—national pride, happiness, identity positivity, as well as (marginally) disidentification and dimensional pride—were qualified by unpredicted gender × cohort interactions: Within the older cohort more pro-German attitudes were reported by women than men, while the reverse was true in the younger cohort. Given the overall finding that men expressed more pro-German attitudes relative to women, the lower scores of older men relative to older women could be related to many men's status as WWII veterans or more instrumental roles in Nazi Germany.

Distinct dimensions of national identity emerged: dimensional pride, cultural preference, and progressive orientation. The first two, also the most reliable, positively predicted national pride for both groups, although dimensional pride was substantially more predictive of pride than was cultural preference for the young. National pride for older people appears pervasive and incorporates cultural embeddedness, love of German culture, and preference for familiar over foreign goods. For young people, by contrast, national pride is rarer and more related to pride in specific dimensions of Germany, such as the economy, military, or technology.

The pattern of correlations between affective attitudes predicted by SIT was obtained: National pride and happiness correlated positively and strongly with each other and dimensional pride and cultural preference, while correlating negatively with shame and disidentification. Despite rhetoric about feeling happy but not proud to be German, national pride and happiness were strongly and positively correlated. Only older women demonstrated some ambivalence (a non-significant negative correlation) between national pride and shame, perhaps indicating that their national identities integrate national pride and shame.

Consistent with SIT, identity strength and positivity were tightly coupled, showing little evidence of a "contra-identity":[80] a strong, but explicitly negative national identity. For both cohorts, identity strength and particularly positivity predicted national pride. In fact, controlling for identity positivity and strength statistically eliminated the national pride difference separating younger people and women (who tended to be relatively less positively or strongly identified as German) from older people and men.

As for the nationalism-patriotism question animating Germany's national pride debate and much social scientific research, this research suggests that German national pride is indeed associated with outgroup derogation, at least for younger Germans. National pride—as well as identity positivity—strongly predicted endorsement of subtle measures of symbolic nationalism and ethnocentrism among individuals raised in a climate that proscribes pride. The findings for younger but not older Germans support SIT's postulate that pro-ingroup and anti-outgroup attitudes coincide.

Proponents of patriotism might emphasize that controlling for national pride statistically eliminated the link between mere happiness to be German and ethnocentrism or symbolic nationalism. Even if the incidence of non-proud happy Germans is low, this distinction matters for Germans wanting to feel positive, albeit not chauvinistic, about their nation. J. Christopher Cohrs,[81] however, critiques the use of regression or structural-equation approaches that control for variance shared by patriotism and nationalism in predicting outcome variables.[82] Given that patriotism and nationalism—like happiness and pride to be German in the current work—are typically correlated positively with each other and with the outcome measure, ignoring substantial shared variance may make results difficult to interpret. In the present analysis, if happiness to be German predicts greater ethnocentrism except when controlling for national pride, such happiness does not appear benign. Moreover, adding other mediators failed to eliminate the link between identity positivity (a more predictive composite measure than happiness alone) and symbolic nationalism or ethnocentrism.

One possible limitation of this work arises in light of findings that ingroup identification and outgroup derogation coincide only after a relational orientation has been primed.[83] This study's comparative questionnaire items and American authorship may have primed a relational orientation that together elicited patriotism, symbolic nationalism, and ethnocentrism. Moreover, these associations might be different in work using more extensive or direct measures of ethnocentrism and nationalism: What the present measures gained in unobtrusiveness, they may have lost in susceptibility to confounds.

Conclusion

In the context of prior work on patriotism and nationalism in Germany,[84] the present analysis provides converging evidence that expressing pride to be German—unlike expressing pride to be American, Israeli, or Japanese—is positively associated with outgroup derogation. That German national pride, in contrast to national pride in some other countries, is more closely linked to symbolic nationalism and ethnocentrism than to critical patriotism highlights the need for emic or context-specific analyses of national identity and nationalism. Cross-national studies, such as an international analysis that included Germany and predicted that feeling "proud of your country's history" would indicate patriotism rather than nationalism,[85] may overlook the sociocultural and historical realities of the specific nations examined.

German national pride remains controversial, ideological, political, and embedded in sociocultural and historical discourses. It varies between generations, both in absolute levels and in its correlates or components, relating differently to pride in specific dimensions of Germany, cultural preferences, and progressive political attitudes. Also, although overt national pride appears closely linked to symbolic nationalism and ethnocentrism in contemporary Germany, particularly for the younger cohort, that relationship is grounded in a particular social, historical, and political context and may change with time. Future research should incorporate longitudinal instead of cross-sectional designs, to test for shifts in national pride and nationalism across the lifespan, rather than across generations. Experimental manipulations of norms relating to national pride and nationalism or of situational cues that prime different aspects of identity could also provide valuable causal confirmation of the correlational relationships documented in the current work.

Notes

This research was supported by an Intellectual Exploration Grant from Stanford University, as well as by the Krupp Foundation and TU Center for Anti-Semitism Research. Many thanks to Steven Bergsieker, Amir Eshel, Susan T. Fiske, and Hazel Rose Markus for comments on the manuscript; Andrew Conway and Julie Turchin for statistical support; and Ulrike Friemann, Wolf Junghanns, and Karen Kramer for assistance with materials and logistics. This research would not have been possible without the 41 schools, youth centers, and retirement homes that permitted and facilitated participant recruitment and data collection on their premises.

1. Ralf Beste, Tina Hildebrandt, Jürgen Leinemann, Christoph Mestmacher, and Gerd Rosenkranz, "Absurdes Getöse" [Absurd Bluster], *Der Spiegel* 13 (26 March 2001): 22-27.

2. Henri Tajfel, *Social Identity and Intergroup Relations* (New York: Cambridge University Press, 1982).

3. Thomas Blank, Peter Schmidt, and Bettina Westle, "'Patriotism'—A Contradiction, a Possibility, or an Empirical Reality?" (paper presented at the ECPR Workshop 26 "National Identity in Europe," Grenoble, France, 6-11 April 2001); Elisabeth Noelle-Neumann and Renate Köcher, *Die verletzte Nation. Über den Versuch der Deutschen, ihren Charakter zu ändern* [The Wronged Nation. On the Attempt of the Germans to Alter Their Character] (Stuttgart, Germany: Deutsche Verlags-Anstalt, 1987).

4. See Russell F. Farnen, ed., *Nationalism, Ethnicity, and Identity: Cross National and Comparative Perspectives* (London: Transaction Books, 1994).

5. Minoru Karasawa, "Patriotism, Nationalism, and Internationalism among Japanese Citizens: An Etic-Emic Approach," *Political Psychology* 23, no. 4 (December 2002): 645-666.

6. Karasawa, "An Etic-Emic Approach."

7. Richard Kosterman and Seymour Feshbach, "Toward a Measure of Patriotic and Nationalistic Attitudes," *Political Psychology* 10, no. 2 (June 1989): 257-74.

8. Jim Sidanius, Seymour Feshbach, Shana Levin, and Felicia Pratto, "The Interface between Ethnic and National Attachment: Ethnic Pluralism or Ethnic Dominance?" *Public Opinion Quarterly* 61, no. 1 (Spring 1997): 102-133.

9. Karasawa, "An Etic-Emic Approach"; Kosterman and Feshbach, "Toward a Measure"; Sidanius et al., "Ethnic Pluralism."

10. See Thomas Blank and Peter Schmidt, "Verletzte oder verletzende Nation? Empirische Befunde zum Stolz auf Deutschland" [Nation Wronged or Wronging? Empirical Findings on Pride in Germany], *Journal für Sozialforschung* 33, no. 4 (1993): 391-415.

11. Henri Tajfel and John C. Turner, "The Social Identity Theory of Intergroup Behavior," in *Psychology of Intergroup Relations*, ed. Stephen Worschel and William G. Austin (Chicago: Nelson-Hall, 1986), 7-24.

12. See Marco Cinnirella, "A Social Identity Perspective on European Integration," in *Changing European Identities: Social Psychological Analyses of Social Change*, ed. Glynis M. Breakwell and Evanthia Lyons (Cornwall, England: Hartnolls Limited, 1996), 253-54.

13. Tajfel, *Social Identity*.

14. Jennifer Crocker and Riia Luhtanen, "Collective Self-Esteem and Ingroup Bias," *Journal of Personality and Social Psychology* 58, no. 1 (December 1990): 60-67.

15. Leon Festinger, "A Theory of Social Comparison Processes," *Human Relations* 7, no. 2 (May 1954): 117-40.

16. Bettina Westle, *Kollektive Identität im vereinigten Deutschland—Nation und Demokratie in der Wahrnehmung der Deutschen* [Collective Identity in Reunited Germany —Nation and Democracy in the Perceptions of Germans] (Opladen, Germany: Leske & Budrich, 1999).

17. Blank, Schmidt, and Westle, "Patriotism."

18. Thomas Blank, "Determinants of National Identity in East and West Germany: An Empirical Comparison of Theories on the Significance of Authoritarianism, Anomie, and General Self-Esteem," *Political Psychology* 24, no. 2 (June 2003): 260.

19. Micha Brumlik, "Stolz sein, stolz sein über alles" [Be Proud, Be Proud above All], *Die Tageszeitung*, 26 March 2001, 11; "'Ich liebe Menschen': Bundespräsident Johannes Rau über richtigen und falschen Nationalstolz" ["I Love People": President Johannes Rau on Right and Wrong National Pride], *Der Spiegel* 13 (26 March 2001): 29-30.

20. "Die Deutschen und ihr Nationalgefühl" [The Germans and Their National Feeling], *Goethe-Institut Inter Nationes* 2001, <http://www.goethe.de/in/d/frames/film/d/kubus-39-2.html> (23 May 2003).

21. Blank and Schmidt, "Verletzende Nation."

22. Michael Kohlstruck, "Bekenntnisse einer Gegengemeinschaft" [Confessions of an Opposed Community], *Die Tageszeitung*, 27 March 2001, 13.

23. Karasawa, "An Etic-Emic Approach."

24. Kosterman and Feshbach, "Toward a Measure."

25. Sidanius et al., "Ethnic Pluralism."

26. Ulrich Seiler, Jurgen Maes, and Manfred Schmitt, "Korrelate und Fassetten des Nationalgefühls" [Correlates and Facets of National Feeling], in "Sozialisation und Identitäten—Politische Kultur im Umbruch?" ed. Helmut Moser, special issue, *Zeitschrift für Politische Psychologie* 7 (1999): 121-36.

27. "Ich liebe Menschen"; Ludwig Thomas, letter to the editor, *Süddeutschezeitung* 30 March 2001, 40.

28. For example, see Michael Billig and Henri Tajfel, "Social Categorisation and Similarity in Intergroup Behaviour," *Journal of Social Psychology* 3, no. 1 (March 1973): 27-52.

29. See Rupert Brown, "Social Identity Theory: Past Achievements, Current Problems and Future Challenges," *European Journal of Social Psychology* 30, no. 6 (November -December 2000): 745-78.

30. See Catherine E. Amiot and Richard Y. Bourhis, "Discrimination and the Positive-Negative Asymmetry Effects: Ideological and Normative Process," *Personality and Social Psychology Bulletin* 29, no. 5 (May 2003): 597-608; Marilynn B. Brewer, "The Psychology of Prejudice: Ingroup Love or Outgroup Hate?" *Journal of Social Issues* 55, no. 3 (Fall 1999): 429-44.

31. Amélie Mummendey, Andreas Klink, and Rupert Brown, "Nationalism and Patriotism: National Identification and Out-Group Rejection," *British Journal of Social Psychology* 40, no. 2 (June 2001): 159-72.

32. Rupert Brown, Steve Hinkle, Pamela G. Ely, Lee Fox-Cardamone, Pam Maras, and Laurie A. Taylor, "Recognizing Group Diversity: Individualist-Collectivist and Autonomous-Relational Social Orientations and Their Implications for Intergroup Processes," *British Journal for Social Psychology* 31, no. 4 (December 1992): 327-42.

33. Mummendey, Klink, and Brown, "Out-Group Rejection."

34. Heribert Prantl, "Vom Stolz, Deutscher zu sein" [Of Pride to Be German], *Süddeutsche Zeitung*, 20 March 2001, 4 (Opinion).

35. Randolf Bourne, "The State," in *The Radical Will: Randolf Bourne (Selected Writings 1911-1918)*, ed. Olaf Hanson (New York: Urizen, 1919/1977), 355-95.

36. Floyd H. Allport, "The Psychology of Nationalism: The Nationalistic Fallacy as a Cause of War," *Harper's Monthly* 155 (August 1927): 291-301.

37. See Robert T. Schatz, Ervin Staub, and Howard Lavine, "On the Varieties of National Attachment: Blind versus Constructive Patriotism," *Political Psychology* 20, no. 1 (March 1999): 151-74.

38. Blank and Schmidt, "Verletzende Nation."

39. Kosterman and Feshbach, "Toward a Measure."

40. Kosterman and Feshbach, "Toward a Measure."

41. Sidanius et al., "Ethnic Pluralism."

42. Karasawa, "An Etic-Emic Approach."

43. Mummendey, Klink, and Brown, "Out-Group Rejection."

44. Schatz, Staub, and Lavine, "Varieties of National Attachment."

45. See Noelle-Neumann and Köcher, *Versuch der Deutschen*.

46. Blank and Schmidt, "Verletzende Nation."

47. Severin Weiland, "Wettstreit der Stolzen" [Competition of the Proud], *Die Tageszeitung*, 20 March 2001, 7 (National).

48. See Thomas Blank, *Gemeinnutz oder Eigenwohl? Motive und Erscheinungsformen nationaler Identität im vereinigten Deutschland* [Collective Utility or Individual Well -Being? Motives and Manifestations of National Identity in Reunited Germany], (Mannheim: Forschung Raum und Gesellschaft e.V., 2002); Blank, "Determinants of National Identity."

49. See Blank and Schmidt, "Verletzende Nation."

50. Blank, Schmidt, and Westle, "Patriotism."

51. Karasawa, "An Etic-Emic Approach."

52. Karasawa, "An Etic-Emic Approach," 645.

53. Blank and Schmidt, "Verletzende Nation"; Blank, Schmidt, and Westle, "Patriotism."

54. Blank, Schmidt, and Westle, "Patriotism."

55. Sidanius et al., "Ethnic Pluralism."

56. Jim Sidanius, Felicia Pratto, and Lawrence Bobo, "Social Dominance Orientation and the Political Psychology of Gender: A Case of Invariance?" *Journal of Personality and Social Psychology* 67, no. 6 (December 1994): 998-1011.

57. Daniel Goldhagen, *Hitler's Willing Executioners: Ordinary Germans and the Holocaust* (New York: Knopf, 1996).

58. Martin Walser, "Erfahrungen beim Verfassen einer Sonntagsrede" [Experiences in Writing a Sunday's Speech], in *Die Walser-Bubis-Debatte: Eine Dokumentation*, ed. Frank Schirrmacher (Frankfurt a. M.: Suhrkamp Verlag, 1998), 7-17.

59. Blank, *Gemeinnutz*; Blank, Schmidt, and Westle, "Patriotism."

60. For example, see Mummendey, Klink, and Brown, "Out-Group Rejection."

61. Blank, "Determinants of National Identity."

62. Blank and Schmidt, "Verletzende Nation."

63. Karasawa, "An Etic-Emic Approach."

64. Five-point scales are common in national identity research, to avoid bi- or trimodal distributions, for instance, see Blank and Schmidt, "Verletzende Nation."

65. See Schatz, Staub, and Lavine, "Varieties of National Attachment."

66. Jeanne L. Tsai, Yu-Wen Ying, and Peter A. Lee, "The Meaning of 'Being Chinese' and 'Being American': Variation among Chinese American Young Adults," *Journal of Cross-Cultural Psychology* 31, no. 3 (May 2000): 302-32.

67. See Blank, *Gemeinnutz* and "Determinants of National Identity"; Blank and Schmidt, "Verletzende Nation."

68. Nicola Brüning, Henning Krumrey, Olaf Opitz, and Wolfgang Stock, "Schwarz-Rot-Stolz" [Black-Red-Pride], *Focus* 13 (March 2001): 21-27.

69. Beste et al., "Absurdes Getöse."

70. Item loadings under .32 are not reported in table 8.1, as recommended in Barbara G. Tabachnick and Linda S. Fidell, *Using Multivariate Statistics*, 5th ed. (Boston: Allyn and Bacon, 2007).

71. Initially, five-way ANOVAs were conducted including occupational status and religious activity, but these variables accounted for little variance and were dropped from further analysis. For ANOVAs in which Levine's test revealed heterogeneity of variance, a more conservative alpha level ($p < .025$) was adopted to minimize Type I errors. Type III sums of squares were used to compensate for uneven cells.

72. Initially, eight factors with eigenvalues over 1.0 emerged, but only three accounted for substantial variance, so a second analysis extracted three factors. These factors each had theoretical meaning and comprised at least three items loading over .32, as recommended in Tabachnick and Fidell, *Using Multivariate Statistics*. Four items were dropped: "Sometimes in my family or circle of friends we discuss national pride"; "I feel closer to residents of my state than to Germans"; and "I don't concern myself with the question of German national pride" for low factor loadings, and "I am familiar with German cultural practices and customs" for moderate cross-loading on all factors.

73. Leona S. Aiken and Stephen G. West, *Multiple Regression: Testing and Interpreting Interactions* (Newbury Park, CA: Sage, 1991).

74. Older women showed a little ambivalence, with all such correlations less than -.30 and one (between national pride and shame) failing to attain significance, $r(78) = -.21, p = .057$.

75. One item intended to assess identity strength, "I feel closer to the residents of my state than to Germans" (R), was dropped because it reduced the index reliability.

76. Reuben M. Baron and David A. Kenny, "The Moderator-Mediator Variable Distinction in Social Psychological Research: Conceptual, Strategic, and Statistical Considerations," *Journal of Personality and Social Psychology* 51, no. 6 (December 1986): 1173-82.

77. Blank and Schmidt, "Verletzende Nation."

78. In addition to predicting ethnocentrism, identity positivity also served as a suppressor variable obscuring the relationship between cohort and ethnocentrism. Initially, ethnocentrism appeared to be the only variable among 11 critical outcome measures that showed no significant cohort differences; however, regressing ethnocentrism on cohort (dummy coded: 0 = old, 1 = young) and identity positivity revealed that among Germans with a comparably positive German identity, the younger Germans were significantly more ethnocentric than the older Germans.

79. Contrary to predictions, Easterners did not report less shame than Westerners.

80. Blank, "Determinants of National Identity."

81. J. Christopher Cohrs, "Patriotismus—Sozialpsychologische Aspekte" [Patriotism—Social-Psychological Aspects], *Zeitschrift für Sozialpsychologie* 36, no. 1 (March 2005): 3-11.

82. Cf. Blank, *Gemeinnutz* and "Determinants of National Identity."

83. Mummendey, Klink, and Brown, "Out-Group Rejection."

84. Blank, "Determinants of National Identity"; Blank and Schmidt, "Verletzende Nation"; Blank, Schmidt, and Westle, "Patriotism."

85. Rui J. P. de Figueiredo, Jr., and Zachary Elkins, "Are Patriots Bigots? An Inquiry into the Vices of In-Group Pride," *American Journal of Political Science* 47, no. 1 (January 2003): 171-88.

Chapter 9
Nationalism in Italy

Andrzej Marcin Suszycki

Introduction

Examining the recent nationalist developments in Italy, this chapter defines nationalism as a discursive legitimization of political action through commitment to the three nationalist principles: The principle of popular sovereignty, the principle of the uniqueness of the people, and the principle of fundamental equality among all strata in the community.[1] Usually, political actors do not commit directly to these principles, but refer instead to the narratives of national identity which are developed on the basis of these principles.[2] The narratives of national identity can differ from state to state. This chapter argues that the stronger the commitment to the narratives of national identity is, the stronger the political actors' nationalism is.

This definition adopts the liberal notion of nationalism. Liberal nationalists put forward three main arguments. First, they claim that nationalism plays a fundamental role in providing continuity and context at the level of individual lives.[3] Intertwined with this argument is, second, the assertion that nationalism exhibits "boundary mechanisms" which are required for the delineation and maintenance of a shared national public space.[4] Third, liberal nationalists argue that nationalism provides a necessary contextual and motivational basis for the implementation of egalitarian policies, such as redistributive justice within a society.[5] On the basis of these arguments, they assert that nationalism is an inherent and organizing part of a democratic political order of the liberal state.[6]

Consequently, the liberal notion of nationalism maintains that the three nationalist principles remain an essential source of political legitimization[7] and the particular narratives of national identity which are developed on their basis codify the subjective features of the nation.[8] Hence, political actors' commitment to the referential framework of national identity renders the legitimization of their choices more coherent, applicative, and effective.[9]

Against this background, this chapter examines the extent of practices of discursive legitimization of political action through commitment to the referential framework of national identity in Italy. In this respect, Italy is an interesting case study for research on nationalism in contemporary Europe for at least three reasons. First, since the beginning of the 1990s the main narratives of Italian national identity (approached in the second part of this chapter) have been put into question by the separatist movement Lega Nord. Some of the national narratives have also been usurped by Lega Nord. This discourse of Lega Nord is addressed in the third section of this chapter. Second, as a reaction to the political discourse made by Lega Nord, an overwhelming proportion of the political elites have attempted to enlarge the referential framework of the Italian national identity by the narratives connected with European integration and, at the same time, to modify some old narratives. These aspects are addressed in the fourth section. Third, Italian nationalism has had a "fluid" contextual character. This problem is approached in the fifth part.

Narratives of National Identity in Italy

On the basis of the three nationalist principles mentioned above, it is mostly argued that four main mega-narratives have been developed in the discourse of the political and cultural elites in Italy.

The narrative of belonging to the West portrays Italy as a prominent member of the Western cultural community. Despite Italy's geographical borderline position between Western Europe and Eastern Europe as well as between the Northern and the Southern Mediterranean, and despite the century-old close ties between Italy and several non-Western countries, in the middle of the nineteenth century Italy began to be perceived as a bastion of Western European civilization.[10] As a result, non-Western sources of identity are inexistent or obscured in the Italian self-understanding.

The narrative of Risorgimento portrays Italy as a nation born out of a strong popular will to be and to remain united, at times against the will of foreign imperators.[11] It presents the Italians as a nation unified by a common language and culture. This narrative has tended to obscure the fact that the Southern Italian regions were forced into a North Italian nation-building project which was unwilling to include them on equal terms.[12] It has also tended to downplay the enormous socioeconomic and sociocultural differences between the Italian regions or, as and when required in the political discourse, to interpret them as a strengthening factor rather than a threat to the cohesion and unity of the country. In contrast to the time of Italian imperialism and fascism, in the whole period between the end of the Second World War and the end of the Cold War, neither the narrative of belonging to the West nor the Risorgimento narrative placed Italy among the leading world powers.

The narrative of openness and tolerance constructs the Italians as a specific society giving a particularly high value to personal and political freedom and as a model for liberal attitudes to different lifestyles and cultures. Intertwined with this narrative is the widely accepted myth of Italians as good or nice people (*italiani brava gente*). This myth was constructed in post-Second World War Italy and contributed to Italians' postwar memory and identity as victims of war. According to this myth, the Italians become involved in wars, crimes, or intolerance by accident rather than by choice.[13] The myth of the Italians as good people, which over the years became a significant identifying myth, made the public discourse in postwar Italy resistant to a sincere examination of conscience regarding its responsibility for aggressive or criminal behavior toward other nations.[14]

The narrative of life quality constructs Italy as a country with high living standards, which is symbolized not so much by a relatively high GDP per head as by excellent foodstuffs and commodities, stunning landscapes, trend-setting fashion design, the presence of a rich and varied cultural heritage, and the general pleasures of life.[15] This narrative depicts Italy as a *bel paese* (beautiful country) and implies an aesthetic superiority of Italy compared to other nations and cultures.[16]

These four narratives have shaped the Italian national identity. However, as shown in the literature, the Italian national identity has remained rather weakly developed despite the efforts of the Italian political elites over more than the past century to strengthen it.[17]

Questioning and Appropriation of Italian National Narratives by Lega Nord

The rise of the separatist Lega Nord (Northern League)[18] to a significant political actor after the end of the Cold War was accompanied by a sharp questioning and appropriation of the main narratives of the Italian national identity.[19]

Above all, Lega Nord strongly challenged the narrative of Risorgimento. The unification of the country in 1861 was presented as a historical artificiality and a mistake because of the "obvious impossibility to unite the North and the South." Lega Nord emphasized the dysfunctional features of the Italian state, in particular the bureaucratic inefficiency and the corruption of the political and economic elites.[20] In addition, the movement accused the central government of conducting unjust redistribution policies favoring the "corrupt" and "economically and socially incapable" South to the disadvantage of the "productive" and "effective" Northern regions.[21] Ignoring the fact that the unification of the country in the nineteenth century was largely a result of the political forces coming from Northern Italy, Lega Nord argued that the claims to national self-determination have not yet been realized in the North and presented the North as colonized and enslaved by the South. Consequently, it put the very existence of the Italian nation into question and claimed that the socio-economic differences between the North and the South made the maintenance of the Italian state impossible.[22] According to the party leader, Umberto Bossi, the Italian state deserved the same fate as the Austrian Habsburg Empire, i.e., it should be dissolved into several parts.[23] To emphasize their aversion toward the Italian state, high representatives of the party refused to demonstrate respect for the most important symbols of the Italian state.[24] The fact that Lega Nord itself three times—in 1994, between 2001 and 2006, and after the elections of 2008—formed part of the Italian government was presented as a necessary step to transforming Italy into a federal state (since the end of the 1990s, the party replaced its calls for independence for the "North" by this more moderate demand) and the path of "Padanian" nation-building.[25]

As far as the narrative of the Italian belonging to the West is concerned, Lega Nord again emphasized the North-South dichotomy. It argued that the North, through its history and culture, belonged to Western civilization and was even one of its main pillars. In contrast, the Southern regions were placed outside the Western civilization and were referred to as a part of "Africa" or the "uncivilized" Maghreb region. Lega Nord thus limited the application of the narrative of the West to Northern Italy.[26]

The self-understanding of Italians as open and tolerant people was made to look ridiculous by Lega Nord. Openness and tolerance toward other people and cultures was presented as a disadvantage due to the increasing numbers of immigrants from countries not belonging to the European Union coming to Italy since the beginning of the 1990s.[27] The meaning of the *brava gente* myth was reinterpreted and used as a metaphor both for Italians' naivety toward immigrants' alleged abuse of the Italian welfare system financed by the taxes raised in the North and for Italians' lacking will to act against immigrants committing crimes in Italy.[28] Hence, according to the reconstructed narrative, the good and honest people in Italy were in Northern Italy, which underwent exploitation not only by Southern Italians but also by millions of dangerous immigrants.[29] This discourse implied two demands. In relation to immigrants, i.e., the foreign "Others," Lega Nord demanded their immediate expulsion from Italy. Domestically, the party representatives confined the notion of "citizens" within the boundaries of "Padanian" political communities, excluding Italians from the South from the privilege of being referred to as "citizens."

The narrative of Italy as a country with a high quality of life was not put into question by Lega Nord. However, in the same way that the representatives of the party processed the narrative of the West, the party clearly limited the area of validity of this narrative to the Northern regions, i.e., the invented "Padania." A modern, creative, ingenious, and clean North was contrasted with a backward, old-fashioned, and extremely polluted South.[30] In other words, the North was portrayed as the perfect antipode to the South. In general, Lega Nord argued that the fact that the life model in the South bore some resemblance to that in the North was only made possible by huge financial transfers from the North. Consequently, Lega Nord interpreted it as another example of exploitation of the North by the South which had to be eliminated.

The political discourse made by Lega Nord thus countered the efforts of a broad majority of the Italian political spectrum to maintain a national solidaristic public culture with its obligations to provide assistance for economic and social welfare in the South. Consequently, it seriously challenged the cohesion of the referential framework of the Italian national identity.

Constructing New and Modifying Old Narratives

The fact that the discourse of Lega Nord gained electoral support from a significant part of the voter base in Northern Italy made the legitimization of important political decisions through a simple commitment to the old narrative framework of national identity problematic. This took place at a time when the challenges resulting from European integration and economic globalization, as well as the immediate geopolitical location of the country to the areas with considerable socioeconomic problems in Southeastern Europe and North Africa, directly affected the essential functions of the Italian state. The challenge for the political elites was to find narratives more hospitable to Northern Italians, in particular to potential voters of Lega Nord, without—with regard to the voters in the South—emptying these narratives of content and destroying the underpinnings of national unity and solidarity. Accordingly, the referential framework of the Italian national identity was enlarged by new supranational narratives, and, at the same time, the old organizing narratives of Italy being part of the West and of Risorgimento (narrative of national unity) were modified.

First, the discourse of the political elites resorted to supranational narratives linked to Europe and European integration. In the dominant Italian understanding the term "Europe" stands for Northern Europe and merges with the term "European Union," and both terms are used almost synonymously. As the opinion polls have regularly shown, the term "Europe" has a particularly positive meaning in Italy.[31] As far as the national narrative of belonging to the West and the narrative of Risorgimento are concerned, "Europe" has constituted the inspiring "Significant Other" of the Italians.[32] People have ascribed to "Europe" the attributes they have not ascribed to Italy: The high level of socioeconomic development; the stability of the political system; bureaucratic efficiency, intelligibility, and transparency; as well as gender equality. The dominant discourse thus considered the Northern

European welfare and democracy models as alternatives constructed differently and better.[33] These positive connotations have decreased slightly since the end of the 1990s. As far as the narrative of Italians as *brava gente* and the narrative of a high quality of life are concerned, Europe has even functioned rather as a neutral or even threatening "Significant Other" and the Northern European models have no longer been viewed as more valuable. In sum, however, the general positive connotations of Europe as the inspiring "Significant Other" have continuously outweighed the recent neutral or negative connotations of Europe within the referential framework of national identity.

Against this background, the narrative which portrayed Europe (the European Union) based on the principles of unity, solidarity, and parity between the member states and their citizens as a new broader homeland of all the Italians has been used by Italian decision-makers since the mid-1990s to legitimize actions which touched the core fields of the Italian monetary and economic system as well as its foreign policy.[34] For instance, the political elites presented the efforts to fulfill the Maastricht convergence criteria for membership of the European Monetary Union (EMU) as necessary steps to bring Italy into its "European home." They argued that effective solutions to the fundamental problems of currency stability, national economic growth, unemployment, and social wealth could be found only at a European level, not at a national level.[35] The common European currency was defined as a way of building a common future life, security and stability for the whole of Europe, and as the most important symbol of the member states' unity. At the same time, references to the national narratives such as the narrative of national unity (Risorgimento narrative) were eclipsed, even though the highest representatives of the government were aware of the fact that the unity of the Italian state could have been questioned by the separatist Lega Nord in the event that Italy failed to qualify for the EMU.[36] In this respect it must be added that the fulfillment of the Maastricht convergence criteria was particularly difficult in Italy because of the country's enormous public deficit and high consumer price inflation rates, and it required significant budget adjustments through tax increases and social expenditure cuts which could have led to electoral losses for the governing left-wing coalition, had they not been explained convincingly to the voters. Hence, without the European narrative, the process of fiscal and monetary consolidation had been slower and less effective.[37] Against this background, it is not surprising that Lega Nord first tried to exploit the question of Italy's EMU membership for its separatist demands, arguing that the strong economic and financial interdependence between the Italian North and the rest of the EU made the adoption of the Euro in Northern Italy necessary and that, since Italy as a whole could not take part in the EMU, the North, which would easily fulfill the Maastricht convergence criteria, should become a member of the EMU alone, leaving the rest of Italy to its "non-European" fate.[38] The enthusiasm of Lega Nord for the EMU ended as it became clear that Italy would fulfill the convergence criteria and qualify for membership of the EMU from the beginning in 1999. From that point onwards, representatives of the party argued that the EMU was a project of an undemocratic European "superstate" which strengthened the power of the Brussels bureaucrats and undermined the sense of regional democracy and economy.[39] In the same supranational vein, an overwhelming majority of the Italian political elites explained their strong support for the European constitutional treaty which was signed in Rome in October 2004. Without referring to the national referential framework, they presented the treaty as a necessary step to strengthen the cohesion between the EU member states and their sense of common belonging in view of the problems resulting from globalization and security risks.[40] In addition, they argued that the European Constitution would strengthen the parity and equality between the member states. At the same time, representatives of Lega Nord strongly criticized the European constitutional treaty, arguing that the treaty was a political adventure of the elites which constructed a Europe of "bankers and judges" based on no popular legitimation, strengthened the corrupt Italian central bureaucracy and ran counter to the needs of the European regions.[41]

Another example of legitimizing an important political decision through commitment to the narrative of Europe became evident in July 2006 when the Italian center-left government led by Romano Prodi decided to remove restrictions on the free movement of the labor force from the new Eastern European EU member states imposed by the former center-right wing government led by Silvio Berlusconi.[42] As stated by the Minister of the Interior, Giuliano Amato, the decision to lift the transitional restrictions corresponded to the European principles of parity and equality between the citizens of old and new member states.[43] At the same time, since the opinion polls showed a negative attitude of most Italians toward immigrants from Eastern and Southern Europe, no references were made either to the national narrative of a high quality of life, for which the influx of thousands of workers from the new EU member states could probably have beneficial effects, or to the narrative of the Italians' openness and tolerance toward other nations. In this regard, it can be argued that the discourse of the Italian political elites using the technologies of limited discursive enlargement of the referential framework of national identity propagated a particular form of nationalism which some observers label supranationalism or Euronationalism (as discussed by Ireneusz Paweł Karolewski in this volume). The Italian decision-makers hence forged a European collective identity in a way that followed the integrative logic of national identity and attempted to generate a supranational sense of belonging in a traditional nation-state environment.[44]

Second, as a reaction to the separatist discourse of Lega Nord, the dominant discourse of the political elites modified the narrative of Italy belonging to the West and the narrative of Risorgimento. As stated in Section 2, the narrative of Italy as part of the West assigned to Italy a rather modest role on the international stage and appealed more to the cultural potentials of the country than to its political weight. Since the middle of the 1990s, however, the discourse left the modest self-understanding and claimed that Italy should be treated in international politics as one of the major Western powers, on equal terms with Germany, France, and Great Britain. The legitimization of important decisions, especially in the field of foreign policy, through commitment to this modified narrative generated a new phenomenon in the Italian political discourse which can be called "big power nationalism." Such was the case in 1997, when Italy took over the leadership of a coalition aimed at providing humanitarian aid and stabilizing the political situation in Albania, which included sending multinational military peace troops. Although Italy's EU partners rejected joint direct military involvement in Albania, the Italian government decided to undertake the operation *Alba* by itself, explaining proudly to the Italians that the success of the operation provided evidence that Italy had the ability to provide humanitarian services to other nations, and that the action served to "regain the credibility" of the country as one of the major European powers.[45] This "big power nationalism" became the more vigorous the more it was contrasted to the discourse of Lega Nord, which spoke in a depreciatory way of the Italian government's action and emphasized the international powerlessness of the Italian state.[46] A similar discursive emphasis on the important role of the country in world politics was evident during the long debate on the reform of the Security Council of the United Nations. Italy has been one of the most active participants in this debate and first advocated the addition to the five permanent members of the present Council of new non-permanent seats, to be taken, for rotating terms, by the top contributors to UN activities, including Italy, and moved later to a new proposal, providing a stronger role for regional groups in the Security Council. However, the openly declared objective of all Italian governments since 1994 has not been a reform of the Security Council—quite the contrary; since the Italian government was aware of the minimal chances of Italy becoming a permanent member of the Security Council, Italy could easily accept the continuation of the present world power distribution. The main goal has constantly been to prevent the enlargement of the Security Council to include Germany. A permanent seat for Germany was viewed as a degradation of Italy, since Italy in this event would be the only one of the four "major European powers" without a permanent seat on the Security Council. The firm opposition of the Italian political elites to this "humiliation" of the country can be explained not only by the pursuit of political interests in the international system (the maintenance of the relative power position) but also by the domestic context:[47] The more the separatist Lega Nord questioned the unity of the Italian state and downsized the international significance of Italy, the stronger the Italian governments and the opposition leaders emphasized the narrative of Italy as an important European power which should be treated on equal terms with Germany, and the stronger the prevention of a disadvantageous reform was declared to be a "national task."[48] At the same time, the Italian decision-makers combined the "big power nationalism" with Euronationalism as discussed above, since the opposition to Germany's ambitions was accompanied by a strong reference to the narrative of European unity and solidarity. Italian President Napolitano argued that the EU member states could better pursue their global interests if the "united Europe" spoke unanimously in the Security Council.[49] Following this logic, the second Italian reform proposal would have implied a common seat of the European Union in the Security Council (in addition to the British and French seats).[50] Another example of "big power nationalism" through reference to the modified narrative of the West was provided by Italian Prime Minister Prodi at the end of 2007 after the Spanish Prime Minister Zapatero had triumphantly announced that Spain had overtaken Italy in terms of GDP per head according to EU statistics.[51] Whereas representatives of Lega Nord interpreted the official statistics as more evidence of the general economic incapability of the Italian state, Prodi rejected the Eurostat figures and described Italy as being far ahead of Spain and as having a good chance of remaining one of the leading Western economies thanks to the successful policies of his government.[52]

Moreover, against the background of the massive immigration to Italy from North Africa and Southeastern Europe, especially from Albania and Romania, the Italian political elites modified the narrative of Risorgimento insofar as the foreign imperators were replaced by immigrants as the threatening "Significant Other." In the old narrative, foreign powers threatened the political unity of the Italian state; now the reference to immigrants was used to strengthen the unity threatened by the discourse of Lega Nord.[53] For instance, the Italian decision-makers portrayed the negative phenomena associated with the massive influx of North Africans, Albanians, and Romanians as a threat to the whole country and the elimination of these threats as a common nationwide task.[54] In 1997 the flood of several thousand Albanian refugees led to the declaration of a state of emergency by the left-wing Prodi government over the whole Italian state territory and not just over the affected parts of the country. In the same exaggerated way, the center-left government generated a sense of a national emergency after the public had been alarmed by several crimes committed by Romanian immigrants in 2007.[55] Prime Minister Prodi described "the psychological and social impact" of the presence of the large numbers of Romanians in Italy as "incredible"[56] and his government undertook extensive measures at the national, bilateral, and European level to reduce the arrivals of Romanian immigrants to Italy.[57] The state-cementing aim of this nationalist discourse becomes clear when considering the fact that the Northern regions were statistically affected by the negative aspects of the immigration to a much greater extent than the Southern regions, and Lega Nord continuously alleged that the central state authorities were incapable of actions securing law and order in the Northern regions.

Contextual Nationalism

Conventional studies present nationalism as a holistic phenomenon and assume its ideological consistency. On this basis, they distinguish between nationalist and non-nationalist actors. An analysis of recent Italian political discourse makes it clear that representatives of all the main political groups used to legitimize their decisions toward the voters alternately in a nationalist and non-nationalist way. They committed to national narratives in some policy fields and, often at the same time, did not appeal to national narratives in other issues. They thus did not represent any strong ideological consistency—the use of the narratives of national identity took place in a selective way. Consequently, in the Italian case it does not make sense to distinguish between "nationalist" and "non-nationalist" actors.[58]

For instance, the left-wing governments led by Prodi, D'Alema, and Amato often accused the center-right opposition of propagating racism and the exclusion of immigrants. At the same time, however, in order to strengthen the unity of the state, they exploited the dominant public perception of immigrants as the threatening "Other." By doing this, they supported the anti-immigrant trends of public opinion. The same holds true concerning their attitude toward European integration. In June 2007 the center-left Italian government of Romano Prodi declared itself "pro-European" during the negotiations on the new EU treaty and accused the opponents of the treaty of having lost the "European spirit" and falling into nationalism.[59] In October 2007, however, as the proposed redistribution of seats in the European Parliament saw a reduction of Italian parliament members from 78 to 72 and the loss of parity with France (74 seats) and Great Britain (73 seats), the Italian government threatened to block the reform treaty unless Italy obtained an additional seat even though both France and Great Britain have more inhabitants than Italy.[60] In this case, the Italian government demonstrated nationalism based on the reference to the narrative of Italy as a big European power (equal to France and Great Britain).

Representatives of the center-right parties also showed contextual nationalism. For instance, as far as the crucial issue of immigration is concerned, Forza Italia e Allenaza Nazionale, being in power in 2003, proposed giving legal immigrants the right of administrative voting. This proposal was explained not by reference to the narratives of national identity but by the appeal to general human values such as justice.[61] However, in 2006, the same parties firmly opposed the plans of the center-left government to liberalize the rules for obtaining Italian citizenship, accusing the government of devaluing Italian citizenship and threatening national cohesion.[62] Hence, they demonstrated nationalism based on the reference to the modified narrative of the West (Italian citizenship as a "valuable" citizenship of a big Western country) and to the modified narrative of national unity (new citizens as the threatening Others).

The highest representatives of the state also showed contextual nationalism. For instance, the Italian president Napolitano on the one hand repeatedly criticized "nationalist" policies and discourses in Italy and in the EU. On the other hand, in 2007 he strongly appealed to the Italian national myth of Italians as "good" people (*italiani brava gente*) and described the displacement of Italians from Istria and Dalmatia after the Second World War as ethnic cleansing and the expelled Italians as innocent war victims.[63] Napolitano was accused by

Croatian President Stjepan Mesic of supporting racism, historical revisionism, and political revanchism, and his statements led to a serious diplomatic crisis between Italy and Croatia.[64]

Explaining the phenomenon of contextual nationalism, i.e., actors' selective use of national narratives, we should consider four factors. The first factor is the short time horizon ("short memory") of the voters and their limited ability to sanction political actors' programmatic or ideological fluctuations in a longer time perspective.[65] Obviously, this aspect is characteristic not only to Italy but to all democratic systems. The second aspect is the disorientation of the voters caused by issues connected with the radical changes within the political system of the country since 1992[66] as well as with issues arising from European integration. In this regard, horizontally, the new organization of the political system has reopened a great number of political, economic, and social issues to be approached by Italian politics. According to many commentators, Italy presents a case of a "never-ending transition," as it has not developed into a stable and effective democratic system.[67] In contrast, after 1992 the political system in Italy has showed high levels of political fragmentation, lack of accountability and anti-elitist, anti-political populism.[68] Vertically, Italian voters' field of vision has been strongly limited by the multi-layer decisional system of the EU, which has become more and more complex in recent decades.[69] The third aspect is the continued extension of boundaries of political and cultural discourse, which meets the increasing need for a national public sphere that is as large as possible and the need to clarify and (re) define a broad range of issues which previously used to be excluded from conventional discursive frameworks.[70]

These three factors have reduced the vulnerability of political actors in front of their voter base and, consequently, have strengthened the incentives for a less ideological and a more strategic use of national narratives. The fourth aspect is connected with the need for the preservation of distributive justice at the national level, and with the increased vulnerability of national actors to sanctions at the international level. On the one hand, as depicted by Walzer, the idea of distributive justice presupposes "a bounded world." Hence, distributive justice can be developed only within closed social and cultural frameworks and must favor members over non-members (according to Walzer, every substantive account of distributive justice is a local account)[71] and membership must be (de)limited.[72] Therefore, in order to retain legitimacy at the national level, political actors must delineate the borders of the distributive policies by means of a strong commitment to the narratives of national identity. On the other hand, in contemporary Europe the use of national narratives has become discernible and vulnerable beyond the boundaries of the nation-state. National actors demonstrating nationalism on a regular basis therefore might face retaliatory actions at the European level. Given the strong political and economic interdependence, these sanctions might endanger the just domestic distribution of social and economic benefits and burdens and, consequently, weaken their own domestic power position. Consequently, international sanction mechanisms have also reduced the incentives for persistent nationalism (in the form of a permanent use of national narratives) and made contextual nationalism more attractive for the Italian political elites.[73]

Summary

This chapter examines the recent nationalist developments in Italy. It adopts the liberal notion of nationalism and defines nationalism as a legitimization of political action through commitment to the narrative framework of national identity.

Three factors which have changed the character of nationalism in Italy since the beginning of the 1990s are the rapid and far-reaching changes of the Italian political system connected with the fight against corruption, the calls of the separatist movement Lega Nord for a secession of the Northern Italian regions from the Italian state, and the process of European integration.

The political discourse made by Lega Nord was aimed, above all, at countering the efforts of a broad majority of the Italian political spectrum to strengthen a national solidaristic public culture with its obligations to provide assistance for economic and social welfare in the poorly developed South. Repeatedly, Lega Nord argued that the claims to national self-determination have not yet been realized in the North and presented the North as colonized and enslaved by the South. It also limited the application of the narrative of the West to Northern Italy. In doing so, the party questioned or usurped the main narratives of the Italian national identity and made the legitimization of political decisions through a simple commitment to the old referential framework problematic. Consequently, it made old forms of nationalism difficult for an overwhelming proportion of the Italian political and cultural elites.

In response to the discourse of Lega Nord, the political elites of the country tried to enlarge the national referential framework by introducing new supranational narratives linked to the process of European integration. Here, the narrative which portrayed Europe as a new homeland of all the Italians and the united Italian state as an indispensable part of a united European Union was used to explain decisions regarding important issues of monetary, economic, and foreign policy, such as the adoption of the common European currency and the support of the European constitutional treaty.

Besides, some old narratives of national identity were partially modified by the political elites. The narrative of belonging to the West no longer ascribed to Italy a modest second range place, but claimed a prominent position among the world powers. The narrative of national unity (Risorgimento narrative) was modified insofar as immigrants now became the threatening "Significant Others" and the reference to them was used to strengthen the unity of the state threatened by the discourse of Lega Nord. The enlargement of the referential framework of national identity and the modifications of old narratives made possible the emergence of new forms of Italian nationalism, especially Euronationalism and big power nationalism.

This chapter also argues that representatives of all the main political parties committed to national narratives in some policy fields and, often at the same time, did not appeal to national narratives in other issues—they legitimized their decisions toward the voters alternately in a nationalist and non-nationalist way. They thus did not represent any strong ideological consistency. Consequently, in the Italian case it does not make sense to distinguish between "nationalist" and "non-nationalist" actors. These results confirm the tendencies observed in other European countries.

Notes

1. See the three nationalist principles coined by Greenfeld in Liah Greenfeld, *Nationalism. Five Roads to Modernity* (Cambridge, MA; London: Harvard University Press, 1993), 8-11.

2. Cf. Andrzej Marcin Suszycki, "Contextual and Nordic: The Case of Swedish Nationalism," in *Nation and Nationalism: Political and Historical Studies*, ed. Andrzej Marcin Suszycki and Ireneusz Paweł Karolewski (Wrocław: Willy Brandt Center for German and European Studies, 2007), 90.

3. For a description of the main arguments made by liberal nationalists see Albert W. Dzur, "Nationalism, Liberalism, and Democracy," *Political Research Quarterly* 55, no. 1 (2002): 191-211, esp. 192-194.

4. See also Sune Lagaard, "Liberal Nationalism and the Nationalisation of Liberal Values," *Nations and Nationalism* 13, no. 1 (2007): 37-55.

5. See also David Miller, *Citizenship and National Identity* (Cambridge: Polity Press, 2000). For the general framework of redistributive justice see Michael Walzer, *Spheres of Justice: A Defense of Pluralism and Equality* (New York: Basic Books, 1983).

6. For this argument see Yael Tamir, *Liberal Nationalism* (Princeton, NJ: Princeton University Press, 1993).

7. Cf. David Miller, *On Nationality* (Oxford: Oxford University Press, 1995).

8. For a similar argument see Craig Calhoun, "Nationalism and Civil Society: Democracy, Diversity and Self-Determination," *International Sociology* 8, no. 4 (1993): 387-411, esp. 390.

9. Of course, political actors' strong commitment to the national narratives might also actuate or strengthen processes of exclusion, indoctrination, and national mythologization. Negative phenomena such as racism, chauvinism, forced assimilation or authoritarianism might result from them and undermine the democratic and liberal character of nationalism. For this argument see also Ray Taras, *Liberal and Illiberal Nationalisms* (Basingstoke: Palgrave Macmillan, 2002). In accordance with liberal concepts of nationalism, however, it can be assumed that advanced democracies possess sufficient control and sanction mechanisms to prevent these negative manifestations of nationalism.

10. See also Enrica Di Ciommo, *I confini dell'identita. Teorie e modelli di nazione in Italia* (Roma-Bari: Editori Laterza, 2005), 157-161.

11. The movement of national revival in the first half of the nineteenth century which primarily aimed at freedom from foreign control and the unification of Italy. Other goals were the propagation of liberalism and the establishment of a constitutional system of citizens' liberties and rights.

12. Cf. Pasquale Verdicchio, *Bound by Distance. Rethinking Nationalism through the Italian Diaspora* (Madison, NJ: Fairleigh Dickinson University Press, 1997), 22.

13. For this aspect see Angelo Del Boca, *Italiani, brava gente? Un mito duro a morire* (Vicenza: Neri Pozza Editore, 2005). For the myth of Italians as *brava gente* see also Filippo Focardi, *L' immagine del cattivo tedesco e il mito del bravo italiano* (Edizioni Rinoceronte, 2005).

14. Cf. Filippo Focardi and Lutz Klinkhammer, "The Question of Fascist Italy's War Crimes: the Construction of a Self-acquitting Myth (1943-1948)," *Journal of Modern Italian Studies* 9, no. 3 (2004): 330-348, esp. 344.

15. Beverly Allen and Mary Russo, eds., *Revisioning Italy. National Identity and Global Culture* (Minneapolis: University of Minnesota Press, 1997), 1-19 (Introduction).

16. See Stephen Gundle, "Il bel paese: Art, Beauty and the Cult of Appearance," in *The Politics of Italian National Identity*, ed., Gino Bedani and Bruce Haddock (Cardiff: University of Wales Press, 2000), 124-141.

17. William Brierley and Luca Giacometti, "Italian National Identity and the Failure of Regionalism," in *Nation and Identity in Contemporary Europe*, ed. Brian Jenkins and Spyros A. Sofos (London: Routledge, 1996), 172-197. See also Ernesto Galli Della Loggia, *L'identita italiana*, (Bologna: Il Mulino, 1998).

18. La Lega Nord per l' indipendenza della Padania, (the Northern League for the Independence of Padania) was founded in 1991 as a federation of regional parties from North Italian regions such as Lega Lombarda and Liga Veneta. The Lega Lombarda and the Liga Veneta have continued to act as regional and local sections of the "federal party"

19. For this aspect see also Benito Giordano, "A Place Called Padania?," in *European Urban and Regional Studies* 6, no. 3 (1999): 215-230.

20. See for instance the statement by the party leader Bossi: Bossi rispolvera la secessione. 'Dovremo fare la Marcia su Roma,' in *La Repubblica* 29 October 2006. For this argument see also Cf. Michel Huysseune, "A Nation Confronting a Secessionist Claim: Italy and the Lega Nord," in *Contextualizing Secession. Normative Studies in Comparative Perspective*, ed. Bruno Coppieters and Richard Sakwa (Oxford: Oxford University Press, 2003), 22-48, esp. 30.

21. See for example the statements by the representatives of the Lega Nord in Camera dei Deputati, *Atti Parlamentari, Discussioni, Seduta del 7 Ottobre 1997*, 36-39; Senato della Repubblica, *429 e 430 Resoconto sommario, 21 Luglio 1998*, 34-35; see also Daniele Albertazzi, " 'Back to Our Roots' or Self-Confessed Manipulation? The Uses of the Past in the Lega Nord's Positing of Padania," *National Identities* 8, no. 1 (2006): 21-39.

22. See the representatives of the Lega Nord in Camera dei Deputati, *Atti Parlamentari, Discussioni, Seduta del 7 Ottobre 1997*, 36-39; Senato della Repubblica, *429 e 430 Resoconto sommario, 21 Luglio 1998*, 34-35.

23. In 1996 Lega Nord left its original demands for federalism in favor of a strong discourse of secession. The separatist policies of the party culminated on 15 September 1996 as the party leader Bossi announced the secession of Northern Italy under the name *Padania*. However, the renewed government coalition with Forza Italia and Alleanza Nazionale after 2001 forced Lega Nord to deemphasize its demands for independence for the North and to settle for the devolution of Italy, i.e., the transformation of Italy into a federal state.

24. One of the most spectacular cases of the manifest disregard towards the symbols of the state was the statement by the Minister of Justice in Silvio Berlusconi's government in the period 2001-2006, Roberto Castelli. Castelli said he did not sing the Italian national anthem because he did not know the text of the hymn. See Fabio Martini, "La mossa di Walter per spezzare l'asse tra Lega e Cavaliere," *La Stampa* 9, April 2008.

25. For an analysis of the political discourse of Lega Nord see Isabelle Fremeaux and Daniele Albertazzi, "Discursive Strategies around 'Community' in Political Propaganda: The Case of Lega Nord," *National Identities* 4, no. 2 (2002): 145-160.

26. Among several examples of this type of reasoning see the statements made by one of the leaders of the Lega Nord Giovanni Fava in Camera dei Deputati, *Atti Parlamentari, Resoconto stenografico dell'Assemblea, Seduta n. 183 del 4/7/2007,* p. 18-19.

27. For the dimensions and problems of immigration in Italy see Antonio Golini, ed., *L'immigrazione straniera: indicatori e misure di integrazione* (Bologna: Il Mulino, 2005) and Giovanna Zincone, "The Making of Policies: Immigration and Immigrants in Italy," *Journal of Ethnic and Migration Studies* 32 (2006): 347-375.

28. See the statement by one of the leaders of the Lega Nord and vice president of the Italian Senate Roberto Calderoli in "Cinque anni per la cittadinanza italiana. Si del governo al ddl di Amato," *La Repubblica* 4 August 2006. See also the statement made by Roberto Cota, Lega Nord's member of the Italian Deputy Chamber in Camera dei Deputati, *Atti Parlamentari, Resoconto stenografico dell'Assemblea, Seduta n. 187 dell'11/7/2007,* p. 65.

29. Cf. "Su immigrazione ed economia e rissa nella maggioranza," *La Repubblica* 23, October 2003.

30. For example the Lega Nord emphasized that the disastrous waste management in the South was a symbol of the cultural gap between the North and the South. See Camera dei Deputati, *Atti Parlamentari,, Resoconto stenografico dell'Assemblea, Seduta n. 183 del 4/7/2007,* 18.

31. For instance, the response of the Italian citizens to survey questions on European identity/feelings of attachment to the EU has been persistently positive. For this aspect see Anna Triandafyllidou, "Popular Perceptions of Europe and the Nation: The Case of Italy," *Nations and Nationalism* 14, no. 2 (2008): 261-282.

32. For the notion of "significant others" as an analytical tool for studying real or imagined interaction between the nation and others see Anna Triandafyllidou, *Immigrants and National Identity in Europe* (London: Routledge, 2001), 32-54.

33. An analysis of the strong public support in Italy for European integration is offered by Pierangelo Isernia, "Present at Creation: Italian Mass Support for European Integration in the Formative Years," *European Journal of Political Research* 47 (2008): 383-410.

34. The narrative of Europe was preceded by the reference to Italy's active role in the process of European integration which had regularly occurred since the foundation of the EC. However, until the 1990s this reference had had little to do with domestic legitimization of the unity of the Italian state. It had clearly outward functions as a legitimization of the Italians' calls for parity and equality as far as its power position in relation to other big member states like Germany, France, and Great Britain was concerned.

35. For a review of Italy's policies on the EU monetary integration see Lucia Quaglia and Ivo Maes, "France and Italy's Policies on European Monetary Integration: A Comparison of 'Strong' and 'Weak' States," *Comparative European Politics* 2 (2004): 51-72.

36. See the declaration by Prime Minister Prodi in *Wirtschaftswoche*, 22 November 1996; see also *Atti Parlamentari, Camera dei Deputati, Resohconto Sommario, Seduta di 12 Febbraio 1997*, p.6-7.

37. For similar conclusions see Lucia Quaglia and Ivo Maes, "France and Italy's Policies on European Monetary Integration . . .," 68.

38. See also Benito Giordano, "The Continuing Transformation of Italian Politics and the Contradictory Fortunes of the Lega Nord," *Journal of Modern Italian Studies* 8, no. 2 (2003): 216-230, esp. 221.

39. See for instance, "Bossi: l' euro non ha portato bene, non ci ha arricchito," *Corriere della Sera*, 29 June 2003.

40. Marzio Breda, "Carta Ue, appello di Napolitano: "Tutti devono rispettare le intese oppure l' Italia chiedera di piu," *Corriere della Sera*, 11 April 2007.

41. Cf. "Costituzione Ue, si della Camera. Contrari Lega e Rifondazione," *La Repubblica*, 26 January 2005.

42. According to the Treaty of Accession of the new member states, Italy like other old EU member states could maintain restrictions on the movement of the labor force from the new member states for a period of up to seven years after the EU enlargement in 2004.

43. Lorenzo Salvia, "Via libera del governo a 350 mila immigrati," *Corriere della Sera*, 22 July 2006.

44. For a general analysis of the process of "Europeanization" of the public discourse in Italy see Donatella della Porta and Manuela Caiani, "The Europeanization of Public Discourse in Italy: A Top-Down Process?," *European Union Politics* 7, no. 1 (2006): 77-112.

45. For this argument see Andrzej Marcin Suszycki, *Italienische Osteuropapolitik 1989-2000* (Münster, Hamburg, London: LIT Verlag, 2003), 230-255.

46. In this regard the leader of Lega Nord Bossi ironically called Italy "Italietta." See Camera dei Deputati, *Atti Parlamentari, Discussioni, Seduta del 9 Aprile 1997*, 14678.

47. For the domestic context of Italian foreign policy see also Maurizio Carbone, "The Domestic Foundation of Italy's Foreign and Development Policy," *West European Politics* 30, no. 4 (2007): 903-923.

48. See the statement made by the speaker of the Parliament Pier Ferdinando Casini in "Riforma ONU un impegno nazionale," *Corriere della Sera*, 12 August 2004. For a broad consensus in this respect between the government led by Berlusconi and the opposition see for instance Riccardo Bruno, "Napolitano: riforma Onu, Casini ha ragione," *Corriere della Sera*, 13 August 2004.

49. See the statement made by Giorgio Napolitano in a interview with the German newspaper *Die Zeit* on 21 November 2007: *Intervista al Presidente della Repubblica Giorgio Napolitano, del settimanale tedesco "Die Zeit"* at http://www.quirinale.it/Discorsi/Discorso.asp?id=34429.

50. Gianna Fregonara, "Frattini: riforma Onu il seggio europeo per ora e un sogno," *Corriere della Sera*, 28 August 2004.

51. Cf. "Zapatero stuzzica Prodi dopo il sorpasso. Il premier spagnolo: "Secondo l'Ue, il nostro Paese ha superato l'Italia. A Romano l'avevo detto," *Corriere della Sera*, 18 December 2007.

52. See Sergio Rizzo, "E Prodi smentisce il sorpasso 'Italia davanti alla Spagna,'" *Corriere della Sera*, 2 January 2008.

53. See for instance Roberto Zuccolini, "Napolitano: Severita sui clandestini," *Corriere della Sera*, 23 July 1998.

54. See the statement made by the Chairman of the Defense Committee of the Chamber of Deputies Valdo Spini in Camera dei Deputati, *Atti Parlamentari, Discussioni, Seduta del 9 Aprile 1997*, 14670.

55. Dino Martirano, "Allarme invasione dalla Romania," *Corriere della Sera*, 22 January 2007. Prime Minister Prodi described the case of an infamous murder committed by a Romanian immigrant on an Italian woman in November 2007 as an injury to all Italians, see "Berlusconi: "'Veltroni e Rutelli stiano ziti,'" *Corriere della Sera*, 2 November 2007.

56. Ian Fisher, "Romanian Premier Tries to Calm Italy After a Killing," *The New York Times*, 8 November 2007.

57. Fiorenza Sarzanini, "I romeni espulsi sono 177," *Corriere della Sera*, 18 November 2007.

58. For similar results with regard to Sweden see: Andrzej Marcin Suszycki, "Nationalism in Sweden and the EU Membership," in *Nationalism and European Integration. The Need for New Theoretical and Empirical Insights*, ed. Ireneusz Paweł Karolewski and Andrzej Marcin Suszycki (New York; London: Continuum, 2007), 95-98.

59. Maurizio Caprara, "Prodi: "Molti hanno perso lo spirito europeo," *Corriere della Sera*, 24 June 2007.

60. Ivo Caizzi, "D'Alema: 'Inaccettabile la riduzione dei seggi,'" *Corriere della Sera* 16 October 2007.

61. Cf. "Fini: diamo il diritto di voto agli immigrati," *Corriere della Sera*, 7 October 2003.

62. Fiorenza Sarzarini, "Immigrati, referendum contro la cittadinanza" in *Corriere della Sera*, 6 August 2006.

63. Marzio Breda, "Napolitano: sulle foibe una congiura del silenzio," in *Corriere della Sera*, 11 February 2007.

64. Mara Gergolet, "Foibe, la Croazia contro Napolitano: Un discorso razzista e revanscista," *Corriere della Sera*, 13 February 2007.

65. Cf. Andrzej Marcin Suszycki, "Nationalism in Sweden and the EU membership," in *Nationalism and European Integration: The Need for New Theoretical and Empirical Insights*, ed. Ireneusz Paweł Karolewski and Andrzej Marcin Suszycki, (New York: Continuum, 2007), 97-98.

66. For the background of this argument see Gianfranco Pasquino, ed., *Dall'Ulivo al governo Berlusconi* (Bologna: Il Mulino, 2002).

67. Cf. Gianfranco Pasquino, "The Government, the Opposition and the President of the Republic under Berlusconi," *Journal of Modern Italian Studies* 8, no. 4 (2003): 485-500.

68. Cf. Anna Cento Bull, "The Italian Transition and National (Non)Reconciliation," *Journal of Modern Italian Studies* 13, no. 3 (2008): 405.

69. For this argument see Beate Kohler-Koch, ed., *Linking EU and National Governance* (Oxford: Oxford University Press, 2005).

70. Cf. Sara Mills, *Discourse. The New Critical Idiom* (New York: Routledge, 2004). For the Italian background see Leonardo Morlino and Marco Tarchi, eds., *Partiti e caso italiano* (Bologna: Il Mulino, 2006), 105-243.

71. Cf. Michael Walzer, *Spheres of Justice*, esp. 31-35.

72. See also Jean L. Cohen, "Changing Paradigms of Citizenship and the Exclusiveness of the Demos," *International Sociology* 14, no. 2 (1999): 245-268, esp. 263.

73. For similar arguments with regard to Sweden see Andrzej Marcin Suszycki, "Contextual and Nordic: The Case of Swedish Nationalism," in *Nation and Nationalism: Political and Historical Studies*, ed. Andrzej Marcin Suszycki and Ireneusz Paweł Karolewski (Wrocław: Willy Brandt Center for German and European Studies, 2007), 95.

Part IV
New Nationalism in Eastern Europe?

Chapter 10
Nationalism and Statism in Latvia: The Past and Current Trends

Ieva Zake

Post-Communist Eastern and Central Europe has become an exciting experimental site for scholars of modern nationalism where they can test old theories and create new ones in order to account for the nationalism's diverse and contradictory nature. One such complex case has been Latvian nationalism, which during the late 1980s worked as a liberating force that could mobilize the disillusioned Soviet-ruled masses in the name of ethnic revival and national independence. However, once Latvian nationalism became an instrument of nation-building, it spawned such notorious post-Communist legal policies as the Citizenship Law of 1991. It disenfranchised about a third of Latvia's residents on the grounds that they were not direct descendants of the First Republic (1921-1940), but rather "remnants" of the Soviet occupation.

Due to this and other policies Latvian nationalism came to be known as a classic example of the so-called ethnic (radical or nationalizing) nationalism. Along with other Easten European nationalisms, the Latvian one was also accused by Western academics and media of promoting discrimination, xenophobia, and intolerance. While the ethnic nationalisms of minority groups were often overlooked, the nationalist ideologies of the titular nations were seen as persistent and dangerous.[1] Popular media also became infatuated with the idea of Eastern European states as examples of the growing threat of ethnic nationalism.[2]

This chapter questions some of these assumptions by showing that, first, both Latvian and Russian oriented nationalisms in Latvia had notable elements of ethnic nationalism and, second, that important ideological changes have recently taken place in Latvian and Russian nationalisms. Namely, a new type of nationalism has emerged. It is characterized by "a search for an inclusive national identity that could foster the cohesion of society across class and ethnic boundaries"[3] and by reliance on the state as the source of this new national identity. It is shown here that both Latvian and Russian nationalisms have began to de-emphasize the ethnic meaning of the nation and strengthen the ideological importance of the autonomous state, its redistributive capacity, and its ability to influence as many aspects of social life as possible. This new ideology is not civic nationalism and it also does not fall neatly into other existing categories of nationalism. Its emphasis on strong statehood adds a new dimension to what we know about ethnic nationalisms of small nations. Therefore it is argued here that we need to address the relationship between nationalism and statism and elaborate our categories. To accomplish this goal, the present chapter suggests a categorization which includes nationalisms that fall between the categories of ethnic vs. civic nationalisms. It then applies the proposed typology to the past and present shifts in Latvian nationalism and addresses the most recent tranisition from ethnic to statist nationalism in contemporary Latvia.

Categorizing Nationalisms

The question of whether it is possible to group nationalisms according to some reliable characteristics has long bothered scholars in the field as they grappled with the question of why some nationalisms lead to violence and destruction, while others serve unifying and democratizing purposes. To explicate this difference, Hans Kohn introduced the classical categories of civic vs. ethnic or Western vs. Eastern nationalism.[4] According to Kohn, the Western type of nationalism centered on the formation of modern centralized statehood. It automatically identified all citizens of the state as members of the nation, and it understood nationhood in political and territorial terms. This nationalism preconditioned the development of stable democratic political systems. At the same time, the so-called Eastern nationalism was highly problematic because it was built on ethnic identities whose borders did not coincide with those of the states and who aimed to disrupt the existing states. Ethnic nationalism asserted the primacy of blood-based membership. It was usually created by intellectuals who identified the nation with cultural uniqueness, peculiarities of native folk traditions, language, and shared (frequently traumatic) history. Some researchers have used Kohn's distinction to demonstrate that nationalisms do in fact have foundational differences.[5] Others have employed it to explain why nationalisms of Eastern and Central Europe have been predominately ethnic in the past and incapable of developing civic nationalism in the future.[6]

Kohn's critics argued that this theory was biased against non-Western nationalisms. They claimed that the supposedly inclusive Western nationalisms were as much based on exclusions as the vilified Eastern nationalisms. Some suggested that there was no reason to believe that the current ethnic nationalisms could not gradually evolve from ethnic into civic nationalism in their own time, while others pointed out that no nationalism was ever purely civic or ethnic and so Kohn's theory could not be empirically substantiated.[7]

Rogers Brubaker also was among Kohn's critics.[8] Instead of ethnic nationalism he proposed a nationalist "triad"— (1) nationalisms of the "nationalizing states," (2) nationalisms of ethnic minorities, and (3) nationalisms of the external homelands.[9] According to Brubaker, Eastern European nationalisms of titular nations were "nationalizing," that is, aimed at ethnically homogenizing their population and fuelled by a belief that the state existed solely to protect one ethnicity. The conception of "nationalizing states" became quite popular and was used to analyze a number of post-Communist countries.[10] The critics of Brubaker's theory, however, noticed that it was applied discriminatorily to the newly independent post-Communist countries, while, for example, Russia was consistently spared. Also, ethnic minorities within the new post-Communist states usually were not interpreted as "nationalizing" although in reality their actions were similar to those of the titular nations.[11] In response, Brubaker dropped his earlier concepts and created a categorization of the state-framed vs. counter-state nationalisms. State-framed nationalisms perceived the nation as perfectly merged with the state. Counter-state nationalisms envisioned the nation as distinct from or opposed to the existing states. State-framed nationalisms were not necessarily civic as they could be imbued with ethnic and cultural interpretations of nationhood, while the counter-state nationalisms did not necessarily conceive of the nation in ethnocultural terms.[12]

The most innovative aspect of this recent categorization was the way it brought statism into the study of nationalism. This idea was effectively linked to Robert Nisbet's suggestion that the belief in the strong and centralized state and the subsequent growth of its power was the most important political revolution of modern history. According to Nisbet, almost all political ideologies of the modern times were influenced by statism. They saw the state as the basic form of political organization that should assume control over close to all aspects of human life.[13] This way of thinking characterized some nationalisms, too, while others pursued a purely ethnic and anti-state understanding of the nation. In order to discuss these differences, it is suggested here that the complexity of nationalisms is rooted in the variety of answers that they give to the question of what constitutes a nation. In other words, all aspects including ethnicity, the state and principles of individual freedom need to be accounted for when categorizing nationalisms.

To resolve this problem it is suggested here to combine the approaches of Nisbet, Brubaker, and Kohn by outlining four categories of nationalisms as shown in the table 10.1.

Table 10.1. Types of nationalisms based on the interaction of modern political ideas about the nation, state, and individual.

What makes a nation?	The state	Not the state
Ethnicity	Type 1: Ethnic nationalism	Type 3: Anti-state ethnic nationalism
Not ethnicity	Type 2: Statist nationalism	Type 4: Civic nationalism

Ethnic nationalism (type 1) usually emphasizes cultural ethnicity over the state and sees the state as an instrument serving the interests of the titular ethnicity. This nationalism has the characteristics of Kohn's ethnic nationalism and Brubaker's nationalizing state nationalism. It does not reject the state, yet it prioritizes ethnic belonging over citizenship and it expects the state to protect the ethnic interests (see, for example, modern German nationalism or post-Communist Eastern European nationalisms).

Statist nationalism (type 2) insists that powerful and stable state is the primary political value. This nationalism is close to what Brubaker identified as state-framed nationalism. In this nationalism, the nation evolves from the identification with the state although it does not disqualify completely the importance of ethnicity. It prioritizes citizenship over ethnicity, yet it does not contain enough respect for individual freedom to qualify as civic nationalism (see, for example, Russian or Iranian nationalisms).

Anti-state ethnic nationalism (type 3) promotes a pure and exclusively defined ethnic collective. Similarly to Brubaker's counter-state nationalism, this type does not believe that the existing (or for that matter any) modern state is able to fully realize the ethnicity's essence. It expects individuals to sacrifice themselves on behalf of the ethnic collective (see, for example, German Romantic nationalism or separatist minority nationalisms).

Civic nationalism (type 4) is rare because it does not build the conception of nationhood either on the cultural ethnicity or the state. Instead it promotes the principle of individual liberty. It conceives of nation in open and citizenship-based terms (it has been suggested that the British and American nationalisms are the best candidates for this category).

This integrated categorization offers a number of analytical benefits. First, it enables us to study the complex relationship between nationalism, statism, and ethnic identity thus fully contextualizing nationalism within modernity and its trends. Second, it can serve as a dynamic instrument that reveals how the ethnic, civic, and statist elements of nationalism make it flexible and how all four types of nationalism can co-exist, overlap, and compete with each other. Third, this categorization accounts for the changing power balance, shifting ideas, and the struggle between ethnic nationalists, democrats, pro-statists, and anti-statists within and across nationalist ideologies. Fourth, this approach could be particularly useful in the East and Central European context that is characterized by a complicated relation between nationalism and statism. For example, the early Eastern and Central European nationalisms were affected by the heritage of imperial rule, ethnic diversity, and unsuccessful modernization. All of this translated into ideas that the state belonged to the dominant ethnocultural group who could use it to enforce supposed historical justice.[14] A similar trend was strong during and after the break-down of the USSR when the Central and Eastern European nationalisms argued that democracy was based on each nation's right to political autonomy. At the same time, there have been strong tendencies of purely statist and distinctively anti-state ethnic nationalisms in the history of Eastern European nationalisms. The following pages demonstrate this using the case of Latvian nationalism since its beginnings in the mid-nineteenth century.

Latvian Statism and Nationalism in the Past

Ethnic Nationalism

Among the most distinctive periods of Latvian ethnic nationalism was the mid-nineteenth century. At that time, Latvian nationalism was formed by the early Latvian intellectual elite, and it was characterized by a strong cultural emphasis. Additionally, Latvian nationalism developed a difficult relationship with the state. The early Latvian nationalists were active young men who came from modest peasant origins and obtained higher education in Russian and German universities thanks to the imperial government's attempts to create a modern nationstate with an educated pro-Russian and native middle class.[15] Influenced by both the Slavophiles and German nationalists, they set out to create cultural conceptions that could be used to shape the native peasant population into a self-aware ethnic group.[16] Although some of them believed that it was important to ensure that the new Latvian ethnicity integrated itself into the Russian statehood, most of the early Latvian nationalists wanted to develop a culturally based Latvian identity.[17] In other words, the statist element did not play a significant role in Latvian nationalism of the nineteenth century.

The cultural or ethnic emphasis in Latvian nationalism intensified after the Russian imperial government decided to crush the fledgling nationalist movements during the early twentieth century with government censorship, forced Russification and conversion to Orthodoxy. In response, Latvian nationalists focused on strengthening the cultural essence of Latvianness by collecting peasant folklore and mythology, and building a literary tradition in the Latvian language. This cultural campaign led to political stagnation in the early Latvian nationalism. The political passions of the new generation of Latvian intellectuals did not belong to the nationalist movement, but to the radical Marxism and Social Democratic statism.

Another wave of Latvian ethnic nationalism emerged during World War I, when a number of influential intellectuals and political activists took refuge from the German occupation in Russia, mainly Moscow and St. Petersburg.[18] These nationalists formulated the connection between the Latvian state and ethnicity for the first time. They demanded national autonomy justifying it with the need to protect and develop Latvian ethnic identity.[19]

Finally, the ideas of ethnic nationalism experienced a powerful reawakening during the late 1980s and 90s. At that time, the conception of an independent Latvian state combined such conflicting goals as liberation from the Soviet regime, establishment of a democratic society and free market economy, and protection of Latvian ethnic identity.[20] Latvian ethnic nationalism was influential in this context, therefore, the citizenship legislation, state language laws, laws regarding minority education, and other policies reflected an emphasis on making the new state serve the interests of ethnic Latvians and their identity. At this time, Latvian nationalism defined the state as an instrument of the titular nation. The state was allowed to regulate and control individuals' lives as long as it was to the benefit of Latvianness. This type of ethnic nationalism dominated Latvia's political scene up to 1998.

Statist Nationalism

The first signs of the statist element in Latvian nationalism could be noticed after the abortive revolution of 1905 when some of the Latvian Social Democrats became interested in the idea of national statehood as borrowed from the Austrian Social Democrats such as Otto Bauer and the Swiss federal constitution.[21] They argued that it was possible to have a strong socialist state that would also incorporate ethnic liberation. The remaining majority of Latvian Social Democrats rejected such conceptions as reactionary. The disagreement between these two positions grew into a conflict that consequently prevented the spread of the ideas of statist nationalism among the masses up until World War I.[22]

The demand for a strong state intensified again during the early 1930s. Its most eloquent expression could be found in a book written by a prominent intellectual, politician, and diplomat Miķelis Valters.[23] He rejected democracy, political liberalism, and market economy as selfish. Instead he proposed an ideology according to which the state had the right to ensure that all individual initiatives were subordinated to the needs of the state. He asserted that the state should be the decisive political agent and suggested institutionalizing state supervised forms of cooperation both in economy and politics. He insisted that such measures were the last hope for making Latvians into a great nation. Views such as these became popular during the early 1930s and by the middle of the decade almost all Latvian nationalists promoted the ideals of statist nationalism, that is, a nationalist ideology that declared the state as basis of the nationhood.

This tendency was strengthened by the arrival of the authoritarian regime of Kārlis Ulmanis in May 1934. After disbanding the parliament and all political parties, he placed himself in an authoritarian position as the President of Latvia and pursued an ideology that was outright statist nationalist. Ulmanis made sure that the state and he as the state's utmost representative were seen as the best instrument for perfecting Latvian nation. Latvianness was now defined as a product of a strong authoritarian state with corporatist administrative systems, interventionist economic policies, censorship, and limited freedom of expression. Under Ulmanis' leadership, the Latvian state grew more centralized than ever, while Ulmanis, along with his bureaucracy, came to be seen as possessing almost mystical power to be in charge of people's lives. The state and Ulmanis personally were praised and glorified by Latvian nationalists, while individuals were expected to adjust their interests and needs to those of the state and its leader.[24] During this period, Latvian nationalism became infused with the idea that the powerful state and leader carried the key to the national character of Latvian people. Ulmanis' regime strengthened statist nationalism and allowed it to dominate until 1940 when Latvia was occupied by the USSR.

Anti-State Nationalism

One of the earliest manifestations of Latvian anti-state ethnic nationalism appeared in the publications of Latvian refugees in Siberia during World War I. Their argument was that the state was an "aristocratic formation," which was foundationally oppressive, therefore any state, including a national one, had to be treated with suspicion. Such convictions persisted even after the establishment of the independent Latvian republic in 1921.[25] However, most Latvian nationalists at the end of World War I and during the 1920s were ethnic nationalists and believed in the usefulness of national statehood.

The anti-state sentiments surfaced again in the form of criticism of Latvia's political system during the late 1920s and early 30s. Increasingly more Latvian nationalists perceived democracy and parliamentarism as hostile to the "true" interests of Latvian ethnicity. They were dissatisfied with the compromises that had to be made under democracy and called for a completely different political system that would privilege Latvian ethnicity as the highest political value.[26] Ironically these anti-state sentiments were later coopted by the statist nationalism of Kārlis Ulmanis in the late 1930s. The anti-state nationalism with its desire to find the meaning of the nation outside the statehood ended up justifying a non-democratic and statist ideology of Ulmanis' authoritarianism.

Then during both the Nazi occupation and the Soviet regime, Latvian nationalism exhibited anti-state tendencies again. During this period, Latvianness was seen as primarily a cultural and spiritual accomplishment that existed in literature, art, music, folklore, and mythology, but not in politics. In other words, it could not be framed by the state institutions. Such anti-state political attitudes persisted throughout the period of the Soviet occupation and they changed only when Latvians were faced with the political opportunities of the late 1980s and early 1990s.

In sum, Latvian nationalism throughout its history had shifted from ethnic, to anti-state to statist types. It is remarkable that anti-state nationalism became powerful during the parliamentary period of Latvian national independence, while ethnic nationalism declined and was eventually replaced with the statist nationalism during the authoritarian period. Thus, Latvian statist nationalism appears closely tied to authoritarianism, while the anti-statist nationalism contained an anti-democratic and anti-parliamentary streak. The history of Latvian nationalisms shows that as Latvian ethnic nationalists became disappointed with the democratic statehood, they were likely to support non-democratic politics and help the ascendancy of statist nationalism. Finally, it is also notable that throughout its history, Latvian nationalism did not show any indications of civic nationalism.

Latvian Statism and Nationalism of the Recent Years

Ethnic Nationalism of the Early 1990s

The central political cleavages of the period between 1991 and 1998 concentrated on such issues as the strengthening of national independence, de-occupation, relations between ethnic Latvians and the Russian-speaking population, the state language legislation, education in minority languages, and the rights of citizenship. In other words, both Latvian and Russian ethnic nationalisms dominated the political scene and decision-making. Two strong nationalist forces battled over the meanings of nationhood in this period—the pro-Latvian nationalist *For Fatherland and Freedom* (TB) vs. the pro-Russian nationalist *People's Harmony Party* (TSP). Of course, other political forces had opinions on how to build the new nation, yet it was these two parties that controlled the parameters of the discussion.

TB supported a strict *jure sanguinis* definition of citizenship and harsh state language legislation. Occasionally some of its politicians even talked about the "voluntary deportation" of the Russian-speaking population to Russia. Their main opponents from TSP demanded immediate citizenship to all residents, two state languages, and preservation of Russian-speaking education. Both positions perceived the state as an instrument for protecting particular ethnic interests; however TB was willing to participate in the coalition governments with other political parties, while the pro-Russian nationalists from TSP continuously remained in opposition. Consequently, the Latvian ethnic nationalists had quite a lot of say in the legislation and policies of the newly independent state.

The first notable alternative to the dominating ethnic nationalism was introduced by the neo-liberal People's Party (TP) in 1998. It articulated an ideology where interests of particular ethnic groups were secondary to those of the state as a whole.

TP injected statism in Latvian nationalism as it downplayed the political importance of loyalty to Latvianness and stressed instead more universal values such as the family, morality, and state. In fact, TP rarely used terms such as "ethnic identity." It rather talked about the state as a decisive political agent. As its goal, TP emphasized creating a tranquil political and economic environment, where the state would ensure the safety of families and individuals—not ethnicities.[27] TP won the election in 1998 with 21.19% of the vote, thus announcing the first cracks in dominance of ethnic nationalism.

The political presence of ethnic nationalists still remained quite strong. Actually, both Latvian and Russian ethnic nationalists gained votes in 1998 in comparison to 1995 (in 1998 TB received 14.65% up from 11.9%, TSP—14.12% up from a mere 5.5%). They continued to perpetuate the idea of the state as instrument of ethnic protectionism. In 1998 TB merged with another nationalist movement—Latvia's National Independence Movement and formed a union called TB/LNNK. They identified themselves as "national conservatives" who believed "in a Latvian Latvia," and demanded more support for state language laws, promised to control immigration, and declared that only the citizens of Latvia (most of whom were ethnic Latvians) could have suffrage.[28] TB/LNNK was open about its intention to serve the interests of ethnic Latvians only. Meanwhile, Russian nationalists from TSP continued to demand that Latvia must become multicultural and that cultural and political development of all ethnic groups had to be guaranteed by the state.

The Strengthening of Statist Nationalism

If the elections of 1998 only indicated an emergence of a new type of nationalism,[29] the elections of 2006 demonstrated a distinctive strengthening of this trend. In 2006, TB/LNNK received only 6.94%, the Russian ethnic nationalists from *For the Human Rights in Unified Latvia* (PCTVL) 6.03%, while the statist nationalists such as TP and the *New Era* (JL) gained 19.56% and 16.38% of the vote respectively.[30] Both Russian and Latvian ethnic nationalists received the lowest voter support since the establishment of Latvia's independence, while the new statist nationalists dominated.[31] These shifts in power balance were not coincidental. In fact, they revealed a deeper change in the nature of nationalism in Latvia where the focus on ethnicity had shifted toward the emphasis on strong statehood.

The ethnic nationalists in 2006 still could be grouped in two wings—pro-Latvian vs. pro-Russian. On the Latvian side, TB/LNNK remained loyal to its ethnic nationalist principles. For example, it threatened that ethnic non-Latvians will have to undergo careful scrutiny and pass a variety of tests to receive Latvian citizenship. They continued to see citizenship not as an agreement between the state and an individual, but as a contract between Latvian identity and the individual. TB/LNNK also called for adoption of a Repatriation Law that would encourage and regulate the emigration of non-Latvians. TB/LNNK continued to state that "the protection of Latvians' interests is our most important task," and insisted on Latvian as the only language of instruction in minority schools.[32]

Equally ethnic nationalist attitudes continued to characterize the pro-Russian coalition PCTVL. This political force grew out of TSP's parliamentary faction and took over TSP's 15-year-old ideology. PCTVL propagated the conception of Latvia as a society of two ethnic enclaves and went against the idea of integration. Although PCTVL claimed to be interested in human rights in general, its priority remained the defense of the Russian-speaking population. For example, when they had to cast a vote on a possible law that would limit the human rights of homosexuals, the parliamentarians from PCTVL abstained and later admitted that such issues were not their priority. PCTVL's ideology concentrated on the issues of citizenship, protection of Russian as the second state language, and preserving state-funded education in Russian.[33] Interestingly PCTVL argued against the presence of Latvian soldiers in Iraq and demanded negotiations about decreasing Latvia's both financial and man-power contributions to NATO. Since the core of PCTVL's ideology was still Russian ethnic nationalist, it viewed other issues in relation to the need to shield one's ethnic group.

Importantly, as noted earlier, the elections of 2006 revealed new trends not only in Latvian, but also Russian nationalism such as the emergence of a different pro-Russian force—*The Center of Harmony* (SC). It formed after a split inside PCTVL and declared as its goal to decrease the radical demands on behalf of the Russian speakers in Latvia. Instead, SC stressed the need to create a unified and tolerant society. To demonstrate its novel take on the inter-ethnic relations, SC admitted that ethnic conflict in Latvia was not solely the fault of Latvians and that the Russian speaking population was at least partially to blame, too. Additionally, the leader of SC Jānis Urbanovičs suggested that instead of demanding that Russians learn the Latvian language, Latvians must create conditions where Russians would voluntarily become bi-lingual. SC did not insist on giving the status of second state language to Russian, but asked to grant it a legal position of a minority language. Urbanovičs particularly emphasized the need to prevent extremist hysteria and whining about "oppression" on both sides of the ethnic split.[34]

Moreover, SC suggested that it was important to nurture in the new generation of ethnic non-Latvians strong feelings of patriotism toward the Latvian state. SC advocated social integration that was based on mutual respect and ethnic co-existence. It also consciously tried to expand the meaning of the individual's rights to include such diverse groups as renters in recently privatized buildings, minorities affected by educational reform, and non-citizens not allowed to participate in municipal elections. SC insisted that the meaning of freedom had to be disconnected from ethnic issues and asserted that it was the lack of social protection that threatened democracy in Latvia. SC's pre-election program called for a "responsible, just and effective state, which invests in each person, guarantees social security and supports honest private business." Also, SC's program contained no discussion of two-enclave (Latvian and Russian) society; there was no discussion about automatic granting of the citizenship rights to all residents and no demand for state-funded education in Russian.[35] In sum, although SC perceived the representation of the Russian speaking population as their central political role, they also placed the needs of a unified state over narrowly ethnic issues.

The statist nationalists among the Latvian political groups were represented by TP and a new party *The New Era* (JL). Together they received close to 36% of the vote in 2006. As before, TP insisted that they were a party of pragmatists and realists committed to working hard, being leaders, taking charge, and making difficult decisions. As stated by its leader and Prime Minister Aigars Kalvītis: "the most important thing to us is—to work hard. . . . We are a party of those who get things done. . . . And the people who vote for us are just like that."[36]

In the past, TP advertised the business skills of its leading figures and argued that they had been successful entrepreneurs who were ready to be effective leaders of the state. Recently, their ideology shifted toward an idea that TP offers the best, strong-willed and principled "state managers" regardless of their private business capabilities. Now TP approached the state as the ultimate form of business that had to be led by a particular type of successful administrators—experts. As before, TP paid little attention to ethnic issues and put all emphasis on building a statist nationalist position. Its pre-election program declared that TP's main goal was enlarging the competency and capacities of the state administration, especially with regard to distributing the financial resources received from the European Union. TP asserted that almost all aspects of social, cultural, and foreign policy depended on which candidates were elected to the parliament and how competent they were as politicians. According to TP's rhetoric, the well-being of the people, and stable and predictable state development could be guaranteed only by making long-term political plans. TP also propagated an idea of coordinating state institutions and private initiatives in order to increase Latvia's international competitiveness. In 1998 TP planted the first seeds of an ideology where national identity was based on a notion of a powerful statehood. By 2006 their ideology had graduated to a full-scale statism where the state was a value within itself and it was to have expanded care-taking powers and international prestige. This conception of state-based nationhood was inclusive and non-ethnic.

As noted, TP was not alone in replacing ethnic nationalism with statism. A similar ideology was promoted also by JL, which first appeared in 2001 and won the elections of 2002 under the leadership of one of the former top state administrators—the head of Latvia's Central Bank, and later businessman, Einārs Repše. In 2002, JL assigned to itself a mission to reveal the corruption in the political establishment and revise the current practices. JL focused on dealing with the problems that had resulted from the formation of new post-Communist elites and their privatization of the state. JL re-oriented the public away from ethnic conflicts and de-occupation toward the impact of the ten years of national independence and market economy.

In 2006 Einārs Repše self-confidently asserted that his party had changed the political culture in Latvia by "bringing in new political attitudes, creating new principles for the state budget and the management of the state's financial resources." Repše insisted that the most important characteristic of JL was its commitment to the fair administration of the state, and opposition to the so-called theft of the state and corruption. Repše blamed other parties, particularly TP, for letting the financial matters of the state fall into a "populistic and incompetent free-flow," while his party was determined to put the state's finances into "a complete order" by redistributing them to deserving groups and carefully planning their use. JL presented itself as a decisively statist force focused on state management, redistribution of state's resources, and regulation. [37] In its pre-election program JL stated that it will "take care of the people, the salaries, jobs, social needs. . . . We will take care of the elderly, the disabled and other protected groups. Our goal is to renew the society's faith in the power of laws, justice and courts without which a person cannot feel safe in their country." Interestingly, although both JL and TP insisted that they were right-wing conservatives and portrayed Latvian Social Democrats as their opponents, they promoted a highly interventionist, care-taking and anti-free market approach to politics. The only difference was that the Social Democrats used statism to acquire social equality, while JL and TP employed statism to strengthen Latvia as a nation-state. Thus, JL and TP were statist nationalists, who did not define the state and nation in ethnic terms.

Although due to personal disagreements TP and JL could not create a coalition government, they had notable ideological similarities. Politicians from TP presented themselves as "the people of action," while JL described themselves as "assertive decision makers." TP emphasized its ability to manage the state and get quick results, while JL highlighted its professional politicians-experts fighting corruption.[38] Both parties dedicated themselves to strengthening the state's ability to influence economic and social processes and re-distribute the financial resources granted by the European Union. In principle, both parties promised to decrease the state bureaucracy, while in practice they approached the state as the only source of political agency.

Discussion

The failure of ethnic nationalists such as TB/LNNK and PCTVL and the success of statist nationalists such as SC, TP, and JL in the parliamentary elections of 2006 was not only a transfer of power to new political actors. It was also a sign of important ideological changes. Since 1998, the issues of state administration, the state's ability to distribute the EU's money and regulate social and economic processes took precedence over concerns of ethnic protectionism, so the conceptions of ethnic nationhood lost ground to the state-based understandings of the nation.[39]

Interestingly, similar tendencies have been noted in other public discourses, too. For example, a study of the postings on the popular web forum *Delfi* regarding the athletes from Latvia in the 2004 Olympic Games showed that both self-identified Latvians and Russians were actively seeking new ways to define "Latvianness." Their strategies included downplaying in-born ethnicity and emphasizing such criteria as individual achievement, how proud one made their compatriots, how well one knew the Latvian language and whether one was a citizen.[40] The findings of this study indicated a notable decline in purely ethnic understandings of who was a Latvian and some early signs of a more open-ended notion of national belonging. Another study showed that exclusively ethnic discourse has moved to a predominately symbolic position as in, for example, the political speeches of the past President of Latvia Vaira Vīķe-Freiberga.[41] However, it is important to note that all of these tendencies do not signal a growth of civic nationalism. Instead we see an expansion of statism. In other words, although ethnic identity is no longer seen as the essence of the Latvian nation, the principles of individual freedom do not take its place. In its stead we see identification with a strong, regulative, internationally competitive, and assertive statehood. It is the connection to one's state—both feeling pride about it and being dependent on it—that would make one a member of the Latvian nation today.

As shown here, the most notable period of statist nationalism in Latvia was during the authoritarian rule of Kārlis Ulmanis in the late 1930s. This, of course, brings up the question of whether the current statist tendencies could invoke an authoritarian or quasi-authoritarian political system in Latvia. Certainly, such political leaders as Einārs Repše from JL and Andris Šķele from TP have promoted themselves as the care-taking fathers, charismatic leaders, and potentially authoritarian rulers. Putin's example in Russia may have served as an inspiration to some of the Latvian politicians, too. However, usually their ambitions had resulted in internal crises within their parties, followed by governmental problems, vehement criticism in the media, and loss of political prestige. It is very likely that these political figures hold a lot of political and economic power from behind the scenes; however, there have been no open attempts to centralize all power in one person's hands. Nevertheless, the growth and strengthening of the statist nationalism in Latvia must serve as an alarming signal for those worried about the onslaught of authoritarianism.

The concern about statist nationalism in Latvia must also be linked to an influence that was not there during the 1930s, namely, the power of the European Union and everything it stands for. A majority of Latvia's population favored Latvia's entrance into the EU and considered it a guarantee to Latvia's independent and safe future. Once the goal of membership was reached, the new task has been to try to benefit from it as much as possible. In this context, it is notable that since the entrance in the EU the state structures have had a chance to grow stronger and more influential than before. It is now expected to be an equal partner with the rest of the EU members. It is supposed to represent and defend the interests of Latvia's residents in relation to the EU and its regulations, legal norms, and bureaucratic directives. The Latvian state is also charged with the redistribution of the EU's financial support and fulfilment of the obligations and responsibilities toward the EU. Membership in the EU has generated moderate success for individual businesses and private initiatives. Only those institutions that have strong and well-established bureaucracies have been able to receive the EU's benefits, while the institutions that administer the EU's funds within the state structure have grown exponentially.

In other words, it appears that the growth of statist beliefs among Latvia's politicians and the public is not coincidental. The majority of them have abandoned the politics of ethnic isolationism; they have been able to examine themselves and re-evaluate their often xenophobic and intolerant nationalist views in the light of the EU's criticisms. In this sense, the positive impact of the EU's regulations, recommendations, and educational programs cannot be denied. At the same time, all of this has led both the political establishment and the public to believe in the power of a strong state more than before. Thus the socialist beliefs had entered the highly anti-Communist political scene in Latvia through the back door. Now it is possible for someone to be a socialist and statist without even noticing it. Latvia's current politics concentrates on the state and its internal matters more than anything else.

This is one of the outcomes of the membership in the EU—it has encouraged the new member states to become stronger and larger with increasingly more administrative offices. Contrary to some earlier predictions, entrance into the EU spurred not so much a backlash of ethnic separatism, as the growth of domestic statism in which, notably, the individual as the fundamental value remains absent. In sum, nationalism *per se* is not disappearing in the post-Communist contexts such as Latvian. Instead, it is moving toward the celebration of the strong state as the basis of a unifying nationhood.

In terms of theoretical implications of this study, it is notable that although we see the decline of ethnic nationalism, civic nationalism is not entering its place. This suggests that Kohn's categorization of "ethnic vs. civic" is too simplistic and therefore—overburdened. Although it does not need to be rejected entirely, it requires to be combined with the analysis of modern statism. In today's Latvia, statist nationalism does not seek a strong leader, but it reflects society's desire for stability, predictability, and national autonomy. And this is hoped to be accomplished not by limiting the state and its various powers, but by actually increasing them.

Notes

1. George Schopflin, "Nationalism and Ethnic Minorities in Post-Communist Europe," in *Europe's New Nationalism*, ed. R. Caplan and J. Feffer (New York: Oxford University Press, 1996), 150-70; Juan J. Linz and Alfred Stepan, *Problems of Democratic Transition and Consolidation: Southern Europe, South American and Post-Communist Europe* (Baltimore, MD: Johns Hopkins University Press, 1996); Andrew Wilson, *Ukrainian Nationalism in the 1990s. A Minority Faith* (Cambridge: Cambridge University Press, 1997); Alexei Arbatov, Abram Chayes, Antonia Handler Chayes, and Lara Olson, eds., *Managing Conflict in the Former Soviet Union: Russian and American Perspectives* (Camb-

ridge, MA: MIT Press, 1997); Vello Pettai, "Estonia and Latvia: International Influences on Citizenship and Minority Integration," in *Democratic Consolidation in Eastern Europe. International and Transnational Factors,* ed. Jan Zielonka and Alex Pravda (Oxford: Oxford University Press, 2001), 257-80; Rusanna Gaber, "National Identity and Democratic Consolidation in Central and Eastern Europe," *International Journal of Sociology* 36, no. 3 (2006): 35-69; Anatol Lieven, "Nationalism in the Contemporary World," *Russian Politics and Law* 44, no. 1 (2006): 6-22; and Anatol Lieven, *Ukraine and Russia. A Fraternal Rivalry* (Washington DC: U.S. Institute of Peace, 1999).

2. See Ciaus Dobrescu, "Conflict and Diversity in East European Nationalism, on the Basis of a Romanian Case Study," *East European Politics and Societies* 17, no. 3 (2003): 393. Dobrescu quotes a random sample of this attitude: "The disintegration of multiethnic states and empires, and the accompanying spectacle of archaic tribal wars on the European periphery, have made Western Europeans wonder whether their pursuit of continental unification might not be a doomed defiance of history's will" (from "The Revival of Long Dormant Vendettas in the Balkans and Caucasus Has Frightened Onlookers in Western Europe," *Boston Globe,* 15 June 1991, 18). Recently, similar doomsday predictions about the threatening revival of radical nationalism together with the conservative right have been appearing, too (see, for example, Roger Boyes "New Europe, Old Dangers," *New Statesman*, 2 October 2006, 30-31; Petrou Michael, "Neo-Neo-Nazis," *Maclean's*, 27 February 2006, 18-19).

3. Sergei Kruk, *Nation-Building, Monument-Building* (unpublished manuscript).

4. Hans Kohn, *Nationalism: Its Meaning and History* (Princeton: Van Norstrand, 1955).

5. See, for example, Liah Greenfeld, *Nationalism: Five Roads to Modernity* (Cambridge: Harvard University Press, 1992); Michael Ignatieff, *Blood and Belonging: Journeys into the New Nationalism* (New York: Farrar, Strauss and Giroux, 1993).

6. See Jack Snyder, "Nationalism and the Crisis of the Post-Soviet State," in *Ethnic Conflict and International Security*, ed. M.E. Brown (Princeton: Princeton University Press, 1993), 79-101; John Gledhill, "The Power of Ethnic Nationalism: Foucault's Bio-Power and the Development of Ethnic Nationalism in Eastern Europe," *National Identities* 7, no. 4 (2005): 347-68; Algis Valantiejus, "Early Lithuanian Nationalism: Sources of Its Legitimate Meanings in an Environment of Shifting Boundaries," *Nations and Nationalism* 8, no. 3 (2002): 315-33; James R. Payton, "Ottoman Millet, Religious Nationalism, and Civil Society: Focus on Kosovo," *Religion in Eastern Europe* 26, no. 1 (2006): 11-23.

7. See Bernard Yack, "The Myth of the Civic Nation," in *Theorizing Nationalism*, ed. R. Beiner (Albany: State University of New York Press, 1999), 103-18; David McCrone, *The Sociology of Nationalism* (London: Routledge, 1998); Taras Kuzio, "The Myth of Civic State: A Critical Survey of Hans Kohn's Framework of Understanding Nationalism," *Ethnic and Racial Studies* 25, no.1(2002): 20-39; Mikael Hjerm, "National Sentiments in Eastern and Western Europe," *Nationalities Papers* 31, no. 4 (2002): 413-429; Stephen Shulman, "Challenging the Civic/Ethnic and West/East Dichotomies in the Study of Nationalism," *Comparative Political Studies* 35, no. 5 (2002): 554-86 and "Sources of Civic and Ethnic Nationalism in Ukraine," *Journal of Communist Studies and Transition Politics* 18, no. 4 (2002): 1-30.

8. See Rogers Brubaker, *Ethnicity without Groups* (Cambridge, MA: Harvard University Press, 2004), 132-46.

9. Rogers Brubaker, *Nationalism Reframed: Nationhood and the National Question in the New Europe* (Cambridge: Cambridge University Press, 1996), 58.

10. See, for example, Charles King and Neil J. Melvin, eds., *Nations Abroad: Diaspora Politics and International Relations in the Former Soviet Union* (Boulder: We-

stview. 1998); Dominique Arel, "Ukraine. The Temptation of the Nationalizing State," in *Political Culture and Civil Society in Russian and the New States of Eurasia*, ed. Vladimir Tismaneaunu (Armonk: M.E. Sharpe, 1995), 157-88; David Laitin, *Identity in Formation: The Russian Speaking Population in the Near Abroad* (Ithaca: Cornell University Press, 1998); Sally N. Cummings, "The Kazakhs: Demographics, Diasporas, and 'Return,'" in *Nations Abroad: Diaspora Politics and International Relations in the Former Soviet Union*, ed. Charles King and Neil J. Melvin (Boulder: Westview, 1998), 133-52; Paul Kubicek, "What Happened to the Nationalists in Ukraine?" *Nationalism and Ethnic Politics* 5, no. 1 (1999): 29-45.

11. Taras Kuzio, "'Nationalising States?' or Nation-Building? A Critical Review of the Theoretical Literature and Empirical Evidence," *Nations and Nationalism* 7, no. 2 (2001): 135-54.

12. Brubaker, *Ethnicity without Groups*, 144, 145.

13. Robert Nisbet, *The Quest for Community: A Study in the Ethics of Order and Freedom* (New York: Oxford University Press, 1953).

14. Marija Obradovic, "The Sociohistoric Roots of East European Nationalism," *Canadian Review of Studies in Nationalism* 24, no. 1-2 (1997): 63-73.

15. Jan Penrose and Joe May, "Herder's Concept of Nation and Its Relevance to Contemporary Ethnic Nationalism," *Canadian Review of Studies in Nationalism* 18 (1991): 6-17.

16. On this process, see Ella Buceniece, *Ideju vesture Latvija: No pirmsakumiem lidz 19.gs. 90. gadiem* (Riga: Zvaigzne ABC, 1995); Agnis Balodis, *Latvijas un latviešu tautas vesture* (Riga: Kabata, 1991), 126-40.

17. Deniss Hanovs, "Rigas Latviešu biedriba: pretruniga realitate?," *Latvijas Vesture* 37, no. 1 (2000): 43-9; Kristine Volfarte, "Rigas Latviešu biedriba un latviešu nacionala kustiba no 1868. lidz 1905. gadam," *Diena*, 3 November 2006, 5.

18. Uldis Kreslinš, "Aktiva nacionalisma ideologija: latviešu nacionalisma idejas kontinuitate vai parravums," *Latvijas Vesture* 37, no.1 (2000): 60-1.

19. Karlis Egle, ed., *Atzinas: Latviešu rakstnieku autobiografijas* (Cesis: O. Jepes Apgads, 1924), 147; Uldis Germanis, "Latviešu politiska nacionalisma izcelšanas," *Latvijas Vesture* 3, no. 6 (1992): 10-15 and "Politiskais noskanojums latviešu sabiedriba 1917. gada sakuma. Autonomijas prasiba," *Latvijas Vesture* 1, no. 8 (1993): 11-3; Edgars Lams, *Mužigais romantisms: Jana Akuratera dzives un dailrades lappuses* (Riga: Zinatne, 2003).

20. Larss Peters Fredens, "Parvertibas," *Diena*, 5 March 2005, 15.

21. Germanis, "Latviešu politiska nacionalisma izcelšanas," 10-15.

22. Lams, *Mužigais romantisms*, 29; Kreslinš, "Aktiva nacionalisma ideologija,"59; Janis Penikis, "Latvijas isais gadsimts," *Diena*, 21 August 2002, 12.

23. Mikelis Valters, *No sabrukuma uz planveidotu saimniecibu: Latvijas atjaunošanas problemas, Latvijas nakotne* (Riga, 1933).

24. Adolfs Šilde, *Latvijas vesture 1914-1940* (Sweden: Daugava, 1976); Nicholas Balabkins and Arnolds Aizsilnieks, *Entrepreneur in a Small Country: A Case Study Against the Background of the Latvian Economy, 1919-1940* (Hicksville, NY: Exposition Press, 1975); Aivars Straume, "Karlis Ulmanis un mazakumtautibu politika Latvija 1920-1940. gada," *Latvijas Vesture* 16, no. 1 (1995): 23-33; Ilgvars Butulis, "Karla Ulmana autoritaras ideologijas ietekme uz Latvijas vestures petišanu," *Latvijas Vesture* 42, no. 2 (2001): 59-63; Ieva Zake, "Etatist Elements in Small Nation Nationalisms: The Case of Latvian Nationalism," *Canadian Review of Studies in Nationalism* 32, no. 1-2 (2005): 77-92.

25. See Kreslinš, "Aktiva nacionalisma ideologija," 61. For example, in 1922 the former refugee Haralds Eldgasts wrote a programmatic article "The Active Nationalism" in which he declared that Latvian society "must be aware that it cannot trust official institutions to be able to fulfill the future of our nation's culture" (*Latvijas Vestnesis*, 7 November 1922, 2).

26. Ieva Zake, "Latvian Nationalist Intellectuals and the Crisis of Democracy in the Inter-War Period," *Nationalities Papers* 33, no. 1 (2005): 97-118.

27. *Diena*, 23 September 1998, 2.

28. Ibid, 3.

29. For a more detailed discussion of the results of the 1998 elections see Ieva Zake, "The People's Party in Latvia: Neo-liberalism and the New Politics of Independence," *The Journal of Communist Studies and Transition Politics* 18, no. 3 (2002): 109-31.

30. Altogether, People's Party won with 19.56%, the Association of the Farmers and the Green Party received 16.71%, *The New Era* received 16.38%, the *Center of Harmony* 14.43%, the First Party together with *Latvia's Way* gained 8.58%. The Association of *For Fatherland and Freedom* and Latvia's National Independence Movement received 6.94% and the association of political forces *For the Human Rights in Unified Latvia* earned only 6.03%.

31. Aivars Ozolinš, "Vienplakšni izlido ara," *Diena*, 16 October 2006, 2. It also has to be noted that since 1991 the Latvian political system was always characterized by a strong presence of populist solicitors of the protest vote. In 2006 the protest vote appeal was re-shaped and concentrated not so much on correcting the effects of social and economic inequalities, but focused on traditional values combined with a call for a stronger state. The two most successful protest vote parties were the Association of The Farmers' Union and the Green Party (ZZS) and a coalition of the First Party and the *Latvia's Way* (LPP/LC). The appeal of ZZS was based on the popularity of its recently acquired leader Aivars Lembergs—the mayor of the port city Ventspils who received popular credit for making the city one of the safest and wealthiest municipalities in the country. The rest of the ZZS' candidate list contained a confusing mixture of political activists, while its program reflected little substance (see, for example, "Asie jautajumi. Intervija ar Induli Emsi. Pilna versija." *V-Diena*, 13 October 2006). ZZS's pre-election program gave a sense of a slogan-like attitude with most distinct emphasis put on pleasing everyone dissatisfied with the current political establishment. When confronted about the vagueness of their program the leaders of ZZS stated "we are not going to push our understanding of the truth upon the people, but instead we will listen to what they have to say and then change our program according to how society perceives it and wants to correct it" ("Viedoklu sadursme: 'bezatbildigi labejie' pret iekartas gazejiem. Indulis Emsis (ZZS) pret Jani Dineviču (LSDSP)," *V-Diena*, 13 October 2006). LPP/LC, on the other hand, was a right-wing political force aimed at protest voters who wanted a more moral and religious state. The First Party's leadership contains a number of priests and religious figures. They stressed that the concept of individual freedom had to be understood in the context of obligations toward God, family, and one's consciousness. One of the strongest "selling points" of the LPP was its intolerance toward sexual minorities (see, for example, "LPP/LC pret TB/LNNK: nodoklu atlaideji pret nodoklu ieviesejiem,"# *V-diena*, 13 October 2006). At the same time, the First Party demonstrated ethnic tolerance and stated that everyone who was loyal and interested should be able to get Latvian citizenship.

32. "LPP/LC pret TB/LNNK: nodoklu atlaideji pret nodoklu ieviesejiem#," *V-Diena*, 13 October 2006; "Asie jautajumi. Intervija ar Robertu Zili. Pilna versija,"# *V-Diena*, 13 October 2006. Quotes from the 2006 pre-election programs come from the website http://

www.vdiena.lv/lat/politics, which is an off-shoot site of the largest daily newspaper *Diena* dedicated primarily to the pre- and post-election issues.

33. "Asie jautajumi. Intervija ar Jakovu Plineru. Pilna versija," *V-Diena*, 13 October 2006; "PCTVL, Saskanas centrs: mes neesam kaškigi." *V-Diena*, 13 October 2006.

34. See "Asie jautajumi. Intervija ar Jani Urbanoviču. Pilna versija," *V-Diena*, 13 October 2006.

35. "PCTVL, Saskanas centrs: mes neesam kaškigi,"# *V-Diena*, October 13, 2006. It has to be noted, however, that some political observers have been able to trace connections between the SC and Putin's government in Russia (see, for example, Aivars Ozolinš "Saskanas Centrs—Kalviša valdibas sabiedrotais," *V-Diena*, 20 November 2006). Apparently, Putin's government was very critical of the failures of the previous pro-Russian political forces and helped to manufacture SC as a new type of Russian party in Latvia and kept it under strict control. There were notable concerns that SC was just an instrument of Russia's foreign policy.

36. "Asie jautajumi. Intervija ar Aigaru Kalviti. Pilna versija," *V-Diena*, 13 October 2006.

37. "Asie jautajumi. Intervija ar Eināru Repši. Pilna versija," *V-Diena*, 13 October 2006.

38. See, "JL pret TP: 'lemt spejigie' pret 'ricibas cilvekiem,'" *V-Diena*, 13 October 2006.

39. The described tendencies are mainly related to political ideas and ideologies. When it comes down to the political realities such as, for example, creating a coalition government and making all of the coalition members happy, things often are different. For example, when the newly elected Parliament started to work on the creation of its committees and hand out their chairmanships such radical Latvian nationalists as Aivars Tabuns from TB/LNNK were selected to lead the important Committee on Citizenship and Naturalization. This chapter wants to point out, however, that notable ideological shifts are taking place.

40. Sergei Kruk, "'Latvians' and 'Latvia's Residents': Representation of National Identity in Public and Private Discourse," *Acta Universitatis Latviensis*, 680 (2004): 101-10.

41. Sergei Kruk, "'Mother Latvia Loves You as Her Sons and Daughters!' Hysterical Discourse of Latvia's President V. Vike-Freiberga" (paper presented at 20th International Conference of Association for the Advancement of Baltic Studies, George Washington University, Washington DC, June 2006).

Chapter 11
The Grass Was Always Greener in the Past: Re-Nationalizing Bulgaria's Return to Europe

Emilian Kavalski

"What was the point, if you give in to sentimental exaggerations about beauty long gone, if you seek in the past the justification for everything present or future. . . . We [Bulgarians] have no present. We have only a 'terrible' past and a 'wonderful' future."

Georgi Markov[1]

The 2007 accession of Bulgaria and Romania into the European Union (EU) effectively brings to an end the 2004 "Eastern Enlargement" round—a process that reiterates the emergence of the *enlarged EU* as a distinct (and in important ways *new*) actor in global life. In Bulgaria (like in other post-communist and post-candidate states), however, the novelty of the condition of membership has been accompanied by discourses of the effect(s) and impact of the EU on the national articulation. Thus, the discursive return to Europe that has dominated the rhetoric of state elites has been mirrored by public perceptions of the reclamation of former status and, thence, a return to a perceived former glory. In Bulgaria, the latter (popular) dimension of this debate has facilitated the legitimation of discourses of *re-nationalism* and their gradual politicization.

It was Rogers Brubaker who, in outlining the ambitious program of the Single European Act, indicated the symbolism of "1992" as a step that might proffer the conditions for transcending the boundaries of national imaginations that have blighted the European continent for at least 200 years. Thus, an incipiently post-national Europe was seen as showing the rest of the world "the image of its own future."[2] Yet, unlike others, Brubaker also acknowledged that the twin forces of European integration and economic globalization have only complexified (rather than blasted into oblivion) the logics of nationalism. Consequently, the reframing of nationalism in the political space of post-Cold War Europe became not only a parallel, but also an integral dynamic to the processes of Europeanization. The interactions between these dynamics has not been straightforward; thus, while the notion of "Europe" percolated into inclusive national attitudes, at the same time it also became the focal point for exclusive forms of group cohesion. In this setting, although a "pan-European identity" has been assumed (and probably practiced) by (and within) EU institutions, national modes of popular legitimation have remained prominent in public debates.[3]

Focusing on an instance of such re-nationalizing practices, this study considers the case of the current patterns of national mobilization in Bulgaria. Thus, rather than engaging in a detailed account of "Bulgarian nationalism," this investigation zooms in on the narratives of the main purveyor of the re-nationalization of popular feeling—the nationalist party ATAKA (Attack). The claim here is that ATAKA's good showing during the 2005 parliamentary, 2006 presidential, and 2007 municipal elections indicates the normative and political vacillation of Bulgarian society and the persisting uncertainty of the direction of the transition process in the country. The claim here is that ATAKA's political platform premised on a conspicuously offensive language against minority groups as well as various "foreign agents" not only articulates popular perceptions of Bulgarian identity, but also represents a confrontation with the reality of a contemporary form of Bulgarian nationalism. The limited (inflammatory) rationality of its articulations gestures toward the possibility of non-democratic and exclusionary ideology.[4]

Most commentators tend to agree that since 1997 Bulgaria has decisively broken with the ambivalence characterizing the beginning of the post-Cold War period and has firmly taken the route toward Europe.[5] Such assertion usually rests on Bulgaria's impressive macroeconomic record as well as its stability, especially when compared with its Western Balkan neighbors.[6] Both these trends have been central to Bulgaria's accession to NATO (in 2004) and the EU (in 2007). These developments, however, have tended to occlude the inability of successive state administrations to impact the normative and material conditions of the society at large. Therefore, the professed "return to Europe" has largely come to be perceived as an elite project driven from above and removed from the reality of a significant part of the population.[7]

In this respect, ATAKA's chauvinistic agenda underscores *the predicament of a nation at conflict with itself over how best to face the future*. In their public statements ATAKA's representatives proclaim a national cohesion premised on the selective use of historical memory, the construction of historical narratives, and the confusion of past and present. The resultant "destructive *gemeinschaft*" suggests the cohesion of a victimhood identity premised on the disassociation from reality through rumor, paranoia, and the demonization of the other.[8] Therefore, ATAKA's popularity seems to indicate that nationalist jingoism still holds a promise for many in Bulgaria not only as a political project, but also as an alternative to the current "European" narrative underpinning Sofia's policy-making. Since ATAKA's representatives regularly resort to the manipulation of history as a platform from which to preach national salvation, this chapter begins by detailing the trajectories of Bulgarian self-identification. In particular, it emphasizes the mythologization of national history as a political project for social mobilization premised on the nostalgia for a past that most likely never existed. This contention prompts an understanding of the "libidinal politics" of ATAKA's nationalism, deriving a righteous satisfaction from being the wronged victim.[9] As it happens, the discourses of ATAKA legitimize the expression of economic, political, and social frustrations through an inflammatory mode of nationalistic language. This chapter claims, therefore, that ATAKA's nationalism is "anti-systemic" both in relational (i.e., vis-à-vis other political parties) as well as ideological (i.e., challenging the character of the transition process) terms.[10] As it will be suggested, these dynamics underwrite the current re-nationalization of public feeling in the country. The contention here is that the idiosyncrasy of ATAKA's discourses derives from the incompatibility which they intimate between the professed Bulgarian national ideal and the project of European integration.

Trajectories of Bulgarian Nationalism

Narrating the past of any state tends to bring forth questions about the motivations and implications from such a historical exploration. Thus, as it often happens, the story of a nation's past tends to be co-opted by particular strategies for the distribution of power in the present. Bulgaria, has not been a stranger to such politicization of history, and, in fact, its history reveals an ongoing story of the politicization of the past. This section, therefore, does not attempt a detailed biography of Bulgarian nationalism. Instead it traces the historical processes shaping the myths of Bulgarian self-identification. It could be argued that just like any other nationalism, its Bulgarian variant has been an elite-driven project aimed at disciplining the non-national consciousness of the "masses" and, thereby, motivating them to political action. In this respect, Bulgarian nationalism is more often than not read back into the past to supply the conditions for state power.[11] Nationalism, therefore, is often seen as the inevitable product of state formation and political transition.

Thus, to borrow from a different context, nationalism is "often a consequence rather than a first cause of political outcomes. As often as not, it is governments that create nationalisms rather than nationalisms that create nation-states . . . we get nationalism and a sense that a given set of human beings are a 'people' or a 'nation' mainly because the accidents of history have given us governments with certain domain. . . . The people in the domain are then given a certain set of experiences by this government and indoctrination in a nationalism that is convenient for the government in question. Even a language is, as the saying goes, usually a dialect backed by an army."[12] Patrick Geary strikes a similar cord by suggesting that "Europe's peoples have always been far more fluid, complex, and dynamic than the imaginings of modern nationalists. Names of peoples may seem familiar after a thousand years, but the social, cultural, and political realities covered by these names were radically different from what they are today."[13] Such sentiments target the cynicism of nationalizing ideologies as vehicles for either challenging or justifying a certain type of rule. In a similar fashion, ATAKA's representatives have exploited the invented imagination of Bulgarian cohesion in order to legitimate their chauvinistic challenge to mainstream politics. The claim here is that such discursive strategies did not emerge in a vacuum; instead they are contingent upon not only specific historical processes but also their interpretation by human agents.[14]

Traditionally, the Bulgarian national historiography traces its origins to the 1762 manuscript, *Slavo-Bulgarian History*, written by Father Paisii at the Hilendar Monastery on Mount Athos. Yet, its significance for the revival of the Bulgarian nation is usually asserted with hindsight rather than with reference to its actual impact on Bulgarian nationhood and, in particular, the educated elites during the Ottoman period.[15] As regards the latter, it is the investigations of James Clark that offer the most detailed accounts of the factors that influenced the construction of a separate Bulgarian identity in the Balkans. Clark ascertains that "it was the Russian, [Iurii] Venelin, who not only fired the historical and national imagination of the young leaders of the patriotic revival but whose meteoric appearance completely overshadowed Paisii."[16] For instance, as Clark notes, Venelin's writings were central to the conversion of Vasil Aprilov—a nineteenth-century educator and founder of the first Bulgarian high school—from a pan-Hellenic zealot to a passionate Bulgarian nationalist.[17] Venelin, however, could also be credited with many of the tropes of grandeur and glory which moulded the Bulgarian national imagination. For instance, the 1853 Bulgarian edition of Venelin's "histories" of Bulgaria consciously included "fifty pages" of errors and fabrications (which had been edited out of the Russian edition) in order to "flatter" the national ego of Bulgarians.[18] Such uncritical re-writing of the past had a significant impact on the nationalist ideology of the influential Bulgarian revolutionary Georgi Rakovski, who, among other things, proclaimed that Bulgarian is the oldest language in the world and the modern form of Sanskrit.[19]

In this respect, the nineteenth-century construction of a national identity by the re-memorized construction of a history that most likely never existed underwrites one of the dominant tropes of Bulgarian nationalism: a perverted sense of nostalgia for a "lionized"[20] past that affected the political projects of the present and informed their future trajectories. According to Richard Crampton, the recourse to the ancient interactions between "Proto-Bulgars," Slavs, and other peoples that have inhabited the mental geography of the nation reflects a projection into the past of contemporary understandings at the expense of occluding the fact that the notions of "'Bulgaria' and 'Bulgarian' have [always] been fluid concepts."[21] To a large extent, this type of discursive strategy has remained part and parcel of Bulgarian policy-formulation and is currently taken to its chauvinistic extremes by ATAKA's proclamations.

Yet, apart from this exclusive form of nationalism that insisted on carving an exclusive separate national space and identity for the Bulgarian nation among the ethnic mix of the Balkans, there was (at least) one other strand that was inclusive in its intentions. This alternative national project attempted to link the political future of the Bulgarian nation to that of the other Balkan nationalities. It also had its origins in the eighteenth-century, but its more significant articulations came during the second-half of the nineteenth century and the beginning of the twentieth century with the promulgation of the idea of a Balkan Federation. This more inclusive form of nationalism imagined Bulgarian self-articulation as part of a larger project of Balkan identification.[22] As a nineteenth-century Bulgarian revolutionary insisted, "But let us [the Balkan peoples] leave our sins behind, and let us lock our ancient history, on which we can look only as a source of evil and misery. . . . The quarrels, which existed between us 450 years ago, are the reason for our plight today. The past should be our example and we should never again fall prey to the lie that alone we can achieve something; instead we should stretch a brotherly hand to one another."[23] This alternative path, however, seems to have been (literally) killed off with the 1923 coup against the Agrarian government of Alexander Stamboliiski and the subsequent terror campaign unleashed in Bulgaria by the government of Alexander Tsankov with the help of the notorious Internal Macedonia Revolutionary Organization (IMRO).[24]

This alternative form of Bulgarian nationalism has been largely overlooked (and forgotten); in particular, in the context of the subsequent re-writing of history during the communist period (1945-1989). The claim here is that the current re-nationalization of the Bulgarian public discourse is ideationally linked to the version of national history produced during the communist period. It has to be noted that Bulgarian historiography from this period emphasized "modern Bulgarian history as a chronicle of unfulfilled hopes and cheated expectations that have bred a deep-rooted psychology of defeat."[25] In this context, Bulgarian communist historiography pursued the exclusive version of Bulgarian nationalism not least because of the country's ideological confrontation with its neighbors—the NATO members Greece and Turkey to the south, Yugoslavia to the west—excommunicated from the Cominform in 1948; and Romania to the north, whose policy-orientation could not always be trusted as exemplified during the 1968 crisis in Czechoslovakia. In many respects, such Bulgarian policy reflected the pattern of development of nationally-specific forms of communism in Eastern Europe; yet, in Bulgaria "traditional nationalism, clumsily camouflaged as 'socialist patriotism,' has become a genuine force in political life [which] acts as a brake on meaningful cooperation with neighbouring countries."[26]

As a phrase which described certain phenomena in what used to be the communist world, the term "national communism" came to suggest "a reaction against the national communism of the Soviet Union."[27] More broadly, it has been interpreted as the legitimation of communist practices through the amalgamation of the language of Marxism with the discourses of national ideology.[28] The Bulgarian national communism, however, occupied a peculiar position among its East European peers. On the one hand, in its domestic and foreign relations it developed a revisionist nationalist line, which targeted minority groups by curtailing their religious and ethnic rights, and also declared as "incorrect" the earlier recognition by the Bulgarian Communist Party (BCP) of Macedonia's right to self-determination.[29] This process was paralleled by a substantial investment of the communist regime in moulding popular perceptions of national selfhood—especially through "folk ensembles"—a development which had to reify the link to pre-history interlaced with an emotional appeal to patriotism. As Donna Buchanan points out, the public performances of collective identity became "the most visible, nationalistic symbols of socialist culture." Therefore, folk music during the communist period was not merely a form of entertainment, but was also "a site for sociopolitical contestation" and performance of the nation.[30]

On the other hand, despite the assertions of Bulgarian national glory, "the official tenets" of communist ideology inculcated an "all pervasive . . . sanctified theology of 'second best,' which states that Bulgarians are great, but which reminds every one from the cradle on that the Russians are even greater."[31] This feature of Bulgarian national communism can be traced back to the Russian origins of Bulgarian nationalism.[32] In this respect, the national expressions of Bulgarian communism were subordinated within the larger framework of Soviet policy and ideology. Thus, communist historiography resorted to the resurrection of the "glorious national heritage . . . to help consolidate the party's hold on the population [and] to act as the single most important counterforce against Western 'bourgeois' influences." In other words, it could be argued that the Bulgarian national communism was perhaps the only one in Eastern Europe that was not an "anti-Soviet nationalism."[33] For instance, the mass expulsion of over 150,000 people of Turkish descent to Turkey during 1950-1951 had almost as much to do with BCP's objective to make Bulgaria a "single-nation state"[34] as it reflected Sofia's willingness to be a Soviet tool for pressuring and destabilizing Turkey over its involvement in the Korean conflict and eventual membership in NATO. In a similar way, the 1968 publication of the *Macedonian Problem: Historical-Political Aspects* by the Historical Institute of the Bulgarian Academy of Sciences, not only revised the BCP position on the "Macedonian question," but also asserted the Soviet interpretation of the Marxist-Leninist principles on nationalities, by denouncing the Yugoslav one as "non-Leninist."[35]

The complex relationship with Russia also dominates Bulgaria's post-communist trajectory. As many commentators have pointed out "the Bulgarian attitude towards Russia continues to be unique. Bulgaria is the only country among East European [states] in which more people think that their future is linked to Russia rather than the EU or the USA."[36] The post-communist form(s) of Bulgarian nationalism have made good use of the residual reverence to Russia. In effect, it can be referred to as *commu-nationalism* as it has its ideational origins in the communist period and, also, because "most nationalist activists originated within the former Communist party, the red intelligentsia, or the state police."[37] Thus, the discourse on nationalism developed by the communist regime—i.e., its aspiration to establish a historical link with the past in order to justify its hold to political power—animate post-communist nationalistic discourses in Bulgaria. At the same time, during the 1990s various nationalistic formations maintained their links to similar Russian organizations reverting to the old reflex of pan-Slavic unity. This was made apparent during the 1993 visit by the Russian nationalist leader Vladimir Zhirinovsky in Bulgaria.[38] Volen Siderov, the leader of ATAKA, has indicated his own subscription to the ideals of pan-Slavism.[39] The Bulgarian sociologist, Haralan Aleksandrov, has furthermore defined ATAKA's nationalism as descendent of the "most primitive form of Russian anti-Semitism mixed with Christian Orthodox fundamentalism and as such is a paranoid expression of a deeply provincial society, frightened by the challenges of modernization and globalization."[40]

In this respect, ATAKA's construction of a Bulgarian identity is in effect a commu-nationalistic manifestation of dissatisfaction with the direction of the post-communist transition. Yet, its popular appeal and the presence of ATAKA's members in the National Assembly legitimizes the expression of economic, political, and social frustrations through the discourses of a chauvinistic form of nationalism. The reliance on the meta-language of popular discontent permits re-nationalizing narratives "to relate practical problems to the symbolic centre of society and its utopian premises."[41] As it will be revealed shortly, what makes these nationalistic discourses distinctive is the suggestion of the anti-systemic nature of the Bulgarian national ideal.

The Libidinal Politics of Nationalist Articulations

ATAKA's discursive strategy largely rests on the emotive language of ethnic nationalism, emphasizing the exclusive uniqueness of the Bulgarian nation, denigrated by various "others." ATAKA's representatives, therefore, have continuously reiterated that it is "the only party, which represents the Bulgarian national interest" and that its "only aim, is to give Bulgaria back to the Bulgarians."[42] According to ATAKA's discourse there are two main perpetrators abusing the cause of the Bulgarian national ideal: foreigners and minorities.

In his first speech at the National Assembly, ATAKA's leader, Volen Siderov, proclaimed that "after a fifteen-year-policy of national betrayal, pillage, and genocide perpetrated against the Bulgarian nation by several parliaments and governments under the dictate of foreign actors, in the end the hour of the Bulgarian revival has come. The Bulgarian nation has woken up from its slumber and has declared to the world that it will no longer allow to be discriminated against, trampled upon, and experimented with. . . . Thus, the Bulgarians have once again proved themselves to be genuine descendents of their glorious forefathers, who have established the first-ever nation state, have originated the oldest culture in Europe, and have subsequently civilized large parts of the continent."[43] Such discursive nostalgia for an imagined past underscores ATAKA's inflammatory remarks against minority groups. This strategy reflects a tendency to identify the national "self" with the notion of a "pure Bulgarian ethnicity," which denigrates the representatives of minority groups not only to the category of the "other," but also to an inferior position.[44] For instance, Siderov has declared that "Bulgaria is a single-nation, unitary state. Bulgaria is not subject to division according to ethnic, religious or any other principle. Ethnic or religious differences cannot take precedence over the national origin. Whoever does this is expelling himself from the Bulgarian nation and state."[45]

In this respect, ATAKA has long insisted that "the abject poverty of Bulgarians is a direct result of the privileged treatment of minorities in the country. We, the Bulgarians, are subjected daily to direct discrimination in our own fatherland."[46] With particular vehemence, ATAKA has targeted the Turkish minority group and its political representatives. Siderov has, therefore, proclaimed that "ATAKA's nationalism is not just phrases and shibboleths, but a practical program . . . aimed at preventing the Turkefication of Bulgaria. There are whole regions of our country, which culturally and administratively are becoming Turkish. Economically, they are also being occupied by either Turkish or pro-Turkish companies. This is a dangerous precedent, which poses the threat of their annexation by Turkey."[47] ATAKA has even resorted to importing Turkish words in its anti-minority discourses in order to sabotage the thinking process and increase its populist leverage.[48] For instance, Siderov declared that ATAKA "would not allow the Prime Minister to put *fezzes* [an Ottoman/Muslim-type of hat] back on Bulgarian heads and would prevent referring to Bulgarians as *gyavur* [a derogatory Ottoman appellation for Bulgarians]. . . . He [the Prime Minister] is no longer a Bulgarian! Down with the Turks!"[49] In a similar fashion, Petar Beron, the Deputy Speaker of the National Assembly and a member of ATAKA, has announced that "if no one restricts the Turks, they are going to turn Bulgaria into a *vilayet* ['province' in Turkish], just as they were doing for five hundred years during the Ottoman yoke."[50]

Such jingoistic statements targeted at "foreigners" abroad and at home reflect the "libidinal politics"[51] of ATAKA's nationalism.[52] In particular, they seem to confirm the assertion that "as long as people are brought up in the memory of the 'Turkish yoke' and told about the 'barbarous' Turks who savagely raped and killed their ancestors, they will react emotionally when it comes to discussing minority rights. . . . The persistence of this unstable environment cannot but bear negatively upon the overcoming of ethnic and religious tensions in Bulgaria."[53] In its content, such discursive strategy suggests the incantation of a collective syndrome articulating a mass-perception that the Bulgarian national group is a "perennial victim of various contemptible 'others' who had sought to overcome their inferiority by uniting in a conspiracy against it. [Therefore, the Bulgarians should] consider themselves 'entitled' to vastly more than is their lot and [should be] determined to punish the conspirators." In this respect, the emphasis on the libidinal aspect of contemporary forms of Bulgarian nationalism suggests that when a society is at the height of nationalistic fervor, "it is like a man driven wild with sexual frenzy: rational judgment is suspended, cost-benefit analysis is held in contempt if it is regarded at all, and all that remains is the collective lust for satisfaction."[54]

However, the question remains as to what made possible the emergence of this kind of libidinal politics during the 2005 parliamentary elections? Most commentators have insisted that during the 1990s, Bulgarian nationalistic formations lacked the political know-how, organizational experience, and financial resources to mount any meaningful political campaigning.[55] Thus, the dominant conclusion has been that "nationalism is not vital and not particularly popular despite all the complexity of inter-ethnic relations in Bulgaria."[56] In particular, "the very spread of anti-Turkish rhetoric led to its banalization, and, hence, to its expansion since it became impossible for any political force to use it as the founding stone for the consolidation of a distinctive political identity."[57] The claim here is that it is exactly this marginalization of radical nationalistic sentiments and their absence from the mainstream public debate during the 1990s, which made it possible for ATAKA to resort to emotive chauvinism at the beginning of the twenty-first century—i.e., the nationalist message was perceived as *novel* and, also, as distinct from the discourse of the dominant political actors in Bulgaria.

In this context, it has to be acknowledged that nationalistic sentiments for the better part of the first post-communist decade remained at the level of popular culture, especially as reflected in the increasing popularity of "popfolk" music (also referred to as "ethnopop" and "chalga") and "Pirin folk" (or "Macedonian") music.[58] This observation relates to the fuzzy origin of Bulgarian nationalism. As Richard Crampton illustrates, the articulation of a distinct Bulgarian identity in the eighteenth and nineteenth centuries was complicated by the geographic proximity to the Ottoman capital. Pragmatically speaking, such closeness to the seat of Ottoman power "meant that when it did emerge Bulgarian nationalism had an unusually weak sense of territorial nationalism . . . [which] combined to ensure that Bulgarian nationalism was primarily cultural rather than political and territorial."[59] The residue of these beginnings can be traced in the current modalities of popular culture.

On the one hand, "Pirin folk" has maintained the symbolic claim—in the words of the then Bulgarian President, Petar Stoyanov—that "Macedonia is the most romantic part of Bulgarian history."[60] The emergence of ATAKA, therefore, bears witness to the pervasiveness of such nationalist sentiments throughout Bulgarian society. This was most vocally expressed in the context of the "public disgust" at the attempts to establish a political formation of the "ethnic Macedonians in Bulgaria," a development which ATAKA labeled an "intrusion into the domestic affairs of Bulgaria funded by Washington and Brussels."[61]

On the other hand, *popfolk* music occupies an idiosyncratic positioning within the space of Bulgarian popular culture. For instance, during the communist period it was largely an underground (if not overtly dissident) genre that challenged the state-sponsored national culture and its proponents (troupes, bands, ensembles, etc.) that became the unwitting purveyors of communist ideology.[62] In the post-communist period, however, the persisting (if not increasing) popularity of *popfolk* was, yet again, constructed as a challenge—this time to the "civilizational choice" of the country.[63] In other words, the perceived "backwardness" of *popfolk* rhythms allegedly confronted the "pro-Western" and "European" direction of the country's transition with their retrieval of "indigenous" traditions. It is often ignored that the appeal of these popular constructions of identity reflect the fact that while "Bulgaria's 'revolution' may have been bloodless, psychologically it was a massacre. The complicated ups and downs of the political climate . . . took a debilitating toll on people's psyches as they strove to make sense of their new world. The public trust was shattered and the idea that everyone was somehow responsible for the mess, unbearable and demoralizing."[64] In this respect, *popfolk* has become the aesthetic site for specific forms of contemporary self-expression that "brought—for many local people—the notion of celebration and a release from the hardships of everyday life."[65] Consequently, these forms of national self-articulation—in particular the quality of both *popfolk* and *Pirin folk* as simultaneously "quasi-private" and "quasi-public" goods[66]—has facilitated the nationalist politicization of popular culture.

Formally, the origins of such re-nationalization of public feeling can be traced back at least to the early 1980s and, in particular, the 1981 celebrations of the thirteen-hundredth anniversary of the establishment of Bulgarian statehood. This was an occasion for the erection of mammoth monuments, the organization of grandiose public celebrations, the publication of monographs, and the directing of films celebrating the glorious past of the medieval Bulgarian empires.[67] Such strategy for political mobilization was underpinned by, what Maria Todorova calls, "logically untenable, scholarly unsupportable, and fantastic assertions" of Todor Zhivkov (the communist dictator) who declared that the Bulgarian state has followed a unique course in European history, "unlike other states then existing in our continent, in being built on the principle of nationality as a state of one people."[68] Thus, by collapsing "pre- and post-1944 lifestyles [and] making the latter seem a natural and nationalistic extension of the former" the communist regime sought to historicize and, thence, legitimize the language of its hegemony.[69]

Such soft policy of heightening national awareness was hardened in 1984 with the initiation of the so-called "Revival Process"—a "government-sponsored cultural blitzkrieg"[70]—which aimed at reclaiming the Bulgarian identity of the Turkish minority.[71] To buttress popular support for this policy, the communist regime released in 1988 the movie *Vreme na nasilie* [*A Time of Violence*], based on the 1964 Anton Donchev's novel *Vreme razdelno* [*A Time of Parting*]. The film—

in almost scatological details—portrays the alleged atrocities committed during a forced Islamization campaign in the Ottoman period. Although such campaigns were part of the life in the Ottoman Empire, Donchev's book itself is based on a fictitious story, first published in the late nineteenth century (that gained popularity, but not much factual confirmation, during the early twentieth century) of large-scale forced conversions of Bulgarians.[72] Such stories of forced Islamization came to justify the nationalist claim that all Muslims living in the country are in fact descendants of these forcibly converted Bulgarians. Thus, the 1984 "Revival Process" had to rescue and liberate this "Bulgarian essence" from the markers of Turkish and Muslim identity.[73] In this respect, the fact that the Bulgarian post-communist transition was initiated from "above" (i.e., as an internal party coup) rather than from "below" (i.e., as some sort of a "velvet revolution") tends to indicate that the majority of the population seemed to accept the "virtues of communism" as well as the "extravaganzas associated with Bulgarian nationalism."[74] In this context, the social commentator, Evgeni Dainov has insisted that the post-communist transition has failed to challenge, let alone change, the "values of the socialist way of life."[75] The normative persistence of national communist lifestyles allows the membership of ATAKA's members to present themselves as "national" representatives, and, thereby, downplay their "state-socialist" affiliations.[76] In this setting, the language of chauvinism offers potent sites for *making sense* of the perceived chaos of democratization.

Apart from the professed ideational freshness of its nationalism, ATAKA also commands the organizational and institutional paraphernalia to propagate its ideas. In its beginning, "ATAKA" was (and still is) the name of a polemical TV show hosted by Volen Siderov. It is his charisma and eloquence that has succeeded to focus the energies of disparate nationalistic formations, by tapping into the libidinal values of society and harnessing popular discontent into nationalistic exaltation. Siderov, himself, is a well-known journalist, who was the editor-in-chief of the first opposition newspaper in post-communist Bulgaria—*Demokratsia* (*Democracy*). However, after his surprise dismissal from the newspaper in 1992, Siderov separated for good with most of his former colleagues. In the following decade he busied himself with journalism, the publication of several anti-Semitic books and a few botched attempts at re-launching his political career (most infamously in 2001 when he was withdrawn from the election race as a candidate in the party of the former king and subsequent Prime Minister, Simeon Saxcoburggotski). In 2000, Siderov was awarded the prestigious award of the Union of Bulgarian Journalists as an editor-in-chief of the newspaper *Monitor* (*Observer*). At about the same time, Siderov started the TV show ATAKA, which quickly gained him popularity with his inflammatory rhetoric. Consequently, he formed the National Union ATAKA as a coalition of several nationalistic organizations, which garnered 21 out of 240 seats in the National Assembly at the June 2005 elections. After the elections, however, Siderov moved swiftly to consolidate his position by registering a party ATAKA and, thus, stamping his authority over the organization.

In many respects, it is this institutional and ideational framework as well as Siderov's charisma that ensure the persistence of ATAKA's popularity. This was evident during the 2006 presidential race, in which Siderov was the runner-up candidate. Thus, the current prominence of nationalistic discourses in the country owes much to the perceived (and real) loss of self-esteem, which has led a substantial number of Bulgarians to subscribe to a chauvinistic program for revamping the processes of transformation.

The Anti-Systemic Character of Nationalist Discourses

Another aspect reflected by ATAKA's emergence during 2005 is its anti-systemic character, which has questioned the content and the direction of the post-communist transition. Its doctrine of collectivism over individual freedom has placed the institutions of civil society at odds with the alleged "national ideal." The ability of libidinal politics to translate societal dissatisfaction into nationalistic claims owes much to the loss of popular legitimacy of mainstream politics. Resentment with the transition has been exacerbated as a result of both the material and ideational disparity between policy-making elites and the society at large. Hence, the intimations of affluence and successful integration into European organizations collided with the popular perception of lowering quality of life. Such attitudes compounded by the substantial emigration of young people convinced many of the corruptive effects of the transition process on the "Bulgarian nation."

As suggested, the lack of rejection of the values of communism ushered in their persistence on the level of domestic practices and beliefs. The social degeneration attendant in the post-totalitarian transitions of countries that have not experienced a normative disengagement with their communist past has been captured by Frances Fukuyama in the phrase "a vacation in Bulgaria." Thus, Fukuyama has used Bulgaria as an epitome of the conflation between a degenerated lack of self-esteem and a pathological desire for recognition: "Communism *humiliated* ordinary people by forcing them to make a myriad of petty, and sometimes not so petty, moral compromises with their better natures. . . . [The] charge against communism is not at all that it failed in its promise to deliver the material plenty of industrial efficiency, or that it disappointed the hopes of the working class or the poor for a better life. On the contrary, it did offer them these things in a Faustian bargain, requiring them to compromise their moral worth in return. And in making this bargain, the victims of the system became its perpetrators, while the system itself took on a life of its own, independently of anyone's desire to participate in it."[77]

The inability to acknowledge the moral compromise forced upon Bulgarian society during the period of communist rule, has underwritten the resilience of its normative grasp in the post-communist period. Thus, the pressure to change the patterns of political behavior in Bulgaria has more often than not come from outside—i.e., from external actors/donors. In this respect, the values of democratization still *remain abstract concepts rather than tangible points of reference for most Bulgarians*. The post-communist transition in Bulgaria can, therefore, safely be regarded as an instance of a democratizing system, but without a similar democratization of the citizens.[78] It is the persistence of the values of national communism, which have allowed ATAKA to recourse to nationalistic proclamations in order to rally support for its populist platform. Thus, some commentators insist that "ethnic nationalism has a future in Bulgaria, because a large number of Bulgarians have lost faith in the promise of 1989."[79]

ATAKA's representatives have been quick to ascertain their distinctiveness from the political establishment. For instance, Stanislav Stanilov, an MP from ATAKA, has declared that "our value system is different from that of other parties. We despise and we are disgusted by suggestions for negotiations with other [parliamentary-represented] political formations, because we are different from the current political class and our voters backed ATAKA because of this unique platform."[80] Likewise, another MP from ATAKA insisted that "ATAKA is different, because we have nothing to apologize for. Our party presents a clean sheet, because we have never been in government."[81] The commu-nationalism of ATAKA, therefore, rehashes the old practices of national communism insisting that its supporters follow the party's leadership because they represent the "genuine national interest."[82] In this respect, the contemporary utterances of chauvinism reiterate the dominant theme of the communist-institutionalized form of Bulgarian nationalism that the essence of the nation "had to be defended by 'heroic deeds' during 'arduous historical tests.'"[83] In this context, Siderov, himself, has openly exploited popular disenchantment with the record of the dominant post-communist parties by referring to all of them as "the political mafia that has exploited Bulgaria."[84]

Such development confirms the suggestion that the recourse to nationalistic policies in Bulgaria tends to exploit popular dissatisfaction with the overall political and economic situation.[85] This article claims, therefore, that ATAKA's populism is anti-systemic both in relational terms—i.e., vis-à-vis other political parties—as well as in its ideological aspect—i.e., challenging the character of the transition process.[86] In this context, it is concerning that an anti-systemic formation is represented in still *democratizing* institutions. ATAKA's commu-nationalism debases the democratic politics by replacing the debate over alternative programs with the debate over alternative strategies for realizing the same program.[87] As Capoccia argues such analytical strategies seriously undermine the ability of democratic actors effectively to respond to anti-systemic threats as it presents them with an impossible dilemma of "tolerance for the intolerant"—that is, "on the one hand, the need for tolerance and, on the other, the danger that the intolerant represents for the very principle of tolerance."[88] The predicaments of this contradiction present a particular challenge to democratizing societies as the institutional infrastructure is not sufficiently consolidated to confront anti-systemic contestation.[89]

The anti-systemic (*commu-nationalist*) challenge underwriting ATAKA's nationalistic proclamations has been evidenced during the formation of the 2005 Bulgarian government. Owing to the fragmented character of the National Assembly as a result of the June 2005 elections, the construction of a governing coalition took more than five weeks of negotiations (and trading) between the three-largest political formations. As it happened, it was with the mandate of the Movement for Rights and Freedoms (MRF)—an ethnic Turkish party—that the new government was formed (although the Prime Ministerial position and the leading role in the coalition were to be played by the Bulgarian Socialist Party—the former communists). In these circumstances, ATAKA resorted yet again to manipulation of history as a platform from which to preach national salvation. Petar Beron, ATAKA's representative in the presidium of the National Assembly, pronounced that this is "a government of the offspring of Kiriak Stefchov."[90] This statement resuscitated into an unlikely political life the literary character of Kiriak Stefchov—one of the central characters in the nineteenth-century novel, *Under the Yoke* by Ivan Vazov. Probably, Bulgaria's most important historical novel, it recounts the Ottoman oppression of the country and offers a graphic depiction of the brutal suppression of the April 1876 Uprising. The figure of Kiriak Stefchov represents the anti-Bulgarian attitudes of some Bulgarians at the time and his name has become a synonym for a traitor to the Bulgarian nation.[91]

Thus, by referring to a fictitious literary character, ATAKA indicated its opposition to a government of the "MRF and its henchmen, regardless of whether they are ethnic Turks or Bulgarians, who have abandoned their national identity by supporting the MRF."[92] Hence, by re-inventing the myth of national suffering within the historical framework of betrayal and treason, ATAKA's construction of the Bulgarian self-understanding attempts the articulation of an exclusive national space by attributing guilt to alleged foes. Such statements have also been underwritten by thinly veiled claims to trans-generational culpability.[93] In this respect, Siderov has declared that "nowadays, we are being governed by the posterity of those that brutally butchered our ancestors when we were under the Ottoman yoke."[94] Anti-systemness here is detected in the attitude and intentions of these statements, which belie an unwillingness to tolerate or accommodate difference, as well as absence of desire for consensual politics.

Thus, it is through such strategies of antagonism and confrontation aimed at encapsulating the Bulgarian national group through discursive platforms for stoking up enmity with various "others" that ATAKA's populist nationalism challenges the direction and process of the post-communist transition in Bulgaria. The suggestion here is that such articulations of alleged communal restoration are inherently anti-political due to their negligence of the plurality of social existence. The discourses of victimhood of ATAKA's commu-nationalism become a token of "lost communities"—that is, communities that are premised on a "fictive past moment in which there was a perfect, even divine fit among subjects, their aspirations, and their situations."[95] By referring to the hoax of an essential national self, ATAKA's narrative of legitimizing chauvinist contentions has undermined the assertion of diversity as a precondition of politics and instead has invoked the figment of national coherence. The inference, therefore, is that such re-nationalization of discourses attests to the possibility of the *erosion of politics*[96] in post-communist countries.

The Conflict between Europe and Nation

This section suggests that ATAKA's libidinal and anti-systemic nationalistic rhetoric has inadvertently brought attention to the impossibility of cohabitation between the mythic narrative of Bulgarian nationalism and the idea of Europe. Such predicament points to the quandary of "managing the past" within the articulation of Bulgarian identity and its interlacing into wider identity-constructs.[97] In contrast, one of the characteristic trends in post-World War II European affairs (also reinforced by the current processes of EU-enlargement) is how the states and nations of the continent have integrated "Europe" into their "we"-concepts. Thus, the notion of "Europe" is not a purely external or dependent matter, but internal —i.e., stability in the continent has come to depend on the compatibility between "the domestic articulation of a project for Europe with long-held concepts of state and nation."[98]

ATAKA's proclamations, however, reflect a tendency to refer to Europe not as a political project based on a set of shared values, principles, or aspirations but rather as an entity, defined negatively (as a dividing line). For instance, populist retractions from European integration declare that "the EU needs us. But what do we get in exchange for our willingness to join the EU? Nothing, as we do not understand our great geopolitical value. . . . The EU needs us so that we can stop those coming to the West from Asia. However, we have to demand the full payment for this service—this is the real Bulgarian interest."[99] This is a discursive strategy, whose origins can be traced back to the period of national revival when Bulgaria has been constructed as the last bastion of "European civilization" in the face of Ottoman depravity as well as an assertion that Bulgaria has always been *in* Europe, hence it should not be expected to return there. In this context, the five centuries of "foreign" Ottoman rule are articulated as an attestation of "the 'kidnapping' of Bulgarians from their natural development,' but at the same time the "inherent Bulgarian 'Europeanness' remained untarnished," if not strengthened by this suffering.[100] The normative claim of contemporary nationalistic discourses, therefore, is that the usurpers of the European appellation should acknowledge Bulgaria's rightful place as one of their own.

For instance, one of ATAKA's MPs has claimed that "although ATAKA is not against [Bulgaria's] membership of the EU, we are opposed to crawling into its basement."[101] In a similar fashion Siderov has insisted that "whenever self-appointed experts from the EU come here to teach us how to behave, we should be reminding them that their countries did not even exist when there already was a Bulgarian state. Bulgaria is the only country in Europe, which for more than a thousand years has not changed its name and has survived all the vicissitudes of history."[102] In fact, Siderov has managed to combine the libidinal and anti-systemic discourses in his insistence that the "current suffering" of Bulgarians stems from "the treasonous acceptance of the European minority rights legislation, which formed the basis of the 1997 Framework Agreement on Minority Rights. At the time, I warned about its anti-Bulgarian character, but the political mafia would not listen."[103]

It should be noted, that ATAKA's nationalistic discourses, although not novel, legitimize the fulfilment of the Bulgarian national ideal as an alternative to the project of European integration. As Siderov has explained, "the Bulgarian national interest makes it imperative that Bulgaria widens its horizons and starts looking to the south and to the east of the EU."[104] In this respect, ATAKA's representatives are not the only ones that have come to express the dichotomy between the national and the European projects. For instance, the Bulgarian President, Georgi Parvanov has stressed on several occasions that "Bulgarians should be proud, because of the historical legacy that Europe owes us . . . because it is our culture that forms the foundation of European civilization."[105] This is a theme that Parvanov intimated in his inaugural address when he declared that "we should remember that individuals and parties come and go, but Bulgaria stays. Let us be, and I am sure we will only be true European citizens if we are true Bulgarians."[106]

Such statements reflect the problematic accommodation of the notion of "Europe" within the narrative of Bulgarian nationalism. For instance, the nineteenth-century Bulgarian revolutionary Luben Karavelov writes that "it is sad, that Europeans have matured so little; it is obvious that the peoples of Europe are doomed for years to come to play an unfortunate role. . . . The reason is that Europe is too *old* and lacks sap for a *healthy* life."[107] According to Clark such sentiment reflects the realization that an emphasis on Europe "led to almost denationalized cosmopolitanism," which threatened fledgling Bulgarian nationalism. This fear together with Russian ideological and material support for the Slavs in the Balkans, "started the trend which drew the centre of Bulgarian (and eventually political) gravity from the West to Russia."[108]

Attesting to the vivacity of this tradition, ATAKA's supporters insist that "the EU tells us that it will accept us and feed us, but only on the condition that Brussels brainwashes us first and makes us forget our national past. But nations have their memory. Therefore, history hinders integration. The current resurgence of nationalism is a response to this and an instinct for self-preservation. Bulgaria needs such self-preserving nationalism."[109] As already suggested, such a stance has also been ideationally corroborated by the popularity of *popfolk* and *Pirin folk* music, both of which serve as a flexible aesthetic territory that reminds us of (and conjurs up) an idyllic past as well as retrieves "the beauty of the fading small remnants of local traditions, which had been excluded and marginalized . . . and are now demonstrating that what is inherited through common memory cannot easily be deleted as if it had never existed."[110] More controversially, however, the "phantasmatic imaginary"[111] of the constructed past has come to dominate the EU-accession project by infusing it with the theme of completing the Bulgarian national integration. Thus, the social commentator Krasimir Uzunov has declared that "European integration is part of the fulfilment of the Bulgarian national ideal. . . . When the Balkan region is Europeanized and regional states become members of the EU, then we can speak of a spiritual unification of all Bulgarians in one political entity."[112] Likewise, President Parvanov has pronounced that the accession of the country into the EU is an opportunity for "proactive engagement in favor of all those who think themselves Bulgarian, because the experience of European integration indicates that the state is not only a territory, but an unbounded moral and spiritual space."[113]

In this respect, the current re-nationalization of political discourses in Bulgaria and their contrasting between the national interest and the European project have evinced the problematic relationship between "state" and "nation." Historically, since its modern emergence in 1878, Bulgarian statehood has consistently fallen short of the expectations of the nation. What was imagined as the Bulgarian national community never inhabited *its* state boundaries (apart from a brief period between the signing of the San Stefano Treaty on 3 March 1878 and the end of the Berlin Congress on 13 July 1878). The dominant interpretation of subsequent Bulgarian history presents it as a narrative characterized by a struggle of the "nation" aimed at the rectification of the "Berlin injustice" through the creation of a suitable "nation-state."[114] Usually, however, these national aspirations were frustrated by the duplicity of particular statesmen, which further undermined the authority of the state and state-institutions.[115] Thus, gradually, the state became a challenge to be handled, not a means for the self-realization of the nation.

It is this context that suggests the incompatibility between the Bulgarian national ideal and the idea of a "united Europe"—that is, the contemporary form of Bulgarian nationalism is a "backward looking struggle, rather than . . . a force leading to the country's future achievements."[116] As Petar Beron has summarized the thrust of ATAKA's nationalism, "one is either a Bulgarian, or a cosmopolitan. There is no middle way."[117] In this way, he has hinted at the impossibility to intricate the dominant narratives of Bulgarian identity into a larger project for self-articulation. Such background also provides an understanding of a largely forgotten 1914 statement at the National Assembly by Alexander Stamboliiski (the leader of the Bulgarian Agrarian National Union and, subsequently, Bulgarian Prime Minister from 1919-1923), who, in retort to a hackle that he is representing Serbian rather than Bulgarian national interests, declared that "You are right, I am no Bulgarian. Neither am I a Serb. I am a Slav from the South—I am a Yugoslav!"[118] In this way, Stamboliiski had recognized that *the ability of Bulgarians to participate in projects involving larger "we" concepts involves the rejection of the myths of their national imagination.* A brutal confirmation of such an assumption is Stamboliiski's murder (although, perhaps, "lynching" would be a more appropriate term), by members of the terrorist IMRO in June 1923, because of his desire to commit Bulgaria to a Balkan Federation and his outspoken rejection of the nationalistic myth of "unifying" all Bulgarian lands.

In this context, the emergence of ATAKA as well as the concomitant re-nationalization of public discourses comes to suggest that the theme of Bulgarian national integration continues to offer potent sources for impacting decision-making in the country. In particular, the radicalization of the renewed construction of nationalist discourses as evidenced by the statements of ATAKA's representatives seems to have legitimized their claims and has also impacted the public perceptions of the direction of the post-communist transition. As it happens, such re-articulation of the national self has reiterated the incompatibility of *the Bulgarian national myths* and *the idea of Europe*.

Whither the Nation?

This investigation has focused on the rise of a particular form of re-nationalization of popular feeling in Bulgaria that has come to dominate public articulations of nationalism. In spite of its idiosyncratic conditions, such patterns are not dissimilar to popular modes of nationalist mobilization across the political space of contemporary Europe. The appeal and support for the self-avowed nationalist party ATAKA in Bulgaria attest to the complexity of contemporary nationalisms. ATAKA's discursive strategies evidence the ability of chauvinism to undermine the assertion of diversity as a precondition for politics by replacing it with the imagination of national unity. Thus, in Bulgaria, the assertion of national essentialism has been constructed as an alternative and a challenge to the European integration project. Such development seems to confirm the insistence that the ideology of nationalism cannot produce a sophisticated national discourse and instead delivers only emotional and intellectually one-dimensional constructs.[119] Yet, despite their simplistic grammars, such articulations are not powerless.

The implication is that the evocation of closer ties with European institutions has been contrasted by a rising public perception of dissatisfaction with the state of affairs in Bulgaria. This chapter, thereby, has asserted that populist articulations of nationalism and the process of European integration are still being construed in the public imagination not only as different, but as alternative projects for the future trajectories of Bulgaria. Such a claim proposes that the persistence of this trend is largely the reason for the continuous vacillation of the country between the alleged legacy of the past and the possibilities of the future (one of which is the reconstruction of the imagined past as instanced by the current rhetoric of chauvinism). The continuities and contingencies of these trends defy any attempts at meaningful prognosis of future patterns.

In this respect, the brief post-enlargement experience of the country indicates the persisting competition between new and old elements in the popular legitimation of policy-making. Nevertheless, this study points toward two observations. Firstly, it is apparent that ATAKA's inflammatory proclamations have rendered acceptable the re-nationalizing discursive practices. As a result, the recourse to "national unity" and "national coherence" has become a normal (if not expected) part of the idiom of mainstream political formations. Secondly, such development reflects the absence of a much-needed debate on the specters of Bulgarian national imagination and the discontent with the post-communist transition. The lack of such open discussion intensifies the political appeal of nationalistic rhetoric as an effective strategy for popular mobilization.[120]

Such a setting provides the context for understanding the claim of the murdered Bulgarian dissident Georgi Markov in the epigraph of this chapter that the construction of the political agenda of the present tends to be disengaged from the immediate reality and instead hesitates between a "'terrible' past and a 'wonderful' future." In this respect, the promise of the past still seems to entice a significant section of the Bulgarian population with its vision of national unity and the bucolic idyll of collective existence. Thus, the last word is left to Markov, whose reflections capture the central predicament in the construction of Bulgarian national identity: "I have always been attracted by the idea of complete rebirth, which is perhaps peculiar to those who have suffered a lot, or sinned a lot. . . . This desire reminds me of Goethe's thought that my fatherland is where I am happiest; it impels me to move to new countries, to meet new people, to learn a new language, to try to think and live in a new way. But the other desire is that of the boy in the fable about King Midas and the ass's ears. This is the uncontrollable, almost painful urge of a man to express himself, to unload everything the years have deposited within him, to pour out what suffocates him because it has to be kept in. *This desire tells me that the past is more real than the present.*"[121]

Notes

1. Georgi Markov, *The Truth that Killed* (London: Weidenfeld and Nicolson, 1983), xvii-xx.

2. Rogers Brubaker, *Nationalism Reframed* (Cambridge: Cambridge University Press, 1996), 2.

3. Lene Hansen and Michael Williams, "The Myths of Europe: Legitimacy, Community, and the 'Crisis' of the EU," *Journal of Common Market Studies* 37, no. 2 (June 1999): 233-49; Emilian Kavalski, "Whether a Nation . . . and Whither if One? The Politics of Selection and Interpretation of the Past," *Ab Imperio* 4, no. 1 (February 2003): 558-68; Katherine Verdery, "Whether 'Nation' and 'Nationalism,'" *Daedalus* 122, no. 3 (June 1993): 37-46.

4. Peter Stamatov, "The Making of a 'Bad' Public: Ethnonational Mobilization in Post -Communist Bulgaria," *Theory and Society* 29, no. 3 (October 2000): 549-72.

5. Kyril Drezov, "Bulgaria: Transition Comes Full Circle," in *Experimenting with Democracy: Regime Change in the Balkans*, ed. Geoffrey Pridham and Tom Gallagher (London: Routledge, 2000), 197. On different representations of Bulgaria see Roumiana

Deltcheva, "East Central Europe as a Politically Correct Scapegoat: The Case of Bulgaria," *CLCWeb: Comparative Literature and Culture* 1, no 2 (June 1999): 1-12; and Sara Brady, "*Cargo Sofia*: A Bulgarian Truck Ride through Dublin," *The Drama Review* 51, no. 4 (December 2007): 162-67.

6. Oscar Clyatt, *Bulgaria's Quest for Security after the Cold War* (Washington, DC: Institute for National Strategic Studies, 1993); Emilian Kavalski, "From the Western Balkans to the Greater Balkans Area: The External Conditioning of 'Awkward' and 'Integrated' States," *Mediterranean Quarterly* 17, no. 3 (October 2006): 86-100; Rossen Vassilev, "De-Development Problems in Bulgaria," *East European Quarterly* 37, no. 3 (October 2003): 345-64.

7. Emilian Kavalski, "Bulgaria: The State of Chaos," *Southeast European Politics* 4, no. 1 (March 2003): 68-90. See also Josette Baer, "The Creation of Polity in Bulgaria: *Realpolitik* or 'Cosmopolitanism by Default,'" *East Central Europe* 31, no. 1 (March 2001): 1-21.

8. Richard Sennett, *The Fall of Public Man* (Cambridge: Cambridge University Press, 1974).

9. Sabrina Ramet, "Under the Holy Lime Tree: The Inculcation of Neurotic and Psychotic Syndromes as a Serbian Wartime Strategy," in *Serbia since 1989*, ed. Sabrina Ramet and Vjeran Pavlakovic (Seattle: University of Washington Press, 2005), 125-42; Sabrina Ramet, "The Sirens and the Guslar," in *Serbia since 1989*, ed. Sabrina Ramet and Vjeran Pavlakovic (Seattle: University of Washington Press, 2005), 395-414; Sabrina Ramet, *Thinking about Yugoslavia* (Cambridge: Cambridge University Press, 2005).

10. Giovanni Capoccia, *Defending Democracy: Reactions to Extremism in Interwar Europe* (Baltimore, MD: Johns Hopkins University Press, 2005).

11. Ellie Kedourie, *Nationalism* (London: Hutchinson & Co, 1960).

12. Mancur Olson, "The Logic of Collective Action in Soviet-type Societies," *Journal of Soviet Nationalities* 1, no. 2 (June 1990): 23.

13. Patrick Geary, *The Myth of Nations* (Princeton, NJ: Princeton University Press, 2002), 13.

14. Rumen Daskalov, *The Making of a Nation in the Balkans: Historiography of the Bulgarian Revival* (Budapest: Central European University Press, 2004); Philip Mosely, "The Post-War History of Modern Bulgaria," *Journal of Modern History* 9, no. 3 (October 1937): 348-66; Kristina Petkova and Valeri Todorov, "Bulgarian National Stereotypes and National Identity," *Sociological Problems* 34, no. 5 (November 2002): 115-28.

15. On the alleged pre-Ottoman "pre-history" of Bulgarian nationalism see Tania Ivanova-Sullivan, "Interpreting Medieval Literacy: Learning and Education in *Slavica Orthodoxa* (Bulgaria) and Byzantium in the Ninth and Twelfth Centuries," in *Medieval Education*, ed. Ronald Begley and Joseph Koterski (New York: Fordham University Press, 2005), 50-67.

16. James Clark, *The Pen and the Sword: Studies in Bulgarian History* (Boulder, CO: East European Monographs, 1988), 101.

17. On "non-Russian" influences on Bulgarian nationalism see Cyril Black, "The Influence of Western Political Thought in Bulgaria, 1850-1885," *American Historical Review* 48, no. 3 (October 1943): 507-20.

18. Clark, *The Pen*, 136. Charles Jelavich, *Tsarist Russia and Balkan Nationalism: Russian Influence in the Internal Affairs of Bulgaria and Serbia* (Westport, CT: Greenwood Press, 1978).

19. Clark, *The Pen*, 102-103. Michael Petrovich, "The Russian Image in Renaissance Bulgaria," *East European Quarterly* 1, no. 2 (June 1967): 87-105.

20. The word "lionized" should be taken here quite literally as it relates to the adoption of the lion as the herald of Bulgarian statehood premised on fictitious historiographical sources. As James Clark points out, the modern origins of the Bulgarian herald are traced to the 1754 volume illuminated by Hristofor Žefarović, who produced "fifty-four largely imaginary heraldic emblems and historical portraits with doggerel captions for all the 'Slav' states. . . . In 1841, Ivan Bogorov published Žefarović's portraits of the Bulgarian kings Ivan Asen and Ivan Shishman, and his Bulgarian lion rampant, which actually became the emblem of the independent Bulgarian state. Thus patriotic fantasy got translated into reality" (Clark, *The Pen*, 99-100).

21. Richard Crampton, *Bulgaria* (Oxford: Oxford University Press, 2007), vii-6.

22. Theodor Geshkoff, *Balkan Union: The Road to Peace in Southeastern Europe* (New York: Columbia University Press, 1940); Emilian Kavalski, "The Balkan America? The Myth of America in the Creation of Bulgarian National Identity," *New Zealand Slavonic Journal* 38, no. 1 (March 2004): 131-58.

23. Luben Karavelov, "Balkanskia poluostrov [The Balkan Peninsula]," *Svoboda*, 10 February 1870: 2. Emphasis added.

24. Nissan Oren, *Revolution Administered: Agrarianism and Communism in Bulgaria* (Baltimore, MD: John Hopkins University Press, 1973).

25. Paul Lendvai, *Eagles in Cobwebs: Nationalism and Communism in the Balkans* (Garden City, NY: Doubleday, 1969), 210.

26. Lendvai, *Eagles*, 210.

27. Thomas Hammond, "The Origins of National Communism," *Virginia Quarterly Review* 34, no. 2 (June 1958): 277. William Carleton, "Is Communism Going National," *Virginia Quarterly Review* 25, no. 3 (October 1949): 321-34. Peter Zwick, *National Communism* (Boulder, CO: Westview Press, 1983).

28. Maria Todorova, "The Course of Discourses of Bulgarian Nationalism," in *Eastern European Nationalism in the Twentieth Century*, ed. Peter Sugar (Washington, DC: American University Press, 1995), 92.

29. Oren, *Revolution*, 172.

30. Donna Buchanan, *Performing Democracy: Bulgarian Music and Musicians in Transition* (Chicago: University of Chicago Press, 2006). See also Deema Kaneff, *Who Owns the Past? The Politics of Time in a 'Model' Bulgarian Village* (Oxford: Berghan Books, 2004), and Carol Silverman, "The Politics of Folklore in Bulgaria," *Anthropological Quarterly* 56, no. 2 (June 1983): 55-61.

31. Oren, *Revolution*, 172.

32. Clark, *The Pen*, 138. Lendvai quotes a "non-Communist Bulgarian historian" who insists that, "There is nothing to fall back on in our modern history. We cannot heave ourselves up out of our historical tragedies. Therefore, we tend to look at Russia as a protector. The result is, of course, that we have become in fact, if not in name, the sixteenth union republic of the Soviet Union." (Lendvai, *Eagles*, 210).

33. Lendvai, *Eagles*, 11, 241-61.Contrary, to such assertion, Georgi Markov (the Bulgarian dissident assassinated in London in 1978) describes an incident in 1964 when nationalism was used as a form of resistance to communism. As he states a group of inebriated Bulgarian intellectuals greeted the former communist leader, Vulko Chervenkov, with "Shumi Maritsa," the anthem of the pre-communist Bulgarian state. Markov writes that "about a hundred voices, strained to the limit, shatter the silence of the Arkutino night with the national anthem of *their* Bulgaria, which they sing in bitter honor of the man who once tried to obliterate it with blood. Never before have I known this anthem to sound so powerful and moving" (Markov, *The Truth*, 105. Emphasis original).

34. Antonina Zhelyazkova, "Bulgaria in Transition: The Muslim Minorities," *Islam and Christian-Muslim Relations* 12, no. 3 (October 2001): 288.

35. Oren, *Revolution*, 154-58. The period of the 1980s is detailed in the following section as it has more immediate bearing on ATAKA's origins.

36. Petar-Emil Mitev, "Popular Attitudes towards Politics," in *Bulgaria in Transition*, ed. John Bell (Boulder, CO: Westview Press, 1998), 57.

37. Nadége Ragaru, "Islam in Post-Communist Bulgaria: An Aborted 'Clash of Civilizations,'" *Nationalities Papers* 29, no. 2 (June 2001): 302.

38. *RFE/RL Daily Report*, 29 December 1993.

39. He has developed his ideas more extensively in the paper "Globalization: The Last Stage in the Colonization of the Orthodox East," given at the 2002 Conference on Global Problems of World History, sponsored by the anti-Semitic *The Barnes Review*. See the conference website at <http://oag.ru/reports/revisionists.html> (21 March 2006).

40. *Mediapool*, 7 July 2005. *BBT*, *BNTnews*, *Focus*, *Mediapool*, and *NovaTV* are Bulgarian electronic news agencies.

41. Stamatov, "The Making," 552.

42. *Mediapool*, 26 June 2005.

43. *Focus*, 11 July 2005.

44. Claire Levy, "Who Is the 'Other' in the Balkans? Local Ethnic Music as a *Different Source* of Identities in Bulgaria," in *Music, Space and Place*, ed. Sheila Whiteley, Andy Bennett, and Stan Hawkins (Aldershot: Ashgate, 2004), 43.

45. *Focus*, 26 June 2005.

46. *Mediapool*, 11 July 2005.

47. *Mediapool*, 20 February 2006.

48. Ramet, *Thinking*, 171.

49. *Focus*, 26 July 2005.

50. *NovaTV*, 14 August 2005.

51. Ramet, "Under," 127-39.

52. It has to be acknowledged that the construction of certain groups of the Bulgarian population as "foreign" in ATAKA's discourses is not limited only to ethnic minority groups, but also to gays and lesbians as well as women who fail to comply with the patriarchal matrix of its nationalism. Some of the reasons for this sense of disempowerment of heterosexual males evidenced by the discourses of extreme nationalist proponents refers to the changing values and ramification of gender roles in post-communist Bulgaria discussed in Kristen Ghodsee, "You '*Can*' Take It with You: Cultural Capital, State Regulation, and Tourism in Postsocialist Bulgaria" in *State and Society in Post-Socialist Economies*, ed. John Pickles (Basingstoke: Palgrave, 2008), 169-90.

53. Ragaru, "Islam," 319. John Georgeoff, "Nationalism in the History Textbooks of Yugoslavia and Bulgaria," *Comparative Education Review* 10, no. 3 (October 1966): 442-50.

54. Ramet, "Under," 126-27.

55. Christo Ivanov and Margarita Ilieva, "Bulgaria," in *Racist Extremism in Central and Eastern Europe*, ed. Cas Mudde (London: Routledge, 2005), 1-29.

56. Zhelyazkova, "Bulgaria," 300.

57. Ragaru, "Islam," 301.

58. See Timothy Rice, *May It Feel Your Soul: Experiencing Bulgarian Music* (Chicago: University of Chicago Press, 1994), and Carol Silverman, "The Politics of Folklore in Bulgaria," *Anthropological Quarterly* 56, no. 2 (March 1983): 55-61.

59. Crampton, *Bulgaria*, 83.

60. *Macedonian Information Liaison Service*, 29 April 1997.

61. *Focus*, 15 December 2006.

62. Buchanan, *Performing*, 437.

63. Levy, "Who Is," 44; Timothy Rice, "Bulgaria or Chalgaria: The Attenuation of Bulgarian Nationalism in Mass-Mediated Popular Culture," *Yearbook of Traditional Music* 34 (March 2002): 25-46.

64. Buchanan, *Performing*, 48. On the transformation of informal networks in post-communist Bulgaria see B.A. Cellarius, *In the Land of Orhpeus: Rural Livelihoods and Nature Conservation in Postsocialist Bulgaria* (Madison, WI: University of Wisconsin Press, 2004).

65. Levy, "Who Is," 47.

66. Elena Triffonova, "Civil Society—A Key Element of the Post-Cold War Zeitgeist: Civic Society Structure in Bulgaria," in *Black Sea Politics*, ed. Ayşe Güneş-Ayata, Ayça Ergun and Işil Çelimli (London: I.B.Tauris, 2005), 128.

67. Ivanka Atanasova, "Liudmila Zhivkova and the Paradox of Ideology and Identity in Communist Bulgaria," *East European Politics and Societies* 18, no. 2 (June 2004): 278-315.

68. Todorova, "The Course," 96.

69. Buchanan, *Performing*, 42.

70. Dimitrina Dimitrova, "The Influence of Command-Style Administration on Ethnic Conflict in Bulgaria," in *Nationalism, Ethnicity and Identity*, ed. Russel Farnen (Piscataway, NJ: Transaction Publishers, 1994), 398.

71. Viktor Bojkov, "Bulgaria's Turks in the 1980s," *Journal of Genocide Research* 6, no. 3 (October 2004): 343-69; Emilian Kavalski, "'Do Not Play With Fire': The End of the Bulgarian Ethnic Model," *Journal of Muslim Minority Affairs* 27, no. 1 (March 2007): 25-36.

72. For a detailed treatment of this issue see Michael Kiel, "Ottoman Sources for the Demographic History and the Process of Islamization of Bosnia-Hercegovina and Bulgaria in the 15th-17th Centuries: Old Sources—New Methodology," in *Ottoman Bosnia: A History in Peril*, ed. Markus Koller and Kemal Karpat (Madison, WI: University of Wisconsin Press, 2004), 93-120.

73. Mary Neuberger, *The Orient Within: Muslim Minorities and the Negotiation of Nationhood in Modern Bulgaria* (Ithaca, NY: Cornell University Press, 2004).

74. Mary MacIntosh, Martha MacIver, Daniel Abele and David Nolle, "Minority Rights and Majority Rule: Ethnic Tolerance in Romania and Bulgaria," *Social Forces* 73, no. 3 (October 1995): 939-68.

75. *Mediapool*, 7 October 2002.

76. Stamatov, "The Making," 563.

77. Francis Fukuyama, *The End of History* (New York: The Free Press, 1992), 168-69. Emphasis original.

78. Ramet, *Thinking*, 69. See also Cellarius, *Land of Orhpeus*; G. Creed, *Domestic Revolution: From Socialist Reform to Ambivalent Transition in a Bulgarian Village* (State College, PA: Pennsylvania State University Press, 1998); Venelin Ganev, *Preying on the State: The Transformation of Bulgaria after 1989* (Ithaca, NY: Cornell University Press, 2007); and Nadia Kaneva, "Remembering Communist Violence: The Bulgarian Gulag and the Conscience of the West," *Journal of Communication Inquiry* 31, no. 1 (March 2007): 44-61.

79. "ATAKA i iskashtite da sa malcinstvo—skacheni sudove [ATAKA and those who want minority status are interconnected]," *24 Chasa*, 21 February 2006: 3.

80. *Focus*, 8 July 2005.

81. *BNTnews*, 15 July 2005.

82. Lendvai, *Eagles*, 13.

83. Buchanan, *Performing*, 286.

84. *Mediapool*, 26 June 2005.

85. Ragaru, "Islam," 301.

86. Capoccia, *Defending*, 28.

87. Ramet, *Thinking*, 397.

88. Capoccia, *Defending*, 5.

89. Michael Mann, *The Dark Side of Democracy* (Cambridge: Cambridge University Press, 2005).

90. *NovaTV*, 14 August 2005.

91. Interestingly, however, Kiriak Stefchov is characterized by his pro-Greek, rather than pro-Turkish attitudes as the current discourses of ATAKA seem to indicate.

92. "Nacionalisti veshtaiat grajdanska voina [The nationalists portend a civil war]," *Monitor*, 24 August 2005: 4.

93. Ramet, *Thinking*, 94.

94. "Siderov, na hod si [Siderov, it's your move]," *Trud*, 23 August 2005: 1.

95. Bonnie Honig, "Difference, Dilemmas, and the Politics of Home," in *Democracy and Difference: Contesting the Boundaries of the Political*, ed. Seyla Benhabib (Princeton, NJ: Princeton University Press, 1996), 257-77.

96. For a comparative assessment of this phenomenon in the nationalistic constructions of "new Europe" see Emilian Kavalski and Magdalena Zolkos, "The Hoax of War: The Foreign Policy Discourses of Poland and Bulgaria on Iraq," *Journal of Contemporary European Studies* 15, no. 3 (December 2007): 381-97.

97. Francois Frison-Roche, "Managing the Past in Bulgaria," in *Stalinism and Nazism: History and Memory Compared*, ed. Henry Rousso (Lincoln, NE: University of Nebraska Press, 2004), 218.

98. Ole Wæver, "Explaining Europe by Decoding Discourses," in *Explaining European Integration*, ed. Anders Wivel (Copenhagen: Copenhagen University Press, 1998), 105.

99. "ATAKA," 3.

100. Evguenia Davidova, "Re-packaging Identities: History Textbook, European Travel and the Untarnished Bulgarian 'Europeanness,'" *East European Quarterly* 40, no. 4 (December 2006): 430.

101. *NovaTV*, 14 August 2005.

102. *Focus*, 11 July 2005.

103. *Focus*, 21 February 2006.

104. *Focus*, 12 February 2006.

105. *Mediapool*, 10 September 2003.

106. Georgi Parvanov, "Inaugural Speech,"<http://www.president.bg/en/news.php?id=7&st=o> (19 January 2002).

107. Luben Karavelov, "Nai-novi izvestia [Latest news]," *Svoboda*, 3 April 1871: 4.

108. Clark, *The Pen*, 102.

109. "ATAKA," 3.

110. Levy, "Who Is," 43.

111. Honig, "Difference," 270.

112. *BBT*, 21 September 2005.

113. *Focus*, 20 October 2006.

114. Marin Pundeff, "Bulgarian Nationalism," in *Nationalism in Eastern Europe*, ed. Peter Sugar and Ivo Lederer (Seattle: Washington University Press, 1994), 93-166.

115. This attitude is poignantly illustrated by the popular saying that "Bulgarian troops have never lost a battle, but Bulgaria has never won a war." According to this narrative, Bulgarian soldiers as representatives of the nation successfully fulfill their duty and win battles, while Bulgarian politicians staying behind in Sofia always manage to undo their feats, while personally profiteering from the national sacrifice. See Snezhana Dimitrova, "'My War Is Not Your War': The Bulgarian Debate on the Great War," *Rethinking History* 6, no. 1 (March 2002): 15-34. Richard Hall, "'The Enemy Is Behind Us': The Morale Crisis in the Bulgarian Army during the Summer of 1918," *War in History* 11, no. 2 (June 2004): 209-19.

116. Buchanan, *Performing*, 37.

117. *NovaTV*, 14 August 2005.

118. Quoted in Kosta Todorov, *Balkan Firebrand: The Autobiography of a Rebel, Soldier, and Statesman* (Chicago: Ziff-Davis Publishing Company, 1943), 194.

119. Todorova, "The Course:" 70.

120. Stamatov, "The Making:" 549.

121. Markov, *The Truth*, xvii. Emphasis added.

Chapter 12
The Importance of Being European: Narratives of East and West in Serbian and Croatian Nationalism

David Bruce MacDonald

"At first we were confused. The East thought we were West, while the West considered us to be East. Some of us misunderstood our place in this clash of currents, so they cried that we belong to neither side, and others that we belong exclusively to one side or the other. But I tell you . . . we are doomed by fate to be the East on the West, and the West on the East, to acknowledge only heavenly Jerusalem beyond us and here on earth—no one."

St. Sava

This chapter critically examines how many Serbian and Croatian nationalists rejected a Balkan identity in the 1980s and 1990s, as leaders like Slobodan Milosevic and Franjo Tudjman sought to create expanded national homelands. Both nations constructed narratives of "Eastern" others and "Western" selves to morally legitimate territorial expansion, and ethnic cleansing. Similarly, both presented themselves as essentially "Western," acting as bulwarks against Eastern expansion. Images of a dangerous expansionist Islamic/Turkish other framed Serbia's desire to create a "greater Serbia" which included chunks of Croatia and Bosnia-Herzegovina. In Croatia, a rejection of eastern Serbs and Muslims played a role in promoting Croatia's Western identity, while legitimating expansion into Bosnia.

In the post-conflict era, both countries seek membership in the European Union—the ultimate proof of their Westernness. Croatia stands an excellent chance of joining in the near future. Serbia will join within the next two decades, possibly sooner. Yet in continuing to promote self-serving narratives of their own histories, both countries display willful blindness about the past, and refuse to confront the crimes their nations committed in war. Ironically, while this glossing of national history is designed to make each nation more attractive to the West, the inability of many Serbs and Croats to responsibly engage with their respective pasts has done the opposite. This chapter engages first with concepts of "Balkanism," "Balkanization," and "nesting Orientalisms" before analyzing how Serbian and Croatian ideologues reinterpreted their respective national identities and histories during the successor wars of the 1990s and after.

In Western historiography, Eastern Europe, particularly the Balkans, has often been portrayed in a resoundingly negative fashion. The Balkans have traditionally been condemned as the locus of passionate violence, blood feuds, despotic kings and communist dictators, and subjugated women, welded together by primitive superstition. In many ways, the Balkans as a quintessential "other" close to home has helped Western and Central Europe define themselves against that which they are not. This chapter posits that both Serbs and Croats have assimilated this otherization of the Balkans and have incorporated the rhetoric of Westernness into their respective national identities—thus distancing themselves from the putative East.

The Geographic Ambiguity of the Balkans

Theorists of nationalism have long observed that the instrumentalization of a threatening "other" can help consolidate in-group sentiments.[1] Trevor-Roper's "normal nationalism," for example, included a sense of persecution and danger, comprising such things as "great national defeat," and "danger of being swamped by foreigners."[2] For Alter, "social groups also tend to define their national identity and national consciousness in negative terms. . . ."[3]

This chapter argues that both Serbs and Croats have employed a form of subaltern discourse which presents the past as a form of "hidden history." Subaltern discourse, as Tosh argues, tends to "demonstrate historical experience of a predetermined kind . . . to the exclusion of material that fits less neatly with the political program of the writer."[4] This promotes a selective reading of the past which omits periods of cooperation between victim and perpetrator, or other shades of grey in the relationship. As a general rule, discourse serves to "define and to enable, and also to silence and to exclude." It does so by "limiting and restricting authorities and experts to some groups, but not others, endorsing a certain common sense, but making other modes of categorizing and judging meaningless, impractical, inadequate or otherwise disqualified."[5]

For many Western Europeans, the Balkans has figured as just such an "other," in cultural, religious, and philosophical terms. As Todorova has explained in *Imagining the Balkans*, the region has often functioned a "Europe's rear door"—

that which faced the East and was in some ways corrupted by its influence.[6] Late nineteenth and early twentieth century accounts typically saw the Balkans as the locus of continual political instability and a culture of violence, which could then be contrasted with a more peaceful west.[7] The warlike and irrational nature of the Balkans could also be ascribed to the influence of the Ottoman Empire, which one early twentieth century historian rubbished as "an alien substance," "embedded in the living flesh of Europe," something akin to a parasite or fungus. He further compared Balkan peoples with those subject to European colonialism, who "resembled Asiatics rather than Europeans, if not in general appearance then certainly by their serfdom and subjugation."[8] The imagery was fundamentally negative and in such accounts the Balkans represented a threat to the West.

Later views would paternalistically describe the potentiality of the Balkans, a region desperately trying to be Western, yet clearly not a part of it. The concept of Balkan evolution became important, an Orient evolving toward Europe. It became "a bridge between stages of growth," a bridge which "invokes labels such as semi-developed, semi-colonial, semi-civilized, semi-oriental."[9] Yet as Todorova astutely notes, while the Balkans can evolve, it can also regress, depending on historical circumstances. Thus can the region be subject to "Balkanization." The term describes not only the carving up of small states by stronger external powers, but can also stand as "a synonym for reversion to the tribal, the backwards, the primitive, and the barbarian."[10] Der Derian too cites the Balkans as an ideological "other," typifying a general rejection of the universalizing ideologies of the twentieth century and an embrace of xenophobic, closed-minded territorial nationalism.[11]

Unlike Orientalism, not all Balkan people are treated in the same fashion by Western observers. Some are more Western, some more Eastern than others allowing Balkan countries to potentially rise and overcome their "easternness." As such there is always the potential for nations to market and represent themselves better as a means of rising above their geography. Some will find this process harder than others. Hayden-Bakic's discussion of "nesting Orientalisms" demonstrates how the West approaches the region as a series of civilizational gradations. Rather than seeing the region in evolution, she argues that many policy makers see Balkan peoples imprisoned in deep-seated primordial "essences," embedded in the social fabric of society and therefore unchanging. Some of these essences are *almost* Western, others hardly so.[12]

The further east you go, the more retrograde becomes the civilization. Going west, the reverse is true. Civil society seems more coherent, democratic institutions better established, religion less superstitious, the people more peaceful and rational, corruption less of a problem, etc. Ottoman society and its inheritors emerge as the worst. By the time one reaches *Mitteleuropa* with its Catholicism and Roman architecture, one has almost attained the heights of Western civilization.[13] In religious terms: Orthodox trumps Muslim; Catholic trumps both Orthodox and Muslim. From a geographic perspective: Slovenia is closest to Western Europe and therefore the most progressive, followed by Catholic Croatia, then

Orthodox Serbia, Macedonia, and Montenegro, then finally Muslim Bosnia and Kosovo. For a study of Balkanism, there seems no better case than Yugoslavia, which sat for five decades on the symbolic borders between east and west, Christianity and Islam, Western capitalism and Eastern communism.

Huntington's *The Clash of Civilizations and the Remaking of World Order* depicted Yugoslavia as an exemplar of violent conflict arising along "fault lines" between competing civilizations. Huntington divided the world into eight discreet civilizations, each possessing its own linguistic, religious, cultural, and other symbols.[14] In his hierarchy of civilizations, he puts America at the top with its "dissenting Protestantism," belief in small government, and other aspects of the "American creed."[15] Islamic civilization, by contrast is the most dangerous and warlike. "The borders of Islam are bloody, and so are its innards," he tells us.[16] Yugoslavia emerged as a "cleft country" *par excellence*, a state made up of "major groups from two or more civilizations" who felt they could no longer live together. Their disdain for members of other civilizations was natural; their membership in a common state was not.

Argued Huntington: "The force of repulsion drives them apart and they gravitate towards civilization magnets in other societies."[17] Such an organic and "scientific" portrayal of the wars in Yugoslavia lends to everything a sense of inevitability. It refutes the false optimism of those like Josip Broz Tito who believed in the Yugoslav project and thought they might defy *civilizational gravity*. That the conflict was the natural outcome of civilizations clashing was almost taken for granted by Serbs and Croats.

In otherizing eastern Yugoslav peoples, both sides pushed for what Lindstrom has termed the return to Europe. Leaving the Balkans and becoming more European was a key goal of Serbs, Croats, and Slovenians.[18] Slovenian identity creation (which I don't examine in detail) involved an active process of otherizing the former Yugoslavia. In evoking images of itself as part of "Central Europe," "the West" or "Europe," Slovenia symbolically and culturally embraced an image of itself as a typical member of *Mitteleuropa*.[19] As sociologist Dimitrij Rupel noted, the first few years of independence marked "a shift from the Balkans to (central) Europe," bringing Slovenia once more into "the company of the civilized nations."[20] Taras Kermauner, writing in the *Nova revija*, would also draw sharp distinctions between Slovenia, and the rest of Yugoslavia, infused with "the spirit of the Ottomans." If Central Europe was Slovenia's future, the Balkans represented "a dead-end street."[21]

Unlike Slovenia, Croatia (like Serbia) had little interest in adopting Western European social and political norms. While both countries paid rhetorical lip service to the ideal of being European, neither country conducted their domestic or foreign policies in typically late-twentieth-century European ways. Both regimes were characterized by authoritarian rule, suppression of independent media and opposition political parties, and ethnic intolerance. Free and frank discussion of the past or of the conduct of the successor wars, was taboo. One might thus speak of a thin veneer of Europe, wholly lacking in any real depth. In what follows, I trace how both Serbs and Croats highlighted their Western identities while sharply differentiating themselves from their Eastern neighbors.

Serbs and the Myth of the Barbarous East

Serbian nationalist narratives from the mid 1980s onwards focused on Serbia as sitting on the dividing line between East and West, a theme which predates St. Sava, the founder of the Serbian Orthodox Church. Kosovar Albanian Muslims and Bosnian Muslims were both problematized as dangerous harbingers of an Islamic conspiracy. Serbia emerged as a valiant defender of Western interests. Throughout the conflict, the Battle of Kosovo was touted as a key moniker of Serbian identity. Fought on 28 June 1389, the basic story surrounds the Serbian Prince Lazar, who in legend allowed the Serbs to be defeated by Ottoman forces in order to obtain a spiritual victory over an earthly one.[22] The details of the battle are sketchy at best, including the identity of the actual winners and losers.[23] Yet in legend, the Serbs consciously chose to lose the Battle, so as to become a holy and chosen nation. They were thereafter subjected to five centuries of Ottoman rule.

The image of a plucky western Serbia facing a hostile and dangerous east emerges prominently from early Serbian texts, as well as in later narratives. During the 1980s, Kosovo was presented as the frontline between East and West, Christianity and Islam.[24] Thus did Metropolitan Amfilohije Radovic of Montenegro warn of "an insane wind tr[ying] ceaselessly to extinguish this sacred lamp." These "insane winds" were to be understood as Catholic and Protestant countries from the west, and Islamic countries from the east. Serbia was sandwiched in the middle of two expansionist forces, both trying to encroach on its territory.[25]

Part of the resurrection of nationalism consisted of assuming control over Kosovo, which under Tito was made into an autonomous province. Deploying a classic Orientalist approach, the Muslim Kosovar Albanians, who comprised 90% of Kosovo's population, were seen as backwards, violent, and dangerous, seeking to subvert Serbia's legitimate claims on the region. Numerous Serbian publications advanced that Albanians had been killing and forcibly expelling Serbs for centuries, acting as the "strong arm of the Ottoman Empire."[26] Such publications also claimed that Albanians, due to their collaboration with the occupying Ottoman armies, were "morally disqualified" from claiming Kosovo as their own.[27] The Ottoman era was then used as a template to understand contemporary Albanian actions.

Nationalist novelist and politician Dobrica Cosic was one of the first to reinterpret Kosovar actions during the lifespan of Yugoslavia as an attempt to create "an ethnically pure Kosovo republic . . . an Albanian state in Yugoslav territory."[28] Others would describe an "open and total war," which was leading inexorably to "the physical, political and cultural genocide of the Serbian population in Kosovo and Metohije."[29] Much of this was pure fiction. Albanians, not Serbs were initially the victims of heavy handed authoritarian rule. Further, there were only five inter-ethnic murders in Kosovo between 1981 and 1987. This region had the lowest crime rate in Yugoslavia.[30] Nevertheless, Serbian propagandists relied on age old stereotypes of Muslims as backwards, violent, and obsessed with large families as a way of morally disqualifying them from exercising any sovereignty over the territory in which they were a predominant majority.

The Muslims as "Traitors"

Bosnian Muslims were targeted in a similar manner, although there were differences. While Kosovo Albanians were seen as ethnic and linguistic aliens, Bosnian Muslims were portrayed as "fallen Serbs," who had embraced Islam and were thus traitors to the Serbian nation. Serbs who converted to Islam were seen to have renounced their chosen status, embracing the religion and culture of the invader. This did not, however, diminish Serbian claims to the region, which could still on ethnic grounds be seen as part of Greater Serbia. The Serbian Ministry of Information, for example, concluded that "most of today's Bosnian Moslems are descended from Serbs," declaring Bosnian Moslems to be "Serbs of Moslem faith."[31] The Serbian government blamed Communism for the spread of an "artificial" Muslim identity. Further, since Communism was itself a major suppresser of authentic forms of nationalism, it was clear that Muslim "nationality" was simply a political tool, nothing more.[32] Serbian archaeologists employed other forms of historical evidence. The use of the Cyrillic script on tombstones, rather than the "Croatian" Glagolytic script, also proved that Bosnia's ancient inhabitants had been Serbs.[33]

Bosnian Serb General Ratko Mladic used such ideas to legitimate his army's conduct, explaining in one interview, "I have not conquered anything in this war. I only liberated that which was always Serbian, although I am far from liberating all that really is Serbian."[34] Muslims would also have the "opportunity" to abandon their constructed identity, embracing their "natural" ethnicity—that of Serbdom. In a radio broadcast, Radovan Karadzic urged Bosnian Muslims to abandon Islam, claiming hopefully that the many Muslims "who are well educated and sensible are being baptized and are becoming Christian in Europe as a way of reacting against fundamentalism and the introduction of militant Islam into Bosnia . . . we must cross the Rubicon since we are dealing with exceptional people in whom the memory of their Serbian origin is alive."[35]

The image of Muslims as "fallen Serbs" helped legitimate a mass program of ethnic cleansing. Miroljub Jevtic, an Islamic specialist at Belgrade University, expressed this view unambiguously when he argued that: "Those who accepted Islam accepted the conquerors de facto as their brothers, and the crimes of the latter are their own. That means that their own hands are also covered with the blood of their own ancestors, the former Bosnian non-Muslim population."[36] Similarly, the fear of a Muslim inspired genocide was linked to the Bosnian youth magazine, *Novi Vox,* which supposedly encouraged its readers to participate in an anti-Serbian game—to collect as many Serbian heads as possible.[37]

The Serbian role in the conflict was thus to save the West from duplicitous and dangerous Muslims. Cosic warned during the conflict of a "pan-Islamic internationalization of war in Bosnia," seeing this as "the greatest danger looming over both the Balkans and south east Europe."[38] Serbs throughout their history had defended the West from the East, had "consented, from the 14th century, to the greatest sacrifices for the defense of Europe and its civilization."[39] Karadzic similarly saw his mission as ensuring that Islamic fundamentalism did not "infect Europe from the south." Middle Eastern countries, such as Saudi Arabia, Iran, and Turkey were trying to use Bosnia as a "springboard for Islamic penetration of Europe."[40] Serbian leaders thus portrayed their people as self-sacrificing warriors, waging war in Bosnia in order to defend the West against a new Ottoman invasion.

This shameful rhetoric needs to be contextualized within a climate of extreme violence and terror. 60 % of Bosnia's inhabitants were forced from their homes, and more than 1.3 million people (some 30 % of the population) were dispersed in 63 countries. This was in addition to a death toll of 280,000 at the war's end.[41] Of course Croatia also contributed to this death toll but Serbs are responsible for the lion's share of the atrocities. Obfuscation through Balkanizing and civilizational rhetoric merely served to obscure a series of extremely bloody policies.

Croatia and Competing Westernization

Geographically, Croatia is west of Serbia. It also contains a predominately Catholic population, making its western credentials impeccable. Yet Croatia too was the enemy during the successor wars over Croatia and Bosnia-Herzegovina. How does a theory of "nesting Orientalisms" account for Serbia's strong denunciation of Croatia? Serbia's strategy here was to label Croatia a backwards colony of the West—a country which because of Catholicism and foreign domination was never able to create a fully formed nation state. Croatia therefore represented not the modern West of today, but a medieval throw-back.

The fear of "Serbophobia" (a historic fear, hatred, and jealousy of Serbs which nationalists have likened to anti-Semitism) allowed nationalists to trace a continuous legacy of Serbian hatred and violence among the Croats. The idea that Serbs were forced into the war, and that Croatia had started the violence, were popular themes—found regularly in the media and in scholarly publications. Cosic claimed in 1994: "We Serbs feel today as the Jews did in Hitler's day. . . . Today, Serbophobia in Europe is a concept and an attitude with the same ideological motivation and fury as anti-Semitism had during the Nazi era."[42] While Cosic never operationalized a working definition of "Serbophobia," its meaning was clearly implied. There were others, however, who did elaborate on the phenomenon, paralleling anti-Serbian and anti-Jewish hatred, with little difference between them.[43]

For many ideologues, a Catholic hatred and jealousy of Orthodoxy had resulted in a centuries long "continuity of genocide" against the Serbs."[44] Like anti-Semitism, Milosevic advisor Smilja Abramov saw Serbophobia stretching back a thousand years. Yet a key theme of Serbian writing was that rather than being part of the West, Croatia had been little more than a colony, doing the West's dirty work for it. Croats historically were subject to "full political dominance by foreign factors." Croats as vassals of Rome, were brought up "as its border guardians towards the East" encouraging them "to exterminate Serbs on the religious basis."[45]

This type of religious-based Serbophobia had seemingly metamorphosed by the nineteenth century, into a more organized and systematized concept of hatred. Historian Dusan Batakovic used comparisons of political and social systems in Serbian and Croatia to argue in favor of Serbian tolerance and Croatian xenophobia. He privileged Serbian concepts of nationhood, and he continually privileged "Greater Serbia"—the now famous Serbian strategy of empire building in the nineteenth century. Batakovic noted that Serbs advocated a strong unified state in the nineteenth century as a bulwark against Bulgarian, Russian, and Turkish expansion, and dreamed of uniting South Slavs into a common homeland.

Rather than condemning this process, he argued that Greater Serbia was a positive form of fraternal unity between Serbs and Croats, who were "but two branches of the same nation, which had become forcibly divided by the foreign domination."[46] Greater Serbia would promote a unitary and democratic state according to the French model.[47] Batakovic elevated the "millet tradition" of self rule under the Ottoman Empire as a great boon for Orthodox nations, as it "proved itself to be a solid base for transition to the standard European type of national integration—the nation-state model, based on the experience of the French Revolution."[48] Thus the Serbian evolution to "democracy" was based on European ideals, and was therefore consonant with enlightenment values.

By contrast, he drew a sharp distinction between desirable Serbian forms of nationalism which were seen as "authentically European," and the supposedly destructive Croatian forms, which Batakovic derided as "clerical nationalism, mixed with feudal traditions . . . colored by an excessive religious intolerance."[49] Contrary to Serbian nationalism, this religious-based nationalism was inimical to the "modern solutions," favored by the Serbs.

Through such a lens, the first Yugoslavia of 1918 failed because of Croatia, to be seen as "undeveloped, predominantly agrarian society, impregnated by various feudal traditions, religious intolerance and often a xenophobic mentality."[50] Cosic would similarly blame the Croatian "hatred for diversity," as a key reason for the Kingdom's breakdown.[51] Both men were clear that the cultural inadequacies of the Croats made the country unworkable, despite the best efforts of Serbian leaders. Furthermore, it soon became apparent that the Croats never accepted Yugoslavia as a permanent solution. Rather, union was seen as a "way-station" on the road to the creation of an "ethnically pure and independent 'greater Croatia.'"[52]

This type of Serbian discourse thus recognized that on the surface, Croats might seem more Western and therefore "superior" according to an Orientalist framework. Nevertheless, Croatia was not really part of the West—and functioned throughout history as little more than the Vatican's hired gun—a mercenary nation devoid of any real identity save their hatred for Serbs. As such the dominant national discourse surrounding Kosovar Albanians, Bosnian Muslims, and Croatians was one of cultural inferiority. Serbs thus presented themselves as being in a unique position—defending the "authentic" European west against the post-Ottoman east, while valiantly defending themselves against the worst elements of unreconstructed "clerical nationalism" as well.

Croatia's Western Origins and Future

Obviously, Croatian nationalists presented a very different account of their own history and identity. A central claim during the conflict was that Croatia (through its "state right" tradition) had enjoyed continuous autonomy/statehood for the past 1,000 years. That the 1990 Constitution described the new state as the realization of "the thousand year dream of the Croatian People" certainly attested to the centrality of this millennial myth.[53] The myth of continuous Croatian statehood stemmed from two very early Croatian institutions: the *Banus* (chief executive), and the *Sabor* (people's assembly), both of which emerged from the seventh century ruling traditions of the Croats. These institutions were ratified by a *Pacta Coventa* with Hungary in 1102, when Croats accepted the indirect rule of the Hungarian king. An elected *Ban*, or Duke, was to be the representative of the Hungarian empire.[54]

This tradition of "State Right" was coupled with the advent of Western European feudalism and the rise of an aristocratic hierarchy, both heavily influenced by the West. Numerous writers thus argued for such a continuous state, even during the Austro-Hungarian period, when Croatia was ruled directly from Vienna and Budapest. Even then, Croatian historians argued that the country had "preserved the characteristics of its constitutional statehood."[55] For some, the *Pacta*, coupled with the later guarantee of free elections from the Habsburgs in 1527 gave clear proof of the continuation of Croatian sovereignty.[56] By contrast, the "Yugoslav" period was "definitely the darkest and most humiliating," leading to the abolishment of Croatian sovereignty.[57] Croats gave up their autonomy and were dominated by Serbs, leading to a dramatic reversal of fortune.[58]

Another aspect of "state right" was the myth of the *Antemurale Christianitatis*, the belief that Croatia was the western-most rampart of Christian Europe—

the primary defender of the west against the east. While the Serbs had also used similar imagery, suggesting that Orthodoxy was the West's defence against Islam, the Croatian interpretation saw *all* former Ottoman colonies as eastern, with Orthodoxy itself as an eastern religion.[59] Croats presented themselves as a noble and benevolent nation because of their Roman Catholic faith. In legend, the Pope sent priests to baptize the Croats in the third century. After this time, Croats made a "covenant" with the Pope, and seemingly with God as well, that in return for living at peace with their neighbors, and never making wars with foreign countries, they would receive both God and "Peter the disciple of Christ's protection" against attack.[60] Yet being defenders of the West had a high price. As Boris Buden argued of the *antemurale* myth: "this title has cost us dearly. . . . Entire generations, one after another, have been sacrificed in defense of the whole European civilization. . . . At the end of the 20th century . . . Croatia is once again defending Europe from this danger from the East."[61]

For contemporary historians, the division of the Roman Empire created an unfathomable gulf between the two nations—who stood at opposite ends of the great divide between east and west. Such divisions were projected into later periods of history, in particular, the 1054 division of the Christian Church into Greek-Orthodoxy and Roman Catholicism. According to Croatian historians, this would further create a civilizational split between "two different civilizations and cultures, that is eastern and western spheres." The River Drina was often portrayed as the real dividing line between these two groups, "figuratively called the border of the two worlds."[62]

Most academics referred to such division, and Tudjman truly believed that a dividing line existed. As he claimed in one speech: "Croats are part of Western Europe, part of the Mediterranean tradition. Long before Shakespeare and Molière, our writers were translated into European languages. The Serbs belong to the east. They are eastern peoples, like the Turks and the Albanians. They belong to the Byzantine culture."[63] He later argued that geographically, Croatia had always been a part of Central Europe, and was culturally a part of this region, except for the "recent past" when "balkanism has constantly subordinated the Croatian State territory to an *Asiatic form of government*."[64] In other words, Croatia's history placed it within the western world, which Serbia was part of the eastern or "Asiatic" world. Any association between these two cultures was purely a historical anomaly.

Tudjman's 1997 presidential campaign was won on the slogan "Tudjman, not the Balkans," suggesting that Tudjman represented everything the Balkans was not. He similarly railed against any initiative which might have brought Croatia back into the "Balkan" fold. He violently rejected Croatia's involvement in the "Southeast European Cooperation Initiative," an economic exchange agreement proposed by the United States and the European Union, including Hungary, states of the former Yugoslavia and other Balkan countries.[65] Curiously, Croatian opposition parties also made use of Balkan stereotypes during the same campaign.

In 1997, Croatian Social Liberal Party presidential candidate Vlado Gotovac denounced Tudjman's own "Balkan tendencies" a shorthand for his rather corrupt and authoritarian tendencies.[66]

Croatia's reinterpretation of history also implied membership in "South-eastern Europe," which formed the basis of a wartime conference held in 1996. For the conference organizers: "being a part of the Balkans means being a part of the backward part of Europe."[67] Croatians wanted to associate with the Serbs, who were seen as nothing better than "Vandals" and "Asian hordes."[68] Like the Serbs, Croats adopted a liminal view of their national territory—the last rampart of the west in the east. Croatian geographer Zalijka Corak expanded upon the *Antemurale* myth, using a social geographer's eye to understand Croatia's history. The shape of the country, he posited, demonstrated Croatian vulnerability, "a kind of visual unrest." At the same time, it could also be interpreted as "a shape of resistance." Thus: "By standing for centuries on the military border of the western world, Croatia is now fighting for a world which can only survive if this historical space survives."[69]

Here, Corak conveyed the image of a Croatia protecting the West from a barbarous East, with the Serbs trying to invade Europe, in a manner reminiscent of Ottoman invasion. As she further described: "This is an attack by the last of the barbarians coming from their darkness to the lights of Mediterranean, to Rome. . . . Their conduct is Eastern and different in the sense of different ethics."[70] Again, the issue of Croatia standing on the border between east and west was a powerful image. It portrayed a sense of heroic struggle, as well as an image of vulnerability, both of which would prove to be positive in Croatia's bid for Western support.

Another aspect of Croatian writing was to stress the chosen or holy elements of the Croatian nation. The myth of Medjugorje was operationalized as part of the Croatian rhetorical arsenal. Describing the apparition of the Virgin Mary to a group of small children in Medjugorje, Herzegovina, in 1981, the myth could not have been better timed. Medjugorje soon became an enduring symbol of the cultural divide between East and West.[71] Tudjman was perhaps the first to instrumentalize Medjugorje, at a peace conference there in May 1993, when he invoked the miracle and heralded "the re-awakening of the Croatian nation."[72]

Mestrovic, Letica, and Goreta successfully operationalized Medjugorje in the service of the Croatian cause, seeing the Virgin's appearance as symbolizing "a growing rupture between Eastern and Western culture."[73] Medjugorje symbolized "the yearnings of Slovenia and Croatia in the west for greater pluralism and democracy versus the Serbian leanings in the East for fascist-like nationalism and monolithic political systems."[74]

The Croats were seemingly recognized from on high as part of a "mother centered culture,"[75] with a passive character orientation, a caring, nurturing identity, in contrast to the "father dominated" Serbs, who were more warlike and destructive.[76] The central aspect of the myth was the goodness of Catholicism, which rendered the Croats more civilized, more peace loving, and more enlightened. If the Serbs seemed to typify the culture of "Eastern European and former Soviet," exemplified by "machismo, totalitarianism and terror," Croatia represented "the "higher," softer, more civilized aspects of Slavic culture."[77] In other words, while Serbs were clearly Eastern Croats were not, promoting a "universalist cultural base" which was "recognizably Western."[78]

Another interesting aspect of the war was the co-option of the psychiatric profession. Several psychiatrists quickly abandoned their professionalism, along with many of the well-established rules of psychiatry, to defend their country against Serbian attack. In a special war issue of the *Croatian Medical Journal* psychiatrists assessed Serbia as a group. Edvard Klein, in his article, "Yugoslavia as a Group," isolated certain Serbian group traits, in order come to terms with the war in Croatia. Through the use of psychiatric language, he concluded:

> The Serbs are burdened with an inferiority complex compared to the peoples of the western part of Yugoslavia, for they are conscious that they are on a lower level of civilization. They try to get rid of that feeling by means of various defense mechanisms, such as negation, projections, denial and destruction. The Serbs are inclined to regress to a schizoparanoid position and exhibit an archaic type of aggression which can explain the torturing of the wounded and massacring dead bodies.[79]

While Klein's theories may well have been useful for analyzing many of the more sadistic Serbian war criminals, he proposed his analysis for all Serbs, not a select group. Psychiatrist Viktor Gruden similarly used the vocabulary of his profession. The Serbs were identified as being in a "vicious circle of frustration aggression" compounded with a "collective paranoia." The Serbian "disintegrated self" was blamed for "their tendency to massacre the Croats," over which they seemingly had no choice. Much of this aggression had to do with the Easternness, and therefore the inferiority of the Serbs.[80]

The Bosnian Muslims

Both Serbia and Croatia had historic claims to Bosnia-Herzegovina. In 1908, Serbian geographer Jovan Cvijic produced "The Annexation of Bosnia-Herzegovina and the Serb Issue," claiming this territory as the "central region and core" of an imagined expanded Serbian state. Similarly, Croatian politician Stjepan Radic published his own study, arguing that Bosnia had only flourished when Austria-Hungary has been in control. The fact that Bosnia-Herzegovina was surrounded on three sides by Croatia, and thus formed "the core of the old Croatian state," only sweetened the argument.[81] However, while some contemporary claims reflected the older musings of Cvijic and Radic, much of the discourse would be entirely new.

As with the Serbs, Croatian propagandists accused the Muslims of trying to take over the Balkans and Europe. Such imagery began in the official media by late 1992. At this stage, it focused primarily on Muslim collaboration with KOS, the Yugoslav military intelligence, and by extension, the Serbs. This soon changed to specific attacks on Islam, with regular news reports decrying the dangers of fundamentalist extremism. By early November 1992, Defense Minister Gojko Susak, in a bid for Israeli military support, tried to drum up fears of an Islamic conspiracy, alleging that there were 11,000 Bosnian Muslims studying in Cairo alone.[82]

Tudjman likewise referred often to a threat of Islamic Fundamentalism and to an Islamic holy war. He justified intervention in Bosnia by maintaining that Alija Izetbegovic's government aimed to "set up an Islamic state in Europe, which was part of a conflict between the Islamic and Catholic worlds, and of a confrontation between the Islamic world and the West."[83] For Tudjman, the Islamic threat was real. In a 1992 meeting with Ambassador Warren Zimmermann, he outlined the dimensions of the Islamic conspiracy, which included the claim that Muslims desired to set up an Islamic fundamentalist state, by "flooding Bosnia with 500,000 Turks." This process was to be coordinated with a certain degree of demographic manipulation and violence, such that "Catholics and Orthodox alike will be eradicated."[84]

Even when Croats and Muslims formed Tudjman-brokered alliances, the local press continued to condemn the Muslims, for trying to destroy their national distinctiveness with multinational federalism. For many Croatian nationalists, even the prefix "Bosnian" implied a Muslim identity rather than the former regional appellation it used to signify. When forced into an alliance with the Muslims in 1995, the Bosnian Croats had an extremely difficult time abandoning their hopes for an internationally recognized Greater Croatia.

Conclusions

In both cases, otherizing perceived enemies as eastern performed a useful role in legitimating the creation of new expanded states. Reflecting a western rhetoric of Balkanism and Balkanization made the conflict appear natural, even expected. Yugoslavia by contrast appeared to be a doomed project from the start—an artificial attempt to bring unlike peoples together. Echoing Huntington's views of an inevitable clash of civilizations, Serbs and Croats played to their own audiences but also courted Western governments with tales of an Islamic conspiracy.

At the very least, perpetrators claiming to be victims of those they were ethnically cleansing served to confuse outside observers. Former U.S. Secretary of State Lawrence Eagleburger in a July 1995 speech asserted that "They have been killing each other with a certain amount of glee in that part of the world for some time now." His successor Warren Christopher similarly viewed the conflict as the result of "ancient ethnic antagonisms," describing the situation as "problem from Hell."[85] The extent to which simplistic historical analysis influenced decision-making was further evidenced by President Clinton's reluctance to send troops to Bosnia, through the argument that "Hitler sent tens of thousands of troops to that area and was never successful in subduing it." He later remarked that "Until these folks get tired of killing each other, bad things will continue to happen."[86]

Eastern anti-Muslim rhetoric also had an effect. While during the conflict Americans and Europeans were apt to see the Bosnians as victims, in the post-9/11 environment, many in the west have forgotten that the Bosnian Muslims were victims at all, especially when links between the Muslims and al Qaeda could be proven. Gordon Bardos for example, who has written balanced reports for Human Rights Watch wrote a scathing piece on the links between al Qaeda and the Bosnian leadership which casts Izetbegovic's government as a near-extremist "regime," with Osama bin Laden as "a prominent supporter."[87]

Despite Serbian convictions for genocide at the Hague, the rhetoric of "nesting Orientalisms" continues still. Muslims of whatever stripe remain targets of hostility and misunderstanding. The Balkans will sadly remain a symbol of retrograde superstition, violent passions, even genocide. Symbolically both Serbia and Croatia seek to leave the Balkans behind them, "evolving" out of the Balkans, as its borders shift ever eastwards. It will certainly be an ironic nod to the Hayden-Bakic thesis if Croatia and Serbia enter the EU before the ever patient Turkey.

Notes

1. For a discussion of the role of negative imagery see David B. MacDonald, *Balkan Holocausts? Serbian and Croatian Propaganda and the War in Yugoslavia* (Manchester: Manchester University Press, 2002), Chapter 2.

2. Hugh Trevor-Roper, *Jewish and Other Nationalism* (London: Weidenfeld and Nicolson, 1962), 12.

3. Peter Alter, *Nationalism* (London: Edward Arnold, 1992), 7; 19.

4. John Tosh, *The Pursuit of History* Fourth Edition (Harlow: Pearson Longman, 2006), 191.

5. Jennifer Milliken, "Discourse Study: Bringing Rigour to Critical Theory," in *Constructing International Relations: The Next Generation*, ed. Karin Fierke and Knud Erik Jorgensen (London: ME Sharpe, 2001), 139.

6. Maria Todorova, *Imagining the Balkans* (Oxford: Oxford University Press, 1997), 81.

7. K. E. Fleming, "Orientalism, the Balkans and Balkan Historiography," *The American Historical Review* 105, no. 4 (October, 2000): 1226.

8. James Marriott, *The Eastern Question: An Historical Study in European Diplomacy* (Oxford: Clarendon Press, 1925), 3.

9. Todorova, *Imagining the Balkans*, 16.

10. Todorova, *Imagining the Balkans*, 3.

11. James Der Derian, *Antidiplomacy: Spies, Terror, Speed and War* (Cambridge, MA: Blackwell, 1992), 149.

12. Milica Bakic-Hayden, "Nesting Orientalisms: The Case of Former Yugoslavia," *Slavic Review* (Winter, 1995): 915-6

13. Hayden-Bakic, "Nesting Orientalisms," 918.

14. Samuel Huntington, *The Clash of Civilizations and the Remaking of World Order* (New York: Simon & Schuster, 1996), 21; 28.

15. Samuel Huntington, *Who Are We: The Challenges to America's National Identity* (New York: Simon and Schuster, 2004).

16. Huntington, *The Clash of Civilizations*, 46.

17. Huntington, *The Clash of Civilizations*, 125; 137-8.

18. Nicole Lindstrom, "Between Europe and the Balkans: Mapping Slovenia and Croatia's "Return to Europe" in the 1990s," *Dialectical Anthropology* 27 (2003): 313-14.

19. Patrick Hyder Patterson, "On the Edge of Reason: The Boundaries of Balkanism in Slovenian, Austrian and Italian Discourse," *Slavic Review* 62, no 1 (2003): 110.

20. Patterson, "On the Edge of Reason," 116-18.

21. Patterson, "On the Edge of Reason," 116-18.

22. Brian Hall, *The Impossible Country: A Journey Through the Last Days of Yugoslavia* (Boston: David R. Godine, 1994) See his chapter on Kosovo, 235-290.

23. See Robert Kaplan, *Balkan Ghosts: A Journey Through History* (New York: St. Martin's, 1993), 35-6; Marriott, *The Eastern Question*, 65; Tim Judah, *The Serbs* (New Haven, CT: Yale University Press, 1997), 31; and Noel Malcolm, *Kosovo: A Short History* (London: Macmillan, 1998), 75-9.

24. Quoted in Michael A. Sells, "Religion, History and Genocide in Bosnia-Herzegovina," in *Religion and Justice in the War Over Bosnia*, ed. G. Scott Davis (London: Routledge, 1996), 74.

25. Quoted in Nebojsa Popov, "La populisme serbe" (suite), *Les Temps Modernes*, May (1994): 35-6. *My translation.*

26. See Michel Roux, *Les Albanais en Yougoslavie: Minorité nationale, territoire et développement* (Paris: Editions de la maison des sciences de l'homme, 1992), 427.

27. Anne Yelen, *Kossovo 1389-1989, Bataille pour les droits de l'âme* (Lausanne: L'age d'homme, 1989), 52.

28. Dobrica Cosic, *L'éffondrement de la Yougoslavie: Positions d'un resistant* (Paris: L'age d'homme, 1994), 45.

29. SANU (A group of members of the Serbian Academy of Science and Arts on current questions in the Yugoslav society), "Memorandum," reprinted in *Roots of Serbian Aggression: Debates/Documents/Cartographic Reviews*, ed. Boze Covic (Zagreb: Centar za Strane Jezike/AGM, 1993), 323-4.

30. Dusko Doder and Louise Branson, *Milosevic: Portrait of a Tyrant* (New York: Free Press, 1999), 39.

31. Serbian Ministry of Information, *Facts About The Republic of Serbia* (Helsinki: Embassy of the Federal Republic of Yugoslavia, February, 1996), 24.

32. Melina Spasovski, Dragica Zivkovic, and Milomir Stepic, "The Ethnic Structure of the Population in Bosnia Hercegovina," in *The Serbian Questions in the Balkans*, ed. Dusanka Hadzi-Jovancic (Belgrade: University of Belgrade—Faculty of Geography, 1995), 264.

33. Djordje Jankovic, "The Serbs in the Balkans in the Light of Archeological Findings," in *The Serbian Questions in the Balkans*, ed. Dusanka Hadzi-Jovancic (Belgrade: University of Belgrade—Faculty of Geography, 1995), 137. The primordialness of Serbian claims were often contrasted with the constructed nature of Muslim identity. Ilic paradoxically claimed that Muslims were Serbs precisely because of their rejection of Serbian ethnicity. He argued that the Muslims possessed the "psychological and ethical handicap of converts," and that their "great aversion towards the ethnicity they come from" constituted

further proof that they were in fact Serbian. Jovan Ilic, "The Balkan Geopolitical Knot and the Serbian Question," in *The Serbian Questions in the Balkans*, ed. Dusanka Hadzi-Jovancic (Belgrade: University of Belgrade—Faculty of Geography, 1995), 16.

34. Norman Cigar, *Genocide in Bosnia* (College Station, TX: Texas A & M University Press, 1995), 81.

35. Cigar, *Genocide in Bosnia*, 59. Summarily rejecting Muslim claims to national identity, he described how Arabs viewed the Bosnian Muslims with disgust, since they were not really "Islamic." See Radovan Karadzic, "Beginnings of a Secular Battle," in *On assassine un peuple—Les Serbes de Krajina*, ed. Patrick Barriot and Eve Crépin (Lausanne: L'age d'homme, 1995), 111; 117.

36. His theories are discussed in Cigar, *Genocide in Bosnia*, 29.

37. Drago Jovanovic, Gordana Bundalo, and Milos Govedarica, eds., *The Eradication of Serbs in Bosnia and Hercegovina 1992-1993* (Belgrade: RAD, 1994), 14.

38. Cosic, *L'éffondrement de la Yougoslavie*, 76.

39. Cosic, *L'éffondrement de la Yougoslavie*, 76.

40. Quoted in: Cigar, *Genocide in Bosnia*, 99-100.

41. Jonathan Glover, *Humanity: A Moral History of the Twentieth Century* (New Haven, CT: Yale University Press, 2001), 127-9.

42. Cosic, *L'éffondrement de la Yougoslavie*, 44.

43. Smilja Avramov, *Genocide Against the Serbs* (Belgrade: Museum of Modern Art, 1992), 18.

44. Bozidar Zecevic, *The Uprooting: A Dossier of the Croatian Genocide Policy Against the Serbs* (Belgrade: Velauto International, 1992), 10.

45. Zecevic, *The Uprooting*, 10-11.

46. Dusan Batakovic, "Frustrated Nationalism in Yugoslavia: From Liberal to Communist Solution," *Serbian Studies* 11, no. 2 (1997): 67-85. <http://www.bglink.com/personal/batakovic/boston.html> (18 June, 1998).

47. Batakovic, "Frustrated Nationalism in Yugoslavia."

48. Dusan Batakovic, "The National Integration of the Serbs and Croats: A Comparative Analysis," *Dialogue* 7-8 (September-December, 1994): 5-13. <http://www.bglink.com/personal/batakovic/national.html> (18 June 1998).

49. Batakovic, "The National Integration of the Serbs and Croats."

50. Batakovic, "Frustrated Nationalism in Yugoslavia."

51. Lenard J. Cohen, *Broken Bonds: The Disintegration of Yugoslavia* (Boulder: Westview Press, 1993), 282.

52. Dusan Vilic and Bosko Todorovic, *Breaking of Yugoslavia and Armed Secession of Croatia* (Beli Manastir: Cultura Centre "Vuk Karadzic," 1996), 3-4.

53. Cohen, *Broken Bonds*, 18.

54. Vatro Myrvar, "The Croatian Statehood and Its Continuity," in *The Croatian Nation in its Struggle for Freedom and Independence*, ed. Antun F. Bonifacic and Clement S. Mihanovich (Chicago: "Croatia" Cultural Pub. Center, 1955), 47-9.

55. Ivan Crkvencic and Mladen Klemencic, *Aggression Against Croatia: Geopolitical and Demographic Facts* (Zagreb: Republic of Croatia Central Bureau of Statistics, 1993), 7.

56. Stjepan Hefer, *Croatian Struggle for Freedom and Statehood* (Argentina: Croatian Information Service/Croatian Liberation Movement, 1979), 25.

57. Myrvar, "The Croatian Statehood and Its Continuity," 53.

58. Marcus Tanner, *Croatia: A Nation Forged in War* (New Haven, CT: Yale University Press, 1997), 99.

59. Gregory Peroche, *Histoire de la Croatie et des nations slaves du Sud 395-1991* (Paris: F.-X. De Guibert, 1992), 9-11. These arguments are reiterated throughout the book.

60. Zeljko Jack Lupic, "History of Croatia: Povijest Hrvatske (200 B.C.—1998 A.D.)" (Zagreb: Croatian Information Center, 21 February 1999) <http://www.dalmatia.net/croatia/history/index.htm> (18 June, 1998).

61. Lindstrom, "Between Europe and the Balkans," 318.

62. Dragutin Pavlicevic, "Persecution and Liquidation of Croats on Croatian Territory From 1903 to 1941," in Alexander Ravlic (ed.), *Southeastern Europe 1918-1995*, ed. Alexandr Cavlic (Zagreb, Croatian Information Center, 1995).

63. Quoted in Robert M. Hayden and Milica Bakic-Hayden, "Orientalist Variations on the Theme Balkan: Symbolic Geography in Recent Yugoslav Politics," *Slavic Review*, Spring (1992): 9.

64. Hayden and Bakic-Hayden, "Orientalist Variations on the Theme Balkan," 2-4. *Italics theirs.*

65. Nicole Lindstrom and Maple Razsa, "Reimagining the Balkans: The Role of Balkanism in the Construction of Croatian National Identity," The 1st Annual Kokkalis Graduate Student Workshop: New Approaches to Southeast Europe (12 February 1999).

66. Lindstrom and Razsa, "Reimagining the Balkans."

67. A. Hauswitschka, "Croatia Cannot Be a Part of the Balkans," *Vjesnik* (24 May 1996) <http://www.cds,neu.edu/info/students/marko/vjesnik/vjesnik7.html> (18 June 1998).

68. Ivo Skrabelo, "They Shoot Monuments Don't They?," in *Documenta Croatica*, ed. Zvonimir Separovic (Zagreb: VIGRAM-Zagreb i VIDEM Krsko, 1992), 100-1.

69. See Zaljka Corak, "Croatian Monuments: Wounds Suffered from Other People's Illnesses," in *Documenta Croatica*, ed. Zvonimir Separovic (Zagreb: VIGRAM-Zagreb i VIDEM Krsko, 1992), 97.

70. Corak, "Croatian Monuments," 101.

71. Stjepan Mestrovic, Miroslav Goreta, and Slaven Letica, *The Road from Paradise: Prospects for Democracy in Eastern Europe* (Kentucky: The University Press of Kentucky, 1993), 131.

72. Ed Vulliamy, *Seasons in Hell: Understanding Bosnia's War* (London: St. Martin's Press, 1994), 60-1.

73. Mestrovic, Goreta, and Letica, *The Road from Paradise*, xiii.

74. Mestrovic, Goreta, and Letica, *The Road from Paradise*, 108.

75. Mestrovic, Goreta, and Letica, *The Road from Paradise*, 111.

76. Mestrovic, Goreta, and Letica, *The Road from Paradise*, 66-67.

77. Mestrovic, Goreta, and Letica, *The Road from Paradise*, 115-6.

78. Mestrovic, Goreta, and Letica, *The Road from Paradise*, 30.

79. Edvard Klein, "Yugoslavia as a Group," *Croatian Medical Journal*, War Supplement 2:21 (1991): 12.

80. Klein, "Yugoslavia as a Group," 9.

81. Dusan Bilandzic, "Termination and Aftermath of the War in Croatia," in *The War in Croatia and Bosnia-Herzegovina, 1991-1995*, ed. Branka Magas and Ivo Zanic (London: Frank Cass, 2001), 85-6.

82. Cigar, *Genocide in Bosnia*, 124.

83. Cigar, *Genocide in Bosnia*, 124.

84. Warren Zimmermann, *Origins of a Catastrophe: Yugoslavia and Its Destroyers—America's Last Ambassador Tells What Happened and Why* (New York: Croan, 1996), 181-2.

85. Sells, *The Bridge Betrayed*, 125.

86. Sells, *The Bridge Betrayed*, 127-8.

87. Gordon N. Bardos, "Balkan Blowback? Osama bin Laden and Southeastern Europe," *Mediterranean Quarterly* 13, no. 1 (2002): 48-9.

Chapter 13
Nationalism in Contemporary Europe: Multiplicity and West-East Similarity

Ireneusz Paweł Karolewski
and Andrzej Marcin Suszycki

This volume has explored new aspects of nationalism in three domains. *First*, at the conceptual level nationalism is referred to as (state) ideology, social movement, and individual attitude. The contributions to the volume reflect these macro-, meso-, and micro-levels of nationalism, which brings us closer to the multidimensionality of contemporary nationalism. Many studies of nationalism are either historicist or reductionist regarding the concept of nationalism. On the one hand, many authors use nationalism in a historic meaning highlighting its longevity, which suggests that today we are facing the same sort of nationalism as in the nineteenth century (as in the ethno-symbolism by Anthony D. Smith). On the other hand, others reduce the notion of nationalism mainly to general motives of elites and individuals, reducing it to an epiphenomenon of rationality (as in the rational choice inspired concepts of ethnic nationalism by Michael Hechter or David Latin).[1]

Second, the multidimensionality of nationalism suggests also its multiplicity, according to which nationalism occurs simultaneously not only in all dimensions as (state) ideology, social movements, and individual sentiments or attitudes, but also assumes numerous forms at the substantial level. The volume offered new foci for the research on contemporary nationalism, in particular in Europe. This refocusing of nationalism research includes trends in the nationalism of the EU, violence-oriented nation-building and regionalism. This suggests that old typologies of nationalism might be obsolete and that the multiplicity of nationalism is associated with a growing complexity of nationalism going far beyond the often simplistic conceptualizations of the past. The simultaneous occurrence of nationalism at several levels and in a new variety of forms entails a functional differentiation of contemporary nationalism, reflecting its multiplicity. Against this background, nationalism can be conceived of as a supra-state integrative endeavor by political elites, as in the case of the EU. However, in other cases it can breed destruction and self-destruction as a response to the globalization or it can generate collective impulses of boundary-creation as a reaction to, for instance, Europeanization. In addition, nationalism can have a fragmenting effect, as some forms of regionalism in Europe suggest. In sum, contemporary nationalism should be explored more deeply against the background of globalization, Europeanization, and new ideologies such as the political Islamism.

Third, the volume juxtaposes empirical studies on nationalism in Western and Eastern Europe. By so doing, it attempts to overcome the traditional dichotomy of Eastern and Western nationalism still present in many studies, and to address the question of dynamics of nationalism. The empirical studies of the volume deal with the issue of the revival and rebirth of nationalism in contemporary Europe. The volume explores cases of the nationalist revival in Western Europe, asking whether we deal here with old and pacified nationalism, only revived as a result of the crisis of the welfare state or stimulated by globalization. The chapters on the rebirth of nationalism in Eastern Europe address at the general level the controversy over whether we are confronted in Eastern Europe with new nationalism associated with nation-building. In this view, the supposedly natural development of nationalism from violence and destruction toward more civilized and pacified modern nationalism, active only as an anomaly in times of crises, has stuck in Eastern Europe as a consequence of state socialism as an intervening factor. This dichotomy of anomaly nationalism and catch-up nationalism is questioned in the volume. It suggests that we should assume an empirical similarity of nationalism, rather than an Eastern-Western dichotomy of nationalism based on a telos of nationalism. In this sense, nationalism in contemporary Europe is evenly dispersed in Western and Eastern Europe, rather than geographically concentrated. For instance, chapters on Belgium and Bulgaria show similarities in nationalism in both countries regarding its historic mythologizing of the nation or anti-European character. Also, the Latvian case exhibits increasingly civic features even though it has been treated for a long time as the classic case of Eastern nationalism. Therefore, we speak of a West-East similarity of nationalism, rather than geographical types of nationalism, derived from a faulty understanding of nationalist dynamics. This concluding chapter recapitulates the theoretical and empirical results of the volume.

Nationalism in Contemporary Europe: Meaning and Focus

While nationalism is not exclusively a European phenomenon, this volume has focused on nationalism in contemporary Europe. The main reason for this is that Europe, as a result of its societal, cultural, and political heterogeneity, is a virtual laboratory of nationalism, which allows for exploration of the diversity of nationalism, its revival, and its new types. In Europe we are confronted with integration changing the character of the nation-states and spawning supranational statehood as well as new collective identities. However, these post-modern and post-national processes are accompanied by state-building and nation-building processes (recently in the Balkans), typical for modernity. In addition, we can observe a revival or an emergence of regionalist tendencies in Europe, depending on whether we regard them as new or old phenomena. All three of these features of contemporary Europe (supranationalism, nation-building, and regionalism) not only add up to a multiplicity of nationalism in Europe, but also relate to three meanings of nationalism we have applied in this volume. *Firstly*, we employ the term "European nationalism" with regard to the collective identity and identity technologies of the European Union. In this perspective, we refer to nationalism of the European Union attempting to weaken national identities of the member states and to generate a supranational nationalism, a term which is only apparently contradictory. This type of nationalism is normatively associated with the EU with benevolent effects, which are expected from integrative community-building beyond the nation-state, while circumventing aggressive forms of the EU member states' nationalism. The *second* meaning of nationalism applies to the traditional nationalism of European nations, frequently based on boundary-making and discrimination of non-members. This nationalism is an antithetical form of supranational integrative nationalism, as it constructs and highlights differences rather than the cross-border commonalities, while spurring negative sentiments toward others. Even though supranationalism also includes boundaries, it claims openness, plurality, and tolerance of diversity. In contrast, the perspective of traditional nationalism stresses the malevolent or dark side of nationalism associated with violence and ethnic cleansing. Both the benevolent integrative and the malevolent sides show the ambivalence of nationalism, characteristic also of other central political concepts such as state, citizenship, and civil society. *Thirdly*, we use the term nationalism with regard to newer forms of regional nationalism that have developed frequently (but not entirely) under the auspices of the EU. The regional nationalism is linked both to the European nationalism of the EU and the more traditional forms of nation-state nationalism: Regional nationalism can be a reaction to the centralist nation-state nationalism, but it is also supported by the EU as an instrument to weaken nationalism among the member-states. In terms of temporality, regional nationalism can be regarded as being entrenched both in the modern reality of state and nation-building with their fragmenting tendencies and in the post-modern reality of multiplicity of identities and political authorities.

The multiplicity of nationalism (supranationalism, nation-building, regionalism) and its functional differentiation (integration, destruction, fragmentation) suggests a new research desideratum for the future to explore the links between the types of nationalism, rather than to seek a unified theory of nationalism as Anthony Smith or Ernest Gellner attempted.

In the remainder of the chapter we will summarize the results of the volume in four steps, corresponding to sections of the volume. First, we recapitulate the chapters questioning the conceptions of nationalism. Against this background, we summarize the findings of the contributors focusing on three theoretical perspectives of the volume. We conclude by reviewing the contributions focusing on the issue of the old nationalism in Western Europe.

Questioning the Conceptions of Nationalism

One of the main contributions of the volume is its critique of both old and new conceptions of nationalism. Here, we focused on the dichotomy of Eastern and Western nationalism as well as the recently popular notion of liberal nationalism. Chapters dealing with both conceptions show limitations of older and newer nationalism approaches to nationalism and suggest a refocusing of nationalism research.

Despite continuous critique, the dichotomy between civic and ethnic nationalism appears to be strongly anchored in contemporary nationalism discourse. Even though there are increasing numbers of attempts to circumvent the simplistic typology developed by Hans Kohn, the civic-ethnic divide in current debates on nationalism still seems to be firmly anchored. One of the recent examples is the typology proposed by Liah Greenfeld, who expands Kohn's model without surrendering its Manichean differentiation. Kohn defined Eastern nationalism as backward, prone to conflict, tribal, and tied to religion, whereas Western nationalism was associated with political rights, individuality, and rationality, rather than with ethno-cultural factors. Greenfeld proposes a typology including individualistic-civic nationalism, collectivistic-civic nationalism and collectivistic-ethnic nationalism. However, this typology of nationalism merely differentiates further the category of Western nationalism, splitting it into collectivistic-civic and individualistic-civic nationalism, which remains strongly rooted in Kohn's model.[2]

In this volume, the contribution by Taras Kuzio attempted to overcome the static character of Kohn's model. The chapter presented a dynamic concept of the convergence between the Western and Eastern nationalism based on the process of societal change, which was evolutionary in the case of the West and revolutionary in the East, mainly as a result of the breakdown of communism. Kuzio criticizes Kohn's model for implying that Eastern European nationalism tends to create authoritarian and culturally repressive states, while in the West liberal and democratic states are likely to flourish. However, the author does not only relate to the implications of different nationalisms for their (in)ability to achieve democracy, but also argues that nationalism in the West and East has probably never been vastly divergent. Therefore, his argument is comparative and empirical in nature, going beyond Rogers Brubaker's critique highlighting the theoretical and normative implications of the Manichean myth of nationalism.[3] The transition to democracy in Eastern European countries as well as their integration into the EU point to a convergence of Western and Eastern nationalism, suggesting that the gulf between the nationalisms was based on a difference of degree, rather than on a difference of type. In this vein, Kuzio argues that the ability of the Eastern European countries to, among other things, fulfill the liberal and democratic requirements of EU membership within only one decade would confirm that nationalism in the East was not fundamentally different from its Western counterpart. In addition, according to Kuzio the static model of nationalism ignores the evolution of the civic nationalism of the European and North American states from the late eighteenth century, as the transformation of these states into civic nations occurred only in the second half of the twentieth century. Therefore, both Western and Eastern nationalisms transformed into civic variants during the same century separated by only a few decades, whereas the major difference between West and East was the period of occurrence of consolidated democracy.

Against this background, the chapter suggests an alternative, dynamic theory of nationalism, arguing that all types of nation-states became in general more inclusive and civic in the twentieth century. In order to prove his point, Kuzio applies three categories of analysis including citizenship, gender, and immigration. Regarding citizenship rights, in the inter-war years Eastern European states granted voting rights to larger parts of the society around the same time as Western Europe and North America. While social rights expanded during the "1960s revolution" in the West, these components of citizenship were broadened also under communism in the East, even though political rights were not guaranteed to the same degree as in the West. However, by focusing on the dynamics of citizenship the major difference in the West and East has been the time factor. Kuzio argues that voting rights were expanded to cover increasingly larger parts of the society in the West over the course of two hundred years, lasting from the late eighteenth to the second half of the twentieth centuries. In Canada and Australia the process was only completed in the 1960s, when indigenous minorities became subject to universal suffrage. In the case of Germany, citizenship policies became more inclusive (and for that matter more civic) only in the late 1990s, when the strongly ethnic and restrictive *ius sangunis* excluding non-German denizens from full citizenship was liberalized. In Eastern Europe the granting of citizenship and the vote took place immediately after the collapse of the communist regimes within a short time frame in the 1990s.

Apart from citizenship, Kuzio uses the specific category of gender to define the civicness of nationalism. He argues that nation-states cannot be defined as civic if women are denied the vote, as they were until the First World War in Europe and North America. In this sense, gender-specific voting rights violate the principle of the inclusiveness of civic nationalism. In both West and East, gender rights were introduced at the same time following World War I. For instance, France—defined by many authors as the best example of civic nationalism—granted women voting rights later than many Eastern European states. Western nationalism does not have a better historical record on gender rights than the East, while female representation in North American and Western European parliaments is no higher than in the Eastern European assemblies. As the third category of his analysis, Kuzio uses immigration policy to show that similar tensions between civic and cultural aspects of nationalism occur both in East and West. In Western Europe, immigration issues have recently been high on the political agenda, inducing the parties of the center-right to incorporate policies espoused hitherto mainly by the radical right. Therefore, the civic nationalism of the West has put a stronger emphasis on ethnic identity politics, as the centre-right and the radical nationalist right came to present themselves as guardians of the majority culture against immigration and multicultural policies. In this sense, we are facing in the West growing pressure toward assimilation policies and more restrictive migration policies. In the process, the evolution of Western nationalism assumes stronger ethnic characteristics, blurring the ethnic-civic-distinction and leading to a convergence between Western and Eastern nationalism.

Whereas Taras Kuzio questions the usefulness of the classical but still popular dichotomy of nationalism, Enric Martínez-Herrera examines the more recent concept of liberal nationalism that has dominated the nationalism discourse in the political theory. "Liberal-nationalists" such as Yael Tamir and David Miller argue in the tradition of benevolence and usefulness of nationalism.[4] Two virtues often associated with "good nationalism" are citizens' political confidence and support for the welfare state, which are expected to generate the perception of national common good and national solidarity. The liberal nationalist position argues that the values of a national community are necessary for the good performance of liberal democracy as well as for the survival and legitimacy of the welfare systems. Since lack of confidence in political authorities is supposed to reduce citizens' consent and compliance toward public decisions, it diminishes democratic institutions' performance and is related to the weakening of social trust. Therefore, liberal nationalists have turned attention to nationalism as a possible remedy for the crisis of social trust and the confidence decline in political authorities. Nationalism is expected to make citizens contribute more willingly to the provision of redistributive policies aimed at helping other citizens, as it generates reciprocity and social trust. Since in the context of mass societies trust and reciprocity are unlikely to be based on interpersonal relations between the individuals, nationalism is believed to provide the ties within an imagined community. Instead of the individual definition of common good, a nation comes to be perceived by the citizens as an entity with its own autonomous existence transcending individual interest calculations. In the process, individuals become able to develop a sense of national interest, whereby the redistributive policies are seen in tune with the well-being of the national community. Therefore, nationalism produces national identification, which leads to a feeling of mutual responsibility and mutual concern as well as a sense of bonding among citizens.

Against this theoretical background, Martínez-Herrera evaluates empirically the claims of liberal nationalism that nationalism has a benevolent side and generates community resources of social trust and confidence. His chapter advances an empirical validation, which is based on a multivariate research analysis of data on political and social attitudes in Great Britain. Since David Miller, as one of the main proponents of liberal nationalism, relates his arguments mainly to the British political and cultural context, Martínez-Herrera uses data from England and Scotland for his empirical examination. The results show that liberal forms of support for Britain do not have any effect on either political confidence or support for the welfare state in that country. Instead, it is British illiberal nationalism that has a positive effect on political confidence in Scotland—but no effect in England—and it has a negative effect on support for the welfare state in England, but none in Scotland. Citizens showing a greater reluctance toward any influence of other countries on British politics as well as holding an uncritical British pride, and citizens showing the stronger British identification and stronger wish to keep Great Britain united, tend to be the least supportive of the welfare state. Therefore, the theory does not have any explanatory value in Britain at large, and holds only partially in Scotland. As the British political community is frequently portrayed as an example of real civic nationalism, it is expected to espouse liberal nationalist virtues rather than non-civic nationalisms. As a result, the chapter by Martínez-Herrera shows that, even in such a case, the liberal-nationalist arguments proclaiming the virtues of nationalism and national identification remain claims without much adequate evidence.

Against this background, a new conceptual elaboration of nationalism seems necessary. Neither older nor newer concepts reflect the multiple character of nationalism, which should open the nationalism research to new debates on contemporary nationalism.

Three Perspectives on Nationalism in Europe

Beyond questioning the classical and contemporary conceptions of nationalism, the volume offered three perspectives on nationalism in Europe which attempt to transcend the conceptual debates at hand. These are European nationalism, the boundary-making perspective, and regional minority nationalism. They reflect the multiplicity of contemporary nationalism.

The *first perspective on nationalism* is presented in the chapter by Ireneusz Paweł Karolewski focusing on the issue of collective identity in the EU as a marker of European nationalism. The author argues that the strategy of European nationalism espoused by the EU intends to construct collective identity in a way that emulates the integrative logic of national identity. It attempts to generate a nation-like sense of belonging in a non-nation-state environment, since the EU does not fulfill any definition of a nation-state. The chapter departs from the theoretical skepticism of nationalism theories, questioning the ability of the EU to reproduce national identity at a higher level. The EU applies identity technologies toward its citizens in an attempt to solve this dilemma. As the political elites of the EU appear to be aware of the stabilizing effects of collective identity, they undertake attempts to generate it, albeit in a more restrained manner than traditional forms of nationalism would offer. This "nationalism light" of the EU uses either selected identity technologies of nationalism or uses them at a more subtle level, as the EU cannot exactly emulate nationalism regarding its strength, sacrificial appeal, and aggressiveness.[5] Karolewski's chapter focuses in particular on two identity technologies applied by the EU—the manipulation of symbols and the construction of positive self-images. One of the ways in which the EU manipulates cultural symbols is the introduction of the common currency. This construction of a tangible symbol of the Euro increases the everyday visibility of Europeanness without homogenizing European cultural diversity, as the Euro allows for different iconographic connotations. At the same time, a common currency establishes a perception of commonality and therefore promotes collective identity. The identity technology of the common currency is in tune with the European multiplicity of national identities, since it is open to national interpretations of their own subjective vision of the European "community." In this sense, European "nationalism light" tends toward abstraction, which is also visible with regard to other European collective symbols such as the flag and the anthem.[6]

A further technology of collective identity in the EU is a production and diffusion of positive self-images. One of various types of positive imaginary tools used to describe the EU substantive identity is cosmopolitan Europe. It highlights positively the historical and institutional peculiarities of Europe. An additional positive image of the EU pertains to the notion of the EU as a civilian power, which the EU uses to distinguish itself from other global powers, such as the United States. As the notion of civilian power refers to the methods of international politics rather than the substance, the EU is expected to pursue post-national or ethical interests by using methods of normative change rather than use of force. Therefore, even in a conflict environment, the EU member states are believed to remain attached to deliberation and cooperation. A further self-image of the EU relates to the idea of normative power, which is closely associated with the cosmopolitan and civilizing image. In this context, the EU stresses its progressive policies of promoting and implementing global human rights and environmental policies. In the process, it asserts its leading role and defines the U.S. as a laggard, thus claiming its own moral supremacy. Against the background of the EU, identity technologies of "nationalism light" relate to soft methods of identity generation. This European nationalism, precisely because it has no certain roots, is associated with a necessity of the EU elites to engage in propaganda actions and strategic socialization with the aim of changing the attitudes of European citizens. However, this social engineering *qua* manipulation of symbols and generation of positive self-images raises questions concerning the EU's legitimacy. As the state nationalism developed in Europe largely under non-democratic circumstances of elite-driven mobilization, it could imply that any European nationalism would shift the focus within European citizenship more strongly from active citizen toward compliant subject, which would be counterproductive regarding the democratic deficit of the EU and further exacerbate the EU's legitimacy problems.

Karolewski shows that the EU is at pains to create nationalism with an integrative outcome. Despite possible negative implications for the EU democratic deficit and manipulative nature of the EU identity politics, the perspective on European "nationalism light" suggests mainly integrative workings of identity technologies, which relate to nationalism as a supra-state ideology at the macro-level. In contrast, Daniele Conversi argues in his chapter that nationalism represents one of the most powerful processes of boundary-building. This represents the *second perspective on nationalism* offered by the volume. This perspective emphasizes that attempts at defining, inventing, or reviving a nation always imply a process of inclusion-exclusion, and for that matter the construction of boundaries between in-groups and out-groups. In this vein, Conversi's chapter explores theoretically and comparatively the links between violence, nationalism, and boundary-making. In the process, the chapter investigates how the Western legacy of destruction and self-destruction intersected with a continuous stress on boundaries and the creation of homogeneous identities as defined by these boundaries. Conversi uses the anthropological and sociological discourses to argue that boundaries exist not only to enclose and delimit, but also to highlight who "the other" is. In this sense, the in-group is defined primarily by constant comparison with the "other."

According to Conversi, this focus on boundaries can be applied to all forms of nationalism. Nationalism remains central to processes of boundary-building aimed at inclusion/exclusion, although the nationalist discourse may relate to the issues of national security, which imply boundary-maintenance rather than boundary-construction. In addition, the chapter argues that ties of ethnic kinship across state boundaries suggest that ethnic boundaries are often more important and durable than state boundaries. Ethnicity becomes reinforced by neo-liberal globalization which interacts with the persistence of ethnic ties, rather than solely with the process of individualization. At the theoretical level, Conversi argues that the role of the boundary should be analyzed in relation to its content. Content would point to the substance enclosed in a boundary representing the tangible and objective repertoire, while the boundary itself would include the subjective perception of ethnicity, separating in-group from out-group. Content provides human skills, which enrich the cultural experience of ethnic belonging. While boundary relates to psychology as an invisible resource, content relates to culture as the visible aspect of boundaries. Against this background, Conversi investigates the relationship between boundaries, content, and political violence. He relates the term "ethnic boundary" to the study of ethnogenesis and nationalism, in particular in the context of ethnic violence, while violence is related to cultural assimilation, or lack of cultural contents. Here, the case of the former Yugoslavia is used as an illustration for the use of violence as a tool of boundary-building. In conclusion, Conversi presents a thesis emphasizing that a stress on boundaries, rather than content, is to be viewed as an indicator of deep feelings of threat and instability leading to violence.

As a result, the chapter argues that the study of nationalism should focus on how elites strive to defend, strengthen, or even construct the sense of distinctiveness. Therefore, the homogenizing workings of modernity are related to the spread of war and ethnic cleansing, thus highlighting the destructive workings of nationalism. In the process, the hitherto permeable boundaries were transformed into insurmountable barriers. Globalization has generated an unprecedented destruction of traditional boundaries accompanied by the simultaneous rise of particularistic ideologies, among other things nationalism, whereas destruction and division have not been accompanied by "deep pluralism" with respect for cultural diversity. As globalization has become an ideology which, like past totalitarian forms of nation-building, has stressed the need to unify, particularistic ideologies such as nationalism became strengthened, rather than weakened. As a consequence, boundaries and boundary theories are also relevant to current trends and patterns of European integration. Conversi stresses that the relationship of European integration should be analyzed in a relation to more traditional forms of nationalism, together with the widespread sense of threat caused by globalization.

With its emphasis on boundary-making and destruction, the uncertainty generated by globalization and trends of ethnic violence, the chapter reflects a specific angle of contemporary nationalism research represented for instance by work of Michael Mann and Mary Kaldor. Michael Mann argues, for example, that mass-scale killings on the basis of ethnic belonging are an offspring of modernity and occur during democratization processes, where particular ethnic groups advance conflicting state-building projects relating to the same territory.[7] As the state-building assumes a form of ethnic boundary-making, the project of democratization is carried out as ethnic homogenization, blurring the meaning between demos and ethnos. This confusion of ethnos and demos creates circumstances under which mass-scale ethnic violence becomes possible, whereby democratization fosters these processes by strengthening powerful social movements. In this perspective, highlighting the destructive potential of nationalism, genocide cannot be regarded as a feature of authoritarian and totalitarian systems, as it is more likely to occur under the conditions of imperfect democratization and liberalization.[8] The chapter by Conversi also argues in a similar vein as Mary Kaldor, who suggests that it is precisely globalization which has triggered the current wave of national sentiment, believed by many to be a phenomenon of the past. She elucidates it through the prism of global changes in the division of labor and in communication processes. Since digital communication is currently becoming more important than print, it perforates the traditional form of nationalism, unleashing new forms of violence supported by new militant nationalist and religious ideologies. Whereas wars between states become rather an anachronism, the traditional nationalism gives way to new horizontal boundary-making ideologies with an exclusive and fundamentalist character, including sub-state and trans-border nationalism.[9]

The *third perspective on nationalism* presented in the volume focuses on the rise of regionalism and regionalist ideologies, in particular the regional minority nationalism. The chapter by Anna Olsson discusses various theories about the emergence and maintenance of sub-state regionalism and regional minority nationalism in Europe. The chapter starts out from a debate on the concept of the region showing its complexity and variety and moves on to exploring the basic distinction between old and new sub-state regionalism. Whereas old regionalisms are often described as traditionalist and cultivating separatism, new regionalisms are believed to seek other ways to increase their autonomy than solely through secession. This dichotomy of sub-state regionalisms divides their features between exclusion and inclusion, national focus and European focus, backward-looking and future-oriented.

Drawing on the research by Michael Keating, Olsson discusses the distinction between ethnic and civic minority nationalism.[10] The comparison of ethnic and civic minority nationalism leads to a conclusion about the predominance of civic minority nationalism, bringing about the term "new minority nationalisms" (also called regional minority nationalisms) which accept the dispersion of power and the decreasing relevance of state sovereignty rendering regional minority nationalism post-national and inclusive.

Furthermore, Olsson explains the emergence of sub-state regionalism in the light of diverse theories, one of which is the competition theory. Inspired by the social movement theory, it emphasizes the importance of a power struggle for limited resources. This rationalist and instrumentalist approach rejects ethnicity as an inherent source of conflict and argues instead that ethnicity is merely one possible instrument utilized by competing groups to define their allies and enemies. In this context, the rise of minority nationalism in post-industrial states is caused by the greater economic security enabling people to satisfy "higher order needs" such as identity, whereby class conflict and ideology are left behind. This makes minority nationalism a phenomenon pertaining to affluent societies while having little relevance for economically under-developed regions. This view contrasts the boundary-making and violence-prone perspective of nationalism represented by Daniele Conversi by focusing on rationality, inclusiveness, and cooperation.

A specific variant of regional minority nationalism is applied to the EU. For instance, the bypass theory of regionalism posits that regions increasingly seek to sidestep their central governments to achieve their policy goals at the EU level by forging direct links with the EU. Olsson shows that numerous scholars apply the bypass theory to explain the paradox phenomenon of traditionally protectionist minority nationalist regions becoming among the strongest supporters of European integration. Some of them elucidate this transformation in the context of the transformation from old to new regionalism. An alternative approach explains sub-state regional mobilization in terms of social movements. It is based on the work of Charles Tilly and Sidney Tarrow, who argued that social movements emerged in response to the modern state. This theory is reflected in the argument that the European Union provides the regions with a new political opportunity structure which they were not given in the context of the nation-state. However, more recent social movement theory argues that political opportunities provided by the EU are just the beginning of a "social movement cycle," which would need an underpinning in terms of the framing of issues and identities. The issue of identity leads to the debate whether there is a parallel between regional identity and national identity, as they both often rest on "imagined communities." In this sense, regional identity would resemble national identity as, rather than reflecting experience, it requires citizens to relate to an abstract idea of a community, whose members remain personally unknown to each other. Nonetheless, regional identity remains an alternative to national identity, in particular in the context of the EU, which facilitates the construction of alternative identities. This occurs in the process of weakening the established states and by generating opportunities for regional leaders to establish their regions as political projects in the European framework. This perspective mirrors the meso-level of nationalism relating to social movements situated between the micro-level of individuals and the macro-level of nationalist state ideology.

Revival or Rebirth of Nationalism?

Against the background of the three perspectives on nationalism, two empirical sections analyze cases of nationalism in Europe. In these case studies, issues of European integration, national-boundary-making and regional nationalism are reflected. The first empirical section focuses on cases of nationalism in Western Europe including Belgium, Germany, and Italy. It oscillates around the issue of "old" nationalism, and explores the modernizing Flemish nationalism and ethnic connotations of national pride in Germany. The revival thesis suggests that nationalism in Western Europe is just an anomaly stemming mainly from the crisis of the welfare-state. Nonetheless, the civilized and civic nationalism of the West remains dominant and ethnic eruptions are only marginal, since nationalism in the West is an advanced and not backward-looking nationalism. This, however, cannot be supported by the case studies of the volume.

In her chapter, Janet Laible examines Flemish nationalism in the context of the European Union. With the example of the Flemish party of the radical right, Vlaams Belang, she explores two conflicting logics about sovereignty and political space, embodied in the practices of the European Union and the political discourse of Vlaams Belang. She argues that the core of the political agenda of Vlaams Belang is the aspiration to regain space and sovereignty for a Flemish nation-state. In this sense, Vlaams Belang utilizes the modernizing ideals of traditional nationalists, which exhibits a conflict with the post-modern project of the European Union. Laible examines the conflict between a "modernizing" agenda of Vlaams Belang and the post-modern EU by focusing on issues of political territory, in particular on the party's understandings of EU citizenship and the freedom of movement as a fundamental freedom of the EU. The chapter argues that even if the party's right-wing ideology reflects the party's commitment to modernity, the major points of contention between the party political program and European integration do not lie in the political demands linked traditionally to the extreme right, such as immigration and crime, but more in the deeper commitment of the party to modernist understandings of territorial authority, which contradicts the cross-border and transnational character of the EU. Against this background, Vlaams Belang is in many respects an anomaly among contemporary European nationalist movements, as other nationalist parties such as the Catalan, Irish, and moderate Flemish nationalists have accommodated the project of European integration, transforming their independence-seeking ideologies toward pursuit of cultural, economic, and political goals in the regional context. In contrast, Vlaams Belang maintains a vision of a minimal European Union, in which nation-states based on ethnic identities are the dominant political actors and in which the transnational and supranational challenges to state sovereignty are limited or even nonexistent. Therefore, the party rhetoric emphasizes territorial sovereignty for the ethnic Flemish community, thus attempting to revive the modernist project of the nation-state. However, there is a contradiction between the party's rhetoric and the party's strategy, which in turn admits to the value of a collective European approach to defending Flemish values and interests. This internal contradiction situates the Vlaams Belang neither fully in the "past" of nationalism nor in the pro-integrationist "present" of many other Western European nationalisms, making it an anomaly both in the light of the classical theories of nationalism and the recent regional minority nationalism discussed in the chapter by Anna Olsson.

Hilary Bergsieker examines a further specific case in the nationalism research. German nationalism is of particular interest because of its distinctive historical and social context associated with extremity and prevalence. For many scholars, Germany occupies a unique position in twentieth-century history as a result of unleashing two world wars and of carrying out massive genocides, which makes the nature of German nationalism not only highly controversial but also singular. While a collective effort to disavow nationalism and adopt a critical perspective on German national identity became part of the German political discourse, German political philosophy pioneered the project of constitutional patriotism, aimed at engineering civic nationalism abstracting from an ethnically-biased concept of the German nation. At the same time, the legal traits of German citizenship remained largely ethnic until the late 1990s, as is argued by Taras Kuzio in his chapter, even though according to cross-national studies in the latter part of the twentieth century Germans have reported less national pride than citizens of other countries. Bergsieker's chapter adopts an etic-emic approach in order to examine national pride and nationalism in Germany, reflecting the notion of nationalism as a micro-phenomenon of individual attitudes. She synthesizes etic (global) theory from political and social psychology with the emic (particular), contextual elements emphasized in cultural psychology. Rather than presuming cross-national consistency in indicators of national pride, Bergsieker focuses on variations in the particular, potentially negative national identity of Germans, both those who lived through the Nazi era and those born decades later. As opposed to the bulk of research on German nationalism exploring East-West contrasts, the chapter intentionally uses generational cohorts, highlighting a comparison across time rather than space.

By exploring the distinction between patriotism and nationalism, Bergsieker's analysis provides evidence that expressing pride of being German is positively associated with out-group derogation. Therefore, German national pride is more closely linked to symbolic nationalism and ethnocentrism than to critical patriotism, as opposed to national pride in countries such as the United States, Israel, and Japan. These surprising findings highlight the need for an emic or context-specific exploration of nationalism, as many cross-national studies that included Germany predicted that the feeling of national pride indicates patriotism rather than nationalism. Against this background, the effects of the constitutional patriotism as an inclusive and open project remain uncertain, while German national pride remains controversial, ideological, and embedded in socio-cultural and historical discourses. While national pride appears closely linked to ethnocentrism in contemporary Germany, particularly among younger people, that relationship is grounded in a particular social, historical, and political context and may change with time. This highlights the dynamic character of nationalism, not only questioning its linearity from emphasis on ethnicity toward focus on civicness, but also stressing its dependence on historical discourses. A revival of historical national pride discourses may for instance lead in Germany to stronger demands for "ethnitization" of the nation, as would be the case in other countries.

In contrast to Bergsieker's chapter, Andrzej Marcin Suszycki uses the discourse analysis in order to examine the recent nationalist developments in Italy. He defines nationalism as a discursive legitimization of political action through commitment to the three nationalist principles: The principle of popular sovereignty, the principle of the uniqueness of the people as well as the principle of the fundamental equality among all the strata in the community. The chapter argues that three factors have changed the nature of nationalism in Italy since the beginning of the 1990s. These are the rapid and deep changes of the Italian political system associated with the fight against corruption, the separatist movement for a secession of the North Italian regions from the Italian state (embodied by Lega Nord), and the process of European integration. Suszycki demonstrates that the political discourse of Lega Nord aimed at sabotaging the political efforts to strengthen national solidarity with obligations to provide assistance for the economically and socially underdeveloped South. By doing so, Lega Nord argued that national self-determination has not yet been realized in the North, while presenting it as colonized and enslaved by the South.

In response to the discourse of Lega Nord, the political elites of the country tried to enlarge the national referential framework by introducing new supranational narratives linked to the process of European integration. Here, the narrative which portrayed Europe as a new homeland of all the Italians and the united Italian state as an indispensable part of a united European Union was used to explain decisions regarding important issues of monetary, economic, and foreign policy, such as the adoption of the common European currency and the support of the European constitutional treaty.

Moreover, some old narratives of national identity were partially modified by the political elites. The narrative of belonging to the West no longer ascribed to Italy a modest second range place, but claimed a prominent position among the world powers. The narrative of national unity (Risorgimento narrative) was modified insofar as immigrants now became the threatening "Significant Others" and the reference to them was used to strengthen the unity of the state threatened by the discourse of Lega Nord. The enlargement of the referential framework of national identity and the modifications of old narratives made possible the emergence of new forms of Italian nationalism, especially Euronationalism and big power nationalism.

Against this background, the Italian case of nationalism exhibits competing functions of nationalism, some of which espouse a political agenda of nationalism *qua* fragmentation or destruction, while others maintain the integrative claim of nationalism. Italy is particularly appealing as a case study for the multiplicity of nationalism, since all three aspects of contemporary nationalism (Euro-nationalism, nation-state nationalism, and secessionist nationalism) are strongly represented in the Italian nationalism discourse. In addition, as Suszycki shows, the main nationalist discourse in Italy does not reflect a strong ideological consistency, suggesting an instrumentalist feature of Italian nationalism (contextual nationalism).

The chapters on Western Europe confirm that nationalism in Belgium, Germany, and Italy can be backward looking and mythodologizing. Therefore, the thesis on the temporary revival of nationalism in Western Europe cannot be supported. Of course, the limited number of cases does not allow for a generalization of the results. Nonetheless, the results warrant a greater skepticism regarding the perspective suggesting an advance of nationalism in Western Europe toward a more "civilized" and post-modern nationalism.

Concerning nationalism in Eastern Europe, the volume includes case studies of countries seldom analyzed in the mainstream studies on nationalism in Eastern Europe such as nationalism in Latvia, Bulgaria, Serbia, and Croatia. Not only are all these countries located at the fringe of Europe, but some of them have also only recently become EU members (Latvia, Bulgaria), while others aspire more (Croatia) or less (Serbia) to EU membership. This makes their cases particular, if we consider nationalism in the context of European integration. This part of the volume raises the question of whether we can indeed speak of "new" nationalism in Eastern Europe, a thesis put forward in the context of new nation-building and a post-communist regime transformation in this region of Europe. This rebirth thesis of nationalism in Eastern Europe suggests that communism/state socialism suppressed national sentiments without transforming them into a more civilized and civil nationalism. The rebirth of ethnic and destructive Eastern nationalism mirrors the underdeveloped nature of Eastern European societies, as they need to catch up with their Western counterparts. This simplistic view also could not be confirmed by the chapters on Eastern Europe. Instead, we argue in favor of a West-East similarity of nationalism in Europe.

In her chapter, Ieva Zake explores the little-known intricacies of Latvian nationalism, which is depicted by some authors as an example of the so-called ethnic nationalism with radical connotations: Latvian nationalism is associated in particular with policies of discrimination, xenophobia, and intolerance. Zake argues that the majority of analyses of Latvian nationalism (often as a typical case of Eastern nationalism) focused solely on the nationalist ideologies of the titular nations, while ignoring the ethnic fixation of the minority groups. Against this background, the chapter questions the validity of these analyses. First, it demonstrates that both Latvian and Russian oriented nationalisms in Latvia exhibit visible elements of ethnic nationalism. Second, it argues that important ideological changes have recently occurred in Latvian and Russian nationalisms, including a new type of nationalism. This new nationalism can be characterized as seeking an inclusive and encompassing national identity that could foster the cohesion of society across ethnic boundaries. In this context, the Latvian state is conceived of as the source of this new national identity. At the empirical level, Zake shows that both Latvian and Russian ethnic nationalisms have already begun to de-emphasize the ethnic meaning of nation and strengthen the ideological relevance of an autonomous and strong Latvian state, in particular regarding its redistributive capacity. However, this new national ideology neither reflects civic nationalism nor does it fall neatly into other categories of nationalism known from the scholarly debates, as its emphasis on strong statehood adds a new dimension to what we know about nationalisms. The chapter argues that this state-framed rather than community-framed nationalism demonstrates that the research on nationalism needs to pay more attention to the relationship between nationalism and statism.[11] In this vein, the chapter suggests a categorization which includes nationalisms that fall *between* the categories of ethnic vs. civic nationalisms. This new categorization is applied to the past and present shifts in Latvian nationalism and addresses the most recent transition from ethnic to statist nationalism in contemporary Latvia.

While Zake's chapter highlights the Latvian particularity of state-building and its post-communist legacies, the chapter on Bulgarian nationalism draws stronger on the nationalism-EU nexus. As Emilian Kavalski argues, in Bulgaria the novelty of EU membership has been accompanied by the discourse of the return to Europe as a reclamation of the former status of a perceived former glory. In this sense, European integration was not conceived of as a superseding of the nation-state, but rather its rescue and strengthening. Therefore, Bulgaria is a case in which the debate on EU membership has facilitated the legitimizing of re-nationalization. The chapter argues in accordance with the perspective presented by Daniele Conversi that the twin forces of European integration and economic globalization have only enhanced the complexities of nationalism, rather than suppressed it. As a consequence, a reframing of nationalism in the political space of post-Cold War Europe became an integral dynamic to the processes of Europeanization. Against this background, Kavalski's chapter focuses on re-nationalization practices and current patterns of national mobilization in Bulgaria. By doing so, the chapter zooms in on the political narratives of the main actor of the re-nationalization, the nationalist party ATAKA (Attack). Kavalski argues that ATAKA's success during recent parliamentary, presidential, and municipal elections points to the normative and political uncertainty of the Bulgarian society concerning the direction of the transition process in the country. This confirms the thesis by Daniele Conversi that exclusionary boundary-making of nationalism can be understood as a reaction to uncertainty. In this sense, ATAKA's political narratives utilize offensive language against minority groups not only to articulate its perception of Bulgarian identity, but also to represent a confrontation with the reality of a contemporary form of Bulgarian nationalism by making gestures toward the possibility of non-democratic and exclusionary ideology. Kavalski argues that ATAKA's chauvinistic agenda reflects the dilemma of a nation at conflict with itself. ATAKA's representatives proclaim a national cohesion by using selective historical memory and by constructing historical narratives which confound the past and the present. This results in a vision of a destructive community based on the demonization of the "other." Furthermore, the chapter emphasizes the mythologization of national history, which becomes a political project for social mobilization underpinned with the nostalgia for a past that never existed. In particular, ATAKA's political discourse highlights the incompatibility between the Bulgarian national ideal and the project of European integration, whereby it shares a certain similarity with Flemish nationalism, analyzed in Janet Laible's chapter. However, Kavalski argues that ATAKA underwrites dynamics of the current re-nationalization of public feeling in Bulgaria. In this sense, the implications of Bulgarian nationalism may be radically different from those in Belgium, precisely because ATAKA's nationalism is "anti-systemic" both in relational (vis-à-vis other political parties) as well as ideological (challenging the character of the transition process) terms.

The chapter by David MacDonald explores a particularly controversial case within the scholarly debate on nationalism. MacDonald critically examines the rejection of Balkan identity in the 1980s and 1990s by Serbian and Croatian nationalists seeking to create expanded national homelands. Nationalist political elites in both countries constructed narratives of "Eastern" others and "Western" selves to morally legitimize territorial expansion and ethnic cleansing. Similarly, nationalist elites in both countries presented themselves as essentially "Western," acting as bulwarks against eastern expansion. Images of a dangerous expansionist Islamic/Turkish "other" framed the desire to create a "greater Serbia" which included parts of Croatia and Bosnia-Herzegovina. In Croatia, a rejection of eastern Serbs and Muslims played an essential role in promoting Croatia's so-called Western identity, while legitimizing expansion into Bosnia. The chapter explores concepts of "Balkanism," "Balkanization," and "nesting Orientalism" and analyzes how Serbian and

Croatian ideologues reinterpreted their respective national identities and histories during the wars of the 1990s and after. In both cases, we deal with expanding and boundary-making nationalism, which starkly contrasts with the contraction-prone and boundary-making nationalism of Western European countries. As the ultimate proof of their Westernness, both Serbia and Croatia sought membership in the European Union. However, as MacDonald argues, political elites of both countries continue to promote self-serving narratives of their own histories, which display blindness about their recent past, in particular about the crimes their nations committed in war. This reflects the early nation-building processes of the nineteenth century, where political elites construct and invent the national past, aiming at generating narrative cohesion of the society. While this glossing of national history is designed to make each nation more attractive to the West, the unreflective stance of Serbian and Croatian elites to engage with their respective pasts has done the opposite. Nevertheless, MacDonald posits that both Serbs and Croats have assimilated an "otherization" of the Balkans and have incorporated the rhetoric of Westernness into their respective national identities, whereby they distanced themselves ideologically from the putative East. In both cases, otherizing perceived enemies as "Eastern" performed a useful role in legitimizing the creation of new expanded states. Reflecting a Western rhetoric of Balkanism and Balkanization made the conflict appear natural. By contrast, Yugoslavia was depicted as a doomed project, which represented an artificial attempt to bring unlike peoples together. In this context, Serbian and Croatian elites not only projected the vision of an inevitable clash of civilizations to their own audiences, but also courted western governments with imagery of an Islamic conspiracy. At the same time, symbolically, both Serbia and Croatia were seeking to leave the Balkans behind them, as its borders shifted ever eastwards.

The theses on Western revival and Eastern rebirth are often based on the faulty choice of cases, which are selected on the dependent variable. In other words, studies arguing in favor of the return of the repressed nationalism in Eastern Europe focus on specific cases of boundary-making and violent nationalism, such as in the Balkans. Other cases such as the Czech Republic or the Baltic countries are ignored. In order to remedy this problem, more comparative approaches to nationalism bridging the obsolete dichotomy of Eastern and Western nationalism are needed.

Implications for Further Research

In conclusion, the volume suggests that the triangle of three perspectives (supranationalism, boundary-making nationalism, and regional nationalism) may be promising as an explanatory framework for the analysis of nationalism in Europe. The volume has distanced itself from older dichotomies such as civic and ethnic nationalism and questioned one-sided normativity of nationalism, in particular in the concept of liberal nationalism. A promising approach to contemporary nationalism would include exploration of links between supranationalism, boundary-making nationalism, and regional nationalism. In addition, the relationship between the three perspectives on nationalism explored in this volume and the three main functions of nationalism—integration, destruction, and fragmentation—should be considered. Even though the preliminary insights of the volume do not appear to support the thesis on the correspondence between the conceptual and functional levels (supranational-integrative, national-violent, regional-fragmenting), more research is needed here. This multiplicity of nationalism should be examined in more depth, both at the theoretical and empirical level. The linearity of nationalism proposed by Anthony Smith and Ernest Gellner needs to be replaced with more complex approaches to contemporary nationalism, in particular regarding its dynamics.

The multiplicity of nationalism and the West-East similarity suggest future research foci which should be subject to further exploration. *Firstly*, the volume argues that, notwithstanding the controversies on the possibility and necessity of European identity as European nationalism, the concept of European nationalism is linked to technologies of collective identity departing from the analytical and methodological template of the nation-state. This warrants more research on European nationalism, rather than European supranationalism as a circumvention of nationalism, which has hitherto dominated the research on Europeanization.

Secondly, the volume demonstrated that boundaries are relevant to current European trends and patterns of integration, which correlate with patterns of nationalism. The relationship of European integration to nationalism should be explored in more depth, together with the impact of globalization. As some of the chapters suggest that a stress on boundaries indicates deep insecurity connected in particular to the projects of societal transformation, the triangle of nationalism (supranationalism, nation-building, regionalism) implies that Globalization and Europeanization can be decisive factors in the research on contemporary nationalism.

Thirdly, besides cases of traditional and violent nation-building nationalism, the volume documented new forms of nationalism. Some of these, as in the case of Latvia, are state-oriented; others reflect the increasing importance of sub-state regionalism. In this context, a promising possible theoretical development could attempt to relate these different forms of nationalism and shift the discourse beyond the traditional civic-ethnic divide. The volume suggests that innovative ways of classifying nationalism are necessary. Neither older nor newer concepts seem to be capable of capturing the multiplicity and the West-East similarity of nationalism in contemporary Europe.

Notes

1. Anthony D. Smith, "Ethno-Symbolism and the Study of Nationalism," in *Nations and Nationalism*, ed. Philip Spencer and Howard Wollman (New Brunswick: Rutgers University Press, 2005), 23-31; Michael Hechter et al., "A Theory of Ethnic Collective

Action," *International Migration Review* 16, no. 2 (1982): 412-434; David D. Laitin, "The Game Theory of Language Regimes," *International Political Science Review* 14, no. 3 (1993): 227-239.

2. Liah Greenfeld, "Is Nation Unavoidable? Is Nation Unavoidable Today?," in *Nation and National Identity: The European Experience in Perspective*, ed. Hanspeter Kriesi et al. (Zürich: Rüegger, 1999), 37-54.

3. Rogers Brubaker, "Myths and Misconceptions in the Study of Nationalism," in *The State of the Nation: Ernest Gellner and the Theory of Nationalism,* ed. John Hall (Cambridge: Cambridge University Press, 1998), 272-305.

4. Yael Tamir, *Liberal Nationalism* (Princeton: Princeton University Press, 1993); Yael Tamir, "Is Liberal Nationalism an Oxymoron? An Essay for Judith Shklar," *Ethics* 105, no. 3 (1995): 626-64; David Miller, *On Nationality* (Oxford: Oxford University Press, 1995).

5. Cf. Cris Shore and Annabel Black, "The European Communities and the Construction of Europe," *Anthropology Today* 8, no. 3 (1992): 10-11.

6. Cf. Peter Niedermüller and Bjarne Stoklund, eds., *Europe: A Cultural Construction and Reality* (Copenhagen: Museum Tusculanum Press, 2001).

7. Michael Mann, *The Dark Side of Democracy: Explaining Ethnic Cleansing* (Cambridge: Cambridge University Press, 2005); Cf. also Jacques Semelin, "Taking Mann Seriously," *Political Studies Review* 4 (2006): 279-289; Daniele Conversi, "Democracy, Nationalism and Culture: A Social Critique of Liberal Monoculturalism," *Sociology Compass* 2, no. 1 (2008): 156-182.

8. Cf. Daniele Conversi, "Demo-Skepticism and Genocide," *Political Studies Review* 4 (2006): 247-262.

9. Mary Kaldor, "Nationalism and Globalization," *Nations and Nationalism* 10, no. 1/2 (2004): 161-177.

10. Cf. for instance Michael Keating, "Minority Nationalism and the State: The European Case," in *Contemporary Minority Nationalism*, ed. Michael Watson (New York: Routledge, 1990), 174-94.

11. A similar need for a stronger incorporation of statehood into the analysis of nationalism was expressed by Rogers Brubaker. Rogers Brubaker, "The Manichean Myth: Rethinking the Distinction between Civic and Ethnic Nationalism," in *Nation and National Identity: The European Experience in Perspective*, ed. Hanspeter Kriesi et al. (Zürich: Rüegger, 1999), 55-72.

Index

O

P

R

S

T

U

V

W

X

Y

Z

About the Contributors

Hilary B. Bergsieker earned a master's degree in psychology from Princeton University, where she is currently pursuing a PhD in psychology and public policy. Her research examines stereotyping, prejudice, and interracial interactions, as well as their intersection with racial, cultural, or national identity. Her recent publications include: "My Choice, Your Categories: The Denial of Multiracial Identities," *Journal of Social Issues* 65 (2009): 185-204 (together with S. S. M. Townsend and H. R. Markus); "Interracial Friendship Development and Attributional Biases," *Journal of Social and Personal Relationships* (in press, together with J. N. Shelton, J. A. Richeson); "Emotions as within or between People? Lay Theory of Emotion Expression and Emotion Inference across Cultures," *Personality and Social Psychology Bulletin* (in press, together with Y. Uchida, S. S. M. Townsend, and H. R. Markus).

Daniele Conversi received his PhD at the London School of Economics. He taught in the Government Departments at Cornell and Syracuse Universities, as well as at the Central European University, Budapest. He is now Senior Lecturer at the University of Lincoln (UK). His current research explores the role of culture in the process of state-building from 1789 to the present day. More specifically, his studies address the relationship between nationalism and culture, with particular attention to the concept of cultural homogenization. In addition, he works on the relationship between nationalism and democracy, globalization, genocide, militarism, and war. His books include *The Basques, the Catalans, and Spain* (London: Hurst, 1997) and the edited volume *Ethnonationalism in the Contemporary World* (London: Routledge, 2004). Recent articles: "Art, Nationalism and War: Political Futurism in Italy (1909–1944)," *Sociology Compass* 3, no. 1 (2009): 92-117; "We Are all Equals!: Militarism, Homogenization and 'Egalitarianism' in Nationalist State-building (1789-1945)," *Ethnic and Racial Studies* 31, no. 7 (2008): 1286-1314; and "Demoskepticism and Genocide," *Political Science Review* 4, no. 3 (2006): 247-262.

Enric Martínez-Herrera is "M. García Pelayo" Senior Research Fellow at the Centro de Estudios Políticos y Constitucionales (Spain), with a PhD from European University Institute (Italy) and an MA from the University of Essex (UK). His research is concerned with political behavior, institutions and public policies in comparative perspective. His recent publications include: "From Nation-Building to Building Identification with Political Communities," *European Journal of Political Research* 41 (2002): 421-453; and "Government Restructuring and Resources Reallocation in the Face of Ethno-Nationalist Insurgency in the Basque Country," in *Resources, Governance, and Civil Conflict*, ed. M. Öberg and K. Strom (London: Routledge, 2008), 101-124.

Emilian Kavalski received his PhD from the Loughborough University. He is Lecturer in Politics and International Relations at the University of Western Sydney (Australia). His research focuses on the security governance of complexity and the interactions between China, India, and the EU in Central Asia. He is the author of *India and Central Asia: The Mythmaking of a Rising Power* (forthcoming); *Extending the European Security Community: Constructing Peace in the Balkans* (New York: Macmillan, 2007); and co-editor of *Defunct Federalisms: Critical Perspectives on Federal Failure* (Aldershot: Ashgate, 2008).

Ireneusz Paweł Karolewski is Professor of Political Science in the Willy Brandt Center for German and European Studies, University of Wrocław (Poland) and Adjunct Professor in the Department of Politics, University of Potsdam (Germany), where he received his PhD in Political Science. His research interests include European citizenship, collective identity in Europe, nation and nationalism in Europe, and constitutionalisation of the EU. His recent selected publications: *Citizenship and Collective Identity in Europe* (London: Routledge, 2009); *Nationalism and European Integration* (with Andrzej Marcin Suszycki, New York: Continuum, 2007); "Constitutionalisation of the European Union as a Response to the Eastern Enlargement: Functions vs. Power," *Journal of Communist Studies and Transition Politics* 23 (2007): 501-524; and "Why We Should Not Believe Every Lesson Andrew Moravcsik Teaches Us: A Response," *Politische Vierteljahresschrift* 4 (2007): 740-757 (with Viktoria Kaina).

Taras Kuzio is Adjunct Professor in the Department of Political Science, Carleton University, Ottawa (Canada), and editor of *Ukraine Analyst*. He received his PhD from the University of Birmingham. His research interests are national identities and democratic transition, democratic revolutions and regime change, and communist successor parties. He is the author and editor of 14 books and 5 think tank monographs, and has guest edited 6 special issues of academic journals, the latest on "Comparative Studies of Communist Successor Parties in Central and Eastern Europe" (*Communist and Post-Communist Studies*, 2008). He has published 25 book chapters and 60 political science articles on nationalism, democratization, and post-communist and

European politics. His latest book is *Theoretical and Comparative Perspectives on Nationalism: New Directions in Cross-Cultural and Post-Communist Studies* (Hannover: Ibidem-Verlag, 2007). His recent articles include "National Identity and History Writing in Ukraine," *Nationalities Papers* 34, no. 3 (2006): 407-427; and "Comparative Perspectives on Communist Successor Parties in Central-Eastern Europe and Eurasia," *Communist and Post-Communist Studies* 41, no. 4 (2008): 1-23.

Janet Laible is Associate Professor of Political Science at Lehigh University (United States), with a PhD from Yale University. Her research interests include statehood and sovereignty, nationalism in the European Union, and the politics of cultural production in the context of European integration. Her recent publications include: *Separatism and Sovereignty in the New Europe* (Basingstoke: Palgrave Macmillan, 2008); "Producing 'Ever Closer Union'? The Rhetoric of Legitimacy and Regional Participation in the EU Constitutional Convention," in *The Rise and Fall of the EU's Constitutional Treaty*, ed. Finn Laursen (Leiden: Martinus Nijhoff Publishers, 2008); and "The Scottish Parliament and Its Capacity for Redistributive Policy," *Parliamentary Affairs* 61, no. 1 (2008): 160-184.

David B. MacDonald holds a PhD in International Relations from the London School of Economics. His research focuses on the fields of international relations, genocide studies, and nationalism. He was Senior Lecturer in Political Studies at the University of Otago, New Zealand, before taking up his current appointment in the Political Science Department at the University of Guelph. He is the author of *Thinking History, Fighting Evil: Neoconservatives and the Perils of Historical Analogy in American Politics* (Lanham: Lexington Books, 2009); *Identity Politics in the Age of Genocide: The Holocaust and Historical Representation* (London: Routledge, 2008); and *Balkan Holocausts? Serbian and Croatian Propaganda and the War in Yugoslavia* (Manchester: Manchester University Press, 2002). He is also co-editor of and contributor to *The Ethics of Foreign Policy* (London: Ashgate Press, 2007).

Anna Olsson earned an MSc in Political Science from the University of Gothenburg, Sweden. She is currently working on her PhD dissertation in Political Science at American University in Washington DC, where she is also a lecturer in the Department of Government. Her research focuses on sub-state regionalism, identity, Euroskepticism, and regional representation in the EU. She has recently published "Regional Minority Nationalist Attitudes toward European Integration" in *Nationalism and European Integration: The Need for New Theoretical and Empirical Insights*, ed. Ireneusz Paweł Karolewski and Andrzej Marcin Suszycki (New York: Continuum, 2007), 52-66.

Andrzej Marcin Suszycki received his PhD in Political Science from the Humboldt University of Berlin in 2002. Between 2003 and 2005 he was Research Fellow in the Department of International Studies at the University of Padua (Italy).

Since 2006 he has been Senior Lecturer at the University of Potsdam and since 2007 at the University of Passau. Between 2007 and 2009 he also taught courses in International Relations at the Humboldt University Berlin and the Collegium Civitas University in Warsaw. In 2008 he was Research Fellow at the Centre for Welfare State Research at the University of Southern Denmark in Odense.

His research interests include the theory of international relations, foreign policy of European states, nationalism, and welfare state. He has recently published *Italienische Osteuropapolitik 1989-2000* (Münster: LIT Verlag, 2003); "Three Dimensions, Continuity and Change in Foreign Policy," *International Affairs Review* 2, no. 154 (2006): 73-94; and "Political Support, European Values and European Identity," in *Politics and Identity*, ed. Robert Szwed (Lublin, 2007), 108-116. He has recently edited *Nationalism and European Integration: The Need for New Theoretical and Empirical Insights* (New York: Continuum, 2007) (with Ireneusz Paweł Karolewski); and *Nation and Nationalism: Political and Historical Studies* (Wrocław: Willy Brandt Center for German and European Studies, 2007) (with Ireneusz Paweł Karolewski).

Ieva Zake is Assistant Professor of Sociology at Rowan University, New Jersey (United States). She earned her PhD at the University of Massachusetts, Amherst. Her research and teaching focuses on the areas of political sociology, sociology of intellectuals, and immigration. Her recent publications include "Controversies of US-USSR Cultural Contacts: The Perspective of Latvian Refugees," *Journal of Historical Sociology* 21, no. 1 (2008): 55-81; *Nineteenth-Century Nationalism and Twentieth-Century Anti-Democratic Ideals: The Case of Latvia, 1840s to 1980s* (New York: Edwin Mellen Press, 2008); and *Anti-Communist Minorities in the U.S.: Political Activism of Ethnic Refugees* (Basingstoke: Palgrave Macmillan, 2009).

Breinigsville, PA USA
24 February 2010

233132BV00004B/5/P

9 780739 123072